UNFREE LABOUR IN THE DEVELOPMENT OF THE ATLANTIC WORLD

Studies in Slave and Post-Slave Societies and Cultures

CO-EDITORS:
GAD HEUMAN
JAMES WALVIN

UNFREE LABOUR IN THE DEVELOPMENT OF THE ATLANTIC WORLD

Edited by

Paul E. Lovejoy and Nicholas Rogers

Routledge
Taylor & Francis Group

LONDON AND NEW YORK

First published in 1994 in Great Britain by
Routledge
2 Park Square, Milton Park, Abingdon, Oxon, OX14 4RN

and in the United States of America by
Routledge
270 Madison Ave, New York NY 10016

Transferred to Digital Printing 2006

Library of Congress Cataloging in Publication Data

Unfree labour in the development of the Atlantic world / edited
by Paul E. Lovejoy and Nicholas Rogers.
(Studies in slave and post-slave societies and cultures)
Includes bibliographical references and index.
ISBN 0-7146-4579-6 (hard)   ISBN 0-7146-4152-9 (pbk,)
1. Slavery – North Atlantic Region – History.   2. Slavery –
South Atlantic Region – History.   3. Forced labor – North Atlantic
Region – History.   4. Forced labor – South Atlantic Region –
History.   5. Colonies – American – History.   6. Colonies – Africa
– History.   7. Labor laws and legislation, Colonial – History.
I. Lovejoy, Paul E.   II. Rogers, Nicholas.   III. Series.
HD4865.N67U53 1994   94–31528
305.3'62'097 – dc20   CIP

British Library Cataloguing in Publication Data

Unfree Labour in the Development of the
Atlantic World. — (Studies in Slave &
Post-slave Societies & Cultures)
I. Lovejoy, Paul E.   II. Rogers, Nicholas
III. Series
331.1173

ISBN 0-7146-4579-6 (hb)
ISBN 0-7146-4152-9
This group of studies first appeared in a special issue on 'Unfree
Labour in the Development of the Atlantic World' in *Slavery &
Abolition*, Vol. 15, No. 2 (August 1994), published by Routledge.

Typeset by Regent Typesetting, London

Publisher's Note
The publisher has gone to great lengths to ensure the quality of this reprint
but points out that some imperfections in the original may be apparent

Contents

Introduction

Between 1500 and 1900, the various parts of the Atlantic world became more and more integrated into an expanding capitalist economy. The purpose of this collection of essays is to examine the different forms of unfree labour that contributed to the development of this world and, by extension, the debates and protests that emerged concerning the conditions and humiliations of labour servitude. The volume grew out of a small conference held at York University, Toronto, in April 1993, at which most of these papers were presented.[1] It is comparative in perspective, drawing on specialists who concentrate on particular regions and specific types of labour. Geographically, the contributions cover Britain, Africa and the Americas, including the regions of European and African settlement and the colonized areas of highland Amerindia. Martin Klein's essay includes a comparison of different labour regimes in Asia as well as in Africa and the Americas.

The involvement of such a range of scholars of European and non-European societies around the Atlantic basin has enabled a dialogue that is comparative. By examining forms of labour in Britain, Amerindia, plantation America, Africa, and Asia, our discussion bridges the gaps that separate specialists of different geographical regions. By focusing on the emergence of the Atlantic world as a complicated process that depended upon various forms of unfree labour, we have attempted to share the various approaches and concerns that are common in each geographical area of specialization. The range of unfree labour regimes that are examined include slavery, indenture, apprenticeship, pawnship (debt bondage) and impressment.

We take as a starting point the comparative historical approach pioneered by Philip D. Curtin, who developed a theory of empire and European expansion that brought the internal dynamics of non-European societies and economies into focus.[2] Curtin examined the intercontinental interconnections that resulted in the emergence of the 'plantation complex' of the Americas; how productive resources (land, labour and capital) were concentrated in the fertile tropical lands of the Americas to form what he initially referred to as the 'South Atlantic System'. This approach emphasized the destruction of Amerindian societies and economies, the enslavement of Africans and their forced

migration to the newly vacated lands of the Americas, and the transfer of
European capital and entrepreneurship to the Americas to run this
complex. From this perspective, systems of labour mobilization in Amer-
india, Spanish America, the plantation complex of the Americas, and
Africa all become relevant to an understanding of the emergence of the
Atlantic complex, and these are best examined comparatively.

This collection is theoretical as well as comparative. It is theoretical in
the sense that it raises questions about the various combinations of unfree
labour that contributed to the development of the capitalist world order.
We pose the question of how different modes of production co-existed
and even contradicted one another, an important issue in the debate over
the transition to capitalism and in discussions about the complex modes of
production and productive relations within different social formations.

Any discussion of this last point must inevitably address in some
manner the panoramic interpretations of Immanuel Wallerstein and
dependency theorists who have sought to integrate a study of Atlantic
slavery into the analysis of the emergent capitalist world economy. In
Wallerstein's own work there is a structural articulation between the
modes of production that dominate the core and the periphery, in the
sense that capitalist expansion at the core is predicated upon self-
evidently coercive modes of production at the periphery. Thus slavery is
seen as 'pre-eminently a capitalist institution, geared to the early pre-
industrial stages of a capitalist world-economy'.[3] Quite apart from the
provocation this has offered to more orthodox Marxists, who have
insisted that slavery is quintessentially a 'relation of domination' rather
than a strictly capitalist relation involving the purchase of labour power,[4]
Wallerstein's paradigm has had the effect of often over-simplifying the
modes of production that operated at the core and periphery in the early
modern period.

Several papers in this collection address the historical specificities of
this problem. To begin with, it is important to recognize the degree to
which unfree notions of labour persisted in the core where 'free' labour
first made its appearance. Britain may have been the first capitalist nation
with an unmistakable proletariat, but, as Paul Craven and Douglas Hay's
paper shows, labour relations were frequently governed by master-and-
servant laws that dramatically reinforced the asymmetrical power relations of the labour contract and larded them with coercive powers against
workers. Such laws, with their pre-capitalist connotations of servile,
contract labour, persisted well into the so-called liberal era of industrial
capitalism.[5] In fact, precisely at the time when the Smithian ethos of
'economic man' was making headway, a battery of sanctions derived from
feudal notions of personal service was extended to break worker resis-

tance to capitalist innovation and the heavy weight of customary expectations that still informed labouring attitudes to agriculture and industry.[6] Thus Nicholas Rogers reveals how the vagrant laws were increasingly extended to resolve pressing problems in productive relations, and, moreover, how the defence of the state and the expanding imperial economy of the eighteenth century were only made possible with substantial inputs of coerced labour from Britain's ships and ports. In Wallersteinian terms, the pre-eminent core state of the capitalist world-system required a substantial array of coercive, extra-economic sanctions within Britain itself to render its workers proletarians and to sustain its international status. Rogers' study raises questions about the relative importance of coerced labour at the core and on the periphery. Coercion was essential to labour regimes throughout the emerging world order, whether it was to control impressed gangs of seamen for the British navy, Irish indentured servants in the West Indies, as Hilary Beckles discusses, or enslaved Muslims from the Sokoto Caliphate in Brazil, as examined by Paul Lovejoy.

If discussions of the British case make one reflect on the 'freedoms' of free labour, the papers on the labour regimes of early Central America make one reconsider the intensity of coercive productive relations at the periphery. In one sense, Nigel Bolland reaffirms in glaring detail the conventional wisdom concerning the harshness of Spanish colonization and enslavement in the Central American isthmus and the severe depopulation of the indigenous population that resulted from disease and brutal exploitation. As Orlando Patterson has remarked, 'this was one of the most savage and deadly slave systems of all time'.[7] Yet Bolland also notes the very significant export of slaves from Nicaragua to the Caribbean and Peru in the early sixteenth century – according to his survey, perhaps as many as 500,000 people – and the subsequent development of cacao and indigo plantations along the isthmus until high mortality rates undermined their labour supply. In so doing he modifies the conventional wisdom that the dramatic decline of the Amerindian population was more attributable to the unintended impact of disease than to the severity of the *encomenderos*. The drastic depopulation of Central America was caused by a 'holocaust' as much as a series of pandemics.

Whereas Bolland stresses the severity of the labour regimes of the early Spanish colonizers in Central America, Elinor Melville and Cynthia Radding emphasize the relative ease with which Amerindians adapted to the pull of market forces arising from the colonial regimes. Coerced labour emerged in specific contexts, but wage labour and peasant production were alternatives that only disappeared after the colonial regime stabilized. Melville points to the existence of wage labour on the *estancias*

of the Valle del Mezquital, long before its better-documented appearance on the *haciendas*. From this evidence she argues that Amerindians
took an active role in sheep farming, both as skilled labourers and
pastoralists, in ways that belie historical orthodoxies about the coercive
character of labour regimes in the era of the *encomienda* and *repartimiento*. Similarly, Radding stresses the shifting strategies of labour
organization among the Sonorans in the pastoral settings of northern
Mexico. The Spaniards had difficulty in mobilizing the semi-nomadic
peoples of the region in a manner similar to the more sedentary and
stratified populations of central Mexico. Sonorans moved back and forth
between 'traditional' forms of labour allocation and recruitment that are
familiar in the anthropological literature and wage employment, sometimes coerced, in the Spanish colonial project. It is useful to remember
that the emergent Atlantic world not only had a core and a periphery but
also a frontier. Clearly one needs to integrate an Annaliste perspective to
the overly-schematic typologies of world-systems theory in order to
examine the effect of terrain, technology and demography upon the
coercive and determinative character of early colonial labour regimes. In
the more dispersed settlements of the Spanish empire or in the pastoral
settings 'outside' the *encomienda* or *repartimiento*, Amerindians had
some room to negotiate the terms of their survival.

Radding and Melville, like some of the other contributors in this
collection, raise the methodological issue of what historians and anthro-
pologists might reasonably infer from the legal and institutional character
of different labour regimes concerning their coercive power and practice.
The question is most starkly put by Hilary Beckles, who questions
whether the experience of indentured servitude on the early Caribbean
frontier was radically different from that of chattel slavery or *encomienda*
bondage. Historians enamoured of strict denotative definitions of slavery
would certainly argue that it was, presumably on the grounds that
indentured servants, unlike slaves, were neither themselves nor their
children perpetually alienable pieces of property, nor 'socially dead' in
Orlando Patterson's understanding of the term.[8] And yet Beckles, drawing upon a different reading of Patterson, argues compellingly that the
similarities between Irish indentured servants, African slaves and Amerindian bondsmen in this particular conjuncture outweighed the differences. Indeed, he suggests that in the first 150 years of Caribbean
colonialism the marginal status and 'lived experience' of these groups
often brought them together in opposition to their colonial masters.

Local and metropolitan influences could counteract race, ethnic origin
and religion, and thereby lead to joint action among white indentured
servants and African slaves. In the case of Irish indentured servants, the

dynastic struggles of England and Ireland reverberated through the islands and recharged the quotidian resistance of coerced labour to their rulers. African slaves were motivated to collaborate with their oppressed Irish breathren in this specific historical context. The interrelationships among different categories of unfree labour were clearly complex.

In a similar fashion Paul Lovejoy stresses the degree to which the African slaves who worked on the Bahian sugar plantations and on the streets and docks of Salvador retained their identity as Muslim or Yoruba in ways that crucially informed the rebellion of Muslim slaves and former slaves in 1835. Through a careful examination of the social affiliations of the rebels and the general pattern of slave migration from West Africa to Brazil, Lovejoy is able to establish the fact that an influential proportion of the rebels had been political prisoners who had been enslaved in the course of the expansion of the Sokoto Caliphate and sent to Brazil from the Bight of Benin. This group of Muslims, known locally as Males, formed a critical core in a slave rebellion that had all the cultural rites and accoutrements that extended the holy war against the infidel from West Africa to Brazil.

Lovejoy's paper thus points to the dangers of over-emphasizing the deracinating tendencies of slavery; specifically, the degree to which slaves were dispossessed of their culture and heritage in the very act of slavery itself. Like the Irish indentured servants active in 1689 in the Caribbean, Brazilian slaves of Yoruba and Hausa descent reaffirmed their religious and cultural traditions, fashioning new identities under slavery that informed their modes of resistance.

The theme of resistance is also taken up by Elizabeth Elbourne in her study of the Khoikhoi of the Eastern Cape. Elbourne movingly charts the injustices, indignities and discriminatory practices that the Khoi faced in their dealings with the white settler regimes of the early nineteenth century. In particular, she shows how Khoi nomadism was used as a signifier of 'listless activity', lawless disposition, and consequent marginality in a discourse that privileged the virtues of 'economic man' within a liberal political economy. In a manner analogous to the mobile poor in Britain, the vagrancy laws were used to disfranchise the Khoi, to dispossess them of their lands and to force their children into long-term indentured service lest they be 'tainted' with the same roving disposition and disinclination to work. The process moved the Khoi to the status of slave, despite the *de jure* recognition of their 'freedom'.[9] Elbourne shows how the Khoi fought back by appropriating the language of freedom used by liberal reformers and accenting it in the direction of racial equality before the law, land reform, and the morality of 'free' as opposed to bonded labour. These were dangerous waters for a group known for its nomadism, but its efforts helped forestall a return, if only briefly, to the vagrant and pass-law system that had been repealed by the liberal colonial lobby in 1828.

Elbourne underscores the ambiguities of the discourse of freedom in the abolitionist era and the manner in which it was appropriated not only by the Khoisan but by conservative as well as liberal whites. James Walvin adds another dimension to this story; the domestic ramifications of emancipation discourse within Britain itself. He shows that emancipation was a 'defining moment' in the history of British nationalism, an event that added a new moral dimension to the prevailing British definitions of freedom, hitherto pre-eminently libertarian and anti-revolutionary in character. It set this self-confident capitalist power on a global civilizing mission to free the world from slavery. Emancipation not only shored up a specifically nationalist political culture and arguably helped to reaffirm the bonds of nation over those of class; it set the stage for a new era of cultural imperialism in which Britain would be the crusader for a freedom that felicitously and unproblematically coupled Christianity with free enterprise.

Toyin Falola's paper casts light on the consequences of this mission. As Falola demonstrates, the closing down of the Atlantic slave trade intensified the development of slavery and pawnship among the Yoruba. Abolition altered the relationship of the Yoruba economy to the larger Atlantic world. Rather than export workers as slaves, the Yoruba shifted to the export of palm oil and palm kernels to Europe. Both slavery and pawnship were important sources of labour in this transition but, as Falola demonstrates, the external market should not be over-emphasized. Slaves and pawns were important markers of wealth and prestige for reasons related to kinship and the political system. Neither form of unfree labour was harmoniously integrated into African kinship networks as some historians have argued. Changes in labour mobilization were complex, moving not from slavery to freedom but from one form of unfree labour to another, with wage labour occasionally surfacing as well. This eclectic pattern of change characterized all parts of the Atlantic world, including areas from where African slaves were drawn for the plantation complex.

Martin Klein suggests that attitudes to the abolition of slavery and other forms of unfree labour were often highly pragmatic. As British practice demonstrates, colonial officials did not wish to disrupt their cordial relations with indigenous elites and regimes that depended upon domestic and administrative slavery, pawnship, and other forms of unfree labour. Indeed, because slavery was abolished in the British colonies at a time when it was still profitable, the British had to tolerate the expansion of indentured labour systems within its dominions to satisfy the demand for a servile, low-paid labour force in the plantation economies. Approximately 28 million East Indians left their homelands to work as 'coolie' labourers in the tropical colonies of the Americas in the period 1846–1932. This migration was almost two and a half times the number of African slaves who made the trans-Atlantic passage to the Americas from the sixteenth century onwards. Such migrations required the master-and-servant statutes, as Hay and Craven emphasize. Much of this legislation was attuned to local conditions and, although within the ambit of common law, frequently framed without English precedent. In Africa and Asia, absentee or recalcitrant workers could be whipped under these laws, just as slaves had been typically dishonoured. In the Caribbean there were strict quotas on the gender ratios of immigrant indentured labour to ensure that single young males could be exploited to the full. Servitude frequently continued under a different name.

The situation was not necessarily any better in non-British territories. In Brazil, where the trans-atlantic slave trade ended in 1851 and where emancipation came only in 1888, planters took advantage of a marginal but demographically vibrant non-white population to stabilize their workforce through the vertical networks of clientage. Although the early stages of the coffee boom in southern Brazil had enabled sharecroppers and tenant farmers to establish a stake in this export economy, Nancy Naro argues that controlled access to land and demographic growth ultimately sustained the power of the more progressive planters in the transition from slavery. As she concludes, 'rigidly hierarchical social relations, defined by the harshness of slavery, persisted in post-emancipation areas'. As in Asia, slavery was not a necessary source of production where population densities were high and tillable land limited. Provided the international price of the export was buoyant, wage labour, what Marx termed '*indirect* forced labour' could fit the bill.

NOTES

1. We should like to thank the Social Science and Humanities Research Council of Canada and the Faculty of Arts, York University, for funding this conference. We should also like to thank Mandy Banton, Herman Bennett, Russell Chace, Philip D. Curtin, Brooke Larson, T.J. LeGoff, Catherine LeGrande, David Levine, Mohammed Mbodj, David Trotman and Mary Turner, who commented on papers or presented papers which are not reproduced here. Their participation was essential in making the conference such a success. Finally, we are grateful to Diane Jenner and Jean Levy of the Department of History for their organizational and editorial assistance, and to David Trotman, the Master of Founders College, for hosting the conference. The paper originally presented by Lovejoy has been substituted by the one published here, which was presented at Boston University, April 1994.

2. Philip D. Curtin, *The Rise and Fall of the Plantation Complex: Essays in Atlantic History* (Cambridge, 1990).
3. Immanuel Wallerstein, *The Modern World-System* (New York, 1974), Vol. I, p. 88.
4. See Marx's own discussion of labour relations in post-emancipation Jamaica in the *Grundrisse*, trans. Martin Nicolaus (London, 1973), pp. 325–6, in which he distinguishes '*direct* forced labour' or slavery from '*indirect* forced labour' or wage labour, noting that 'Wealth confronts direct forced labour not as capital, but rather as relations of domination'.
5. For an illuminating discussion of how precapitalist notions of contract labour informed capitalist labour relations in the 'liberal' United States, see Karen Orren, *Belated Feudalism: Labor, the Law and Liberal Development in the United States* (Cambridge and New York, 1991).
6. For the importance of such attitudes, see E.P. Thompson, *Customs in Common* (London, 1991) and J.M. Neeson, *Commoners: Common Right, Enclosure and Social Change in England, 1700–1820* (Cambridge, 1993).
7. Orlando Patterson, *Slavery And Social Death* (Cambridge, 1982), p. 471.
8. For a concise exploration of this concept, see Orlando Patterson, *Slavery and Social Death*, pp. 5–9.
9. For further discussion of the convergence of different forms of unfree labour in the southern African context, see Elizabeth A. Eldredge and Fred Morton (eds.), *Slavery in South Africa* (Boulder, 1994).
10. For further discussion of pawnship in Africa, see Toyin Falola and Paul E. Lovejoy (eds.), *Pawnship in Africa: Historical Perspectives on Debt Bondage* (Boulder, 1994).

Part I

Frontiers

Colonization and Slavery in Central America

O. NIGEL BOLLAND

In the development of the 'Atlantic World' after 1492, Central America was always as peripheral as it remains today. Yet it is precisely the peripheral nature of its relationship to this emerging world that is the key to understanding the particular patterns of colonization and varieties of slavery that existed in the three centuries following the conquest. The relationship between colonization and slavery in Central America from the early sixteenth century to the mid-nineteenth century was affected by the fact that the region remained, throughout this period, at the periphery of the Spanish and British empires.

The demand for labour in the early Spanish settlements of Hispaniola, Cuba, Panama, and Peru resulted in a large-scale Indian slave trade in Central America in the second quarter of the sixteenth century. Indeed, the first colonial economy of the region was based on slave trading. Supported by the colonial officials themselves, this odious commerce, more accurately conceived as 'looting' than as trade, remained the principal colonial economic activity until the decline in population reduced the supply.

The export of as many as half a million enslaved Indians prior to 1550 contributed to the rapid and severe depopulation of Central America in the sixteenth century. Subsequent demands for labour, particularly by British woodcutters interloping in Spanish territory in the eighteenth century, depended on the import of slaves of African origin, chiefly via West Indian markets. The abolition of slavery in the newly independent Central American republics in 1821 contributed to undermining the institution in the remaining British settlement at Belize, where it was finally abolished in 1838. Thus, the peripheral nature of the colonies and changes in the colonial economies of Spain and Britain were reflected in changing patterns in the institution of slavery in Central America.

THE ENSLAVEMENT OF INDIANS

Slavery existed in the indigenous societies of Central America, as in Mexica society, but it exhibited a new form and scale with the European conquest of the region.[1] The existence of slavery in the indigenous societies was important to the Spaniards, as it helped them find justifications for continuing the institution, on their own terms. Though the Indians were familiar with the notion, particularly with a pattern of servitude following conquest, the Spaniards found new pretexts for enslaving them. Moreover, the ways in which they obtained slaves, and the scale on which they exported them, had a more devastating effect, especially when combined with the impact of pandemics, than anything experienced during the pre-hispanic period.

Moreover, we should be cautious in interpreting the Spanish sources on indigenous slavery, precisely because the Spaniards were motivated to equate the indigenous forms of servitude with their own. It seems likely that servitude in indigenous societies, though widespread, was more often temporary than under the Spanish, and that the children of slaves were less likely to inherit their mother's status. This is not to suggest that indigenous slavery was somehow 'less oppressive', but simply to warn that the Spaniards had a purpose in translating *tlacotli* and *ppencatob* into 'slavery', in order to try to justify their own cruel and violent actions.

A holocaust devastated Central America in the sixteenth century. When Spaniards undertook the conquest of the region in 1523–4, they found a land teeming with indigenous peoples of many and diverse cultures. In the area between present-day Panama and Mexico (Belize, Guatemala, El Salvador, Honduras, Nicaragua, and Costa Rica) there lived, by conservative estimates, some two and a quarter million people in pre-conquest times. While we will never know exactly how many people there were, we do know that, even taking the more conservative estimates, there was an appalling loss of population within a short period of time of two or three generations. By the early 1570s, only half a century after the Spanish invasion, there were perhaps no more than half a million native people left, most in the highlands of Guatemala.

Many of these people died from diseases, such as pulmonary plague and smallpox, even before the Spanish invasion. Indian traders, messengers, and ambassadors brought infection from Mexico to people who, having no immunity to diseases previously unknown in the region, were devastated. MacLeod says that, 'it is safe, indeed conservative, to say that a third of the Guatemalan highland populations died during this holocaust'.[2] Pedro de Alvarado, on his first intrusion in 1523, encountered the 'sickly survivors' of this disaster.[3] As a result of indigenous long-distance trade and communication throughout the region, similar effects were surely felt elsewhere, such as in Nicaragua even before Pedrarías Dávila and his men arrived from Panama in 1523–4. Cortés found dense Indian populations on the shores of the Gulf of Honduras during his epic march of 1524, but these were also hit by diseases. Further epidemics of smallpox, plague, typhus and measles followed in 1529–31, 1532–4, and 1545–8, resulting in very high mortality rates. The native population of what is now Nicaragua and Honduras was reduced from more than a million before the conquest to 20,000 or 25,000 by the mid-century, and possibly to less than 10,000 by the end of the century.[4]

The Spanish invasion, often preceded by such epidemics, resulted in further disruption and death. Entire communities, and perhaps cultures, disappeared in this period. Native sources in Yucatán describe these incomprehensible epidemics as the time of sickness when the dead lie about everywhere untended. The consequent disruption of normal life promoted famine, which in turn made people weaker and more vulnerable to disease and conquest. In MacLeod's words, 'The conquest of the Mesoamerican part of Central America was itself an unusually destructive and protracted process, especially when compared to that of Mexico.'[5]

In the course of this demographic disaster, and contributing to it, the Spaniards began hunting, enslaving and exporting Indians. The Greater Antillean islands suffered drastic population losses in the early sixteenth century, so Spaniards from Cuba and elsewhere began slave-raiding expeditions to the Yucatán coast and the Bay Islands in the Gulf of Honduras in 1515 to replenish their labour force.[6] Some of the Bay Islands Indians seized a ship in Cuba and returned to their homeland, but the raids continued, undoubtedly because they were lucrative.[7] By 1525 the Bay Islands had been depopulated by raids from Cuba, Hispaniola and Jamaica.[8]

The transport of Indians from Central America to the Caribbean was soon exceeded by their export via the Pacific coast to Panama and Mexico. The Spanish conquest of the rich Inca empire in 1533, in particular, created labour needs not only in Peru itself but also in Panama. As the original inhabitants of Panama were rapidly reduced, the Spaniards faced the problem of replacing them to provide labour for the Spanish settlements and to staff transportation across the isthmus. African slaves were brought in, but there were not enough of them and they were expensive. Instead, as the Spaniards did not at that time perceive of Central America as an attractive area to colonize, they saw the Indians of the region as a large, available and expendable reservoir of labour for their wider colonial designs. Nicaragua became the chief centre of this trade soon after the conquest, and by the 1530s, 'slaving was the basic industry of Nicaragua'.[9] Over two-thirds of the foreign Indian slaves in Peru between 1531 and 1543 were from Nicaragua, the remainder coming equally from Mexico and Guatemala.[10]

In the first half of the sixteenth century, Spanish attitudes towards and treatment of the Indians were full of contradictions. As early as 1512, a dozen years before the conquest of Central America, the Laws of Burgos required Indians to be well treated and converted to Christianity. Though they could be required to work for Spaniards for nine months, they were to be allowed to work for themselves or for wages during the remaining three months, and they were not to be struck or abused. Between 1526 and 1542, several royal edicts proclaimed that Indians were free and not subject to servitude unless they engaged in pagan practices, such as cannibalism, or rebelled. Indians who refused to submit to Spanish authority were called *esclavos de guerra*, while those who were legally purchased from their native owners were known as *esclavos de rescate*.[11] Indians who rose in rebellion against their conquest and ill-treatment thus provided the excuse for their enslavement.

Despite these formal regulations, the enslavement of Indians in Central America that followed the conquest occurred almost without constraint. To some extent, this may be blamed on the 'strong men', Pedro de Alvarado and Pedrarías Dávila, the quintessential *caudillos* who maintained control over most of the region until their deaths, in 1541 and 1531, respectively, and Pedrarías' son-in-law, Rodrigo de Contreras, who ran Nicaragua between 1534 and 1544. Offenders against the law generally went unpunished because the highest colonial officials were themselves in collusion with the slave trade. These peoples' power depended to an extent on their allowing their followers unrestricted access to Indians, with the result that this was 'a period of violence and unrestrained oppression of the native population'.[12]

When the New Laws of the Indies for the Good Treatment and Preservation of the Indians was proclaimed in 1542–3, a new court, the Audiencia de los Confines, was established. From 1544 to 1548, according to Sherman, there was 'better administration and some measure of justice', but 'the plight of the Indians remained much as before'. In 1548, however, a new *audiencia*, formed under Alonso López de Cerrato, substantially enforced the laws to improve the Indians' lot. Nevertheless, 'life for the Indians remained that of servitude to their white masters throughout the sixteenth century and beyond'.[13] The slave trade was reduced to a trickle after 1550, but this was less the result of humane Spanish laws and dedicated judges than that 'there were simply no Indians left to send'.[14] Central America, in the first quarter century after the Spanish invasion, was a 'conquest society', in which 'the *conquistador-encomendero* had little opposition, living off the labor of the conquered people'.[15]

By 1550 the Indian slave trade, in combination with the series of epidemics and famine, had resulted in the severe depopulation, and subsequently the persistent underdevelopment, of the region. Some of the Spanish settlements themselves declined, while others disappeared, in part because of greater attractions in Peru and elsewhere, but also because the continuing decline of the Indian population reduced the supply of labour on which the Spanish settlers depended.[16] Yet another pandemic, probably of pulmonary plague, swept through Central America between 1576 and 1581, again with high mortality rates. Numerous pandemics and local epidemics continued to take a dreadful toll of Indian lives throughout the seventeenth and early eighteenth centuries, shattering the fabric of many Indian societies.

The numbers of Indians enslaved and exported are hard to estimate, as is the number who died in the course of the slaving expeditions. Between 1536 and 1540, more than twenty ships sailed regularly from the Pacific coast of Nicaragua, as often as six times a year to Panama and once or twice a year to Peru. The number of Indians in their cargoes varied but was frequently as high as 400 per ship, and most of the crews were Indian slaves. On this basis, MacLeod estimates, 'ten thousand slaves per year for the decade between 1532 and 1542 would certainly seem to be a low figure, and a total of two hundred thousand Indians for the whole Nicaraguan slaving period appears to be conservative'.[17] Radell estimates that 450,000 to 500,000 Indians were removed by the slave trade from Nicaragua between 1527 and 1548, and another 400,000 to 600,000 died of disease and war, or fled from Spanish domination,[18] while Sherman believes that no more than 150,000 Indians were made chattel slaves between 1524 and 1549 and that fewer than a third of these were exported.[19] Newson estimates that in the decline of the Nicaraguan population, 'the Indian slave trade and disease were of equal importance, perhaps accounting for one third each of the total decline', the remainder dying from overwork, ill-treatment, and the disruption of their communities.[20]

Many other Indians were transported from further north, along the coasts of San Salvador (now El Salvador) and Guatemala. Honduras, too, suffered huge losses to the slave trade. In 1526 the governor of Honduras, López de Salcedo, argued that it was only the traffic in slaves that allowed the Spanish settlement to exist, as the Indians were traded for food from the Caribbean islands. Twenty-five pounds of salted meat or a bushel and a half of maize could be obtained in return for two slaves, worth a couple of pesos each.[21]

The slaving expeditions were hugely wasteful, resulting in many more deaths than live slaves. In 1527 Salcedo led an expedition south into Nicaragua, taking with him hundreds of Indian slaves as bearers. *En route*, he punished by execution and mutilation two hundred Indians who had rebelled. He enslaved a further two thousand Indians, but most died on the way, only a hundred arriving in León. Those enslaved were placed in neck chains, and if they weakened on the journey they were decapitated. The Bishop of Honduras reported that a major expedition from Guatemala, involving three thousand Indian auxiliaries, had resulted in six thousand Indians being killed or enslaved, three thousand of them being taken to Guatemala or sold to the Caribbean islands.[22] While it is difficult to estimate how many were killed as distinct from those who were enslaved, Newson suggests that between 100,000 and 150,000 Indians were enslaved and exported from Honduras, while some 30,000 to 50,000 were killed in the conquest and the raids.[23]

The dramatic decline in the native population concerned those local Spanish officials and *encomenderos* who resented the export of what they saw as their labour supply, a supply that it was hard and expensive for them to replace. By 1545 most labour in the extraction of gold in the Guayape River valley in Honduras was by African slaves, who numbered about 1,500, but most local enterprises could not afford such labour.[24]

López de Cerrato, who arrived after the Nicaraguan and Honduran slave trade had dried up for lack of supplies, was largely successful in using the New Laws to stop the Indian slave trade in Guatemala. At least as important, however, was the fact that the demand for slave exports declined as local Indians in Peru became increasingly subjected to coerced labour after 1548, while mules and horses largely replaced Indian bearers in Panama. By the early 1550s the export of enslaved Indians, the first major staple of the colonial economy of Central America, had virtually disappeared.[25] But attempts to have surviving Indians returned to their homelands from Panama and Peru were unsuccessful. When the Indian slaves were freed in Panama in 1550, only 185 of the 821 brought forward were survivors from the Central American holocaust.[26]

Though relatively large populations survived in the highlands, the Spaniards in Central America could no longer count on what they had falsely assumed to be limitless supplies of Indian labour. While Spanish freeholders still fought against the abolition of Indian slavery, the *encomienda* became 'the most important method of organizing and coercing Indian labor' in the second half of the sixteenth century. So, when López de Cerrato enforced the abolition of Indian slavery in the years after 1548, he 'was not attacking the powerful in Central America, nor was he improving the lot of the majority of Indians who were by this time nearly all in Crown hands or private encomiendas'.[27]

Given the serious labour shortage and the Indians' unwillingness to be ill-treated and exploited voluntarily, it seems inevitable that a variety of forms of forced labour, though not precisely slavery, would continue.[28] The use of *tamemes*, Indian bearers who transported loads on their backs supported by tumplines, contract labour in which the terms sometimes extended for several years, *repartimiento* labour, and other forms of personal service, more or less unfree, persisted. Moreover, some Spaniards continued to hold and act on the idea that Indians who resisted could be enslaved, so 'the issue of Indian slavery was not completely closed in Central America' after the mid-sixteenth century.[29]

So long as surface gold or Indian labour could be grabbed and sold they offered quick fortunes, but once these resources were exhausted those Spaniards who had not moved on had to search for alternatives. Thus, the typical monoculture economy, with its associated cycles of booms and depressions, was established at the beginning of Central American colonization, stimulating 'a constant search for a single key to wealth'.[30]

The problems of the cacao economy illustrate the consequences of the catastrophic decline in the native population. The Spaniards in Guatemala, San Salvador and Nicaragua turned to cacao production in the 1560s. Soconusco, along the Pacific coast, from where cacao had been sent to the Aztecs before the conquest, was the greatest cacao province of all. Its population declined from 30,000 tributaries at the time of the invasion to 1,600 in the 1560s and 1570s. 'Desperate efforts to recruit fresh labor were made, but the new laborers died as rapidly or more rapidly than the original inhabitants.'[31]

Though the cacao economy depended on the skill as well as the hard labour of Indian workers, bad conditions and overwork continued to reduce the labour supply. Indeed, as MacLeod points out,

> overwork in the cacaotales, or cacao plantations, did not begin in a severe form *until* the Indian population had declined so drastically that the labor situation had changed from one of overabundance to one of scarcity. Then indeed the Spaniards forced the remaining Indians to work harder in a desperate attempt to prevent the plantations from becoming overgrown, aged, and gradually unproductive, as they were doing increasingly by the early seventeenth century.[32]

Moreover, as the remaining Indians were forced to work on the plantations, they neglected production of such staples as maize and beans; by 1570 famine was widespread. Facing this shortage of manpower, the Spaniards began coercing large numbers of Indians out of the highlands, where there were still numerous survivors of the holocaust. Though highland Indians poured into Soconusco every year, the population of the area remained around two thousand. 'The long journey, the drastic change in climate, and the exposure to the murderous diseases of the coast quickly killed many of these new arrivals' and among the survivors who returned home were some who carried infections.[33] Soconusco was a depressed area by the end of the sixteenth century, and the high mortality rates promoted by its short-lived 'development' continued well into the seventeenth century.

Forced labour was still widespread when Thomas Gage lived in Central America between 1627 and 1637, and he refers to the extreme violence used against Indians. Nevertheless, as Sherman concludes, while 'unjust exploitation continued in familiar vein until at least a century following the conquest, the vicious atrocities and chattel slavery of the early decades after the conquest were far less in evidence'.[34]

THE ENSLAVEMENT OF AFRICANS

As high mortality rates reduced the Indian slave gangs in Honduras and Guatemala, the Spaniards began to import African slaves. By the 1540s they were arriving in quite large numbers, though not in comparison to the number of Indian slaves being traded. Of the 62,500 African slaves imported into the whole of Spanish America between 1551 and 1600, only about three thousand ended up in Central America. As Burkholder and Johnson have noted, 'African slavery prospered only where a diminished Indian population could no longer sustain alternative forms of labor,'[35] but in Central America, despite the demographic catastrophe, Indian labour was still cheaper than enslaved Africans.

The disastrous decline of the cacao economy by the end of the sixteenth century confirmed a serious and prolonged depression in Central America. The search for new industries and trades resulted in expanding indigo plantations, but shortages of labour remained a persistent problem. The indigo growers, if they had the capital and opportunity, bought African slaves, but purchase prices were high and Central America was not such a good market for slavers as New Spain or Tierra Firme. Moreover, the colonial authorities were anxious about slave revolts and saw the largely unpopulated interior as a dangerously inviting refuge for maroons. The authorities even feared that slaves might join with Indians, free blacks, mulattoes and mestizos in revolt.[36] In any case, few Spanish entrepreneurs could afford African slaves, few were imported after 1635, and the African slave population of the Spanish Central American colonies remained small. Instead, despite legal constraints, fresh expeditions were mounted to enslave previously unconquered Indians. Any sign of rebelliousness became the pretext of slave raids; in 1620 governor Alonso de Guzmán of Costa Rica invented a rebellion among the

Aoyaque Indians in order to attack and enslave them.[37] Though such raids, called *entrada y saca*, increased in the first two decades of the eighteenth century, they did not resolve the Spaniards' labour problem and the shortages continued.

Meanwhile, the peripheral, underpopulated and depressed nature of the Spanish Central American colonies provided an opportunity for their British rivals to intercede, establishing a series of minor settlements along the Mosquito Coast and at Belize, as well as on the Bay Islands in the Gulf of Honduras and on Providence Island off the coast of Nicaragua. Though these settlements were also peripheral to the British empire, they became increasingly important after Britain seized Jamaica from Spain in 1655, as Jamaica became the centre for British trade and piracy in the western Caribbean and Central America. One consequence that was typical of such colonial rivalries was that the British sought allies among the local Indians and maroons who were hostile to Spain.

In the second half of the seventeenth century, small groups of British adventurers, with some African slaves, settled on these Caribbean coasts to engage in small-scale planting and trade with the Indians. By the 1680s, some of these Africans, sent to trade with or raid Indian communities inland from the Mosquito Coast, had mixed with local people. The result was a new people, the Miskito Indians or Zambos Mosquitos, who became feared by the Spaniards and other, less aggressive or less well-armed Indians. These people, who remained largely dependent on the British into the middle of the nineteenth century, inhabited the Caribbean coast between the eastern tip of Honduras and northern Costa Rica. Their principal settlement was at Sandy Bay, near Cap Gracios a Dios.[38] Nineteenth-century chroniclers attested to the persistent power of the Miskito Indians over the 'pure Indians' of the interior, from whom they continued to obtain tribute and even slaves.[39] These Miskito Indians and their persistent slaving activities resulted from the particular patterns of colonization of this region.

For the most part, however, the British settlers along the Caribbean coast depended on imported African slaves, chiefly obtained in West Indian markets such as Jamaica, from the early seventeenth century until the end of the slave trade in 1808. Though they were an expensive source of labour – the compensation money given for freed slaves in 1838 being higher in Belize than in any other colony – the British had better supplies than the Spaniards. Moreover, the British developed a lucrative wood-cutting trade, first in logwood and then mahogany, that made the import of such slaves worthwhile. Consequently, before the middle of the eighteenth century, these slaves became the majority of the population in the British settlements. When the Spaniards captured the settlement at

Belize in 1779 there were about three thousand slaves, who were about 86 per cent of the population. After the resettlement following the peace of 1783, about 75 per cent of the population was slaves, 14 per cent was free blacks and 'coloured', and about 10 per cent was white. After 1787, when 2,214 people, over three-quarters of whom were slaves, were evacuated from the Mosquito Coast to Belize, the British hold on those parts of Honduras and Nicaragua became weaker,[40] while the settlement at Belize became a colony in all but name.[41]

The initial *raison d'être* of British settlement at Belize, sometime in the 1630s, was the exportation of logwood, a tree from which a dye valuable in the woollen industry was extracted. In 1763, the Treaty of Paris conceded the right of the British to cut logwood on what was still defined as Spanish territory, but by then logwood production was only marginally profitable. By 1770, when the depression in the logwood trade was acute, the settlers were exporting mahogany, an enterprise which was legalized by the Convention of London in 1786. Used in the making of luxury furniture and shipbuilding, and later in the construction of railway carriages, mahogany remained the chief export of Belize until the mid-twentieth century.

The shift from logwood to mahogany reinforced the tendency for a few of the wealthier settlers to dominate the economy and control the settlement, as the extraction of mahogany was a much larger-scale operation, requiring more land, labour, and capital. Consequently, while logwood was first cut by British settlers with one or two slaves, the concentration of slave ownership by a handful of 'Principal Inhabitants' who also claimed possession of four-fifths of the land, became marked.[42] By 1816 some 3 per cent of the free heads of families owned 37 per cent of the slaves, and in 1820, the five biggest owners possessed 669 slaves, or over a quarter of the total.[43] Since land tenure remained insecure in the eighteenth century because of Spanish claims to sovereignty, most of the Belizean settlers' capital was invested in slaves.

There was an unusually marked division of labour by gender among the slaves in Belize: in 1834, 795 of the men, over 80 per cent of those over ten years of age, were woodcutters, whereas virtually all the women were involved in domestic work of some kind. Residence patterns, too, were unusual in that men spent the long logging season in more or less temporary camps in the forest, while the women and children were clustered in Belize Town. In this way, the social organization of labour shaped the social and cultural life of the slave population, with the period around Christmas, when all the slaves came together in the town at the end of the logging season, being the climax of the year.[44]

The slave population in Belize, like most in the Americas, did not reproduce itself. There was a marked imbalance of the sexes (generally two or three men to each woman), and high mortality rates resulted from such factors as disease, malnutrition, overwork, and ill-treatment. Some slaves killed themselves and abortion was said to be 'extremely common', having 'its avowed professors' among the slave women.[45] The slave population became increasingly older, as those who were forty years old or more increased from about one-fifth in 1820 to about a third in 1834. From a peak of around three thousand at the beginning of the nineteenth century, the slave population declined after the abolition of the slave trade, and their proportion to the rest of the population declined dramatically. In 1834, the 1,923 slaves constituted less than half the total population of the settlement, not counting the Maya Indians in the interior or the Garifuna in the south. By that time, men outnumbered women by only seven to six under the age of forty, compared to ten to three at age forty years or more. These figures suggest that the slave population had attained greater demographic stability by the time of emancipation in 1838.[46]

Two further factors contributed to the decline in the slave population of Belize in the early nineteenth century. One was the rate of manumission, which was unusually high for a British colony. Almost three hundred slaves were manumitted between 1808 and 1820, and 210 between 1821 and 1830, a total of about one-fifth of the slave population in 1834. Less than a quarter of the manumitted slaves were adult males, despite the fact that they constituted the majority of slaves, and the most common forms of manumission, by gift or bequest of the owner, suggest that many of those being freed were the slave mistresses and children of their owners. However, a surprising number of slaves purchased their own freedom, often at considerable expense; one slave paid £450 for his freedom in 1829.[47]

The other cause of the decline of the slave population was simply that many slaves escaped. The British settlers repeatedly complained that the neighbouring Spaniards gave asylum to runaway slaves, and the organization of timber extraction, with many small gangs scattered throughout the forest, facilitated flight. Most of the slaves who escaped in the eighteenth century went north across the Rio Hondo into Yucatán, where the commandant at Bacalar offered them freedom and protection. When the mahogany cutting expanded to the west and south in the early nineteenth century, pushing the Maya further back into the forests, the slaves tended to escape through the bush into the Petén in northern Guatemala or by boat down the coast to Omoa and Trujillo in Honduras. Most of the slave revolts that occurred, in 1765, 1768, 1773 and 1820, ended with slaves escaping, either over the border into Spanish territory or to maroon communities in the interior of Belize. In 1817 the Magistrates expressed the fear that runaway slaves would join with Indians, overpower the British and destroy the settlement, but there is no evidence that this was ever attempted. The most serious instance of Maya resistance did not develop until a decade after slavery was abolished.

Complaints of escaping slaves increased after the neighbouring Spanish territories became independent and abolished slavery. In a little more than two months in 1823, for example, 39 slaves 'absconded' to the Petén, where they knew there was 'a Town of black People' who had fled from Belize in former years. In 1825, the settlers were desperate, 'having just learnt that 19 slaves have left their employments up the river in a body, and taken the road to the Town of Petén at the head of the River, and 12 to Omoa ... instant ruin stares us in the face'.[48] The facility with which slaves could escape also inhibited ill-treatment. George Hyde, a leading free coloured merchant and slave-owner, complained in 1825 that 'as for punishment or ill-usage, you are aware (if ever so deserved) we dare not inflict it, so easy is their retreat to the Spaniards'.[49] James Stephen, in the Colonial Office, commented in 1830 that, '[British] Honduras is now in the centre of countries which have declared Slavery illegal, and if we persist in maintaining it we must look for a rapid depopulation of the settlement by slaves passing the border line, and returning no more.'[50]

There is no doubt that many slaves took advantage of the opportunities available and, by voting with their feet, contributed to undermining slavery in Belize. The Abolition Act, passed in June 1833, was applied to Belize as if it were a colony (though this was not officially declared until 1862), instituting the 'apprenticeship' system in 1834 and ending it in 1838, just as in the British West Indies.

Varieties of coerced labour persisted in Belize, as elsewhere in Central America, long after slavery had been made illegal. The extreme concentration of land ownership ensured a dependent population,[51] and forms of debt servitude, backed by an expanding police system to enforce the labour laws, disciplined the workers of Belize effectively for more than a century after 1838.[52]

CONCLUSION

The fact that Spanish conquistadores demanded labour outside Central America more than they required it within resulted in the huge export trade in Indian slaves in the 1530s and 1540s, which in turn contributed to depopulation, persistent labour shortages, and the subsequent under-development of the region. The holocaust, in which some three-quarters of the indigenous population of Central America was lost in the fifty years after the conquest, condemned the region to persistent underdevelopment and confirmed its peripheral status within the Spanish empire. The effect was most severe in Nicaragua and Honduras, where the combination of disease, warfare, enslavement, and social disruption reduced the native population by over ninety per cent in the second quarter of the sixteenth century. The Spaniards' motives in the region were to accumulate wealth as quickly as possible, and few thought of long-term settlement or economic development. MacLeod has aptly characterized the conquest of Central America and the two following decades as 'a large raid', rather than an occupation.[53]

Meanwhile, the relative lack of Spanish interest in settling the Caribbean coast enabled the British to establish small settlements from the mid-seventeenth century, expanding them with the importation of slaves of African and West Indian origin. After Spanish power waned in the eighteenth century, the British colony of Belize developed on the basis of African slave labour, while the Spanish colonies of Central America continued to stagnate. Finally, the independence of the Spanish territories and their abolition of slavery helped undermine the institution of slavery in Belize by faciliting the escape of slaves.

After the legal end to slavery in Belize in 1838, varieties of coerced labour persisted in much of Central America. Even today, over 150 years after the abolition of slavery, many people, whether of African, Indian, or mixed descent, continue to struggle against the persistent legacies of colonization and slavery in the region.[54]

NOTES

1. Murdo J. MacLeod, *Spanish Central America: A Socioeconomic History, 1520–1720* (Berkeley, 1973), pp. 27–8, 32; Sylvanus G. Morley, *The Ancient Maya* (Stanford, 1956), pp. 159–61; William L. Sherman, *Forced Native Labor in Sixteenth-Century Central America* (Lincoln, 1979), pp. 15–19; Eric Wolf, *Sons of the Shaking Earth* (Chicago, 1959), pp. 142–4.
2. MacLeod, *Spanish Central America*, p. 41.
3. Ibid., p. 41.
4. David R. Radell, 'The Indian Slave Trade and Population of Nicaragua During the Sixteenth Century', in W.M. Denevan (ed.), *The Native Population of the Americas in 1492* (Madison, 1976), p. 76.
5. MacLeod, *Spanish Central America*, p. 41.
6. Ruth Kerns Barber, *Indian Labor in the Spanish Colonies* (Albuquerque, 1932), p. 110.
7. MacLeod, *Spanish Central America*, p. 50.
8. Linda Newson, *The Cost of Conquest: Indian Decline in Honduras Under Spanish Rule* (Boulder, 1986), p. 108.
9. MacLeod, *Spanish Central America*, p. 51.
10. James Lockhart, *Spanish Peru, 1532–1560: A Colonial Society* (Madison, 1968), p. 200.

11. Newson, *The Cost of Conquest*, p. 108.
12. Sherman, *Forced Native Labor*, p. 10.
13. Ibid., p. 12.
14. MacLeod, *Spanish Central America*, p. 54.
15. Sherman, *Forced Native Labor*, p. 9.
16. Ibid., p. 7.
17. MacLeod, *Spanish Central America*, p. 52.
18. Radell, 'The Indian Slave Trade', p. 75.
19. Sherman, *Forced Native Labor*, p. 82.
20. Linda Newson, *Indian Survival in Colonial Nicaragua* (Norman, 1987), pp. 123–4.
21. Sherman, *Forced Native Labour*, p. 68.
22. Newson, *The Cost of Conquest*, pp. 109–10.
23. Ibid., pp. 127–8.
24. MacLeod, *Spanish Central America*, pp. 60–61.
25. Ibid., p. 56.
26. Sherman, *Forced Native Labor*, p. 81.
27. MacLeod, *Spanish Central America*, pp. 111–12.
28. Sherman, *Forced Native Labor*, p. 208.
29. Ibid., p. 216.
30. MacLeod, *Spanish Central America*, p. 47.
31. Ibid., p. 71.
32. Ibid., p. 73.
33. Ibid., p. 77.
34. Sherman, *Forced Native Labor*, p. 338.
35. Mark A. Burkholder and Lyman L. Johnson, *Colonial Latin America* (New York, 1990), p. 118.
36. MacLeod, *Spanish Central America*, pp. 190–91.
37. Ibid., pp. 300, 451.
38. Center for Research and Documentation of the Atlantic Coast, *Trabil Nani* (Managua, n.d.[1984]), pp. 11–14.
39. C. Napier Bell, *Tangweera: Life and Adventures Among Gentle Savages* (Austin, 1989); Orlando W. Roberts, *Narrative of Voyages and Excursions on the East Coast and in the Interior of Central America* (Gainesville, 1965); see also O. Nigel Bolland, 'Indios Bravos or Gentle Savages: 19th Century Views of the Indians of Belize and the Miskito Coast', *Revista/Review Interamericana*, 22 (1992), pp. 36–54.
40. Robert A. Naylor, *Penny Ante Imperialism: The Mosquito Shore and the Bay of Honduras, 1600–1914: A Case Study in British Informal Empire* (Rutherford, 1989).
41. O. Nigel Bolland, 'The Social Structure and Social Relations of the Settlement in the Bay of Honduras (Belize) in the 18th Century', *Journal of Caribbean History*, 6 (1973), pp. 1–42; *The Formation of a Colonial Society: Belize, From Conquest to Crown Colony* (Baltimore, 1977); *Colonialism and Resistance in Belize: Essays in Historical Sociology* (Benque Viejo del Carmen, 1988).
42. Bolland, *Foundation of a Colonial Society*.
43. Bolland, *Colonialism and Resistance*, pp. 58–9.
44. O. Nigel Bolland, 'The Extraction of Timber in the Slave Society of Belize', Paper given at the conference, 'Cultivation and Culture: Labor and the Shaping of Slave Life in the Americas' (University of Maryland, College Park, 1989).
45. Captain G. Henderson, *An Account of the British Settlement of Honduras* (London, 1809), p. 75.
46. Bolland, *Colonialism and Resistance*, p. 47.
47. Ibid., p. 57.
48. Magistrates to Supt. Codd, 28 Jan. 1823, CO 123/36, Public Record Office (PRO), Kew.
49. Frederick Crowe, *The Gospel in Central America* (London, 1850), p. 321.
50. James Stephen to Horace Twiss, 13 Oct. 1830, CO 123/41, PRO.
51. O. Nigel Bolland and Assad Shoman, *Land In Belize, 1765–1871* (Kingston, 1977).

52. O. Nigel Bolland, 'Systems of Domination After Slavery: The Control of Land and Labor in the British West Indies After 1838', *Comparative Studies in Society and History*, 23 (1981), pp. 591–619; 'Labour Control and Resistance in Belize in the Century After 1838', *Slavery and Abolition*, 7 (1986), pp. 175–87.
53. MacLeod, *Spanish Central America*, p. 47.
54. Rigoberta Menchu, *I, Rigoberta Menchu: An Indian Woman in Guatemala*, edited by Elisabeth Burgos-Debray, translated by Ann Wright (London, 1984).

Land-Labour Relations in Sixteenth-Century Mexico: The Formation of Grazing Haciendas

ELINOR G. K. MELVILLE

Spaniards introduced sheep into New Spain immediately following the defeat of the Mexica in 1521 and the collapse of the Aztec empire, and by the middle of the sixteenth century vast flocks grazed the central highlands.[1] During the same period the Spaniards developed a woolen textile industry that dominated markets in New Spain and Peru and challenged the monopoly of Spanish textile supply by the end of the sixteenth century.[2] In the context of the Spanish conquest and the formation of a colonial regime, it would not be too surprising to find that gangs of Indian labourers were coerced into shearing the huge flocks that supplied the woolen industry; and it is possible this did happen in the early years of sheep raising. But evidence from a major sheep grazing region demonstrates that Indian shearers were selling their skill freely and individually to the owners of the small holdings which formed the base of operations for pastoralism in the formative conquest era: the *estancias*. Taken together with evidence of quite extensive Indian involvement in sheep raising, the presence of free wage labourers in this era suggests a rather more active role for Indians in the formation of the mature colonial system of production, the *hacienda*, than is generally acknowledged.

The presence of wage labour has been taken as a definitive indicator of the appearance of the hacienda since the publication in 1967 of Charles Gibson's classic study of Indian and Spanish relations. Gibson not only demonstrated that wages were used to recruit labour for colonial rural estates, but he also suggested that the profit motive shaped estate-owners' actions; that estates were acquired and managed to produce for market exchange, not simply for subsistence or prestige.[3] The extraordinary amount of research stimulated by Gibson's work has transformed our understanding of colonial Mexico as a rigid tradition-bound neo-feudal world. The colonial political economy is now depicted as a dynamic commercial world driven by profit and markets.[4]

Perhaps the reaction has been somewhat too far in the direction away from the traditional model, so that colonial Mexico seems at times to be too modern, too developed to be true. None the less, research focusing on hacienda organization and its role in the colonial political economy has confirmed Gibson's propositions by demonstrating that estates were, to a greater or lesser degree, part of a system of market exchange and were managed to make profits; with varying degrees of success according to the individual capacities of the owner and his or her agent-overseer.[5] Wage labour was indeed a major form of labour recruitment and labour costs were far and away the largest expense faced by any type of great estate, whether it was producing grains, livestock or sugar. In fact, in some regions rural estates owed more money to labourers than the reverse during the seventeenth century – indicating the considerable bargaining power of the Indians.[6] On the grazing haciendas in the Isthmus of Tehuantepec, for example, 'promptly paid, relatively good wages, rather than high-level debts, induced local Indians and mullatoes to work on the haciendas'.[7]

Wage labour, however, was only one among many different types of colonial labour relations. These same hacienda studies, together with studies of textile manufacturers and mines, have demonstrated an extraordinary variety of labour regimes in place by the end of the sixteenth century. Various forms of coerced labour, such as debt peonage, slavery and work gangs existed side by side with wage labour- and cost-sharing arrangements.[8] Indeed, this sort of variety has come to be accepted as the distinguishing characteristic of the colonial systems of production.[9]

Current models of the development of colonial labour regimes link the appearance of different forms of labour recruitment to the demographic collapse of the indigenous population. The means used to obtain labour immediately after the military defeat of the indigenous elites in the central regions were predicated on huge populations and included outright slavery and the *encomienda* (grant of access to labour and tribute of Indians in specified areas). With direct and virtually exclusive access to the labour pool (at least amongst the Spanish population) the *encomenderos* effectively controlled the colonial economy. In the 1540s the crown moved to restrain the growing power of the *encomenderos* by, among other things, restricting access to personal service.[10] The *encomenderos* resisted this curtailment of their power base; but in 1550, immediately following a severe four-year pandemic (1545–8) and, it appears, in response to the abrupt decline in indigenous populations, a system of government-controlled draft labour known as the *repartimiento* was formally instituted. A number of labourers was to be taken weekly from each community (starting at 2 per cent of the adult males and increasing thereafter) to work in the mines, on government work projects, and on Spanish landholdings. Workers were collected on Monday mornings and walked to their place of work where they worked from Tuesday to Tuesday, with Sunday as a day of rest; in this way a continuous flow of labour was ensured. Each labourer was to work on the *repartimiento* not more than three or four times a year and, theoretically at least, he was to be paid for his labour. It was intended that the *repartimiento* replace *encomienda* service, and it was hoped that it would encourage the development of voluntary wage labour. But in many instances *encomienda* service remained in place despite the prohibition, and it is clear that the *repartimiento* never functioned as a voluntary paid labour draft.[11]

The next stage in the sequence links the appearance of both wage labour and the *hacienda* system of production with the abrupt decline in indigenous populations during the pandemic known as the Great *Cocolistle*, which ravaged New Spain from 1576 to 1581. The demographic collapse associated with this epidemic drastically reduced the pool of labourers available for the *repartimiento*. At the same time Indian production declined precipitously and Spanish production took up the slack. The combination of a shrinking labour pool and increasing demand for labour, it is argued, forced Spanish landowners to look outside the *repartimiento* to supply their needs; and, as had already occurred in the mining regions, they began to offer inducements to workers in the form of wages, tribute payments, food and sometimes residence on the hacienda. The hacienda and wage labour are thought to have appeared on the rural scene at the same time. The monopolization of labour by estate owners who were concurrently moving to monopolize land is seen as a defining characteristic of hacienda formation.[12]

Hacienda studies appear to confirm this model by demonstrating the extent of wage labour present on haciendas in all regions of Mexico. Most of these studies focus on the structure and function of haciendas, however, and do not deal explicitly with developments in the pre-hacienda era. They invariably begin with a discussion of the acquisition of the holdings which formed the land base of the hacienda, then describe the labour regimes used to work that land.[13] Despite Lockhart's caution that historians begin at the beginning, historians of the hacienda do not address the question of the nature of land-labour relations prior to its appearance.[14]

When we look more closely at the pre-hacienda era, however, or simply consider carefully the implications of regional variations in land and labour relations on haciendas, we find a great deal of carry-over from earlier systems of production.[15] For example, the sixteenth-century history of land and labour relations in the Valle del Mezquital demonstrates the importance of the small holdings which appeared prior to the hacienda as both the territorial units out of which the hacienda was formed, and as units of production where labour regimes characteristic of the hacienda were developed.[16]

Grazing dominated regional production in the Valle del Mezquital by the 1570s. Large numbers of individual livestock owners who based their operations in the *estancia* (station) of ca. 7.8 km^2, grazed huge numbers of sheep in common in all parts of the region. Agriculture was less important, but the small-scale intensive agricultural unit, the *labor*, was present in certain parts of the region by the same date. *Labores* were formed by coalescing two to six *caballeras de tierra* (48.5 ha agricultural land grants) into one holding where irrigation and relatively intensive management practices were used to grow primarily Old World products such as wheat, barley, figs and grapes.[17]

What is particularly interesting about the *estancias* and *labores* from our point of view is the fact that wage labour appears on these holdings. That is, the labour relationship thought to be a defining characteristic of hacienda formation was already in place when haciendas appeared. In the accepted developmental sequence, *estancias* and *labores* are associated with *repartimiento*, slave, or *encomienda* labour, i.e. various forms of coerced labour; and indeed, there is evidence that *encomienda* and *repartimiento* Indians, and some slaves, were used on both *estancias* and *labores*.[18] However, not only are various categories of wage labourers (*sirvientes*, '*gente*', *naboríos*, *gañanes*)[19] resident on these units of production, in a manner reminiscent of later hacienda residence patterns; there is also evidence that Indian sheep shearers freely sold their skill, not simply their labour, outside the *repartimiento*.[20]

As yet this author has not found any similar cases of agricultural specialists living in the villages and selling their skills individually to the *labor* owners; *mayordomos* and other more skilled labourers appear in most cases to have lived on the *labor*.[21] This apparent difference between the labour regimes of the *estancia* and *labores* may be simply a factor of the documentation; but by the eighteenth century the labour regimes characteristic of grazing and agricultural haciendas exhibited intriguing differences. According to Riley,

> Grazing estates employed labourers described as *sirvientes* who were hispanicized and predominantly from mixed-blood groups. Paid monthly, they were rarely deeply in debt and, judging from the rate of turn-over discovered by some researchers, had little attachment to the estates on which they laboured. Agricultural operations on the other hand, employed a few *sirvientes* as *mayordomos* or field bosses, but the remainder of the labour was provided in the

central valleys by tributary Indians who, during the seventeenth and
early eighteenth centuries, fell into one of three categories: the
gañanes, who generally resided on the *hacienda*, but more
important, were included on its tribute rolls; occasional labourers,
called *tlaquehuales* or peons, who resided and paid tribute in
corporate villages; and contract workers, called *indios de cuadrilla*,
who lived in villages and were hired in teams (usually of forty men)
at times of peak need, like sowing and harvesting seasons.[22]

These differences were not simply the result of the different labour needs
of pastoralism and agriculture; rather, they arose in the formative pre-
hacienda era as a result of the different developmental processes by which
grazing and Spanish agriculture evolved in New Spain.

Spanish agriculture was dominated by the *encomenderos* until 1550
when the *repartimiento* system of labour drafts made Indian labour
available, at least in theory, to all landowners. Up to this point *encomenderos* had a virtual monopoly on production: they specified the tributes
they required, the crops they wanted grown, and used their Indian
labourers for a wide range of entrepreneurial activities.[23] But they had no
legal right to the land within their *encomiendas*; and while they did have
indirect access to the land and control over what was produced, the
encomenderos were ultimately dependent on the Indians' labour, land
use and land tenure systems. The crop was grown on Indian lands, by
Indian labour, and most often by Indian land management techniques –
even wheat was, at first, grown according to Indian practices.[24] In the
1530s a system by which individuals obtained formal rights to land within
the Spanish system of land tenure, was formally instituted. The recipient
of an agricultural grant, very often an *encomendero* in the early period,
received title to the land and had exclusive access to the soil during the
growing season; fallow fields were to be open for common grazing. But
they were still dependent almost entirely on Indian labour for all aspects
of the agricultural cycle.[25]

Pastoralists, by contrast, were not restricted to the Indian communities
for their source of labour, since herdsmen and shepherds were almost
exlusively African slaves in the early decades. Nor did they need to
acquire land in order to graze their animals, because grass was a fruit of
Nature and a common resource, and animals could legally graze
wherever grass grew.[26] Pastoralism was thereby able to develop uncon-
strained by Indian land use and tenure rights, or by the need to draw only
on Indian communities for their labour. In contrast to Spanish agriculture, pastoralism existed 'outside' the *encomienda*/village systems of

production, and had all the advantages of untrammeled exploitation of new ecological and social niches. Pastoralists also received land grants, very often confirming squatters' rights, that gave license to build shepherds' huts and corrals and to graze in common the surrounding area.[27] But livestock owners did not move to maintain exclusive access to the lands their stations encompassed, or to define clearly its boundaries, until the range deteriorated in the last quarter of the sixteenth century and land and the pasture on it became a scarce and valuable resource.[28]

This author has suggested elsewhere that if the range had not deteriorated under heavy grazing, small holdings and grazing the range in common probably would have remained the basis of livestock management. With the deterioration of the carrying capacity in the 1580s, however, and the associated decline in the animal populations, stock owners moved to enforce exclusive access and those who could acquired several stations and formed large grazing haciendas. By these means they were able to monopolize ever larger areas of land in order to maintain flock numbers, and thereby profits, and to take advantage of the sellers' market at the end of the sixteenth century.[29] The relations of production that developed as grazing expanded across the region remained to characterise livestock management on the haciendas, and by the eighteenth century labourers on grazing haciendas were considerably less tied to the estate than agricultural labour.[30]

Pastoralism evolved as a parallel system of resource exploitation independent of village production systems. This aided its expansion into even densely populated agricultural regions. The expansion of sheep grazing also seems to have been facilitated by Indian participation in this new form of land use.[31] The Valle del Mezquital, for example, is notable for the number of grants made to Indian nobles and communities for grazing land: between 1560 and 1565 Indians received 78.9 per cent of the grants made for sheep stations in this region. Indian participation in this industry was cut back later in the century when Spanish authorities, reacting to the rapid collapse of the animal populations that occurred during the last quarter of the sixteenth century throughout New Spain, restricted the number of animals Indians could graze. Despite this restriction, however, Indian nobles, and Indian communities to a slightly lesser extent, continued to own land, some 37 per cent of all the land given over to sheep raising in the Valle del Mezquital by the end of the sixteenth century.[32] It is possible that existence outside Indian village production made pastoralism an attractive occupation for Indian nobles; and it may be that the independence of Indian sheep shearers grew out of the possibility of alternative work on Indian stations. Judith Zeitlan makes a similar point when she notes that

although Indian-Afro-Mexican relations were not particularly har-
monious, the nature of *estancia* labour and the presence of free
black and mulatto communities in its midst gave the native population a closer look at the attitudes, behavior, and livelihood of a
segment of colonial society closer in status to itself, one whose very
presence in [the Tehuantepec Isthmus] was tied to the new ranching
economy. For some segments of the Indian population, emulation
of these black *vaqueros* may have been a more appealing alternative
than that of trying to maintain the economic and social norms of the
past.[33]

Developments in the Valle del Mezquital confirm Gibson's understanding of the years between the great pandemics (1544–8, 1576–81) as
a dynamic period of Indian-Spanish relations when the Indians were
actively engaged in the formation of land-labour relations in rural areas,
rather than simply responding to Spanish initiatives.[34] Because hacienda
studies have dominated the study of rural labour relations, the active role
of Indians in the evolution of the early colonial labour regimes has been
obscured. Hacienda labourers have been found to have used their
considerable bargaining power in negotiations for advances and other
perquisites. But the development of rural wage labour is presented as a
Spanish initiative to attract labourers in times of labour shortages. In this
scenario, Indians adapted to, and manipulated, new opportunities
opened up by Spanish initiative; they did not make new opportunities for
themselves. By contrast, the activities of Indians in the early years of
silver mining have come to be viewed as aggresively entrepreneurial. For
example, Steve Stern writes of Indian mine labour in Potosí:

> In a phase lasting until the early 1570s, what was remarkable was the
> dependence of European silver producers on conditions of work
> and technology defined largely by Indians. Indian labourers were
> either *yanaconas*, indvidual Indians who had cut or loosened ties
> with native ethnic-kin groups, or *encomienda* Indians. ... For the
> most part, the *yanaconas* floated independently from employer to
> employer and, in effect, leased rights to mine particular veins in
> exchange for providing a share of the ore to their employers. The
> *yanaconas* assumed responsibility for organizing, provisioning, and
> paying their own work parties. The *encomienda* Indians, theoreti-
> cally a more subject group, in practice turned over the silver needed
> to pay tributes to their *encomenderos* and kept the rest for them-
> selves. ... Moreover, the Indians controlled the smelting of silver.
> Literally thousands of *guayras*, small wind ovens, dotted the great
> silver mountain, and it was through the Indian ore market that

crude ore was bought, refined, and resold as silver. To acquire pure silver, the Spaniards had to sell the ore they received as tribute or as 'shares' back to the Indians.[35]

The implications of such activities, as Stern and others have noted, is that Indians were not passively adapting to Spanish initiatives but actively engaging in the new regime in formation. If Indians were able to manipulate the Andean mining system to their benefit, there is really no reason why they could not manipulate other areas of the evolving colonial political economy as well. In his study of Oaxaca, for example, William Taylor has demonstrated that Indians were fully capable of holding on to their land, and of continuing to dominate regional production at the expense of the Spanish landowners throughout the colonial era. He suggests that distance from the centre, lack of attractive resources or markets accounted for the comparative lack of interest shown by Spaniards in Oaxaca during the colonial era. The implication is that had the Spaniards been interested they would have been in Oaxaca in force, and the Indians would have suffered the fate of the Aztecs in the Valley of Mexico.[36]

At first glance the Valle del Mezquital confirms Taylor's model for central regions: the Mexico City markets lay close to the South, the silver mines of Pachuca were located immediately to the East, and the textile manufacturing city of Queretaro was not too far to the North; and, by the end of the sixteenth century, two-thirds of the land had been transferred into the Spanish system of land tenure. But, as we have seen, this picture of Spanish takeover is misleading: Indians took a very active role in sheep grazing as both skilled labourers and pastoralists. It would appear that even in those rural areas in the centre of Spanish power, Indians were not always content to be led off in gangs to labour on others' lands; that skilled Indian labourers, as well as Indian nobles, took advantage of the freedom offered by the new industry to shape their world.

NOTES

1. See Lesley B. Simpson, *Exploitation of Land in Sixteenth Century Mexico* (Berkeley and Los Angeles, 1952), pp.2–6, for contemporary witness to the increase of grazing animals.
2. Richard J. Salvucci, *Textiles and Capitalism in Mexico. An Economic History of the Obrajes, 1539–1840* (Princeton, 1987), p.9.
3. Charles Gibson, *The Aztecs under Spanish Rule. A History of the Indians of the Valley of Mexico, 1519–1810* (Stanford, 1964), Ch. 9, esp. p.246.
4. For an example of the revisionist synthesis of Mexican colonial history, see Colin M. MacLachlan and Jaime E. Rodriguez O., *The Forging of the Cosmic Race: A Reinterpretation of Colonial Mexico* (Berkeley and Los Angeles, 1980).

5. For a discussion of Mexican rural history, and in particular an examination of the historiography of the colonial hacienda, see Eric Van Young, 'Mexican Rural History Since Chevalier: the Historiography of the Colonial Hacienda', *Latin American Research Review*, 18 (1983), pp. 5–61.

6. James D. Riley, 'Crown Law and Rural labour in New Spain: The Status of Gañanes during the Eighteenth Century', *Hispanic American Historical Review*, 64, 2 (1984), pp. 259–85.

7. Lolita Guttierez Brockington, *The Leverage of Labour. Managing the Cortés Haciendas in Tehuantepec, 1588–1688* (Durham, 1989), p. 168.

8. See Van Young's discussion of the different labour regimes found on the Mexican hacienda during the colonial era, 'Mexican Rural History', pp. 16–23.

9. Steve J. Stern, 'Feudalism, Capitalism, and the World-System in the Perspective of Latin America and the Caribbean', *American Historical Review*, 93 (1988), p. 870.

10. See Gibson, *Aztecs*, Ch. IV, for a discussion of *encomienda* history in the Valley of Mexico.

11. Gibson, *Aztecs*, Ch. 9, esp. pp. 224–36.

12. Ibid., 246 ff; see also Van Young, 'Mexican Rural History', p. 22.

13. Herman W. Konrad, for example, begins his classic study of the huge Jesuit hacienda, Santa Lucia, with a discussion of the acquisition of land between 1576 and 1586; *A Jesuit Hacienda in Colonial Mexico: Santa Lucia, 1576–1767* (Stanford, 1980), pp. 15–45.

14. James Lockhart, 'Encomienda and Hacienda: The Evolution of the Great Estate in the Spanish Indies', *Hispanic American Historical Review*, 49 (1969), p. 428.

15. See, for example, Lolita Gutierrez Brockington's discussion of labour regimes in Tehuantepec, and her comparison of the history of labour regimes in Oaxaca, Morelos, Guadalajara, Yucatan and Tlaxcala, *The Leverage of Labor*, esp. pp. 167–9.

16. This paper is a preliminary attempt to combine my study of the transferral of land rights from the Indian to the Spanish system of land tenure in the Valle del Mezquital with the as yet unpublished results of a study of the evolution of colonial labour relations in this region during the period 1521–1600; Elinor G. K. Melville, *A Plague of Sheep: Environmental Consequences of the Conquest of Mexico* (New York, 1994). Chapter 5 contains a discussion of the land take-over process, and Chapter 6 a discussion of the formation of grazing haciendas in the Valle del Mezquital.

17. Ibid., Ch. 4, 5.

18. *Encomienda*: AGI, Escribanía de cámara, leg. 160–B, #3, fol. 76v; leg. 161–C, fol. 80r. AGN, General de Parte, Vol. 3, fols. 1 24v–125v. AGN, Indios, Vol. 3, fols. 191r. AGN, Tierras, Vol. 2812, exp. 13, fol. 407r. Papeles de la Nueva España Vol. I, p. 218. *Repartimiento*: AGI, Audiencia de Mexico, leg. 111, ramo 2, doc. 12: this document is a census of all Spanish holdings in the Huichiapan and Alfaxayucan Valleys in 1588–9, with an estimation of their labour needs. It also contains a census of the tributary population of the villages, and an estimation of the numbers of labourers each village can supply. Other sources: AGN, Mercedes, Vol. 7, fols. 179r-v, Vol. 8, fols. 50v, 64v–65r. AGN, General de Parte, Vol. 2, fols. 38v, 73v, 86r, 236v, 264v–265r; Vol. 3, fols. 15 v–16r, 124v–125v, 202r; Vol. 4, fols. 12v, 86r–v; Vol. 5, fols 134r. AGN, Indios, Vol. 4, fols. 220v–221r; Vol. 5, fols 2v–3v, 85v–86r; Vol. 6–1, fols. 79r–v. AGN, Tierras, Vol. 2337, exp. 1, fol. 392r. *Slaves*: AGN, Tierras, Vol. 1521, exp. 2; Vol. 1527, exp. 1, fol. 2r, 80. AGN, General de Parte, Vol. 1, fols. 181r, 207v; Vol. 3, fols. 124v–125v,. AGN, Indios, Vol. 5, fols. 2v–3v, 203r–v. AGN, Mercedes, Vol. 4, fols. 370r–v. AGI, Audiencia de México, leg. 11 1, ramo 2, doc. 12.

19. *Gañanes*: AGI, Audiencia de México, leg. 111, ramo, 2 doc. 12. AGN, Tierras, Vol. 2105, exp. 1, fol. 10v; Vol. 2812, exp. 13, fol. 411. AGN, General de Parte, Vol. 5, fol. 26v, 65r–v. *Navoríos*, 'Gente': AGI, Audiencia de México, leg. 111, ramo 2, doc.12. *Sirvientes*: AGN, General de Parte, Vol. 3, fols 202r.

20. AGN, Civil, Vol. 809, exp. 6; AGN, Tierras, Vol. 2713, exp. 18, fol. 8v.

21. AGN, Audiencia de México, leg. 111, ramo 2, doc. 12.

22. James D. Riley, 'Crown Law and Rural Labor in New Spain: the Status of Gañanes during the Eighteenth Century', *Hispanic American Historical Review*, 64, 2 (1984),

pp. 261–2.
23. For a discussion of the activities of the *encomenderos* and the role they played in the formation of the colonial political economy, see José Miranda, *La función económica del encomendero en los origenes del regimen colonial* (Mexico City, 1965).
24. Gibson, *Aztecs*, p. 322.
25. Ibid., pp. 322–6, for a discussion of Spanish agriculture using *repartimiento* labour.
26. François Chevalier, *La formación de los grandes latifundios en Mexico* (Mexico City, 1975), p. 12. David E. Vassberg, *Land and Society in Golden Age Castile* (Cambridge, 1984), p. 6.
27. Simpson, Gibson and Chevalier also note that grants were often issued for lands already in the possession of the grantees; Simpson, *Exploitation*, p. 6. Gibson, *Aztecs*, p. 275. Chevalier, *La formacion*, p. 131.
28. This point is discussed fully in Melville, *A Plague of Sheep*, Ch. 6.
29. A similar process of land acquisition underlay the formation of agricultural haciendas, but in this case the drop in supply of agricultural products that made the markets so attractive was brought about by the decline in indigenous production as a result of the demographic collapse during the 1576–81 pandemic. François Chevalier, *La formación*, p. 44; André Gunder Frank, *Mexican Agriculture, 1521–1630. Transformation of the Mode of Production* (New York, 1979), Ch. 6.
30. In addition to Riley, 'Crown Law and Rural Labor', see also Brockington, *The Leverage of Labor*, esp. p. 168.
31. Gibson notes the importance of sheep grazing within the centre of Spanish power, the Valley of Mexico, *Aztecs*, p. 345.
32. The history of transferance of land from Indian to Spanish land holding is discussed in detail in Melville, *A Plague of Sheep*, Ch. 5. Over the course of the century Indians received 54 per cent of all the land grants (nobles obtained 56 per cent of these grants, communities 44 per cent). Spaniards seem to have been more adept in this region in the fine art of squatting and regularising their rights with titles.
33. Judith Frances Zeitlan, 'Ranchers and Indians on the Southern Isthmus of Tehuantepec: Economic Change and Indigenous Survival in Colonial Mexico', *Hispanic American Historical Review*, 69, 1 (1989), p. 47.
34. Gibson, *Aztecs*, p. 404.
35. Steve J. Stern, 'Feudalism, Capitalism and the World-System in the Perspective of Latin America and the Caribbean', *American Historical Review*, 93 (1988), p. 850.
36. William B. Taylor, *Landlord and Peasant in Colonial Oaxaca* (Stanford, 1972), esp. his conclusions, pp. 195–202.

The Colours of Property: Brown, White and Black Chattels and their Responses on the Caribbean Frontier

HILARY McD. BECKLES

The establishment of colonial dispensations on the Caribbean frontier by rival European imperial powers was conceived and implemented within an ideological framework that sanctioned and mandated the extensive use of servile labour. The creation and survival of economic enterprises across imperial borders, in mining, agriculture, distributive trades and services, depended upon the availability of coerced unfree labour. Entrepreneurial thinking, likewise, was constrained by a set of specific economic references in which the attainment of growth and profitability, and a stable social order, were seen as contingent upon the supply and organization of unfree labour.[1]

This colonial cosmology reflected centuries of cumulative experiences, but emerged specifically from an interpretation of the politics and psychology of conquest, the application of the principles of marginal economics in labour use under frontier conditions, and a pragmatic understanding of how to refashion old managerial concepts to social organization within the empire. It was clear to all with an interest in the colonial mission that by the seventeenth century the options as far as labour use was concerned were reduced to three basic forms. These choices were the reduction of the conquered indigenous population to servitude on lands appropriated from them, the transfer of surplus labour from the imperial centre to the colonial periphery under set contractual conditions, and the trading in chattel labour from the already well established African market. Also, these forms were considered discrete in the sense that their structures were clinically demarcated by racial differences – heightened by clearly distinct methods of recruitment.[2]

Over time and space, entrepreneurial thinking was reflected in decisions made in respect of the dominant form of labour used. Such thinking was influenced by the potency of cultural restraints (with respect to commitment to the ideology of unfreedom), the stage of commodity development within particular localities, perceptions of what was politically and socially viable, and general considerations of relative cost and benefits. The shifting weight of these variables determined for entrepreneurs why, how, where and when brown, white and black bondspersons met at the colonial rendezvous of the North Atlantic capitalist system, and dictated the specific nature of their social relations.[3]

Undoubtedly, the experiences of these labourers were shaped and driven by the application of a complex set of ideological instruments to the process of socio-economic organization. It is remarkable, for instance, how similar were opinions across imperial borders, and over time, on how best to exploit native labour. The ideological position that West Indian natives were a savage lot whose role within the new order (which was replacing their ancient regime) should be limited to servile labour embraced all Europeans in the business of making profits. The enslavement of natives by Europeans, who used different instruments of explanation and legitimation, was assured once the politics of conquest and the economics of accumulation had cojoined within an ideological discourse in which non-whites were defined as representatives of historical inertia and anti-progressive values.

Likewise, the application of the principles of political economy to the arrangements of social life during the seventeenth century suggested that propertyless white workers finding themselves upon the colonial market should pay the price in the form of a measured reduction in their civil liberties. Once the cost of injecting such labour into the colonial market could be expressed in accounting terms, it was no longer problematic for a system of compensation in the form of labour use to be put in place. The precepts for a legal framework that encouraged sponsors of propertyless migrants were already established within a range of domestic apprenticeship/indentureship systems, which required at best a little fine tuning for direct application to colonial circumstances. In addition, the dominance of the ideology of nationalism in seventeenth-century Western Europe created the space within which states could supplement legitimately this voluntary traffic in 'surplus' labour with persons whose labour was considered more valuable to the nation if applied to colonial production. Persons designated by the state as social misfits, outcasts, and generally dishonoured, in addition to those who fell foul of the criminal justice system, were thrown together to fill growing gaps within the colonial labour market.[4]

The use of the labour of enslaved Africans was part of the strategic economic thinking of European wealth accumulators in the pre-Columbian era. Black labour gangs could be found in some Mediterranean and European economies by the mid-fifteenth century, and these Africans were already defined as chattel slaves. This market information, reinforced by awareness of the popular practice of legally subjugating bonded white labourers in Western Europe, arrived in Caribbean space and landed on the heads of natives with the full weight of centuries of accumulated class aggression. Browns, whites, and blacks were trapped in a whirlwind of labour market forces, propelled by ideological currents that promoted the paramountcy of race, colour, class, gender and religion in determining the depth of enslavement and the number of avenues for escape. Within the descending spiral of enslavement, different levels were ascribed for different groups according to their method of recruitment, racial origins and the current nature of economic demand. But subjugated they all were, whether the forms of categorization were *encomienda* slavery, indentureship, or chattel slavery.

Colonial codes defined these institutions as discrete forms of bondage rather than degrees of enslavement. The tendencies have been for historians to accept this false premise, and they have produced a formidable body of literature that highlights institutional differences, structural discontinuities and legal disparities. Recently, however, Orlando Patterson has emphasized the need to focus not so much on the formal structures of labour systems but on the nature of everyday life for subjugated labourers. In so doing he has urged the need for more research into matters such as workers' self perception of honour and social worth.[5] At the same time he has called for less emphasis upon the constitutional provisions established for their governance.

Patterson's analysis urges the following questions: What would it have meant to the Taino people in Hispaniola or the Kalinago in St. Vincent, for example, after smashing their cultural world, appropriating their land, criminalizing their religions, exacting tribute in the form of bonded labour – all of which reduced their numbers by 90 per cent – to be told that they were really not 'slaves' like the African people around them? What would it have meant to the white indentured servants in Barbados, for example, experiencing seven to ten years of bondage in labour gangs on sugar plantations, with no right to leave its premises, marry, transact business, disobey supervisorial commands, and knowing that there was a considerably reduced survival chance, to be told that they were not slaves like the African people since it was their labour 'power' rather than their 'persons' which was the marketable commodity? What was the social value of such a 'fine' technical distinction since it remains phenomenal how to alienate an individual's labour power from his or her personage?

Obviously, the answer to these questions requires a clear understanding of the social details of bondage from the perspective of those persons who lived the reality. This is where, it seems, a comparative analysis should begin.

West Indian planters freely bought, sold, gambled away, mortgaged, taxed as property and alienated in wills their white indentured servants, African slaves and Amerindian bondsmen – all expressions of a highly developed market-oriented conception of labour and its function as capital. Colonial governments recognized the market functions of these labour types as alienable property. Such functions were part of a wider system of property and possessory relations in human beings developed in the colonies in support of capitalist export-oriented plantation production and officially legitimized within the legal-customary superstructure.[6]

In all analyses of property, the concept of appropriation appears central across a wide range of social relations. The total appropriation of a person's social and productive capacity by another in any set of social relations implies the formation of ownership and the establishment of rights in that person. Furthermore, the ultimate proof of the existence of property rights in persons lies in whether those rights and titles can be alienated. No system of slavery could function effectively unless property rights were not only defended but also alienable, especially within a family through the inheritance mechanism. West Indian sugar planters had perfected such systems and mechanisms with respect to the use and alienation of white, brown and black bondspersons.

The question of degrees of unfreedom among browns, blacks and whites is important, even if from the perspective of the relative hope they harboured for redemption. However, the similarities 'on the ground' – the inner feel of the nature of life – bound them together in ways that the chains never did. It is also important not to lose sight of the fact that race and colour differentials within the gangs of subjected labour were used by capitalist planters in order to promote a pattern of material and social distribution that enhanced their own hegemonic status. White bondspersons were beneficiaries of the greatest returns; they were given the best lottery chance at the boon of social freedom – the most prized commodity within the colonial formation.

The use of race as an instrument of social and material distribution functioned as a smoke screen in many respects, and has confused some researchers who, as a consequence, have placed considerably more emphasis on race than class in explaining the nature of colonial society. Robert Miles, it seems, is correct in asserting that, although there is an historical specificity to those circumstances and conjunctures where the appropriation of labour power is accompanied by a process of racialization, it is generally a specificity none the less that relates to the development of class relations within the development of capitalist production.[7]

On the Caribbean frontier the processes of racialization, in which colour was a dominant ideological element, should be explained and understood in the particular context of social relations established within the colonial economy. The concept of racism justified a variety of economic and political practices – such as extreme inequality in material and social distribution – and had considerable influence as an ideological effect within these economic and social relations of production. What slave-owners wanted from black, brown, and white bondspersons were surplus labour, social non-pecuniary return, class recognition and increasing value. These are the things they pursued. What they got, however, were returns differentiated by class considerations and constraint by a range of cultural and ideological factors – including race.

At the base of Caribbean frontier societies, then, could be found these three primary types of bondsperson – each with its own set of concerns, interests, and expectations. Natives wanted to retrieve their ancestral lands and liberty; whites wanted opportunities to realize those socio-economic and ideological ideals that were held high as benefits of colonization; and blacks wanted ontological recognition and a restoration of their social liberty. They all protested the conditions under which they lived and laboured, and driven by rapidly maturing political consciousness, planned to escape, destroy, or better their lives within the oppressing world of the privileged elite. Their motives were essentially different; so, too, were their actions of redress and liberation. None the less, the common social experience of futile and endless servitude produced within them an intensity of belief that drove them to risk their lives in search of the better – or other – life.

The resistance of native Caribbean people to the colonial dispensation has received insufficient attention from scholars. Unlike the case with the experience of enslaved African people, few studies have presented systematic accounts of their anti-colonial and anti-slavery struggle. The reasons for this historiographic imbalance are not altogether clear. No one has suggested, for example, that their fight for liberty, life and land was any less endemic or virulent than that of white bondspersons and Africans. On the contrary, most accounts of European settlement have indicated in a general sort of way their determination and tenacity in confronting the new order in spite of their relative technological limitations with respect to warfare.[8]

In the Greater Antilles, Tainos offered a spirited but largely ineffective military resistance to the Spanish. In 1494 Columbus led an armed party of 400 men into the interior of Hispaniola in search of food, gold and slaves, to which Taino Caciques mobilized their armies for resistance. Guacanagari, a leading Cacique, who had tried previously to negotiate an accommodating settlement with military commander Alonso de Ojeba, marched with a few thousand men upon the Spanish. The native army was decimated. In 1503 another forty Caciques were captured at Hispaniola and burnt alive by Governor Ovando's troops; Anacaona, the principal Cacique, was hanged publicly in Santo Domingo.

In Puerto Rico, the Spanish settlement party, led by Ponce de Leon, was attacked frequently by Taino warriors; many Spanish settlers were killed but Tainos were defeated and crushed in the counter-assault. In 1511 resistance in Cuba, led by Cacique Hatuey, was put down; he was captured and burned alive; another rising in 1529 was also crushed. In these struggles Taino fatalities were high. Thousands were killed in battle and publicly executed for the purpose of breaking the spirit of collective resistance; some rebels fled to the mountains and forests where they established maroon settlements that continued intermittently the war against the Spanish.[9] By the middle of the sixteenth century, however, Taino resistance had been effectively crushed in the Greater Antilles; their community structures were smashed, and members reduced to various forms of enslavement in Spanish agricultural and mining enterprises.

In the Lesser Antilles, however, the Kalinagos (referred to as Caribs) were more successful in defying first the Spanish, and then later the English and French, thereby preserving some political freedom and control over extensive territory. According to Carl Sauer, 'As the labor supply on Espanola declined, attention turned to the southern islands' which from St. Croix, neighbouring Puerto Rico, to the Guianas were inhabited by the Kalinagos. Spanish royal edicts dated 7 November 1508 and 3 July 1512 authorized settlers to capture and enslave Kalinagos on 'the island of Los Barbados [Barbados], Dominica, Matinino [Martinique], Santa Lucia, San Vincente, la Asuncion [Grenada], and Tavaco [Tobago]', because of their 'resistance to Christians'.

By the end of the sixteenth century, however, the Spanish had decided, having accepted as fact the absence of gold in the Lesser Antilles, and the inevitability of considerable fatalities at the hands of Kalinago warriors, that it was wiser to adopt a 'hands-off policy' while concentrating their efforts in the Greater Antilles. As a result, the Greater and Lesser Antilles became politically separated at this time by what has been described as a 'poison arrow curtain'.

The English and French, initiating their colonizing missions during the seventeenth century, had a clear choice. They could either confront the Spanish north of the 'poison arrow curtain' or Kalinago forces south of it. Either way, they expected to encounter considerable organized armed resistance. They chose the latter, partly because of the perception that Kalinagos were the weaker, but also because of the belief that Kalinagos were the 'common enemy' of all Europeans and that solidarity could be achieved for collective military operations against them.[10]

The English and French sought the pacification of the Kalinago for two distinct but related reasons, and over time adopted different strategies and methods; at all times they maintained the ideological position that Kalinagos should be enslaved, driven out, or exterminated. First, lands occupied by the Kalinagos were required for large-scale commodity production within the expansive, capitalist, North Atlantic agrarian complex. Second, European economic activities in the Caribbean were based upon the enslavement of all types of labourers. Europeans in the Lesser Antilles, however, were not as successful in reducing natives to servitude as they were in the Greater Antilles. Unlike the Taino, their labour could not be commodified in economical numbers. It was not that the Kalinago were more militant than the Taino. Rather, it was because the nomadic nature of their small communities, and their emphasis upon territorial acquisition, in part a response to the geographical features of the Lesser Antilles, enabled them to make more effective use of the environment in resistance activities.

The French discovered, like the Spanish before them, noted Père Labat, that it was always best, if possible, 'to have nothing to do with the Kalinago'. But this was not possible. Relations had to be established, and Europeans discovered, he observed, that the Kalinagos knew 'how to look after their own interests very well'. 'There are no people in the world', he stated, 'so jealous of their liberty, or who resent more the smallest check to their freedom'. Altogether, Kalinago world-view was anathema to Europeans, thus the general view, echoed by Labat, that 'no European nation has been able to live in the same island with them without being compelled to destroy them, and drive them out'.[11]

While English settlements in the Leewards struggled to make progress against Kalinago resistance, Barbados alone of the Windwards forged ahead uninterrupted. Unlike their Leewards counterparts, early Barbadian planters rapidly expanded their production base, made a living from the export of tobacco, indigo and cotton, and feared only their white indentured servants and their few black chattel slaves. By 1650, following the successful cultivation of sugar cane with a mixed labour force of white servants and African slaves, the island was considered by mercantile economic theorists as the richest agricultural colony in the hemisphere.

St. Kitts colonists, both English and French, determined to keep up with their Barbarian competitors, were first to adopt a common military front with respect to Kalinago resistance. During the 1630s they entered into agreements, in spite of their rival claims to exclusive ownership of the island, to combine forces against Kalinago communities. They 'pooled their talents', and in a 'sneak night attack' killed over eighty, enslaved captured women and drove the men off the island. After celebrating the success of their military alliance, the French and English continued their rivalry over the island until 1713 when the matter was settled in favour of the English by the Treaty of Utrecht.[12]

The success of Kalinago communities in resisting large-scale enslavement and holding on to a significant portion of the Windwards fuelled the determination of the English and French to break their resolve. By the mid-seventeenth century, European merchants, planters and colonial officials, were in agreement that Kalinagos 'were a barbarous and cruel set of savages beyond reason or persuasion and must therefore be eliminated'.[13] By this time it was also clear that the slave-based plantation system demanded an 'absolute monopoly' of the Caribbean, and tolerated no 'alternative system'.[14] What has been referred to as 'Carib independence and self-reliance', then, constituted a major contradiction to the internal logic of capitalist accumulation within the plantation economy. As a result, therefore, the economic leaders and political representatives of this increasingly powerful production and trade complex were determined to bring the contradiction represented by this oasis of freedom to a speedy resolution by any means necessary or possible.

The severe crisis of labour supply in the formative years of English colonial programmes that resulted from the success of Kalinago resistance to slavery and land appropriation heightened the importance of white indentureship as a principal labour organization. But the behaviour of these servants was typically restless and insubordinate, sparked by the awareness that the indenture system had been refashioned by colonial demands into a form of slave-like relation. Certainly, they experienced servitude as an unfamiliar and oppressive system in which their living conditions were nearer those of enslaved blacks than their counterparts at home. Like blacks, they resisted this unfamiliar subservience when and how they could. Masters complained about their unwillingness to work according to the terms of their contracts and about their hostile reactions to demands of overseers and managers.[15]

To control and discipline servants, masters and their managers established complex systems of authority. If these systems failed, a planter could request the services of parish constables, the provost marshal, or, as a last resort, the parish militia. During the seventeenth century, officials unleashed the full apparatus of law enforcement on their servants, whom some thought as great a threat to peace as their African slaves.

Barbados servant revolts of the 1650s spring from the minutes of the Colonial Council. In 1656, for example, Governor Searle learned that there were 'several Irish servants and Negroes out in rebellion in the Thicketts and thereabouts', plundering estates in a systematic and arrogant manner, and 'making a mockery of the law'. The Council's response reflected the seriousness with which it viewed this information. It ordered Lt. Col. John Higginbottom of the St. Philip parish Militia to raise Col. Henry Hawley's regiment, 'follow the said servants and runaway Negroes', and secure or 'destroy' them. On 15 July 1656 the governor once again ordered Higginbottom to examine a case of a 'riotous and unruly lot' of Irish servants on the estate of Robert Margott in that parish. The investigation led to several arrests and the imprisonment of five Irishmen who had declared themselves opposed to the 'furtherance of the English nation'. On 1 September 1657, the Council heard the petition of Edward Hollingsheade, who stated that, 'his servants, Reage Dunnohu and Walter Welch, have rebelliously and mutinously behaved themselves towards him, their said master, and their mistress, whereby they have been in fear of their lives by the said servants'. The Governor ordered the provost marshal to jail these servants pending a full investigation. It was finally ordered that Dunnohu and Welch should receive thirty-one lashes each, 'soundly laid to their bare backs by the common hangman and returned to the common goal at the pleasure of their master'. On this plantation, as on many others, the planters' system of control proved inadequate.[16]

Governor Searle adopted a four-point programme of control. First, servants found off their plantation of residence without a 'pass', 'ticket', or 'testimonial' signed by their master or mistress were to be arrested and conveyed by any English person to the nearest constable, who was empowered to whip and return them to their plantation. Second, ex-servants found about the island who could not give a good account of themselves were to be arrested by constables and, 'if they be of no fixed abode', put 'to labour for one whole year on some plantation'. Third, it became a legal offense for anyone to 'sell any kind of arms or ammunition' whatsoever to Irish servants especially. Fourth, servants found in possession of arms or ammunition, 'either on their persons or in their houses, shall be whipped and jailed at the Governor's pleasure'.[17]

By the end of the 1650s the Barbados government, accepting the failure of these measures to curb servant insubordination and halt the deterioration of plantation labour relations, moved toward adoption of a tough and comprehensive legal framework that took the form of the Master and Servant Code of 1661. The code reflected English perceptions of the Irish servants in particular as 'a profligate race', 'turbulent and dangerous spirits', who thought nothing of 'joining themselves to runaway slaves'. The preamble illustrated the intentions and attitudes of the legislature.

Since 'much of the interest and substance of the island consists in the servants', who have caused 'great damage' to their masters by their 'unruliness, obstinacy and refractoriness', the peace of the island could only be maintained by adopting a 'continual strict course' to prevent their 'bold extravagance and wandering'. The code covered most aspects of servant life; it was especially explicit on the subject of resistance. Clause four, for instance, states that any servant who shall, 'lay violent hands upon his or her master or mistress, or overseer, or any person put over them in authority to govern them – and being thereof convicted before any of His Majesty's Justices of the Peace shall serve one whole year of service, and double the time for any term of imprisonment or every two hours' absence from work without permission'. Barbados planters were satisfied that this legislation provided a satisfactory framework for the control of servants.[18]

What worried masters in Barbados, above all, was servant involvement in slave revolts. Fear outran fact in this regard: no certain evidence exists that servants or freemen ever attempted to participate in a large-scale violent uprising of slaves. The reality was that the poor whites benefited, though marginally, from black slavery, and the slaves knew it. But the English constantly suspected that they might support the slaves' rebellious designs and debated the need for preventive measures.

Following the discovery by the militia of an island-wide slave conspiracy in 1675, suspicions of servant participation ran deep in Barbados. No servants were arrested on this occasion, but in 1686 Governor Edwin Stede learned that a party of creole slaves was inviting some Irish servants to join in a design to destroy the English. Stede immediately ordered constables in seven of the eleven parishes to 'search the negroes' houses within their parishes for arms and ammunition ... there being signs of an insurrection of negroes and white servants'. Within two weeks of this investigation he informed the Council that some 'servants have been sent to gaol and others are in recognizance touching the suspicions of their being concerned or privy to the late intended rising of the negroes to destroy all masters and mistresses'. Twenty-two Negroes were arrested and executed. Eighteen servants were arrested, then freed owing to insufficient evidence. The arrest of servants was probably no more than a precautionary measure brought about by intense suspicion. Governor Stede, however, asked his constables to tighten the policing of servants.[19]

In January 1692 Barbadian planters believed they had finally found sufficient evidence to implicate servants in large-scale rebellious organizations of slaves. In that month, creole slaves plotted an island-wide conspiracy to defeat the planters and take control of the island. John Oldmixon, an English historian whose account was based on interviews with absentee planters, described the aborted affair as 'the most general the Slaves ever hatched, and brought nearest to Execution'. A small party of Irish servants was arrested and imprisoned for participating in the plot. The Assembly's Commission of Enquiry reported that the slaves' strategy for obtaining arms was to send 'five or six Irishmen' into Needham Fort to intoxicate the guards with strong drink and then unlock the stores. Of the slaves arrested for involvement in this plot, 92 were executed, 4 died of castration, 14 of miscellaneous wounds and 4 of causes unknown. No record, however, has been found pertaining to the trial or punishment of servants, and it can be reasonably assumed that, as on the former occasion, there was no evidence that planter suspicion had reached paranoid levels.[20]

Englishmen in the Leewards mainly feared that Catholic servants would form an alliance with the French. Their anxiety was heightened by political developments in the Leewards during the war years of the 1660s and the 1680s. While Barbadians suspected that their Irish servants were providing the French with military intelligence and took measures to prevent their running away to French settlements in the Windward Islands, in the Leewards Irish servants determined the pattern of international events in a more fundamental way by contributing to important shifts in the balance of imperial power.[21]

In January 1689, however, as information spread through the islands that William of Orange had been crowned King of England, a new Irish-French military assault was launched in the Leewards. During the first week of February, Irish servants and freemen in St. Kitts plundered English estates in the name of King James II. The revolt weakened English forces, and the French were able to seize the colony. On receiving news of the rising, Leewards Governor Codrington hastily arrested a large number of Irish servants and freemen.[22] They were subsequently deported to Jamaica, according to Codrington, 'lest they should serve us as they did' at St. Kitts. The Antiguan policy was to disarm the Irish servants, 300 in all, and 'confine them to their plantations'. The Irish servants at Montserrat, who were 'three to one of the English', openly declared their intention to desert their English masters and give over the island to the French. Sixteen were arrested, charged with treason, and sent for trial to neighbouring Nevis.[23]

The English soon recaptured and pacified their island colonies, but settlers continued to live in fear of servant-assisted French invasions. In June 1689 Joseph Crispe, a colonial official, reported from St. Kitts that 'beside the French we still have a worse enemy in the Irish Catholics, who despite the law to the contrary, remain ... among us and openly exercise their religion'.[24] In 1706 Lt. Governor Anthony Hodges of the Leewards noted that the French still 'flatter themselves' that regaining territory in the Leewards would be an easy matter – an impression 'derived from some confidence that the Irish here are in their interest'.[25]

Against this background of fear, successive governors continuously reported to London that the white English population was growing too slowly. Jamaica's deficiency law contributed to the demand for white labour by requiring that a certain number of white men be kept on each estate in proportion to the number of blacks. This law was strictly enforced. Planters accordingly took whatever servants they could find in order to avoid paying the deficiency fee, and the Irish were most readily available. In 1703 the Assembly exempted from port charges all ships carrying thirty or more servants. The prices planters paid for servants reflected discrimination against the Irish, as was also the case in Barbados and the Leewards.

The Africans, most records suggest, were prepared to accept whatever assistance they could, from natives or white servants, in their anti-slavery struggle. It is now commonly recognized that in the West Indies anti-slavery conflict was of an endemic nature. Orlando Patterson has suggested that the many slave revolts and plots in these territories between 1638 and 1838 could be conceived of as the '200 Years' War' – one protracted struggle launched by Africans and their Afro-West Indian progeny against slave-owners. Such persistent anti-slavery activity represented, furthermore, the most immediately striking characteristic of the West Indian world. Current historiography outlines in detail the empirical contours of this struggle – what amounts to an indigenous anti-slavery movement – though its philosophical and ideological aspects remain less researched.[26]

Anglophone literature on anti-slavery, however, has emphasized above other features, its trans-Atlantic dimension. This perspective has enriched significantly our general understanding of the diverse forces that succeeded ultimately in toppling the region's heterogeneous slave regimes. To some extent, this panoramic vision of the anti-slavery movement results from the need for a closer investigation of slaves' political culture. Such an examination is necessary for fuller evaluation of the consciousness of slaves and their depth of political awareness; also to illustrate more precisely those linkages, real or imaginary, that existed between plantation-based politics and the international anti-slavery ethos.

Many historians have responded to this challenge, and the theme of slave resistance or, more appropriately, the blacks' anti-slavery movement, has now become a leading growth area in Caribbean historiography. It is now possible to demarcate some structural features in the development of Caribbean anti-slavery. Three basic stages can be identified. The first stage relates to early plantation construction and corresponds approximately with the period 1500 to 1750. The second stage is characterized by mature plantation society and declining dependency on slave importation – 1750 to 1800. The third stage relates to the 'general crisis' in plantation slavery; it is linked with the impact of Haitian politics and serious anti-slavery discussions in the metropoles – 1804 to 1848.

Within these three general stages, three types/levels of anti-slavery struggle can be described – though no systematic effort has been made to articulate them within the historical continuum. Firstly, a proliferation of acts of 'day-to-day' resistance; these were generally designed not to overthrow the slave system, but to undermine its efficiency in order to hasten its eventual abandonment. Secondly, evidence indicates a large number of unsuccessful plots and revolts which were characterized by collective organization with reformist and revolutionary objectives. Thirdly, there is the incidence of 'successful' rebellion – from long-term marronage to the St. Domingue revolution.

According to Robert Dirks there are references within the literature to some seventy slave uprisings in British colonies between 1649 and 1833, including large-scale insurrections that engulfed entire colonies and small-scale violence limited to single estates. Of this total, Dirks states that some thirty-two revolts did not materialize due to discovery, and some were undoubtedly the invented product of planter paranoia. Michael Craton's chronology of resistance in these colonies between 1638 and 1837, however, lists seventy-five aborted revolts and actual rebellions; in his computation some of these actions have been grouped together and appear as one event.[27] This record of resistance illustrates that there was hardly a generation of slaves in the English West Indies that did not confront its masters collectively with arms in pursuit of freedom. In this sense, therefore, the relations between slaves and masters in the West Indies was characterized by ongoing psychological warfare and intermittent bloody battles.

The successful colonization of the Caribbean, then, was possible as a result of the effective market mobilization of unfree labour. The commodification of the labour power of natives, immigrant whites and blacks under various forms of property relations and degrees of unfreedom provided capitalist colonizers with the opportunity to establish productive enterprises on a large scale. The denial of these workers' fundamental rights – particularly the right to life – engendered an ideological environment at the frontier in which endemic conflict and warfare determined the nature of social life. The reduction of all unfree workers to various forms of property relation within the context of large-scale productive operations was necessary if capitalist producers were intent on accumulating on a grand scale within a short period under frontier conditions of resource and spacial openness. The institutionalisation of race ideology and its use as a principle in the economics of resource distribution ensured that these forms of labour organisation were considered politically and constitutionally discrete. The official use of the terms – tribute bondage, indentureship and slavery – to define the social conditions of brown, white and black workers, respectively, was at specific moments for many of them more significant as distant legal categories than indicative of their 'lived' experience. What these labour institutions offered their subjects were the denial of their right to liberty, a survival-oriented share of material produce, a view of themselves as chattels, and an overwhelming sense of social regression. They rebelled when they could, and in ways peculiar to their specific social consciousness and circumstances.

NOTES

1. See Evsey D. Domar, 'The Causes of Slavery or Serfdom: A Hypothesis', *Journal of Economic History*, 30, 1 (1970), pp.18–32; Bent Hansen, 'Colonial Economic Development with Unlimited Supplies of Land: A Richardian Case', *Economic Development and Cultural Change*, 27, 4 (1979), pp.611–27; David Eltis, 'Free and Coerced Transatlantic Migrations: Some Comparisons', *American Historical Review* 88, 2 (1983), pp.254–5.
2. See William D. Phillips, Jr., 'Sugar Production and Trade in the Mediterranean at the Time of Crusades', in V.P. Goss and C.V. Bornstein (eds.), *The Meeting of two Worlds:Cultural Exchange between East and West during the Period of the Crusades* (Kalamazoo, Mich. 1986), pp.393–406; J.H. Galloway, 'The Mediterranean Sugar Industry', *Geographical Review*, 67 (1977), pp.177–94; Felipe Fernandez Armesto, *Before Columbus: Exploration and Colonisation from the Mediterranean to the Atlantic 1229–1492* (Philadelphia, 1987); Sidney M. Greenfield, 'Madeira and the Beginning of New World, Sugar Cane Cultivation and Plantation Slavery', in Vera D. Rubin and A. Tuden (eds.), *Comparative Perspectives on Slavery in New World Plantation Societies*, Annals of the New York Academy of Sciences, vol. 292, (New York, 1977), pp.536–52; also, 'Plantations, Sugar Cane and Slavery', *Historical Reflections/Réflexions Historiques*, 6, 1979, pp.85–119; Philip D. Curtin, *The Rise and Fall of the Plantation Complex: Essays in Atlantic History* (Cambridge, 1990).
3. On Native Caribbean Enslavement see Jerome Handler, 'The Amerindian Slave Population of Barbados in the 17th and 18th Centuries', *Caribbean Studies*, 8, 4 (1968/69), pp.38–63; David L. Radell, 'The Indian Slave Trade and Population of Nicaragua during the 16th Century', in W. Denevan (ed.), *The Native Population of the Americas to 1492* (Madison, Wisc., 1976), pp.67–76; Marie Helmer, 'Cubagua: L'île des perles', *Annales ESC*, 17, 4 (1962), pp.751–60; David Henige, 'On the Contact Population of Hispaniola: History as Higher Mathematics', *Hispanic American Historical Review*, 58, 2 (1978), pp.217–37.
4. Hilary Beckles, *White Servitude and Black Slavery in Barbados 1625–1715* (Knoxville, 1989); David Galenson, *White Servitude in Colonial America: An Economic Analysis*

(Cambridge, 1981); A. Smith, *Colonists in Bondage: White Servitude and Convict Labour in America 1607–1776* (Chapel Hill, NC, 1947); Richard Dunn, *Sugar and Slaves: The Rise of the Planter Class in the English West Indies, 1624–1713* (New York, 1973); John J. McCusker and Russell R. Menard, *The Economy of British America, 1607–1789* (Chapel Hill, NC, 1985).

5. Orlando Patterson, *Slavery and Social Death: A Comparative Study* (Cambridge, Mass., 1982).

6. Hilary Beckles, 'Plantation Production and "White Proto-Slavery": White Indentured Servants and the Colonisation of the English West Indies, 1624–1645', *The Americas*, 41 (1985), pp. 21–45.

7. Robert Miles, *Capitalism and Unfree Labour: Anomaly or Necessity* (London, 1987), pp. 7–8. See also R. Bean and R. Thomas, 'The Adoption of Slave Labour in British America', in H. Gemery and J. Hogendorn (eds.), *The Uncommon Market: Essays in the Economic History of the Atlantic Slave Trade* (New York, 1979); Sidney Mintz, 'Slavery and Emergent Capitalism', in L. Foner and E. Genovese (eds.), *Slavery in the New World* (Englewood Cliffs, 1969).

8. In the early European literature the Tainos of the Northern Caribbean are referred to as Arawaks, and the Kalinagos of the East and South as Caribs. See Michael Craton, *Testing the Chains: Resistance to Slavery in the British West Indies* (Ithaca, 1982), pp. 21–3; Hilary Beckles, 'Kalinago Resistance to European Colonisation of the Caribbean', *Caribbean Quarterly*, 38, 2–3 (1992), pp. 1–15.

9. On Kalinago assistance to Tainos in Puerto Rico see Carl Sauer, *The Early Spanish Main* (Berkeley, 1966), pp. 58, 192.

10. Sauer, *Early Spanish Main*, pp. 35, 180, 193; see also G.K. Lewis, *Main Currents in Caribbean Thought: The Historical Evolution of Caribbean Societies in its Ideological Aspects 1492–1900* (Kingston, 1983), p. 64.

11. John Eaden (ed.), *The Memoirs of Père Labat. 1693–1705* (London, 1970), pp. 83, 98, 104, 109.

12. Dunn, *Sugar and Slaves*, p. 8.

13. Lewis, *Main Currents*, p. 104.

14. Ibid., p. 105.

15. See Hilary Beckles, 'Rebels and Reactionaries: The Political Responses of White Labourers to Planter-Class Hegemony in 17th Century Barbados', *Journal of Caribbean History*, 15 (1981), pp. 1–19; 'A "Riotous and Unruly Lot": Irish Indentured Servants and Freemen in the English West Indies, 1644–1713', *William and Mary Quarterly*, 47 (1990), pp. 503–21.

16. Minutes of the Barbados Council, 6 Nov. 1655, Box 12, No. 1. Davis Transcripts, Bridgetown Public Library, Barbados.

17. Ibid., 22 Sept. 1657, 21 Dec. 1657, 3 Jan. 1658.

18. Expedition of Admiral Penn and General Venables to the West Indies, Lucas MSS, Misc. Vol. v, 342; Minutes of the Barbados Council, 16 Oct. 1660; 'An Act for the Good Governance of Servants, and Ordaining the Rights between Masters and Servants' in Richard Hall, *Acts Passed in Barbados. 1645–1762* (London, 1764), No. 30, 35–40.

19. Minutes of Council of Barbados, 16 Feb. 1686, Calendar of State Papers, Colonial Series (CSPC) 1685–1686, p. 155; also, CO 31/1, fol. 675.

20. John Oldmixon, *The British Empire in America* (London, 1741; reprinted, New York, 1969), II, p. 53; Hilary Beckles, *Black Rebellion in Barbados: The Struggle Against Slavery* (Bridgetown, 1984), pp. 42–8.

21. Francis Sampson to John Sampson, 6 June, CSPC, 1661–68, pp. 386; Report of William Willoughby on Montserrat, Feb. 1668, CO 1/24, No. 71.

22. Ibid.; also William Willoughby to King, Jan. 1668, CO 1/22, No. 17.

23. Henry Carpenter to Thomas Belchkamber, 19 Aug. 1689, CSPC, 1689–1692; Christopher Codrington to Lords of Trade, 31 July 1689, CSPC, 1689–1692, No. 312.

24. Colonel Joseph Crispe to Colonel Bayer, 10 June 1689; ibid., No. 193.

25. Gov. Hunter to the Board of Trade, 13 Nov. 1731, CO 137/19, Vols. pp. 108–9.

26. See Orlando Patterson, 'Slavery and Slave Revolts: A Socio-historical Analysis of the

First Maroon War, Jamaica, 1655–1740', *Social and Economic Studies*, 19, 3 (1970), pp. 289–325; Hilary Beckles, 'Caribbean Anti-Slavery: The Self-Liberation Ethos of Enslaved Blacks', *Journal of Caribbean History*, 22, 1–2 (1990), pp. 1–19.
27. See Robert Dirks, *The Black Saturnalia: Conflict and Its Ritual Expression on British West Indian Slave Plantations* (Gainesville, 1987), p. 167; and Craton, *Testing the Chains*.

Work, Labour and the Market: The Responses of Farmers and Semi-Nomadic Peoples to Colonialism in North-West Mexico

CYNTHIA RADDING

The Pima, Eudeve and Opata-speaking peoples of Sonora (*sonoras*) in the western foothills of the Sierra Madre Occidental were drawn into the Jesuit mission system during the early decades of the seventeenth century. These highland peasants, whose livelihood depended on the combined resources derived from horticulture, hunting and foraging, sustained their villages by adapting to both the missions and the incipient market for goods and labour which developed around the mining camps of Sonora and Chihuahua. Behind these outward forms of accommodation, the *sonoras* maintained significant levels of resistance to colonialism which reveal opposing sets of cultural values.[1] This article examines *serrano* attitudes towards work, time and wealth which clashed with the Spanish colonial project. It explores the theme of 'social ecology' by showing that the highlanders' means of reconstituting their households and communities under colonial rule comprised both a defence of their autonomy and a claim to vital resources.

Work and productivity comprised a central arena of conflict between Spanish and Indian cultures in the western foothills of the Sierra Madre Occidental. Eighteenth-century Sonora was a settled colony, where numerous mining camps and ranching operations sustained a permanent Spanish population of *vecinos* and gave rise to an incipient market for labour and goods which increasingly drew native villagers into its orbit. Nevertheless, this province of north-western New Spain remained part of the *gran septentrión*, a frontier where Spanish dominion was precarious in the face of persistent nomadism. Whereas the Spaniards were able to draw on highly stratified sedentary populations for their labour needs in central Mexico, here they faced the problem of developing a stable labour force.

This study explores the cultural meaning of *work* which underlay the internal organization of ethnic polities in the western foothills of the Sierra Madre Occidental. The cluster of related activities which comprised the productive and ceremonial labour of different social groups was central to local resistance to external subjugation. The pattern of quotidian resistance to colonial demands on the time, energy and productive resources of native peoples developed in the context of the ongoing struggle for survival. To a greater or lesser extent, indigenous systems of exchange of goods and labour collided with but ultimately blended with European markets and commercial standards emanating from Spanish enterprises on this colonial frontier. Because the *serrano* peoples and Spanish colonists defined subsistence and surplus differently, and they each perceived of the methods for the allocation of tasks and the distribution of the fruits of labour in different ways. This frontier society became increasingly complex, especially since colonialism changed the ecological relations which governed the interaction of the *sonoras* with their environment.

CULTURAL PARADIGMS CONCERNING LABOUR

Scholars who have studied Indian-European relations and colonialism in Latin America have raised a number of issues concerning the political and social dimensions of work, specifically in relation to pre-conquest and Hispanic systems for distributing separate tasks among individuals and communities and on the complementarity of ritual and productive labour. Charles Gibson has contrasted indigenous regulation of communal labour in central Mexico with Spanish institutions designed to redirect the flow of Indian productive energy to colonial enterprises. The Nahuatl institution of *coatéquitl*, 'which implied a division of tasks among the *calpulli* subdivisions ... with a high ratio of labourers to labour units', was essentially subverted by *encomienda* and *repartimiento*, which alloted workers to Spanish claimants of Indian labourers. As Alonso de Zorita reported, 'the "merriment" and "great rejoicing" that attended [communal labour in pre-conquest Mexico]' stood in stark contrast to the harsh conditions imposed by the conquistadores.[2]

In a similar vein, John Murra has shown how the Inca extracted labour by distributing different tasks among numerous *ayllús*, assigning a large number of workers to particular kinds of labour on a rotational basis. In the Andes, as in Mesoamerica, work involved productive activities such as cultivating Inca lands, gathering coca leaves, and transporting produce from one area to another, as well as ceremonial duties like guarding sacred shrines and escorting the Inca and his royal entourage.[3] The labour demanded of Andean commoners by both the ethnic *kurakas* and the lords of Tawantinsuyu was understood as personal service, exemplified most pointedly in the separation of *yanakuna* from the peasant base of the *ayllú*.[4] Yet within the peasant community, households exchanged labour on a reciprocal basis, codified as the *ayni*, a practice which persists in the Andes today.[5]

Nancy Farriss's magisterial study of the survival of Mayan communities in colonial Yucatán has highlighted the importance of ceremonial work carried out by indigenous elites. Likewise, Alfonso Ortiz's description of contemporary Tewa Pueblo culture in New Mexico demonstrates how the ritual calendar of Made people, according to which ceremonial duties are performed, is linked to the Tewa subsistence cycle of agriculture and hunting. For both activities, religious leaders organized work around ceremonies and feasts which the community deemed necessary to maintain the cosmic order.[6]

In addition to these distributional and ceremonial aspects of work, a number of authors have underscored the division of labour across age and gender lines. Agriculture, the foundation of village peasant life, required the labour of both men and women in diverse cultural settings. As Felipe Guaman Poma de Ayala discovered in the Andes, tasks associated with cultivation were complementary according to the sexes, which was symbolically perceived in terms of the rotating spheres of the sun and moon.[7] Similarly, in the highland villages of North-west Mexico men and women worked together to plant fields and harvest crops. Among hunter-gatherers of the Sonoran Desert, the Tohono O'odham ceremony of 'Throwing Up the Clouds' exemplified the close association of physical and ceremonial work and the complementarity of the sexes. O'odham women worked by gathering the *sahuaro* fruit in the heat of the desert; men worked by singing ancient songs, and both sexes drank and threw up the fermented wine in order to bring on the summer rains.[8]

In contrast, Ramón Gutiérrez's portrayal of Pueblo society in colonial New Mexico has emphasized the distinctive roles assigned to men and women and to juniors and seniors. Children who received ritual gifts from their parents discharged their debts or obligations through obedience and labour. Indeed, age constituted one of the principal standards of inequality in Pueblo communities. In this matrilineal and matrilocal society, women were heads of household and controlled 'all food and seed reserves'. Although men tended the fields, hunted and traded, and dominated most of the ceremonial societies, women processed the harvested grain and 'fed' all the members of their extended kindred.[9] That food processing, particularly grinding maize on stone *metates*, was a female task among the sedentary peoples of Mexico (and by extrapolation elsewhere in the Americas) has been aptly noted by Arnold J. Bauer.[10] Women assumed a burden that was physically exhausting and enormously time-consuming, but which conferred on them a central role in the distribution of food within and among households.

This gendered distribution of specific tasks took its meaning from indigenous peasant cosmology and ritual, which linked sexuality to notions of work and productivity. Ramón Gutiérrez has argued that Pueblo women controlled household production because '[they] were empowered through their sexuality'.[11] With less emphasis on the struggle for power between the sexes, Campbell Pennington has argued that *sonoras* peoples related human sexuality and reproduction to the life-giving fertility of the land, and that women performed central roles in the rituals enacted to assure bountiful harvests. Jesuit and Franciscan missionaries tried vigorously to suppress these rituals, but some of them survived until recent times.[12] For example, the Pima of central Sonora made their planting ceremony, called *usiabagu*, correspond to the Catholic Feast of Saint John. A special women's dance highlighted *usiabagu* to bring sufficient rainfall and make the seeds fertile. The women chosen for each year's rite left the village and spent several days in seclusion. When they returned to the village they danced on a board placed over a large vessel buried in the ground, containing maize, squash and bean seeds. At the conclusion of their dance, the women ran past a line of men and bathed in the river. When the planted corn began to sprout, men and women participated in additional feasts to help the growing season along. *Tesgüino* (fermented corn drink) was consumed in copious amounts, while the deer dancers and ritual clowns performed to the music of violins, rasping sticks, and gourd drums.[13]

Serrano villagers conserved these ceremonies, albeit in altered form, within the economic and religious structures imposed by mission life. They placed wooden crosses in their *milpas* and celebrated the onset of the summer rains on prominent feast days of the Catholic calendar. Frequent *tesgüinadas* and *borracheras* were carried out in the relative seclusion of the scrub forest, despite the missionaries' indignant condemnation. Their persistence under the mission regime implies that native agriculturalists never separated ancient ritual from the ongoing cycle of planting and harvesting. Hunting and gathering, as vital to Indian livelihood as farming in this semi-arid environment, required another set of rites to assure the continued bounty of game and seed plants.[14] In hunting, as in agriculture, technique, ceremonialism and magic were closely linked in the popular mind.

Pre-conquest *serrano* and desert peoples developed a variety of techniques for growing cultigens in open fields and garden plots. Experienced horticulturalists, their knowledge of plant selection, soil conservation, and water management enabled them to produce sufficient food for themselves in this semi-arid environment. Native agricultural practices established three distinct patterns, each adapted to different ecological zones, which have survived to the present day. The *papawi o'odham* ('bean-eating Pimas' or the historic Papago) planted ephemeral crops at the mouths of *arroyos* during the summer rainstorms and created *'ak-ciñ* fields by diverting water from a number of washes to alluvial flatlands in the desert. Papago subsistence maintained a close link between cultivation and wild food gathering. It has been estimated that the desert *o'odham* obtained only about one-fifth of their total food supply through cultivation.[15] Their livelihood rested mainly on wild plant and animal products, supplemented by their harvests and foodstuffs received in trade from the riverine Pima and Yuma. These nomads extracted from the bountiful desert the fruit of the *sahuaro* and *pitahaya*, nopal, cholla buds, mesquite pods, tepary beans, sand roots and tubers, wild greens, and ironwood and paloverde seeds. Most *o'odham* cultigens have their counterparts in closely related wild plants.[16] To a lesser degree, highland peasants depended on gathering and hunting as well as farming for year-round sustenance.

Mountainous Pima developed swidden agriculture dependent on seasonal rains. Their habitat over a thousand metres above sea level supplied sufficient summer rains for seasonal plantings on natural terraces set back from highland river channels, despite the narrow soil deposits along the mountain streams which limited possibilities for irrigation. Floodplain farming, using diversion weirs, living fence rows and irrigation canals, characterized the major river valleys of the Opata and Eudeve in the heart of Sonora. Indigenous agricultural techniques in this area, which channeled the flow of water from *arroyos* and main river courses to soil deposits along the river banks, established the productive base for a durable village economy. Following conquest, from the seventeenth century onward, native horticulture and community structures supported the most prosperous missions in these alluvial valleys. Not surprisingly, Spanish mining and ranching operations gravitated to this area in search of a ready supply of labourers and foodstuffs.

There follows a summary of some of the historical evidence concerning indigenous *sonoras* attitudes toward work and exchange, and their adoption of Spanish standards of work and payment, in their struggle to survive under the exigencies of colonialism. The term 'survival' is used here to connote the procurement of the means to sustain material life and the endurance of cultural norms through dual strategies of resistance and accommodation to alien rule.

WORK, PRODUCTIVITY, AND GIFT EXCHANGE

In eighteenth-century Sonora, *serrano* peoples worked in three distinct work environments, moving seasonally among them: agriculture in their home villages, planting and harvesting their own *milpas* as well as working required labour shifts in the fields reserved for the missions; hunting and gathering in the *monte* of scrub forest and desert growth which dominated the landscape beyond the fertile floodplains; and wage labour in the Spanish economy. As individuals shifted from one place to another, households and communities garnered resources from each of these environments.

The central concept which governed native practice rendered work meaningful as labour or service exchanged for food. Exchange was an essential component of the Sonoran economy, inseparable from work itself as a means of resource procurement. Trade took on the apparent simplicity of a gift. The ritualized exchange of gifts regulated the Indians' relationship to the environment and strengthened the bonds which held communities together. Indigenous conventions concerning gift-giving nurtured widely held values of generosity and abundance. Trade among kin groups and between ethnic provinces took place in the form of gift-giving, foodstuffs constituting the principal medium of reciprocal exchange. For example, the Sand Papago, who lived mainly by fishing and gathering wild plant foods, journeyed annually to Yuma villages in the Colorado delta and bartered baskets and sea shells for maize, teparies and squashes.[17]

This ethic of gift-giving did not necessarily mean the exchange of goods and services of equal value. At times some trading partners operated under a perceived disadvantage due to the harshness of their environment or depleted supplies, and reciprocity came to embrace different forms of service and even the subordination of one group to another. For instance, the Tohono O'odham travelled long distances to the Gila, San Pedro and Altar valleys, where they traded candied fruit and beverages made from the fruit of the *sahuaro* and worked in exchange for wheat, maize, beans, mesquite pods, and cotton. In times of hunger, these desert dwellers would perform a 'Begging Dance' for the Gila villagers lasting several nights before receiving presents of food.[18] Similarly, the semi-nomadic Joba, who lived on the eastern margins of Sonora in the rugged *barrancas* of the Sierra Madre, wove mats from the plant fibres of the palmilla which they traded in the mission villages for food and clothing. Missionaries observed that Opata villagers treated the Jobas 'as servants', exacting labour for a share of their food surpluses.[19]

Practices of subordination and inequality were common among the different Sonoran peoples. There was a trade in *nijoras*, captive slaves, during both pre-conquest and colonial times. *Nijoras* – children, youths and women – were taken from non-Piman villages in repeated raiding forays along the porous western frontier of the Colorado and Gila valleys, and the captives were bartered for prescribed amounts of goods, including merchandise originating in the Spanish economy. *Nijoras* became domestic servants in both Indian and *vecino* households, and their demographic presence was systematically registered in the eighteenth-century missions of the Pimería Alta. Those who survived to adulthood married and were integrated into their adoptive communities. *Nijoras* figured significantly in the ethnic and social fabric of colonial Sonora. As servants, these captives conferred prestige on elderly members of Pima communities. Furthermore, Spanish demand for household service fuelled the capture and trade of *nijoras*. However, these dependent youths, separated from their kinsmen, did not constitute a central part of the productive labour force in Sonora.[20]

The confrontation between indigenous values of *work* and European notions of wealth and productivity first occurred in this frontier province around the Christian missions. In the early decades of the seventeenth century, the newly-implanted Jesuit regime came in contact with peasant traditions which associated prestige with consumption rather than in marketing surplus. Highland villagers possessed the physical and technological capability for producing agricultural surpluses, but the coercive structures for exacting levels of production beyond the needs of subsistence remained weak in a natural environment of contrasting microclimates and uncertain conditions for agricultural yields. The household constituted the basic unit of production and distribution of essential goods. Consumption, rather than the accumulation of property or the maximization of rent, was the primary goal of indigenous work. *Serrano* horticulturalists and desert gatherers perceived a tension between the toil exerted and the benefits accrued to each domestic unit, exhibited in their reactions to the missionaries' demand for disciplined labour measured in a certain number of days of service in mission fields.

Within the Spanish sector, wage labour involved a number of different physical settings and contractual arrangements. Indians worked for varying periods of time in mining camps and on private ranches and haciendas. While a significant minority of Indians became professional mineworkers – most notably Yaquis from the adjacent Province of Ostimuri – the mining placers of Sonora typically drew labourers for a few months a year outside the growing season.[21] Similarly, most of the Sonoran ranches of this period were not sufficiently large to sustain a resident population of tenants; rather *vecinos* called on mission Indians to work for them during peak seasons. Although *repartimiento* (forced recruitment of labourers to perform specified stints of paid labour) had ceased to function by the second half of the eighteenth century, individuals frequently sent requests to the missionaries for small groups of Indians to perform routine tasks associated with fencing, planting and harvesting. Skilled Indians were in especially high demand: carpenters, masons, shepherds, muleteers, and cowboys. These *tapisques* left their villages for short periods of time, but their absences reduced available manpower in the villages. Although nominally required to pay a minimum wage of two *reales* a day, little information is available on the customary wage for *tapisques* who were contracted from the missions. It is probable that the *vecinos* who hired labourers converted most of the payment to the Indians into mere subsistence, namely shelter and the food consumed during the time of employment.[22]

The *sonoras* approached the colonial market cautiously, retaining their ingrained patterns which closely linked work and exchange in case involvement in the market collapsed. As the accounts of Jesuit missionaries from the seventeenth and eighteenth centuries amply demonstrate, the *sonoras* were simple commodity producers. The most prosperous villages traded with Spanish settlements, exchanging surplus grain and craft wares for Spanish goods. However, when faced with scarcities of land and labour, Sonoran villagers had to retreat from surplus production. They operated in the three types of markets theoretically open to them – exchange, labour and land – to the extent that was possible but never to the point that traditional values were abandoned.

The tension between surplus and subsistence heightened as the eighteenth century drew to a close. In the 1780s the mission of Ures, a large Pima village located at the crossroads of major trade routes, became an important centre, with the consequence that there was increasing pressure on the land, as ever greater numbers of *vecinos* settled in the fertile valley. In 1784 the bishop denounced 'continual discord' between natives and unruly squatters who occupied floodplain lands and allowed their cattle to roam through the Indians' *milpas*. When the Pimas appealed to provincial authorities, they were told to fence their fields and gardens, but since fences cost more than what the harvested crops would bring, many Pimas abandoned farming altogether.[23] During these same years, the mission for the Eudeves of Opodepe refused to provide the rations that were considered standard. The Eudeves and Nacameri complained that instead of giving them food the mission was exporting the harvests and furthermore was not providing an account of how the earnings were spent. Since mission harvests were declining during this period, one infers from these complaints that Indians had calculated a relative advantage in terms of the market value of their crops in deciding how much to plant. A decade later numerous missionaries (now converted into the caretakers of newly secularized parishes) complained of the impossibility of collecting the tithe which the bishop had ordered. Indians and *vecinos* alike refused to pay the half-*fanega* (approximately ¾ bushel) designated per household, claiming that this exaction would force many marginal farmers to abandon agriculture and turn to foraging and wage labour.[24] And, indeed, as the colonial period drew to a close, the market most readily open to the *sonoras* was the labour market.

These attitudes toward work and market exchange resonate with some of the issues raised in the current debate over peasant behaviour.[25] Opposing views on peasant responses to the market, seen either as a threat or as an opportunity, may be reconciled in the following way. Peasants do not reject the market on principle; quite the contrary, they seek ways to enhance their livelihood through commercial exchange and paid labour. However, when conditions become adverse, they reserve the right to retreat to foraging and production for subsistence. They defend the freedom to move in and out of the market, for this mobility assures their physical survival and the social reproduction of their domestic unit and community.

In order to apply this interpretation to the Sonoran data, it is necessary to explicate what we mean by *markets* and *marketing systems* over time. Pre-Columbian trade patterns of highland villages across north-west Mexico involved the extensive redistribution of surpluses, featuring decorated pottery, cotton mantas, salt, slaves, ornamental shells, turquoise and parrot feathers.[26] While the movement of significant quantities of these goods over a large geographic region implied the existence of chiefdoms with sufficient power to appropriate village products, this network essentially sustained the exchange of products for their use value, whether that use was utilitarian or ceremonial. Indigenous trade practices were qualitatively different from colonial *commerce*, the latter based on the sale of commodities whose exchange value was defined by one pre-eminent commodity: money in the form of silver and gold coin. *Sonoras* and Spaniards who entered the colonial marketplace as unequal partners or as adversaries, operated with different rationales. Indians accepted the goods (usually cloth) offered them through the missions or in the mines in return for their labour. This approach conformed to traditional exchanges of labour for food between farmers and nomads described above. By way of contrast, Spanish and Mexican proprietors sought a favourable price differential between what they paid for labour and the value of the products they sold.

The missions themselves constituted the main vehicle through which native peasants entered colonial markets. Missionaries were heavily involved in selling grain and cattle to the mines, receiving merchandise, silver bars, or gold dust in payment. They exchanged the products of

Indian labour for religious statuary to adorn the churches and cloth, tools and other consumer goods to give to the Indians. While the missions generally exchanged goods for goods, they kept elaborate account books, noting the monetary value of sales and purchases.[27] Furthermore, missionaries dealt frequently with local merchants and participated in colonial credit systems characterized by the *libranza*, or letter of credit. Thus, native and Spanish notions of market exchange first clashed in the missions. Indian farmers derived their livelihood from the missions, but these same villagers under Jesuit tutelage subordinated the value of their work to European commercial practices based on monetary pricing.

In addition to the hundreds of sacks of wheat and maize leaving the pueblos each year under the missionaries' direction, Indians of their own accord bartered smaller amounts of grain in the mining centres or surrendered a part of their harvest to itinerant peddlers who travelled through the villages. Missionaries and colonial governors alike fretted that the Indians more often than not bargained away their produce for a trifle and fell prey to those grain merchants who advanced them goods against the following year's harvest. In Spanish eyes, the Indians were irrational and childlike, oblivious to timing and price differentials in the market.[28]

Yet we can better understand the native peasants' rationality if we focus on their defence of subsistence. Sonoran peasants did not distinguish sharply between subsistence, as the physical minimum necessary for sheer survival, and surplus, as an expendable amount of produce. Rather, they sought to obtain through a variety of means the quantity of goods sufficient for both their material sustenance and ceremonial needs; for example, the celebration of community feasts and the exchange of gifts among their extended kin. Their approach to the market may also be understood in terms of a cultural imperative to personalize economic exchange: they approached the *presidios* and mining camps not only to sell grain and craft wares but also to seek patrons who might give them employment or provide other favours.

The participation of Sonoran peasants in Spanish commercial networks effected changes in their cultural values concerning work and exchange. The longstanding pattern by which the Sonorans rendered service in exchange for food was vulnerable to exploitation; the Spanish were able to impose excessive labour demands in return for mere sustenance. In response, the highland peasants who trekked to the mines or worked as muleteers and presidial auxiliaries increasingly demanded payment in both goods and money.[29] Furthermore, controversies arose over remuneration for labour performed in the missions. Indians now expected to be paid for construction work on churches, skilled tasks, or jobs that took them away from their pueblos. Despite the decline of surplus production in the second half of the century, the mission ledgers of the Franciscan order reveal that the friars had to expend greater sums in paying Indian shepherds, gardeners and masons than their predecessors had.[30]

The cultural values which Indians acquired in the marketplace were at odds with the traditional relations of production in their communities. Indian mine workers learned the value of Spanish money and were exposed to forms of patronage and occupational ranking that were different from those which operated in the missions. Many Indians found employment as common labourers (*jornaleros* or *operarios*) who were recruited in *cuadrillas* (gangs) that worked under the direction of an entrepreneur or his hired overseer. Other Indians migrated to the mines as independent, small-scale prospectors. They actually owned their own mines and built small ovens for refining ore, and sometimes employed other workers. Whether as *jornaleros* or as prospectors, native mine-workers travelled widely throughout the province and even as far away as Nueva Galicia and Nueva Vizcaya.[31]

Serrano peasants combined seasonal labour in the mines with the annual cycle of planting and harvesting. They were drawn to the larger *reales* as permanent workers or roamed from one camp to another as part of a *cuadrilla*. Some Indians found the itinerant life of mining to be an attractive alternative to the discipline of field work in the missions. While migration in search of work brought Indians more fully into the market economy of the Spaniards, long-term migration seriously affected the availability of labour in the pueblos. Consequently, there was a shortage of manpower to undertake the co-operative work of repairing irrigation systems and of maintaining agricultural production. Spanish recruitment of presidial auxiliaries made the shortage even more acute.

The problem of labour scarcity and the changing attitudes towards work in the pueblos are illustrated in Opata petitions to the Comandante General de Provincias Internas in 1777. Opata regiments had been organized to patrol the frontier and prevent incursions of hostile Apaches, but the pay that the Opatas received was not sufficient to compensate for the labour that was lost to the pueblos. Therefore, the war captains approached Spanish military authorities with demands for higher pay or for greater support from the mission *común* of their home villages. They alleged that they were forced to pay other community members to tend their crops and guard their possessions while on campaign. Furthermore, they argued that women and children could not do fieldwork because of the ever-present danger of Apache raids. Militia service may have provided Opata men with a monetary wage, but it drew male workers away from their villages during the peak growing season.[32]

As the Opata petitions disclose, paid labour displaced the communal obligations of kinsmen which had regulated social relations in their villages. The assimilation of Spanish standards of individualized and commoditized work introduced new forms of inequality and social stratification in the pueblos. Because of the pressures and opportunities of the colonial regime, migration diminished the human resources necessary to sustain the traditional economy of the highland communities. Conversely, physical movement enabled Indians to resist colonialism. Spatial mobility brought *serrano* peasants into the Spanish orbit of commercial exchange but at the same time allowed them to elude the full impact of the colonial project.

THE SOCIAL ECOLOGY OF RESISTANCE

The character of *sonoras* resistance was rooted in the ecology of their subsistence patterns. The social bonds of community nurtured in shared productive and ceremonial work constituted the nucleus of their culture and ethnic identity. The *social ecology* of this specific environmental setting of north-west Mexico encompassed a living and changing complex of cultural values that shaped the character of resistance to external subjugation.[33] The responses to colonialism were complex and, at times, contradictory. Like nearly all Amerindians, *serrano* peoples opposed initial European conquest in armed combat. After suffering defeat, their ongoing struggle for survival required a dual stance of accommodation and resistance. Highland villagers came to terms with the dominant institutions of colonialism but periodically renegotiated the conditions of their subjugation. These agricultural peoples accepted mission life; they none the less modified the Jesuit programme of concentrated settlements by forming breakaway hamlets. Opata and Pima warriors formed an uneasy alliance with Spaniards in the ongoing Apache wars. Presidial service brought them wages and legitimized social and political ascendency based on military rankings. At the same time, Sonoran peasants sought out colonial markets, but balanced the sale of their services with subsistence agriculture and foraging. As the repeated complaints of Spanish colonists demonstrate, the Indians refused to work if wages were too low or if compensation only consisted of food. Low wages were one reason for the inconstancy and scarcity of labourers for the mines and haciendas during peak seasons. As long as the *monte* was a viable alternative, Indian labourers could pursue a strategy that sometimes brought them into the colonial project but other times enabled them to

stay beyond its immediate reach. This strategy even received legitimiza-
tion from traditional norms because *sonoras* conceived of seasonal work
in the placers and wheat fields of Spanish proprietors as another form of
'gathering', whether it was the harvest or gold-laden sand, and in the
traditional world view the product of this 'gathering' could be exchanged
for food.[34] In this way, *serrano* peasants placed limits on the exploitation
of their labour and effectively resisted proletarianization until the end of
the colonial period in the early decades of the nineteenth century.

Sonoras were seldom united in their confrontation with the Spanish.
Different ethnic groups fought each other, sometimes as allies of the
Spaniards and sometimes separately. Perhaps more telling than ethnic
differences, social stratification shaped the options of people in the
colonial economy. Indians who acquired property or, more typically,
accepted permanent status as mineworkers, melted into the racially
mixed population of *vecinos*. Furthermore, increasing numbers of
Indians classified as *hijos de campana* ('children of the bell') under the
mission regime opted to leave their ethnic communities by petitioning
colonial authorities for the status of *vecino*. Thus, they abandoned
communal labour in the pueblos and cast their luck in the marketplace.[35]

Undeniably, the efficacy of resistance was limited by the conditions of
conquest. 'Resistant adaptation' became the strategy of *sonoras* and poor
vecinos in their efforts to achieve marginal advantages under colonial
oppression.[36] *Sonoras* defended modes of spatial and cultural mobility
which forced Spanish authorities and settlers to redefine the territorial
configuration of this imperial frontier and their own economic ambitions.
Serrano peoples upheld the cultural integrity of their basic social unit: the
extended family which brought together consanguine and ceremonial kin
folk. In native communities authority flowed from internally-defined
criteria of hierarchy based on the traditional merits of chieftaincy. This
political system fused with the colonial regime introduced by the
Spaniards to regulate town government. Indigenous cultures changed
over time as peasant cultivators and gatherers adapted to certain elements of the colonial project, endured others they could not avoid, and
resisted still others through negotiation, flight and revolt.

The ability of people on the frontier of European expansion to move
back and forth between the colonial economy and its ties to the emerging
world order of the greater Atlantic world is an important factor in
examining 'free' and 'unfree' labour systems in colonial settings. The
efficacy of the term *subsistence* can be enhanced by defining it not merely
as a quantitative indicator of physical survival but also as a complement of
resources necessary to satisfy both the social and ceremonial needs of
community life.[37] Furthermore, *community* can be defined in terms of the

ethnic and political relationships that bind individuals to different kinds of social units. If indeed subaltern peoples conserve a 'hidden transcript', as James Scott has argued, how can we discern its existence historically? The search for a culture of resistance is tempered by a sobering reminder of the severe limits placed on subaltern peoples.[38] In the clash of superordinate and subordinate ideologies, what are the opposing sets of values concerning work and productivity, equity and the outer limits of exploitation that emerge from alternative discourses? Here we turn to the creative analysis of language and to sources of information outside the written text in order to infer from recorded actions the cultural values which define the peasants' world and mediate between local polity and alien governance.[39] Finally, we can give these values historical specificity through the notion of social ecology, rooted in a specific time and place.

This brief overview of work, labour and market relations of production in north-west Mexico illustrates the ambiguity of freedom in a colonial periphery. Indian-Spanish relations in this region evolved not through chattel slavery, nor within the institutional constraints of *encomienda* or *repartimiento*, but rather through multiple layers of coercion and negotiation. *Sonoras* retained a significant degree of physical mobility throughout the colonial period; yet this outward expression of autonomy should not blind us to the impoverishment of native communities through the loss of watered land and the decline in the number of effective workers resident in the pueblos. The Spanish sector absorbed Indian labourers, albeit gradually, and garnered the wealth their work produced. Gift exchanges remained an important part of *serrano* ceremonial life, but the value of Indian labour was measured increasingly by the standards set in the market, expressed metonymically in silver *reales* and bolts of cloth. Opata, Pima, and Eudeve villagers still derived their subsistence from cultivation and foraging, but increasingly as well from paid militia service, labour stints in mines and the haciendas and, for a minority, sharecropping and tenantry. Tradition kept them close to the land, but their notion of work shifted from communal values to contractual relations between individual *sirvientes* and *patrones*. This individualization of labour constituted the major transformation of the social ecology of highland Sonora during three centuries of European colonial rule.

NOTES

1. I have defined *resistance* broadly, following James C. Scott's theoretical argument developed in *Weapons of the Weak: Everyday Forms of Peasant Resistance* (New Haven, 1985) and *Domination and the Arts of Resistance. Hidden Transcripts* (New Haven, 1990). The fine line between resistance and accommodation is often open to interpretation; see Steve J. Stern, 'New Approaches to the Study of Peasant Rebellion and Consciousness: Implications of the Andean Experience', in Stern (ed.), *Resistance, Rebellion, and Consciousness in the Andean Peasant World, 18th to 20th Centuries* (Madison, 1987), and Ward A. Stavig, 'The Past Weighs on the Minds of the Living: Culture, Ethnicity, and the Rural Lower Class', *Latin American Research Review*, 26, 2 (1991), pp. 225–46. In addition, the efficacy of different modes of resistance carried out by subaltern classes has been called into question. See, for example, Timothy Mitchell, 'Everyday Metaphors for Power', *Theory and Society*, 19, 5 (1990), pp. 545–77.
2. As quoted in Gibson, *Aztecs under Spanish Rule. A History of the Indians of the Valley of Mexico, 1519–1810* (Stanford, 1964), pp. 220–22.
3. John V. Murra, 'The *Mit'a* Obligations of Ethnic Groups to the Inca State', in George A. Collier, Renato I. Rosaldo, John D. Wirth (eds.), *The Inca and Aztec States 1400–1800. Anthropology and History* (New York, 1982), pp. 237–62.
4. Murra, 'The *Mit'a* Obligations', pp. 240–45; Karen Spalding, 'Social Climbers: Changing Patterns of Mobility among the Indians of Colonial Peru', *Hispanic American Historical Review*, 50 (1970), pp. 645–64.
5. Steve J. Stern, *Peru's Indian Peoples and the Challenge of Spanish Conquest* (Madison, 1982); David Lehmann (eds.), *Ecology and Exchange in the Andes* (Cambridge, 1982).
6. Nancy Farriss, *Maya Society under Colonial Rule. The Collective Enterprise of Survival* (Princeton, 1984); Alfonso Ortiz, *The Tewa World. Space, Time, Being & Becoming in a Pueblo Society* (Chicago, 1969).
7. Guaman Poma de Ayala, *Nueva crónica y buen gobierno* (1615), as cited in Stern, *Peru's Indian Peoples*, p. 19.
8. Charles C. DiPeso, *The Upper Pima of San Cayetano de Tumacacori: An Archaeohistorical Reconstruction of the Ootam of Pimereía Alta* (Dragoon, 1956); Campbell W. Pennington, *The Material Culture. The Pima Bajo of Central Sonora, Mexico*, Vol. I (Salt Lake City, 1980); Ruth Underhill, *Papago Indian Religion* (New York, 1946); Underhill, *Papago Woman* (New York, 1979); Ignaz Pfefferkorn, *Descripción de la Provincia de Sonora* (Hermosillo, 1983–1984 [1795]).
9. Ramón A. Gutiérrez, *When Jesus Came, the Corn Mothers Went Away. Marriage, Sexuality, and Power in New Mexico, 1500–1846* (Stanford, 1991), pp. 3–38.
10. Arnold J. Bauer, 'Millers and Grinders: Technology and Household Economy in Meso-America', *Agricultural History* 64, 1 (1990), pp. 1–17.
11. Gutiérrez, *When Jesus Came*, p. 17.
12. Jean B. Johnson, 'The Opata: An Inland Tribe of Sonora', in Basil C. Hedrick, J. Charles Kelley and Carroll L. Riley (eds.), *The North Mexican Frontier. Readings in Archaeology, Ethnohistory, and Ethnography* (Carbondale and Edwardsville, 1971).
13. Pennington, *Material Culture*, pp. 149–50. Today, the rural mestizo of Sonora await the beginning of the summer rains on the Feast of Saint John (24 June) and recall a tradition of bathing in the river on that day.
14. DiPeso, *Upper Pima of San Cayetano*, p. 443; Bernard L. Fontana, 'The *Vikita*: A Biblio History', *Journal of the Southwest* 29, 3, (1987), pp. 259–72.
15. Castetter and Bell, *Pima and Papago Agriculture*, pp. 48–63, 74–113; Gary Nabhan, *The Desert Smells Like Rain. A Naturalist in Papago Indian Country* (San Francisco, 1982), pp. 75–86.
16. Gary Nabhan, *Gathering the Desert* (Tucson, 1985), 93–184; Pennington, *Material Culture*, pp. 143–7 and *passim*.
17. Underhill, *Papago Woman*, p. 68; Edward F. Castetter and Willis H. Bell, *Pima and Papago Agriculture* (Albuquerque, 1942).
18. Castetter and Bell, *Pima and Papago Agriculture*, pp. 45–6; Frank S. Crosswhite,

'Desert Plants, Habitat, and Agriculture in Relation to the Major Pattern of Cultural Differentiation in the O'odham People of the Sonoran Desert', *Desert Plants* 3, 2 (1981), pp. 47–76.

19. P. Juan Nentvig, *Descripción Geográfica, Natural y Curiosa de la Provincia de Sonora*, edited by Germán Viveros (Mexico, 1971 [1762]), p. 118; Correspondence of P. Joseph Roldán, P. Thomas Pérez and P. Manuel Aguirre to Jesuit *visitador* Ignacio Lizassoaín, AGN *Jesuitas* II–29, exp. 19, 1762 (Documentary Relations of the Southwest, University of Arizona, microfilm R III–C–4).

20. Henry F. Dobyns, Paul H. Ezell, Alden W. Jones and Greta S. Ezell, 'What were Nixoras?', *Southwestern Journal of Anthropology* 15, 2 (1960), pp. 230–58; Julio Montané, 'De nijoras y "españoles a medias"', *Memoria del XV Simposio de Historia y Antropología de Sonora*, Hermosillo (1991), Vol. I, pp. 105–24.

21. Thus Pedro Tueros, the Spanish *teniente* who administered the gold placers of San Ildefonso de la Cieneguilla at the height of its first bonanza in 1771, reported that of the estimated 1,500–2,000 Indians who worked there, most left the mines during the short growing season of Pimería Alta (June and July, during the summer rains) to plant and harvest their crops. Governor Francisco Antonio Crespo added that the mines' slack season lasted from late May to October, owing to the mineworkers' absence to tend their crops. Archivo General de la Nación [AGN] *Provincias Internas*, exp. 245A, ff. 325–7, translated and published by Kieran McCarthy, *Desert Documentary* (Tucson, 1976), pp. 19–24.

22. On *repartimiento*, see Ignacio del Río, 'Repartimientos de indios en Sonora y Sinaloa', *Memoria del VII Simposio de Historia de Sonora* (Hermosillo, 1982); Susan Deeds, 'Rural Work in Nueva Vizcaya: Forms of Labour Coercion on the Periphery', *Hispanic American Historical Review* 69, 3 (1989), 425–50; José Cuello, 'The Persistence of Indian Slavery and Encomienda in the Northeast of Colonial Mexico, 1577–1723', *Journal of Social History* 21, 4 (1988), pp. 683–700. Evidence for the eventual hiring of tapisques in Sonora comes from AGN *Jesuitas* IV–10, exp. 98, f. 130; exp. 116, f. 180; exp. 119, f. 153.

23. Biblioteca Nacional Fondo Franciscano [BNFF] 34/759, f. 23. Informe del Obispo de Sonora Antonio de Reyes, 1784.

24. Gibson estimated that an Indian household in Central Mexico would require from 10 to 20 *fanegas* of maize a year to sustain itself. In that case, the tithe in grain ordered by the Bishop of Sonora represented 5–10 per cent of a household's subsistence needs; see Gibson, *Aztecs under Spanish Rule*, p. 311. Also see Thomas H. Charlton, 'Land Tenure and Agricultural Production in the Otumba Region, 1785–1803', in H.R. Harvey (ed.), *Land and Politics in the Valley of Mexico. A Two-Thousand Year Perspective* (Albuquerque, 1991), p. 254.

25. For the debate over the moral economy of peasants, see James C. Scott, *The Moral Economy of the Peasant. Rebellion and Subsistence in Southeast Asia* (New Haven, 1976); *Weapons of the Weak. Everyday Forms of Peasant Resistance* (New Haven, 1985); Samuel L. Popkin, *The Rational Peasant: The Political Economy of Rural Society in Vietnam* (Berkeley, 1979); Teodor Shanin, *The Awkward Class. Political Sociology of Peasantry in a Developing Society: Russia 1910–1925* (Oxford, 1972).

26. Ethnohistorical and archaeological data on pre-Conquest Sonoran peoples are ably synthesized by Carroll L. Riley, *The Frontier People. The Greater Southwest in the Protohistoric Period* (Carbondale, 1982).

27. Inventories and mission accounts corresponding to the pueblos of San Pedro de Aconchi and San José de Baviácora, Archivo de la Mitra, Hermosillo, Sonora, Archivo del Sagrario, Libro 1, 1666–1828.

28. Archivo de la Mitra, Hermosillo (University of Arizona microfilm 811, roll 3).

29. University of Arizona Special Collections Az 370, Padre Jacobo Sedelmayr to Visitador Padre Balthazar, 1749; AGN *Jesuitas* IV–10, exp. 119, f. 153, 1764; IV–10, exp. 116, f. 180, 1764. Opata presidial auxiliaries were paid 3 *reales* a day: BNFF 34/734, 735, 1777. Capitán General de la Nación Opata D. Juan Manuel Varela to Juan Bautista de Anza in San Miguel de Horcasitas, 30 June 1977.

30. BNFF 35/761, 761. Fr. Pedro de Arriquibar, minister of San Ignacio de Cabúrica, and Fr. Juan Santiestéban of Santiago de Cocóspera, reported to the Presidente de las Misiones de la Pimería Alta and the Franciscan Colegio de Propaganda Fide de la Santa Cruz de Querétaro, 1787–88.
31. Archivo General de Indias [AGI] *Guadalajara* 505, f. 377–8.
32. BNFF 34/734.
33. I have adapted the term 'social ecology' from Juan Martínez-Alier, 'Ecology and the Poor', *Journal of Latin American Studies*, 23 (1991), pp. 621–39.
34. On the gathering mentality of the O'odham, see François Rodriguez and Nelly Silva, 'Etnoarqueología de Quitovac, Sonora', field reports for the Centro de Estudios Mexicanos y Centroamericanos (Mexico, DF) and the Instituto Nacional de Antropología e Historia (1985, 1986).
35. Bishop Reyes, 1784, BNFF 34/759; AGN *Gobernación*, Cajas 3, 4, exp. s/c, s/n (1837).
36. Stern, 'Peasant Rebellion and Consciousness', pp. 3–25.
37. For the importance of quantitative estimates of agricultural productivity and household needs in terms of measurable amounts of maize and price analysis, see Gibson, *Aztecs under Spanish Rule*, p. 311; Charlton, 'Land Tenure and Agricultural Production', p. 254; Richard Garner, 'Price Trends in Eighteenth-Century Mexico', *Hispanic American Historical Review*, 65, 2 (1985), pp. 279–325; Enrique Florescano, *Precios del maíz y crisis agrícolas en México (1708–1810): Ensayo sobre el movimiento de los precios y sus consecuencias economicas y sociales* (Mexico, 1969). Recently David Reher has correlated population and price figures for central western New Spain (Bajío and Michoacán) during the eighteenth century, see 'Population Pressure and Living Standards in Late Colonial Mexico', *Actas. El Poblamiento de las Américas* (Mexico, 1992), Vol. I, pp. 447–76.
38. Scott, *Domination and the Arts of Resistance*, especially pp. 183–202. A recent critique of Scott's approach asserts that methods of domination are so pervasive that they define the limits of autonomous action to which suppressed groups aspire; see Timothy Mitchell, 'Everyday Metaphors of Power', *Theory and Society*, pp. 545–77.
39. For a discussion of the nuances of language in historical documents and offers a thoughtful critique of the 'hyper-agentialism' and rationality which James Scott attributes to subaltern peoples' behaviour, see Eric Van Young, 'Sliding Sideways: Text and Context in the Mexican Wars of Independence', *Colonial Latin American Review*, 2 (1992).

Part II

Old Worlds, New Worlds

The Criminalization of 'Free' Labour: Master and Servant in Comparative Perspective

PAUL CRAVEN and DOUGLAS HAY

A recurrent theme in recent work on slavery is that the rigid boundaries of that juridical category were always blurred in practice. Within slave regimes there were always possibilities (sometimes brutally suppressed, sometimes tolerated or encouraged) for slaves to employ the bargaining strategies of 'free labour'.[1] Within societies with strong artisanal sectors, slaves might act as independent entrepreneurs. When the decay of plantation economies increased the master's incentive to allow slave participation in a wider labour market, even the juridical category could be deformed. In the Bahamas after 1800, for example, masters allowed slaves to work for wages. When masters attempted to use the slave laws to punish those who refused to turn over their wages, the Attorney General decided that only the more limited penalties of the master and servant laws applied. Slave law would only be available to masters if they denied their slaves permission to work for wages.[2]

The fact that a colonial law officer could believe it possible to carve out a temporary legal status of this kind (slaves who could be controlled only by master and servant law) is a reminder that slavery was just one of many legal statuses defining employment relations in the common law world.[3] Apprentices, journeymen, labourers, indentured servants, 'industrial' immigrants, slaves and masters were the main categories, but within each there was a plethora of legal definitions at common law and in legislation, setting the limits of freedom that 'free' servants (and masters) enjoyed.[4] One of the best-studied examples of some of those differences is the use of versions of apprenticeship (1834–8) and then full master and servant law (from 1838) in the ex-slave societies of the British Caribbean. The argument in those jurisdictions about the relative severity of each legal regime is an important one. But it is also important to bear in mind that those successive legal regimes, and similar legislative changes in other slave societies that became part of the British empire, were local variations of a broad body of employment law, an immense corpus of legislation and judicial decisions that left its mark on virtually every British possession.

Legislation in England since at least the Statute of Labourers (1349), and in the colonies since their founding, sharply constrained freedom of contract by 'free' labour and its employers. In many post-abolition colonial regimes (and sometimes in England itself) the coercive powers of masters were little different from those their counterparts had enjoyed under slavery. But in some jurisdictions, at some periods, the law of master and servant could also foster and embody greater equity by enforcing claims for wages and protecting workers from ill-treatment. In the late nineteenth century, with the growth of theories of contractual equality that had their own ideological bite, some of the fiercer provisions of the older law were repealed in England and the white settler colonies, even as they were reproduced in newer parts of the empire.[5]

In short, while current research emphasizes the freedom that could exist within the juridical category of slavery, aspects of unfreedom within 'free' labour make that juridical category no less problematic. It was a powerful ideological construct that encompassed an immense variety of exploitative and coercive, as well as more even-handed, employment relations. And the voluminous and appalling comprehensiveness of the slave codes was paralleled by an immense amount of legislation throughout the empire, that subjected 'free' workers to penal law or to their masters' will legitimated by law. The social continuities between slavery and free labour are the subject of much recent research; the legal continuities are equally important. This paper describes a comparative study of the legal construction of coercion and consent in 'free' labour regimes throughout the British empire from the sixteenth to the twentieth centuries and presents some preliminary findings.

Lawsuits for damages against workers in breach of contract were neither speedy nor effective, and labour discipline was a central concern of legislators. Two salient characteristics of master and servant law were a liberal use of penal sanctions for breach by the worker and summary enforcement before lay magistrates and cognate officials. From an early period in some jurisdictions, the statutes or case law also allowed servants to obtain summary judgements for unpaid wages, or remedies for other breaches by masters. The statutes also set the general terms of employment contracts in a great range of variations. Maximum and minimum periods of employment, requirements for written rather than verbal agreements in various circumstances, the exemption of some groups of workers and special provisions for others are only some of the ways in which the law in scores of jurisdictions narrowed the range of contractual bargaining allowed to the employer and the worker.

It is clear from the extensive and growing literature on 'free' labour in the British empire and Commonwealth that distinctive forms of this legislation, employing only a subset of the whole repertoire of available terms, were to be found in different jurisdictions. White settler colonies, slave economies with contemporaneous indentured white labour, post-slave colonies with large numbers of immigrant Indian workers, and twentieth-century African jurisdictions all appear to show distinctive kinds and uses of master and servant law. For the most part, however, studies of master and servant in particular jurisdictions have ignored or glossed over its prevalence elsewhere. Many such accounts assume either that the colonial statute was cobbled together on a standard metropolitan list, or that it was an indigenous innovation custom-built to suit peculiar local circumstances. But the prevalence and persistence of master and servant legislation, taken together with its variety, suggest that such assumptions should not go unexamined. The scope of its enactment and enforcement, in space and time, presents an unusually promising opportunity for a comparative study of the impact of law on economies and societies, and vice versa.

THE MASTER AND SERVANT PROJECT

Three general problems arise out of the prevalence, persistence and variety of this kind of employment law.[6] These are the *uses* of the law – its administration and enforcement in different jurisdictions; the *dissemination* of the statutes – how particular provisions and formulations were transmitted between jurisdictions, including the role of the metropolitan administration; and the *distribution* of characteristic terms – how master and servant law varied in different political economies. These three broad enquiries are obviously interrelated, but each calls for a different methodological approach.

In all jurisdictions the enforcement of the legislation is one of the most difficult issues, since the summary nature of the remedies, administered in hearings that were not courts of record, means that the actual use of the law was only occasionally documented. In some jurisdictions it appears likely that the statute law was not much more than a façade for more draconian employer self-help.[7] In others, pass laws or other forms of regulation took precedence. In each case, painstaking local reconstructions are required to suggest the nature and extent of use. These must take into account not only the relations of master and servant at work and before the magistrates, but also the extent to which the judiciary and other state agencies were active in interpreting the law, supervising its enforcement, and shaping the local reception of English law and policy.

We are therefore collaborating with a number of specialists who are writing explicitly comparative accounts of the enforcement of master and servant law in different regions, informed throughout by their awareness of the prevalence, persistence and variety of the legislation everywhere in the empire. At present our collaborators include David Arnold (History, School of Oriental and African Studies, University of London), Michael Anderson (Law, also SOAS), Mandy Banton (Public Record Office, London), Hilary Beckles (History, University of the West Indies), Martin Chanock (Law, LaTrobe University), Michael Quinlan (Industrial Relations, Griffith University), and Christopher Tomlins (Law, LaTrobe, currently at the American Bar Foundation). Paul Craven is preparing an account of master and servant and its administration in Canada; Douglas Hay is preparing a similar account for England.

These regional studies will be written in explicitly comparative terms, with each author, so far as local sources permit, seeking to answer the same questions about the enactment, judicial interpretation, enforcement and impact of the master and servant legislation in the relevant group of jurisdictions. One 'regional' study is of a special kind: Mandy Banton's study of the role of the Colonial Office in suggesting, demanding or acquiescing in legislative provisions for the colonies under its mandate. The regional studies are co-ordinated by the range of questions being posed by their authors; they draw as well on aspects of the project conducted centrally at York University, under the direction of Craven and Hay. These are the creation of an archive of all, or nearly all, the master and servant legislation enacted in almost 100 imperial jurisdictions since the sixteenth century; the preparation of computer inventories and cross-indexes to these holdings; the creation of a computer database containing the full text of the more significant statutes; the representation of the meaning of their provisions by means of a conceptual coding scheme; and the computer-assisted analysis of these materials. As findings emerge we are distributing the results to the authors of the regional studies to assist them in their archival research and writing; at the same time we are conducting studies of the dissemination of the legislation throughout the empire and of the distribution of its characteristic terms. The rest of this article describes the methodology employed in these centrally-conducted aspects of the project. We present some preliminary findings that help illustrate these approaches.

COLLECTING THE LEGISLATION

Studies of the dissemination of the legislation and the distribution of its terms require, first of all, that a comprehensive collection of the statutes be made. This has proved a more difficult undertaking than we had reason to anticipate, and after nearly three years of investigation and enquiries some statutes remain elusive. Nevertheless, we have so far identified and obtained copies of statutes from 96 jurisdictions (a few of these are the same place with changes of name).[8] We currently hold 1,025 statutes dating from the mid-sixteenth to the mid-twentieth centuries from all regions of the empire.[9] These include master and servant provisions embedded in other legislation as well as brief amending statutes.[10] We expect eventually to have in the data set about 1,300 statutes and sections of statutes, varying from single clauses to voluminous enactments.

On receipt at York University, each statute is numbered and read to determine whether it is a *principal statute* (providing a fairly comprehensive statement of employment law at the point of adoption), an *amending or consolidating statute* (usually modifying, repealing or adding to a pre-existing statute), or a *related statute* without express master and servant content.[11] The first reading is also used to decide whether all, or only parts, of principal statutes are to be processed (by coding and full-text entry, described below) for further computer analysis, and that information is added to the inventory, which is also used to track the subsequent stages of processing. In this phase of research wehave used only principal statutes; we will incorporate terms from amending statutes in the near future. To complete this preliminary processing, a research assistant records all references made in the text of the statute to other statutes in another computer database, the cross-reference file: if we do not already have them, these statutes in turn become candidates for collection. The whole body of statutes, together with computer-based indexes and supporting materials, will be deposited in the Osgoode Hall Law Library (York University) upon completion of the project.[12]

COMPUTER ANALYSIS OF STATUTES

Dissemination: Lexical analysis

There are so many statutes, and they are so diverse, as to defy systematic comparison by traditional methods. We employ computer-based comparative techniques for our approaches to the dissemination and distribution problems.[13] One key to tracing the *dissemination* of statutes and provisions through the empire is identifying the recurrence of specific words, phrases and other collocations across time and space. This is accomplished by applying the tools of literary and linguistic scholarship to these statutory materials.[14] We have recently begun using *TACT*, developed at the University of Toronto's Centre for Computing in the Humanities, to help analyse the texts of several hundred significant statutes (and parts of statutes), amounting in all to half a million words.[15] *TACT* permits us to view every instance of a word or phrase of interest in its context, and provides tools for generating word lists, concordances and lists of common phrases. In addition to the sophisticated word- and phrase-tracing that *TACT* permits, we have developed tools for identifying and calculating the overlap of different statutes' lexicons. Similar vocabularies are an internal clue that the statutes may be related.

Lexical analysis therefore explores what the statutes themselves reveal about their dissemination. Using such techniques, we can find and map the movement of chunks of language over decades or centuries and between continents. We can identify how much of a statute has been copied from earlier ones in other jurisdictions and in what sequence such borrowing took place, so that we may construct family trees of statutes within and across jurisdictions. To give one example from a pilot study of these techniques, we have shown that the 1856 Cape Colony statute has language in common with an 1828 statute from the same South African jurisdiction (two lines only), an 1839 statute from St. Vincent (a standard form for contracts, and an apprenticeship clause), and an 1850 statute from Natal (the greater part of which is identical to the 1856 Cape Colony Act). It also shows immediately that the framers of the Cape statute chose not to adopt a section of the Natal predecessor that provided compensation to servants and apprentices whose master failed to live up to his part of the employment bargain. Instead, the Cape statute merely gave the magistrate discretion to cancel the contract in such circumstances.[16] In working out appropriate techniques of lexical analysis, we have launched pilot studies of three approaches.

The first involves identifying particular terms that are known to have particular significance in the history of master and servant legislation, and tracing their emergence and reappearance in the corpus. In the pilot study we are working with constellations of words: shortly we expect to be able to work with lemmatized forms (word roots). The pilot study traces two constellations, one having to do with menial or domestic labour (which is expressly excluded by master and servant statutes in some jurisdictions and included in others) and the other with mistreatment or ill-treatment, a fairly common master's offence. A graduate student assistant has been using *TACT* to identify every occurrence of the terms of interest, and to link each use to its specific context. We anticipate that by investigating a relatively small number of middle-ranked terms of interest we will be able to link a large number of statutes into 'family groups'.

The second approach uses lexical overlap as an indicator of dissemination links. Every statute can be reduced to a list of unique words. By performing a series of pair-wise comparisons, we can derive an index of overlap between each pair of statutes, expressed as the ratio of the common vocabulary to the total vocabulary of the pair (or as a pair of ratios, one for each member). The greater the overlap, the more likely the two statutes are to be related by a dissemination link. We have generated the source data for this approach, and are currently refining the measurement technique. There are several issues here: for example, should words that appear in only one statute be counted? Should function words – prepositions, auxiliary verbs, etc. – be excluded? Should words be weighted by their frequency of appearance in the database, so that common words 'count for less' than uncommon ones in assessing the degree of similarity of two statutes? We anticipate that lexical overlap will be a useful and inexpensive heuristic for identifying candidates for more detailed comparisons.

The final approach uses *TACT*'s collocation generator to identify and trace middle-frequency sequences that function as 'rote phrases' in groups of master and servant statutes. This approach is similar to the first approach above, extending the analysis from words of interest to phrases. One difference is that phrases are subject to reorganization during dissemination. So far we have looked at a few collocations with a view to designing a pilot study. We are awaiting a revised version of the *TACT* collocation programme before continuing with the evaluation of this approach.

Of course, these techniques do not explain *why* language is found first in one jurisdiction, then in another, often very distant and often much later. But they raise important questions about statutory borrowing and drafting that may find answers in archival sources, and sometimes the statutes themselves are the only evidence of origins where archival sources are missing. Lexical analysis of dissemination can show *where* provisions in the statutes came from and *how* they got there; but to explain *why* one clause was borrowed and another not, we have to turn to the meaning of the legislation. This is the goal of the distribution study.

Distribution: Conceptual Analysis

Like the study of dissemination, the distribution study focuses on the statutes themselves. Here, however, we address them not as collections of words and phrases but as packages of ideas about the proper regulation of employment relations. Several statutes providing imprisonment for disobedient apprentices share the same idea, although some may call the institution of confinement a bridewell, others a jail, and still others a house of correction. Moreover, the lexicons of two provisions may be statistically very similar, suggesting a close relationship from the standpoint of dissemination, yet they may express entirely opposed ideas from the standpoint of distribution simply because one of them prefaces the shared language with the word 'not'.

In order to embark on the distribution analysis, then, we have had to develop techniques for representing the *conceptual* contents of the master and servant legislation, and also for identifying various *types* of master and servant law according to the concepts they contain. The former aspect involved developing a coding scheme and protocols, and writing a suite of computer programs to aid student assistants in coding the statutes, to support the validity and reliability of the coding process, and to allow *ad hoc* queries against the code base. At the outset, our research assistants prepared brief abstracts of some 300 statutes to assist us in developing the initial coding categories; these abstracts are maintained in machine-readable form for ease of retrieval. From them we first developed an elaborate, hierarchically-structured coding scheme with approximately 1000 individual nodes or decision points; extensive testing and development reduced its complexity to 225 points.

The code captures information about 13 aspects of the employment relationship dealt with in the statutes: related provisions; employees covered by the statute; who may contract; forcible recruitment; assignment and transfer of the contract; duration; consideration and wages; the form of contract; continuing and ending the contract; administration of the law at first instance; appeals and writs for judicial review; masters' offences and penalties; workers' offences and penalties; and third-party offences and penalties. Each of these main headings branches out into many alternatives. Coders first read the statute carefully, using worksheets to note the occurrence of specific terms and the clauses in which they are found. They then code the statute using a computer program which assists them by displaying only the relevant portions of the coding scheme, depending on the choices selected. The statute is coded by highlighting descriptive words on the computer screen.[17] Each statute is coded at least twice, by different coders; a computer-generated comparison then lists differences between versions, and the investigators and coders meet to resolve differences and also to assess the accuracy of the coding where the coders agree. Another program 'reads' the codes for a statute and displays a textual summary, which can be retrieved on disk and is filed in paper form with the original statute and preliminary code sheets.

Once the statutes have been coded to identify their essential contents, we can proceed to identify distinctive types of master and servant statutes in order to test our ideas about the distribution of terms. In the remainder of this paper we describe in a provisional and preliminary way how we go about this, concentrating on the logic of the analysis rather than the technical details of the computer-based tools we use. Findings are reported here for purposes of illustration: the research we are reporting is still under way, and only a subset of the relevant statutes has been included in the analysis so far.[18] Our object in this paper is not to establish a general classification scheme for the legislation, still less to explain the statutes in terms of social forms and labour market conditions, although both of these are among the final goals of the project. We aim to explain an approach that we believe may have broad applications in comparative historical research. We illustrate some of its advantages and difficulties in a sort of guided tour of our encounter with the distribution problem.

THE DISTRIBUTION PROBLEM

Why did any given colonial jurisdiction[19] acquire the type of master and servant statutes that it did?

This seemingly simple question requires a great deal of unpacking. It is based, of course, on the general observations we have alluded to already: that master and servant legislation was pervasive, persistent and extremely varied. The variety seems to cry out for classification. It is as though there was an extensive imperial repertoire of employment law provisions from which each jurisdiction, at various points in its history, selected a few, and to which some jurisdictions occasionally contributed a novel element. What guided the selection? What explains the innovations?

There are many possible accounts, some more plausible than others. Central to many of these is the idea that master and servant legislation was simply imposed on colonial societies by the imperial metropolis. Four informal variants seem to find expression in the literature. While they are intuitively attractive in varying degrees, none explains all the elements. The first is that because English settlers and administrators were familiar with this form of employment regulation they brought it with them to the various corners of the globe. This may explain the pervasiveness of the legislation, perhaps even its persistence, but surely not its variety. The second has it that colonial governors and chief justices simply imposed an inappropriate metropolitan model on their colonial charges: pervasiveness perhaps, but neither variety nor persistence, and still less innovation. According to the third variant, these same historical agents sought to adapt the familiar model to the peculiar circumstances in which they found themselves: this helps explain the variety (and perhaps the persistence), but not the recurrence of similar ideas in widely separated times and places. Finally, it is sometimes suggested that a centralized bureaucracy in the offices of the Secretaries of State and later the Colonial Office (or the India Office or the Foreign Office) tried to standardize employment law throughout the empire. This account probably exaggerates the effectiveness of these bureaucracies. In general, they did not try to standardize employment law, and when the attempt was made it often failed due to bungling, political interference at home, or the wilier ways of their colonial clientele.[20]

Our working hypothesis is that colonial officials and legislatures had a relatively free hand in framing their master and servant statutes, and that they did so in great part by selecting provisions from the common pool in accordance with their understanding of local needs and opportunities, and with some regard to experience elsewhere. We do not discount the idiosyncrasies of the occasional chief justice or colonial under-secretary, but we suggest that grossly inapposite legislation was generally short-lived: unlike England, most colonies repealed old provisions when they enacted new legislation. As a result, we hypothesize that colonies whose local elites faced roughly similar problems and opportunities in recruiting, employing and disciplining labour adopted roughly similar master and servant legislation.

We realize that this working hypothesis assumes that coercive law was, or was believed to be, necessary for the creation and replacement of appropriate labour. It ignores (in this formulation) whether master and servant legislation served multiple ends, including both coercive and more symbolic purposes, and in what proportion. It says nothing about whether long-term changes in the characteristics of employment law everywhere in the empire (perhaps orchestrated from the centre) could generate congruences that otherwise might not be expected; and it simply sets aside questions about levels of enforcement, and about the significance of master and servant law for attitudes toward law in general, and its legitimacy, in these societies.[21] But the simplified hypothesis has the virtue that it can structure an initial comparison of master and servant regimes and their social contexts that is appropriately broad for a first assessment of the legislation; it is also an hypothesis that is implicit in much of the existing literature.

In order to test this apparently simple hypothesis, we need a way of specifying both the dependent variable and the independent variable. That is to say, we have to be able to identify 'roughly similar master and servant provisions' when they occur; we also need a typology of colonies with 'roughly similar problems and opportunities in recruiting, employ-ing, and disciplining labour'. This paper gives only rudimentary versions of the latter; the main distinction we employ here is between England and the white settler colonies on the one hand, and colonial plantation and mining regimes employing native or imported labour on the other, with attention also to white indentured labour regimes in which slavery was also present, such as the American and West Indian colonies of the seventeenth and eighteenth centuries. It is a suggestive and fairly obvious set of distinctions, sufficiently clear at least to serve as a starting point.[22]

In England, after the fourteenth century and even more so after the sixteenth century, the overall supply of labour roughly matched the demand, whatever deficiencies (from an employer's point of view) there might be in particular trades in particular years. In other jurisdictions to which the law of master and servant was extended in the empire, this was emphatically not the case. The American mainland colonies used slave labour in part because the demands of plantation sectors were far greater than capital was prepared to command by the use of free labour, but the effects could also be seen in the determination to make even free labour less free through indentures. The intensive labour demands that were largely responsible for extraordinarily high depletion rates among slaves in the sugar islands of the mid-eighteenth century still existed in the post-emancipation British Caribbean, especially in light of the declining profits in sugar. They had much the same results in the mahogany forests of Belize, to take but one example of many.[23] In some African colonies, such as Northern Rhodesia, the constant loss of mine workers to better wages and working conditions in South Africa or back to their villages meant that recruitment, organized through the mine owners' associa-tions, was a constantly unsolved problem.[24] In Assam tea gardens after the mid-nineteenth century, the consumption of lives in producing greater and greater amounts of tea at lower and lower cost was appal-ling.[25] Capital in many other highly exploitative industries, especially new ones attempting to forge new kinds of labour forces, shared the problem. The demand for labour in some sectors in some colonies was, in effect, inexhaustible. One response was the informal or illegal use of a great deal of force. But other responses can be found in legislative innovations, in pass law, poor law, criminal, and master and servant law. We are concerned in this paper only with the last.

To test the proposition that the law in such regimes differed signifi-cantly from that in England, or in other less harsh environments for labour such as white settler colonies, it is necessary to be able to identify patterns of similarity in the various master and servant acts, and to construct an appropriate typology. The early-modern English regimes of master and servant law provided three principal remedies for masters: abatement of wages, dissolution of the contract (dismissal without wages), or imprisonment of the servant until she or he was willing to complete the contract. Imprisonment did not end the obligation to fulfil its terms.[26] While it was conceived, like all master and servant legislation, to compel work from workers who might be tempted to leave for higher wages, or who were unsatisfactory workers in other ways, this body of law none the less addressed demands of both master and servant with summary remedies. The crucial distinction remained, of course, that only workers could be imprisoned for breach; the contract was conceived as one in which the authority of the master was lawful and necessary, and the penal consequences entirely congruent with that fact. Thus in the early nineteenth century Lord Ellenborough held that the presence of a penal provision showed that a statute applied only against servants.[27] But, as will be seen, in comparison with much colonial legislation, the English statutes were closer to being even-handed in their distribution of remedies and penalties.

MARKER PROVISIONS

A first approach to the distinctiveness of regimes can be made by considering individual 'markers' or especially significant characteristics of the legislation, including some that appear as innovations in the general law of master and servant relatively late. Since the penal clauses of master and servant law are among its most distinctive features, and proved most controversial in the nineteenth century before their abolition, they may be expected to serve as discriminators among different varieties of legislation. Imprisonment of servants for breach was one of the most common characteristics in all jurisdictions, but in some it was replaced or accompanied by corporal punishment or servitude (compulsory labour beyond the term of the original contract). For the offending master, a similar extremity of punishment, arising relatively late, was the possibility of jail. Using only simple tests for the presence or absence of single characteristics, we use the coded versions to identify statutes that include servitude or corporal punishment as workers' penalties, or imprisonment for masters' offences.

Masters' Remedies: Servitude

The English legislation used imprisonment to compel the worker to complete the contract if the master so desired, but it did not make service itself a punishment. In sharp contrast, many of the colonial regimes punished the worker's breach by increasing the length of the contract. We have called this 'servitude'. The offences for which servitude was enacted differed among regimes. It applied most commonly (thirty-two of the statutes in the group studied here) to absenteeism, and the usual form required a servant to serve a multiple of the time away. Thus, by a Nova Scotia statute of 1765, the absent worker was obliged to repay his master by twice the labour missed plus additional labour to make up for any 'extraordinary expense' his master had had in bringing him to justice.[28] Less often (fifteen statutes), servitude was used to punish insubordination; this is clearly a more coercive variety of legislation, given the wide ambit and often indeterminate nature, of that offence.[29] Servitude for absenteeism is fairly widespread: there is a heavy concentration in the West Indies and American mainland colonies in the seventeenth and eighteenth centuries, with some further West Indian examples in the nineteenth;[30] but there is also the 1765 Nova Scotia statute mentioned above and several in Mauritius and India between 1854 and 1908.[31] Servitude for insubordination, the more coercive use, is found almost entirely in seventeenth and early eighteenth-century America (1641–1748) and the West Indies: the latest use of it is in a Jamaican statute of 1814.[32]

In summary, servitude for absenteeism is found in both white settler and plantation economies using both slave and indentured labour in the early period: in other words, societies with either somewhat or much higher demands for labour than England, which had no such legislation. Servitude of non-slave labour for insubordination is almost entirely limited to jurisdictions which also gave legal recognition to slavery. By the nineteenth century, servitude for absenteeism is found only in plantation societies with large native or ex-slave populations; in our present sample there are no statutes prescribing servitude for insubordination later than 1814.

Masters' Remedies: Corporal Punishment

Another dimension of comparative interest is the maximum punishment allowed by statute. Here corporal punishment is of particular interest, since it carried heavy connotations of baseness and ignominy from early modern times to the twentieth century. The *Statute of Artificers*[33] (England, 1562) allowed whipping for forging a certificate, and while the penalty certainly applied to servants, it may also have applied to masters (the wording is ambiguous). Corporal punishment of servants, although not as frequent as jail or fine or abatement of wages, was widespread in the centuries following the Statute of Artificers, but there is a great discontinuity in its enactment. Whipping (and some use of the stocks) is found in two broad sets of enactments:

1. *American mainland colonies (none after 1748), West Indian colonies, and Ireland (a statute of 1715)*. Here the variations are that in the northern American colonies whipping could be used only for the insubordinate servant, but in the south it also applied to absenteeism. There was no whipping permitted for master and servant offences in England other than the provision in the Statute of Artificers itself, and it is extremely doubtful that it was ever used after the seventeenth century. The Irish statute is a severe one, in telling contrast to the law in England: stocks or House of Correction for being absent or insubordinate the first time, House of Correction and whipping for a second offence. A certificate offence brought a whipping *and* imprisonment for three months. In all these cases the extent of the whipping is not specified, although in some acts (e.g. Ireland 1715) public whipping is required.[34]

2. *African and Asian statutes dating from 1850 to 1932*. Many of these acts provided whipping as a general substitute for any other penalty, at the discretion of the magistrates, when the offender was a youth. Generally whipping was limited to those under 18 or 16 years; there is frequently a limit of 12, 16, or 24 strokes, and some statutes specify 'a light cane' or similar limitation.[35] A few specify no limits of any kind.[36] Only one statute in this group appears to allow adult whipping. The 1908 North Borneo statute provides for a range of whippings, to correspond for specific absenteeism and insubordination offences, with the unusual feature that whipping is sometimes an alternative to imprisonment at the option of the offender.[37]

There are two points of significance in this pattern. The first is that early-modern acceptance of corporal punishment for employment offences of free servants seems, from the present sample of statutes, to be almost entirely confined to societies in which slavery is also to be found, but also in Ireland and in two exceptions noted below. The second is that the whipping provisions in the African and Asian statutes after 1850 are distinctive; they probably reflect a Colonial Office determination to limit the use of whipping, which was probably widespread, without entirely ruling it out. In short, that legislation replicates in the late nineteenth and twentieth centuries (with qualifications about age and severity) the use of corporal punishment earlier seen in the southern Thirteen Colonies, the West Indies and Ireland – that is, in societies where highly coercive codes existed for slave and free labour and/or societies peopled by groups whom

English planters considered inferior, dangerous, or in need of extra-ordinary discipline – indentured labourers (including transported criminals), manumitted slaves, and the Irish. To this broad pattern there are only two exceptions, both from white settler colonies. The 1765 Nova Scotia act provides a whipping for certificate offences, purportedly following the Irish statute of 1715.[38] An 1842 statute of Western Australia, the last Australian colony to receive English convict labour, allowed a magistrate to sentence juvenile apprentices on second convictions to three dozen lashes (plus imprisonment) for insubordination.[39]

Servants' Remedies: Jail for Masters

As noted, masters were liable to corporal punishment in at most two statutes. If we turn to another penalty with connotations of particular stigma for employers, imprisonment, we find a limited use of it against masters in provisions that help map some of the variations in master and servant law through the empire and through time. Jail is, of course, among the most common penalties for servants' breaches.

The *Statute of Artificers* prescribed jail for paying wages in excess of those set by justices or by statute. This provision is replicated in an English statute of 1720 and an Irish one of 1771; in all these cases offenders would be defying judicial regulation of the trade.[40] This was an offence against the public policy of restraining wage demands. Of more significance for assessing the meaning of master and servant is imprisonment for masters' offences against servants, either for non-payment of wages or for cruelty and other mistreatment.

The chronology is striking: all the statutes providing imprisonment for non-payment or mistreatment are very late, the earliest dating from the mid-nineteenth century. For non-payment, the enactments are with few exceptions mid- or late-nineteenth century Caribbean, or early twentieth century African.[41] We suspect these are the product of Colonial Office attempts to control, to some extent, highly exploitative employment relations, perhaps in the expectation that the penalty would be used in a discretionary manner only against native employers and labour brokers. The statutes that provide imprisonment for mistreatment of servants were all enacted after the middle of the nineteenth century, and here the pattern is more general, and indeed the provision first appears in our sample in a white settler colony and in England. The earliest is a Quebec statute of 1849, providing a penalty of £5 or prison up to thirty days.[42] The next is an English act of 1851 which provided the striking penalty of up to three *years'* imprisonment, with hard labour optional, for harming apprentices or servants bound under the Poor Law; in 1861 this was extended to all servants to whom a master was obliged to provide food, clothing or lodging (apparently a test of dependence), with a penalty of three years' penal servitude or two years' imprisonment with or without hard labour.[43] As statutes became more 'balanced' in the nineteenth century, in the sense that they began to embody notional equality between the contracting parties, it became possible to punish masters, as well as servants, by imprisonment for any offence that was 'aggravated' (defined within narrow limits). But the 1875 *Conspiracy and Protection of Property Act* in England, widely copied in the white settler colonies, expressly provided a £20 fine or six months imprisonment, with or without hard labour, for mistreatment of a servant.[44]

Apart, then, from the Quebec statute, the earliest legislation is the 1851 English statute, and it is replicated, in its various phases, in a scattered range of colonial legislation: in Montserrat,[45] British Guiana,[46] and then the Gold Coast, Kenya, various Australian states, Southern Rhodesia and Sierra Leone. Still, it appears in only 28 of 257 statutes. Ninety-four statutes provide penalties for masters found guilty of mistreatment: the more common penalties are compensation (49 statutes); a fine (51); or simply dissolution of the contract (72), the only provision to be found in the *Statute of Artificers* itself. In short, jail for mistreatment by the master is rare, late, and appears first in cases involving juveniles. It appears in England barely a quarter-century before the abolition, in 1875, of imprisonment for breach of contract.

Thus far we have considered servitude and corporal punishment for servants guilty of absence or misbehaviour, and imprisonment for masters guilty of mistreatment or not paying wages, as the most penal aspects of master and servant law. Some of the findings about their incidence are summarized in Figure 1. Each entry indicates at least one statute having such a provision.[47]

The fact that corporal punishment and servitude are peculiar to colonial rather than English legislation emerges clearly from Figure 1. It also shows the concentration and coincidence of these two penalties in the American colonies and the West Indies, societies deeply influenced by slavery, and the somewhat different use of corporal punishment in early-modern Ireland and late imperial Africa, discussed above. The white settler colonies of Australia and Canada are distinguished by very little use of corporal punishment and servitude and by relatively early use of imprisonment of masters. A high incidence of jail for masters for non-payment is found in Africa and in post-apprenticeship West Indies (the only exception is one Western Australian statute). The influence of the Colonial Office on both West Indian and African legislation is perhaps reflected in the similarity of their legislation, although that paternalism (if that is what it was) also countenanced corporal punishment, albeit

FIGURE 1

MARKER PROVISIONS BY REGION AND PERIOD

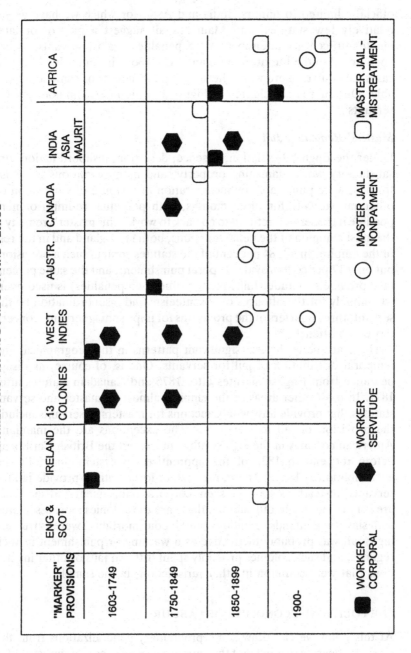

officially limited to minors. India and Asia, for which we have as yet relatively few statutes, and Mauritius all suggest a pattern of late-nineteenth century intensification of penalties against servants, as has been noted in the literature on plantation labour in India. In almost all cases, of course, there were alternative punishments or remedies available. One that is not charted in Figure 1 is the most common: jail for servants.

Masters' Remedies: Jail

Under the English legislation, absence, desertion, insubordination, un-satisfactory work, damaging property, and many variations on those themes, were punishable by incarceration in a House of Correction or other jail, usually for three months, with perpetual re-imprisonment possible if the servant refused to go back to work. This master's remedy is the most common of the penal sanctions, both in England and in the rest of the empire. In all, 84 per cent of the statutes contain such a provision, but only 17 per cent provide corporal punishment, and the same percentage provide servitude. Jail (like the other two penalties) is used overwhelmingly for the offences of absenteeism and insubordination by the servant: three quarters of the provisions for imprisoning servants concern those two offences.[48]

There are none the less significant patterns in the geographical and temporal distribution of jail for servants. One is, of course, its disappearance from English statutes after 1875 and Canadian statutes after 1877. In most other areas of the empire, almost all master and servant statutes that provide any penal sanctions for masters or servants include the provision of jail for servants.[49] The exceptions are the mainland American colonies in the eighteenth century and the British Caribbean before the end in 1838 of the apprenticeship system that followed emancipation in 1834.[50] There, only ten of forty statutes provide jail for servants; instead, as we have seen, corporal punishment and servitude are very common. In our sample, these are the colonies most associated with slavery; demands for labour (and labour mortality) were extremely high; jail was probably ineffective as a warning or punishment in such regimes, and such colonies probably spent little on jails or other institutions that were common in other jurisdictions in the sample.

THE POLITICAL ECONOMIES OF LABOUR

At this point we can draw some preliminary generalizations from the markers, bearing in mind that they are just a small subset of the attributes of interest in the project, and that so far we have examined each of them in isolation from the others. Using broad economic and social generalizations, we might describe their observed incidence as follows:

- *Early modern Britain (broadly, the sixteenth to eighteenth centuries)*
  No corporal punishment and no servitude for workers but jail for workers; no jail for masters.
- *Industrial revolution Britain (c.1800–75)*
  No corporal punishment or servitude for workers but jail for workers; introduction of jail for masters for mistreatment but not for non-payment of wages.
- *White settler colonies without slavery (Canada, Australia)*
  Almost no corporal punishment but some servitude for workers, and jail for workers; jail for masters for mistreatment but not for non-payment.
- *White indentured labour regimes in the presence of slavery (notably the Thirteen Colonies, Nova Scotia, and the West Indies in the seventeenth and eighteenth centuries) and Ireland*
  Corporal punishment and servitude for absenteeism and misbehaviour of workers, but jail for workers fairly rare; no jail for masters.
- *Post-apprenticeship indenture regimes in the British Caribbean and other non-white indentured labour regimes such as Mauritius*
  No corporal punishment, but some servitude for absenteeism by workers, and jail common for worker offences; a few instances of jail for master for non-payment and mistreatment.
- *Plantation/mining economies in other Third World jurisdictions (Africa, Asia in the nineteenth and twentieth centuries)*
  Corporal punishment common and jail for workers universal; servitude for absenteeism but only in India; jail for masters common for both mistreatment and non-payment.

Note that this exercise does not correlate different species of master and servant legislation with particular political economies of labour. It does not specify a typology of the latter, but only notes some of the grossest apparent differences. They are suggestive, but no more than that, and we have used them in fairly cavalier fashion. For example, we have ignored the fact that some of the African jurisdictions are ex-slave regimes, that some colonies clearly had two kinds of regime coexisting (often divided by race), or that Colonial Office interventions probably had considerably more impact on certain colonies, at certain periods, than on others. A convincing analysis linking statutory regimes to the political economy of labour in each jurisdiction, or group of jurisdictions, will only be possible when we have described the types of statutes in far more detail and when we have devised a clear and independent typology of the host societies. Nevertheless, it will be useful for purposes of illustration to pursue this suggestive example somewhat further here.

First, we should note that both Figure 1 and our descriptive exercise chart the incidence of only the few marker characteristics discussed above. They ignore most clauses of most statutes, and even most offences and penalties. They are based on incomplete data: probably fewer than half of the final number of principal statutes we expect to have in the code base. Examination of the cell contents of Figure 1 shows that many of the statutes in 'marked' cells do not themselves contain marker provisions. This leads to a more general point: that it is likely to be the *combinations* of a *range* of provisions in the legislation (rather than the simple absence or presence of a few of them) that will constitute types of statutory regime. In other words, master and servant statutes and regimes may fall into groups according to particular patterns of associations among numerous characteristics of the legislation, but those groups cannot be reconstructed by the presence or absence of any specific set of markers. For this reason, while analysis of markers may suggest the existence of distinct groups of statutes, the groups themselves cannot be constituted simply by looking for the presence or absence of markers. To extend this analysis to the actual constitution of such groups, we have therefore turned to an heuristic known as conceptual clustering.

Conceptual Clustering[51]

Conceptual clustering is a method of classifying groups of items by their similarity to one or another of a set of 'concepts', which may be either real items or ideal types. This method is distinct from statistical cluster analysis in two respects: it focuses on grouping observations (statutes, in our case) where cluster analysis focuses on grouping attributes or variables; and it encourages the development of a theoretically-informed classification scheme rather than a scheme based entirely on statistical regularities.[52] Conceptual clustering is well suited to comparative historical research because it does not rely on precise mathematical measurements; items are described in terms of the attributes they possess, which need not be measurable numerically. We have developed a general-purpose computer program for conceptual clustering, along with more specialized computer-based tools for preparing coded statutes for clustering and for summarizing and analysing the results.

We used conceptual clustering to test the preliminary generalizations embodied in the marker exercise described above. We constructed 'types' corresponding to the observed incidence of the individual markers and used them to 'seed' the clustering. If these 'types' were robust general descriptions of quite different kinds of master and servant law, we would expect statutes from different times and places to cluster around the 'type' corresponding to their distinctive labour political economy. They did not do so.

Fortunately, conceptual clustering is also useful as an heuristic for exploring complex data and suggesting new approaches to classification. Taking the same data-set (less the type descriptions) and specifying a model with six clusters, we derived the grouping summarized in Table 1.[53] In this tabulation, 'Y' means that every statute in the cluster contains the attribute, 'N' means none of the statutes in the cluster has it, and '—' means that some of the statutes possess the attribute while others do not. This is an unambiguous classification of the statutes on the five attributes of interest, as may be seen by the classification tree in Figure 2.

TABLE 1

CLUSTERING OF ATTRIBUTES

Cluster	Number in cluster	Master jail wages	Master jail mistreat	Worker corporal	Worker servitude	Worker jail
A	18	Y	—	—	—	—
B	12	N	N	Y	N	—
C	14	N	Y	—	N	—
D	29	N	N	—	Y	N
E	10	N	—	—	Y	Y
F	34	N	N	N	N	Y

To recap briefly, the marker analysis identified the incidence of specific penal provisions in a group of statutes. Viewed one at a time, each of these provisions was seen to occur in some kinds of economic setting and not in others. This suggested a description of six different forms of labour political economy in the empire. We then used conceptual clustering to ask whether the 'markers' which appeared individually in these various forms could be taken *together* to describe different kinds of master and servant law associated with specific political economies. We found that the markers did not coincide in such a patterned way within the statutes. Next, we used conceptual clustering to determine that there is (at least one) distinctive patterning of the occurrence of these attributes *in combination* within the statutes.

It is instructive to compare the clustering (attributes in combination) with the 'types' derived from the marker descriptions. Figure 3 shows the distribution of 'types' over the clusters. In effect (if this was a precise test rather than an illustrative example) it shows the relationship between

FIGURE 2

CLASSIFICATION TREE FOR THE CLUSTERING IN TABLE 1

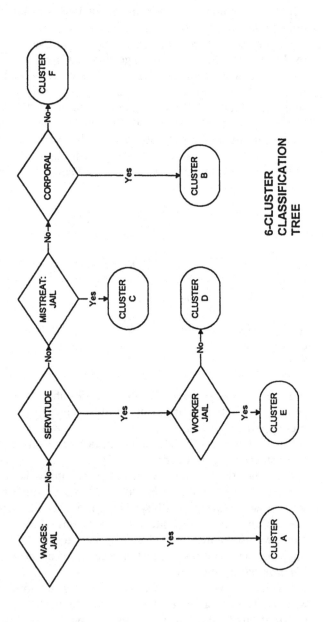

6-CLUSTER CLASSIFICATION TREE

observed groupings (the clusters of statutes) and predicted ones (the 'types' of labour political economy, identified by the incidence of individual markers). Thus Cluster A, consisting of all the statutes by which masters may be jailed for non-payment of wages, contains many of the statutes from Third World plantation and mining economies of the nineteenth and twentieth centuries ('type 6') but also some from post-apprenticeship regimes in the West Indies ('type 5'). Statutes from 'type 6' economies occur in all the clusters but one. This one, Cluster D, is the most homogeneous with respect to 'type'. Consisting of statutes which provide servitude for workers but no jail for workers or masters, it contains the lion's share of the statutes from economies that mix white indentured labour with slavery ('type 4'). Other statutes of those societies are found in Clusters B, E and F. Almost all the statutes from industrial Britain ('type 2') are found in Cluster C (master's jail for mistreatment but not non-payment; no servitude), but so are some statutes from the white Dominions ('type 3') and the Third World plantation and mining economies ('type 6'). The only unique relationship is that all the early modern British statutes ('type 1') occur in Cluster F (jail for the worker but no servitude or corporal punishment, and no jail for masters) and nowhere else; so much for the notion that colonial master and servant acts merely parroted an English original. Nevertheless, Cluster F contains statutes of every 'type'.

Close examination of the contents of each cluster bears out some aspects of the broad geographic-cum-temporal-cum-economic groupings suggested by the marker analysis. The early modern English statutes occur together, as do a majority of those from pre-emancipation America and the West Indies. Every statute in Cluster A provides jail for non-payment of wages. With the exception of one late Western Australia statute, all of the eighteen statutes in this cluster are nineteenth or early-twentieth century African and West Indian statutes. In short, it appears that this legislation occurs where employers may be natives or other non-whites, and that the West Indian legislative pattern of 1854–1907 represented by these statutes is substantially replicated in Africa from 1901 to 1938. The Western Australia statute of 1892 is a notionally 'neutral' statute in which penalties for all offences, including non-payment of wages, are 'balanced'. The West Indian and African statutes are not so constructed.

In Cluster B, the programme grouped statutes in which corporal punishment (but not servitude) coincides with no jail for masters; it is similar to Cluster D, where no jail for masters is always accompanied by servitude for workers, but not jail. These groups, in which masters are never jailed but servants are exposed to corporal punishment or servitude, and sometimes both, include most of those statutes that one would expect to find associated with white indentured labour regimes in association with slavery ('type 4'). They include thirty-two (of thirty-nine) American and West Indian statutes before 1800 and three (of eight) Indian and Asian enactments; there are also two African. However, they also include three statutes from societies without a racial divide: one Irish, one Canadian, and one Australian. The Canadian statute is the

FIGURE 3

'TYPES' BY CLUSTERS

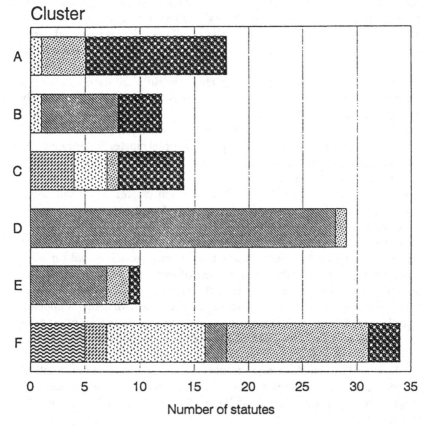

☒Type 1 ☒Type 2 ☶Type 3 ☷Type 4 ☷Type 5 ☒Type 6

short-lived Nova Scotia statute notionally modelled on the Irish one of 1715; the Australian is the Western Australia statute of 1842 – in all three jurisdictions corporal punishment is exceptional.

Other cases are more problematic. There is little to distinguish the great majority of statutes from the white Dominions from those of early-modern England or many of the post-apprenticeship West Indies statutes (Cluster F). Although pre-emancipation West Indian statutes heavily weighted against servants cluster, as expected, with similar American colonial statutes (Clusters B and D, providing servitude, corporal punishment, or both), a group of post-apprenticeship West Indian statutes is grouped with African statutes that imprison non-paying masters (Cluster A). A wide range of jurisdictions in the later nineteenth and twentieth centuries provide jail for cruel masters (Cluster C). The smallest grouping (Cluster E) contains ten statutes that provide both jail and servitude for erring servants: they include statutes from America (1705–1802) and the West Indies (1722–1834) together with much later statutes from Madras (1878) and Mauritius (1908).

We have said that this comparison is instructive. What has it taught us? First, it shows that one cannot safely infer from the incidence of particular provisions in a geographic, temporal or economic region that every master and servant statute or every jurisdiction in the region contains those provisions. Second, it demonstrates that although two provisions may coincide in the region, they do not necessarily occur in association in any particular statute. None of the attributes, and few of their pair-wise combinations, are unique to a particular time and place. Nevertheless, as the clustering demonstrates, it is possible to distinguish groups of statutes with unique patterns of attributes. Despite its significant limitations, this small illustration of our method provides some support for the hypothesis that different sorts of labour regime adopted quite different master and servant legislation.

It is worth reviewing the limitations of the example we have worked through here, because they point most directly to the next phase of the distribution study. There are four main limitations to be addressed. First, our example was based on a fairly small subset of the principal statutes; the full distribution study will incorporate a much more comprehensive collection of enactments. Second, the example was based on a small handful of attributes, the extreme penal sanctions for the most common offences. There are many other aspects of master and servant law to be worked into the analysis and studied in combination with the penal clauses. For example, provisions for the forced recruitment and assignment of workers, for enforcing employment contracts entered into outside the jurisdiction, for regulating the duration of the contract, for requiring discharge certificates, or for prohibiting third-party interference in the employment relation, all bear on the questions of labour supply and discipline that we suggest are central to the distribution problem. The proof of the clustering approach will lie in its ability to manage large numbers of discrete attributes.

The third limitation is the description of the independent variable, the political economies of labour. In this article we relied on broad characterisations gleaned from general reading in the economic and labour history of the regions and informed by the marker analysis. One of the key intellectual tasks of the next phase of the research will be to refine a typology of colonial political economies that is theoretically independent from the typology of master and servant statutes. We envision a model that combines selected demographic characteristics with indicators of the sectoral structure and output of the local economy and that incorporates a measure of change over time. Such a multidimensional model will have to be sufficiently robust to allow us to specify the characteristics of local political economies for which few reliable statistics are available and to cope with the fact that where series are available they are not directly comparable. It will also have to recognize that different labour political economies sometimes coexisted within a single jurisdiction. The most familiar case is the coexistence of white indenture with black slavery, but there are other cases of deep sectoral differences accompanied by racial segmentation and distinct legal regimes. We anticipate that a qualitative model with clear boundaries between types will be more useful in practice than a continuous quantitative measure.

The fourth limitation in this illustrative study is that it makes the statute the unit of analysis. In many places there were numerous statutes in force at the same time. In general, any comparative analysis of the law that relies on patterns of attributes must take account of what we have referred to as the *regime problem*. We use the term 'regime' to refer to the state of master and servant law in a jurisdiction. At any point in time, a jurisdiction's master and servant regime is constituted by the statutes in force, the case law interpreting those statutes, and the practices of magistrates and others administering the law. While all these elements are of interest, we have relegated the main treatment of case law and administrative practice to the regional studies. We will base our comparative overview of case law and administration on the regional studies. The distribution study's focus should not be on individual statutes but on the statute law in force, which we refer to as the statutory regime. Different jurisdictions assembled their statutory regimes in different ways. In England, where there were numerous master and servant statutes in force regulating different trades, older statutes were rarely repealed when new ones were adopted. Some of the American colonies adopted numerous distinct enactments that together added up to much the same range of provisions as could be found in a single comprehensive master and servant statute in the British North American or Australian colonies. Some colonies in Africa and elsewhere subsumed their master and servant provisions in more general statutes covering employment, immigration and race relations. Moreover, there was in most jurisdictions a continuous process of amendment and consolidation. To describe the state of the statute law in any jurisdiction at any point in time is therefore not a simple matter. We have sketched out a technique for building dynamic regime descriptions, which we propose to implement in the next phase of the project. Once again, it will be necessary to recognize that some jurisdictions had separate statutory regimes covering different sectors, usually with racial or other barriers to mobility between them.

Finally, to repeat some interim conclusions, it is now clear that much of the colonial master and servant legislation was without English precedent. Within the empire, there were extensive similarities of policy and pronouncement among statutes widely separated in time and place. None of the common explanations of colonial master and servant law withstands scrutiny. Few of these statutes were mere copies of metropolitan acts; fewer still were local innovations. While there was some copying and some innovation, it is apparent that policy and pronouncement spread through the empire by a complex process of borrowing, selection and adaptation. Where provisions were borrowed from and by what vectors they were spread; why some were selected and others rejected; how they were adapted to local exigencies and how well: these are the questions for which we hope to find answers.

ACKNOWLEDGEMENTS

Research reported in this article has been funded by the Social Sciences and Humanities Research Council of Canada, by two York University Faculty of Arts research grants, and by work-study funding administered by York University. We have also benefited from the generous loan of equipment by the Osgoode Hall Law School (York University) IBM project. This article is an extensively-revised and reworked version of papers presented to the Conference on Unfree Labour in the Development of the Atlantic World, York University, 14 April 1993, and to the annual meeting of the Canadian Historical Association, Carleton University, 7 June 1993. We thank Harry Arthurs, Antonio Lechasseur and David Levine for their perceptive comments on these earlier papers.

NOTES

1. For example, Mary Turner, 'Chattel Slaves into Wage Slaves: A Jamaican Case Study' in Malcolm Cross and Gad Heuman (eds.), *Labour in the Caribbean: From Emancipation to Independence* (London, 1988).

2. Howard Johnson, *The Bahamas in Slavery and Freedom* (Kingston, Jamaica and London, 1991), pp. 9 ff.
3. It seems doubtful that the Bahamas opinion would have been accepted in England. However much Lord Mansfield may have wished to avoid pronouncing on the legality of slavery in Somersett's Case, he repeatedly declared that the capacity to contract for wages was clear evidence of free status.
4. We include all these categories under the rubric of master and servant.
5. In England, the ideology of contractual equality that helped justify the repeal of master and servant law (1875) also served to justify the judges' imposition of the fellow-servant rule, greatly increasing employers' defences against claims of vicarious liability for injuries suffered by their servants on the job.
6. For an overview of the larger project and its methodology, including details of what we mean by 'this kind of employment law', see Douglas Hay and Paul Craven, 'Master and servant in England and the Empire: A Comparative Study', *Labour/Le Travail*, 31 (Spring 1993), pp. 175–84.
7. See, for example, V. Samaraweera, 'Masters and Servants in Sri Lankan Plantations: Labour Laws and Labour Control in an Emergent Export Economy', *Indian Economic and Social History Review*, 18,2 (1981), pp. 123–58.
8. Most of the American and many of the Australian statutes were contributed by our international collaborators. Several hundred more were located and copied at the Osgoode Hall Law Library or acquired through inter-library loan from other North American institutions. Having exhausted the North American collections, we employed Dr Ruth Paley, under a grant from the Faculty of Arts of York University, to search the statutory collections of the Foreign and Commonwealth Office Library jurisdiction by jurisdiction; their copies contain handwritten annotations of repeals and amendments. Unfortunately this work was interrupted by the decision of that library to transfer most of the relevant collection to the Institute of Advanced Legal Studies, University of London. We believe that some volumes have been misplaced in the move; fortunately, Paley completed most of the research in those series, except for some gaps, under that grant. The gaps are of two kinds: odd missing statutes from the series already exploited and the statutes of the Indian subcontinent and some far eastern jurisdictions.
9. In this paper we have ignored statutes earlier than the Statute of Artificers, 5 Eliz. c.4 (England, 1562). For the medieval and early modern origins of the legislation see, among other works. L.R. Poos, 'The Social Context of Statute of Labourers Enforcement', *Law and History Review*, 1 (Spring 1983), pp. 27–52; S.T. Bindoff, 'The Making of the Statute of Artificers', in S.T. Bindoff (ed.), *Elizabethan Government and Society* (1961); D. MacCulloch, 'Bondmen under the Tudors', in C. Cross *et al.* (eds.), *Law and Government under the Tudors* (Cambridge, 1988); E. Clark, 'Mediæval Labor Law and English Local Courts', *American Journal of Legal History*, 27, 4 (1983); and R.J. Steinfeld, *The Invention of Free Labor: The Employment Relation in English and American Law and Culture, 1350–1870* (Chapel Hill, 1991).
10. This gives rise in some contexts to a problem in defining the unit of analysis: is it the particular statute (or provision in a statute) or the whole body of master and servant law in force in a particular jurisdiction at a particular point in time? Bear in mind that for most jurisdictions at most times there is no authority other than the statutes themselves for describing 'the whole body of master and servant law in force'. See the discussion of the 'regime problem' below.
11. For the scope of our definition of master and servant provisions, see Hay and Craven, 'Master and servant in England and the Empire', 184f.
12. For much assistance we thank our collaborators and the staff of Osgoode Hall Law School Library at York University in Toronto; in London, Dr Ruth Paley and the staffs of the Foreign and Commonwealth Office Library, the Public Record Office, and the Institute of Advanced Legal Studies.
13. These aspects of the project are being conducted at York University. We would like to acknowledge the research assistance of Sheryl Beckford, Karen Cunningham, Juanita DeBarros, Martha Kanya-Forstner, Craig Morrison, Carey Nieuwhof, Adele Perry,

Stuart Swartz, Will Traves and Tracy Wynne (students in history, political science, mathematics and law at York University and Queen's University).

14. Historians concerned with the close analysis of documents would do well to familiarize themselves with work in these areas. A valuable guide is I. Lancashire and W. McCarty, *The Humanities Computing Yearbook* (Oxford, 1988) and seq. C.S. Butler (ed.), *Computers and Written Texts* (Oxford, 1992), is a useful collection of essays on various aspects of computer-aided textual analysis.

15. J. Bradley, *TACT: User's Guide* (Toronto, 1990). For a brief overview see J. Bradley, 'An Introduction to *Tact* and its Design, with Thoughts on its Future', *ALLC-ACH92 Conference Abstracts* (Oxford, 1992), pp. 46–7. A new version of *TACT* is currently in beta-test; documentation is to be published by the MLA.

16. N. 15 of 1856, *An Act to Amend the Laws regulating the relative Rights and Duties of Masters, Servants, and Apprentices* (Cape Colony); no. 49 of 1828 (Cape Colony), *Ordinance for the Admission into the Colony, under certain Restrictions, of Persons Belonging to the Tribes beyond the Frontier thereof, and for regulating the Manner of their Employment, as free Labourers, in the Service of the Colonists*, in s.8; n. 30 of 1839 (St. Vincent), *An Act for regulating the Rights of Masters and Servants, and for the better Enforcement of Contracts*, ss.13, 14; n. 2 of 1850 (Natal), *Ordinance for regulating the relative rights and duties of Masters, Servants, and Apprentices*. The Cape (1856) and Natal (1850) statutes supplied remedies for specific breaches by the master, including non-payment of wages, failure to provide necessities, and other forms of mistreatment.

17. Paul Craven and William Traves, 'A General-Purpose Hierarchical Coding Engine', *ALLC-ACH92 Conference Abstracts* (Oxford, 1992), pp. 98–103; Craven and Traves, 'A General-Purpose Hierarchical Coding Engine and its Application to Computer Analysis of Statutes', *Literary and Linguistic Computing*, 8, 1 (1993), pp. 27–32.

18. Two hundred and ninty-five statutes had been coded and verified when this paper was begun. 257 of these, from 68 jurisdictions, legislate offences (of all kinds), and it is on this group that the 'marker' analysis (below) is based.

19. We are also interested in the development of master and servant legislation in England, and we do not rule out the possibility of colonial influences on reform of the metropolitan legislation.

20. Mandy Banton, 'Colonial Office supervision of the introduction and revision of labour legislation in British Africa, with special reference to the use of penal sanctions in master and servant ordinances' (Ph.D. dissertation, unpublished, University of London, 1993).

21. We intend to discuss all these issues in detail, both comparatively and in the context of specific case studies.

22. See below for some of the considerations involved in constructing a more systematic and independent typology of political economies.

23. J.R. Ward, *British West Indian Slavery, 1715–1834: The Process of Amelioration* (Oxford, 1988), Ch.5 and p. 140 (depletion rates being the excess of crude death over crude birth rates); D. Trotman, *Crime in Trinidad: Conflict and Control in Plantation Society, 1838–1900* (Knoxville, 1986), Ch.7; N. Bolland, 'Systems of Domination after Slavery: The Control of Land and Labor in the British West Indies after 1838', *Comparative Studies in Society and History*, 23 (1981), pp. 591–619.

24. For example, C. Van Onselen, *Chibaro: African Mine Labour in Southern Rhodesia 1900–1933* (Johannesburg, 1980); I.G. Shivji, *Law, State and the Working Class in Tanzania* (London, 1986).

25. R.P. Behal and P. Mohapatra, '"Time and Money versus Human Life": The Rise and Fall of the Indenture System in the Assam Tea Plantations, 1840–1908', *Journal of Peasant Studies* 19, 3/4 (1992).

26. Douglas Hay, 'Masters, Servants, Justices and Judges: the Law of Master and Servant in England in the 18th and 19th Centuries' (paper presented to the York University Seminar in Advanced Research, October 1988 and to the Postgraduate Seminar on Law and Labour in the Commonwealth, Institute of Commonwealth Studies, University of London, November 1988).

27. R. V. Haywood (1813), 1 Maule & Selwyn 624, at 628.
28. 4 Geo.III c.7 (Nova Scotia, 1765).
29. Servitude was also used to punish a certificate offence in Barbados, a recruitment offence in Cape Colony, and a discretionary breach in New South Wales: n.30 (Barbados, 1661); n.49 (Cape Colony, 1828); 10 Geo.IV n.4 (New South Wales, 1829).
30. Province Laws 1694–15, c.23 (Massachusetts, 1694); 11 Geo.III (Pennsylvania, 1771); Statutes at Large (Pennsylvania, 1683); 'Master, Servants and Sojourners' (Connecticut, 1672); 13 Geo.II c.77 (Delaware, 1740); n.61? (Antigua, 1834); Province Laws 1758–9, c.17 (Massachusetts, 1759); n.51 (St. Kitts, 1722); 'Master, Servants and Sojourners' (Connecticut, 1672); Act CIX (East Jersey, 1682); Laws of the Province of Maryland (Maryland, 1718); Laws c.24 (North Carolina, 1741); 13 Anne (New Hampshire, 1715); Laws of the Royal Colony (New Jersey, 1714); 7 Geo. 3, c.1306 (New York, 1766); Laws, 11th Session, c.13 (New York, 1788); Laws, c.11 (New York, 1801); Acts and Laws (Connecticut, 1786); 22 Geo.II n.14 (Virginia, 1748); n.403, in Trott, Laws (South Carolina, 1717); Acts and Laws of His Majesties Colony(Connecticut, 1715); 'Fugitives', Duke of York's Laws (Pennsylvania, 1676);18 Car.I, n.22 (Virginia, 1642); 6 Commonwealth, n.11 (Virginia, 1655); 9 Commonwealth, n.56 (Virginia, 1657); 14 Car.II n.102 (Virginia, 1661); n.1 of 1854 as am. (British Guiana, 1893); n.30 (Barbados, 1661).
31. N.12 (Mauritius, 1878); n.21 (Mauritius, 1854); n.13 (Mauritius, 1908). Several Mauritius statutes deal expressly with Indian immigrant labour.
32. May Session (Massachusetts, 1649); 18 Car.I, n.20 (Virginia, 1642); 11 Commonwealth, n.13 (Virginia, 1659); Car.II, n.104 (Virginia, 1661); 'Masters, Servants and Labourer', Duke of York's Laws (New York, 1665); 4 Anne, n.49 (Virginia, 1705); Laws of the Royal Colony (New Jersey, 1714); Trott, Laws, n.403 (South Carolina, 1717); Laws of the Province (Maryland, 1715); Laws, c.24 (North Carolina, 1741); 22 Geo.II n.14 (Virginia, 1748); n.30 (Barbados, 1661); n.51 (St. Kitts, 1722); 55 Geo.III c.19 (Jamaica, 1814).
33. 5 Eliz. c.4.
34. 2 Geo.I c.17 (Ireland, 1715), Laws, c.24 (North Carolina, 1741); 4 Anne, n.49 (Virginia, 1705); Trott, Laws, n.403 (South Carolina, 1717); 18 Car.I n.22 (Virginia, 1642); 6 Commonwealth, n.11 (Virginia, 1655); 9 Commonwealth, n.56 (Virginia, 1657); 10 Commonwealth, n.3 (Virginia, 1658); 'Children and Servants', Duke of York's Laws (Pennsylvania, 1676); 16 Car.II (Rhode Island, 1676); Laws of the Province (Maryland, 1715); Laws, c.24 (North Carolina, 1741); 'Children and Servants', Duke of York's Laws (New York, 1665); 3 Geo.II (Rhode Island, 1728); n.48 (Nevis, 1701); 22 Geo.II n.14 (Virginia, 1748);14 Car.II n.101 (Virginia, 1661).
35. 16 (Gold Coast/Ghana, 1877); n.11 (Gold Coast/Ghana, 1921); n.2 (Natal, 1850); n.8 (Gold Coast/Ghana, 1893); n.2 (British North Borneo, 1929); n.56 (Northern Rhodesia, 1929); n.24 (South Africa, 1932); n.8 (Kenya, 1906); n.2 (Kenya, 1938); n.10 (Southern Rhodesia, 1926); n.4 (Kenya, 1910).
36. For example, n.11 (Gold Coast/Ghana, 1921).
37. N.4 (British North Borneo, 1908).
38. 4 Geo.III c.7 (Nova Scotia, 1765). Professor Jim Phillips (Law, Toronto) informs us that the probable author of the corporal punishment provision is Jonathon Belcher, first Chief Justice of Nova Scotia, who had earlier practiced at the Irish bar and was a noted authoritarian. A marginal note to the Nova Scotia whipping provision makes reference to the Irish act. There are substantial differences between the two statutes, however, and it is conceivable that having devised the Nova Scotia provision, Belcher cited Irish authority to justify it.
39. 6 Vict., n.8 (Western Australia, 1842).
40. 5 Eliz. c.4 (England, 1562); 7 Geo.I st.I c.13 (England, 1720); 11 & 12 Geo.III, c.33 (Ireland, 1771). There is also a 1796 English statute that provides for dissolution of the contract in the event of excess wages: 37 Geo.III c.73 (England, 1797), for seamen.
41. A highly discretionary, residual clause in a 'balanced' Western Australian statute of 1892 (55 Vict. n.28) is so encrusted with protective language ('aggravation', 'not in the

bona fide exercise of a legal right', etc.) that it is hard to see how it would ever be a threat to any but the most egregious behaviour by a master. The protective language is borrowed from an English statute of 1867 (30 & 31 Vict. c.141).

42. 12 Vict. c.55 (Quebec, 1849).
43. 14 & 15 Vict. c.11 (England, 1851); 24 & 25 Vict., c.100 (England, 1861).
44. 38 and 39 Vict. c.86 (England, 1875).
45. Act of 3 Oct. 1851 (Montserrat, 1851).
46. N.1 of 1854 as am. (British Guiana, 1893).
47. The dividing dates used in Figure 1 have been determined by inspection: groupings of statutes suggest these divisions, although differences of a year or two have sometimes been ignored in assigning statutes; the differing practices in different regimes at different times in dating statutes is our excuse.
48. This discussion of workers' imprisonment is based on a group of 294 statutes.
49. This discussion is based on a subset of 117 statutes that contain at least one of corporal punishment, servitude, master's imprisonment, or a monetary remedy for non-payment of wages. The latter was considered as a marker in an earlier version of the analysis, and the same data set has been used here. As a result, there are a number of statutes that provide imprisonment for worker absence or insubordination but do not contain any of the current markers. This under-represents the number of such statutes insofar as it does not include statutes that contain neither the markers or the monetary remedy for non-payment but that provide jail for worker absence or insubordination. For the limited purposes of the present example, this does not present a serious difficulty. The same group of 117 statutes is also used for the clustering analysis below.
50. Antigua moved directly from slavery to free labour without the intervening period of apprenticeship for ex-slaves imposed in the other islands. For this reason we class the 1834 Antigua statute with the post-apprenticeship legislation adopted elsewhere in the region from 1838 on.
51. R.S. Michalski and R.E. Stepp, 'Automated Construction of Classifications: Conceptual Clustering Versus Numerical Taxonomy', *IEEE Transactions on Pattern Analysis and Machine Intelligence*, v. PAMI-5, n. 4, July 1983; Michalski and Stepp, 'Learning from Observation: Conceptual Clustering', in R.S. Michalski *et al.* (eds.), *Machine Learning: An Artificial Intelligence Approach*, I (Palo Alto, CA, 1983); D. Fisher and P. Langley, 'Conceptual Clustering', in W.A. Gale (ed.), *Artificial Intelligence and Statistics* (Reading, MA, 1986). For an alternative approach, see Stepp and Michalski, 'Conceptual Clustering: Inventing Goal-Oriented Classifications of Structured Objects', in R.S. Michalski *et al.* (eds.), *Machine Learning: An Artificial Intelligence Approach*, II (Palo Alto, CA, 1986). There is an excellent recent summation in Kenneth Haase, 'Automated Discovery', in Richard Forsyth (ed)., *Machine Learning: Principles and Techniques* (London, 1989), especially pp.132–37. A brief account of classification in artifical intelligence research and an illustration of a simple conceptual clustering engine will be found in B. Thompson and B. Thompson, 'Artificial Intelligence: Overturning the Category Bucket,' *BYTE*, 16, 1 (Jan. 1991).
52. For a discussion of a statistical cluster analysis algorithm similar in many ways to the conceptual clustering model, however, see M.G. Kendall, 'Cluster Analysis', in S. Watanabe (ed.), *Frontiers of Pattern Recognition* (New York, 1972).
53. This clustering incorporated 117 statutes at an intracluster similarity score of 94 per cent and an inter-cluster difference of 40 per cent, for an average score of 67 per cent. The similarity score is very good. The intercluster difference is low because the small number of attributes limits how well the data-set can be partitioned *n* ways: in this model there are more clusters than attributes.

Vagrancy, Impressment and the Regulation of Labour in Eighteenth-Century Britain

NICHOLAS ROGERS

We begin with a deposition from Fulham, a parish west of London but in 1793 already part of the metropolitan conurbation.[1] It concerned Esther Gillingham, a parishioner whose 'maiden name was Herbert', who, 'being with child by Samuel Gillingham, was compelled to marry the said Samuel ... by the threat of Mr. Cheesmore, one of the overseers of Fulham, that if she did not marry Samuel she would be sent to Bridewell for a year and a day'. 'By which she was frightened into a consent' she deposed, 'and the man [Samuel Gillingham] was kept in a cage for three days at Fulham, when a license was produced, and both were married in the parish church'. The parish then entertained the 'happy' pair at two inns in the neighbourhood and 'from thence to a lodging in Hooper's Court'. But 'about eight the same evening' Esther related, 'her husband ran away from her, and never bedded with her' again.

Forced marriages of this kind were not that unusual in eighteenth-century England, although this one was coercively dramatic. But what is also interesting about this episode is the very explicit deployment of legal sanctions by the parish authorities to avoid the expense of maintaining illegitimate children. Samuel was incarcerated under a 1733 act which technically empowered JPs to imprison fathers who refused to honour their paternal obligations; Esther was threatened with a stint in the House of Correction under an old Jacobean statute (7 James I c. 4) which allowed magistrates to detain 'lewd women having bastards ... and leaving their children of the parish'. She might also have been detained under subsequent vagrant acts, although doubtfully for a year. While the battery of sanctions failed to achieve the required result and probably stretched the law to its limits, the affair reminds us of the sorts of interventions local authorities could make into the lives of the poor, and the arcana of statutes and summary justice that could be brought to bear to enforce them.

We are no longer accustomed to thinking of eighteenth-century England as an especially regulatory age. The old label 'mercantilism', with its connotations of a planned economy, have largely fallen into disrepute, at least outside of the matrix of international trade. The emphasis has increasingly been on the relative 'freedom' that labouring men and women enjoyed within an advancing capitalist economy. 'The whole industrial climate of the eighteenth century,' wrote Ephraim Lipson many years ago, 'was permeated by a growing economic individualism which resisted or ignored occasional attempts to fetter the unrestricted freedom of action which it henceforth claimed'[2] – a perspective that new generations of historians have largely endorsed. Consequently the social legislation of the era, unlike that of the previous centuries, is no longer seen as playing such a crucial role in the process of primitive accumulation and proletarianization. Freed from central control, it is seen rather as relapsing into local particularism and desuetude. Vagrancy acts lost much of their bite; wage regulations by JPs lapsed after 1725; guild regulations for skilled workers declined; and the Settlement Acts of the Poor Law, which sought to restrict labour mobility and were seen by some justices as a 'sort of imprisonment', were only sporadically enforced.[3] The proletariat itself, which grew a lot faster than the general population from the mid-sixteenth century onwards, was increasingly the product of demographic reproduction rather than expropriation.[4] And its fortunes are seen to be principally determined by the market in the perceptible shift to a laissez-faire economy. Hence the rise of high-wage theorists who no longer believed that labour discipline needed to be enforced by what Mandeville termed a 'middling scarcity'.[5]

There is something to be said for this picture, but it conceals many half-truths, especially when it is set within a developmental mode which sees 'class relations as emerging more or less directly from the [changing] requirements for the generation of surplus and the development of production'.[6] English workers were deeply ambivalent about their proletarian status, however preferable it may have seemed to other forms of servile labour, and they struggled tenaciously to hold on to what little independence they were able to secure in seeking their means of subsistence. This included many non-wage forms of remuneration derived from access to the land and customary rights. It also encompassed trade perquisites, control over the labour process, and in the struggle to maintain traditional apprenticeship regulations, control over the labour supply. Few workers in the eighteenth century were fully proletarian; many eked out a partial living from the land, from fishing, or combined agricultural work with industrial by-employments. And because most major industries were run on a sub-contracting or putting-out basis, in a decentralized and personal context, the customs of a trade could play an important part in determining patterns and roles of production.

The relative independence of many English workers and the coexistence of capitalist and non-capitalist forms of production within the same economy go a long way to explaining why employers, and indeed the propertied class generally, retained a strong interest in extra-economic forms of labour discipline and why legal instruments remained central to the processes of class reproduction and, by extension, to public order and welfare. Although it is true that some of the regulatory machinery of the Tudor-Stuart era was dismantled in the eighteenth century, this was by no means true of all. Powers of summary arrest and bridewells continued to be used to deal with master-servant relations and disagreements about the social wage. Wage regulation was abandoned in general contexts but invoked in an attempt to stabilize the tense relations in specific trades, such as the Spitalfields silk industry, where there had been mounting complaints of labour dilution.[7] The Settlement Acts, for all the opposition they drew from Adam Smith, continued to filter labour mobility to the towns and expanding industrial areas. And they provided the mechanisms by which the early, unpopular spinning mills were provided with a cheap, tractable, indentured labour force – the pauper apprentice.[8] Rather than see such statutes as residual and inconsequential, as anachronisms in a maturing capitalism, it is necessary to explore their mediatory influence, the ways in which they were imbricated within the processes of social reproduction and the selective uses to which they were put.

Within this context I would like to explore just two aspects of this regulatory regime: vagrancy and impressment. With respect to the first it should be noted that historical inquiry has conventionally focused upon the draconian era of vagrant legislation in the sixteenth and early seventeenth centuries when labouring men and women were harshly treated with whippings, brandings, imprisonment and, for a brief moment, enslavement, in an effort to curb idleness and social irregularity and to reincorporate them into the world of labour. With the expansion of the English economy after 1660 and the introduction of the settlement laws, so it is argued, the vagrancy acts lost much of their centrality as a source of labour discipline and served only as an ancillary penal sanction for the most reprehensible of offenders.[9]

There is something to be said for this view, in the sense that the Privy Council took a limited interest in vagrancy after 1660 and subsequently divested many of the problems of labour mobility upon the poor law. Yet the fact remains that between 1700 and 1824 as many as twenty-eight statutes were passed on the subject of vagrancy, twelve before 1760 and fourteen thereafter. Some of these were concerned with rationalizing the relationship between the vagrant and the poor laws with respect to finance, administrative process, judicial appeal and responsibility. But others added a significant accretion of offences to the traditional crimes of vagrancy. Over and above the old categories of wilful idleness, begging, pedlary and the tramp, vagrancy was applied to 'endgathers', that is, to those who travelled the country collecting oddments of wool or cloth (1744), to those *suspected* of commiting a felony (1752), to those apprehended with housebreaking implements (1783), to Thameside pilferers (1799), night poachers (1800), spoilers of wood (1805) and, finally, to the very amorphous category of 'suspected persons' (1802). In addition, the 1744 act brought the 'idle and disorderly', hitherto liable to conviction under the act of 1610 (7 Jas I c.4) under the jurisdiction of the vagrant laws.

The last act might be regarded as simply statutory house-cleaning but the others disclosed a rather different logic. The extension of vagrancy to endgatherers was part of a larger struggle between masters and workers over perquisites in the woollen industry and was quickly applied in the industrial areas of Essex as part of a broader offensive by employers against the customs of the trade.[10] The use of vagrancy to contain Thameside pilfering was part of a strategy employed by London merchants and magistrates to clamp down on riverside perquisites, one that accompanied the formation of a marine police and the building of fortified docks.[11] Similarly, the application of vagrancy to night poaching was part of the battle over wild game that engulfed the countryside with increasing intensity in the wake of enclosures and the final phase in the proletarianization of the agricultural labourer.[12] In other words, the vagrant laws were adapted to address new crises in social relations. At critical junctures in the march of agrarian and industrial capitalism, they were designed to plug loopholes in the existing laws: to buttress the laws against embezzlement in the textile industry; to strengthen the hand of the landed gentry in dealing with poachers; to redefine and regulate the wages of wharfside workers in the interests of merchant capital; and with the introduction of the 'sus' laws, to assist magistrates in their powers of detention and arrest in cases of theft, especially in years of demobilization when public anxieties about property crime ran high.[13] In this context it is instructive to note a perceptible rise in vagrancy prosecutions at the end of each war as local authorities attempted to come to grips with the social dislocations of demobilization and to reintegrate soldiers and sailors back into society.[14]

This is not to imply that the vagrant laws were always applied for reasons that had an explicitly direct relationship to capitalist development. With a catch-all category like vagrancy this would be incorrigibly reductionist. In London the vagrant laws were routinely used as a substitute for poor-law removals, relieving parishes from the burden of providing for destitute people without settlement entitlements in the metropolis. In a century that saw perhaps 8–10,000 migrants flock to the capital each year, as many as 800–1000, that is, about ten per cent, were shipped out again in the wagons of hired contractors. A significant minority, perhaps twenty per cent of the men and ten per cent of the women, were Irish labourers who were part of the seasonal casual workforce for the Port of London and the agrarian counties of southern England.[15] Others included unemployed Scotsmen; old, injured or 'unemployable' workers without a London settlement; and in the flush of demobilization and economic depression, labourers who simply could not find work and were thought likely to steal or pilfer to make ends meet.[16] But in the half-century prior to 1815, the great majority of vagrants passed out of London were women: servants and needleworkers out of employ; abandoned wives; widows; the victims of limited employment opportunities, of economic dependence upon men, of demographic circumstances that might place unbearable strains upon a family in a harsh and perhaps unfamiliar urban environment.[17]

The vagrancy laws were thus used to rid ratepayers of troublesome dependencies and to regulate the ebb and flow of seasonal and surplus labour in London. Saunders Welch, a Middlesex JP and former high constable who was very active in the suppression of vagrancy, believed the monitoring of surplus labour to be one of the most important functions of the laws. Hence he advocated a pass system to control the 'indiscriminate migrations' to the metropolis.[18] Such recommendations were by no means unusual, for a pass system of sorts was officially part of the fabric of the poor laws, and consequently social commentators were quite prepared to advocate their extension to the most reprehensible of wayfarers. Sometimes such recommendations were saturated with the language of servility. In the aftermath of the American war, for instance, when the vagrant problem loomed large, one Yorkshire clergyman thought that vagrants ordered to be passed to their home parishes should wear a 'substantial collar of brass or steel' with the name of the conveying township upon it.[19]

In practice vagrants were never subjected to such indignities in the eighteenth century, although migrant workers who fell under the jurisdiction of the laws were routinely passed and not infrequently whipped. In addition, the vagrant acts were used to discipline runaway apprentices and men who refused to provide for their families.[20] Encompassing the 'idle and disorderly' from 1744, they were regularly applied to police the streets of social undesirables, particularly streetwalkers, beggars and the destitute. And, in the case of Samuel and Esther Gillingham, to chivvy couples into marriage and to avoid the costs of bastardy. Despite the diverse forms of itinerant poverty and social irregularity that were targeted by the authorities under the laws, vagrants were continuously represented as a 'moral pestilence', a violation of public space, as people whose verminous clothes and vulgar imprecations were a blight to respectable society; 'a most indelible disgrace to these enlightened times', wrote one correspondent to the *Gentleman's Magazine* in 1807, 'a dreadful imposition on the public, in which the cause of real charity is not served'.[21] Notwithstanding a few disclaimers to the contrary, such dominant images did much to inhibit any significant public discussion of how the vagrancy laws were in practice applied.

Vagrants could find themselves subject to hard labour in house of correction in the eighteenth century. If they were male, they could also find themselves forcibly recruited into the navy in wartime. The impressment of vagrants was not new. It had clear precedents from the Tudor and Stuart era, if not earlier. Significantly, that purportedly proto-liberal John Locke was a strenuous advocate of such a policy.[22] Yet it was not until the first decade of the eighteenth century that the practice was given explicit statutory endorsement.[23] By the mid-century the bridewells and streets were routinely scoured for potential recruits, and despite the fact that some regarded the impressment of beggars as a 'Species of Tyranny', magistrates had little compunction about doing so.[24] In 1787, the round-up of vagrants in London as part of a pre-war mobilization was said to have 'made a visible change in the streets'. 'All the idle, vagabonding part are removed,' the *Times* reported, 'and an addition thereby made to the safety of the inhabitants. So many poor fellows, without employment, and acting under the combined influence of distress and drink, must be thieves or rogues, if not otherwise provided for'.[25]

The recruitment of such men, many of them landlubbers, none the less testified to the difficulties that the Admiralty had in manning its fleets. At the beginning of the century the government had flirted with the idea of creating a register of voluntary recruits to the service, national conscription being too redolent of continental absolutisms to be politically feasible. But from 1710 until 1833 the navy resorted to the forcible recruitment of seamen and all males between the ages of eighteen and fifty-five who 'used the sea' to man its fleets in wartime, supplementing this experienced workforce with volunteer landsmen, jailbirds and vagrants. Just how many men were recruited is difficult to measure with any precision, partly because desertion and recapture created a revolving-door effect to naval enlistment.[26] But making due allowance for population growth and desertion, it seems likely that during the Seven Years War, when roughly 185,000 men were enlisted at least once, one adult male in eleven, that is nine per cent, was recruited into His

Majesty's navy. Of these, probably half were actually impressed, many at sea from homeward-bound merchant ships, but also from the ports and inland towns with navigable rivers. In some ports the proportion impressed was sometimes higher than these figures suggest; in Liverpool and Newcastle it ran at 70.4 per cent and 66.2 per cent during the American war, and in the case of the latter, enlistment involved nearly 13 per cent of all adult males, by no means an insignificant number.[27]

Impressment was defended as a royal prerogative, grounded in 'immemorial usage', a necessary price to be paid for British liberty, prosperity and trade. Britain required a powerful navy to safeguard the nation against foreign invasion and to protect its overseas possessions and markets. In these circumstances, impressment was a reasonable charge upon the 'lower ranks of life' to whom the 'offensive and disagreeable public duties' properly fell. Just as the 'noble and most opulent of the nation' contributed taxes and governance to the public welfare, wrote Charles Butler in the first sustained defence of impressment, so the poor man should play his part in 'personal labour and service'.[28] As such, impressment was compatible with the common law and the reciprocal obligations and duties of different ranks within a divinely-ordained unequal society. More practically, contemporaries argued that impressment saved seamen from idleness and intemperance; it made 'sturdy beggars' useful to their country. Indeed, it freed the nation of 'idle and reprobate vermin by converting them into a Body of the most industrious People, and even, becoming the very nerves of our State'.[29]

To the more liberal minded, the chain of equivalences that linked social subordination with servitude and coerced labour was disturbing in a society that prided itself on its liberty. 'Poor Sailors,' reflected Captain Thomas Pasley in 1780, 'you are the only class of beings in our famed Country of Liberty really *Slaves* ... tho' the very being of the Country depends upon you'.[30] To the seamen themselves, impressment was a violation of the Englishman's birthright, a species of bondage that tore them from their families for long periods of time, subjected them to the hazards of disease and harsh discipline aboard men of war, and compromised their ability to bargain for their labour. To port workers, fishermen, even Cornish tinners who combined mining with summer pilchard fishing, press gangs were a persistent hazard; as indeed they were for any artisan or tradesman who worked in the vicinity of a 'rondy'. As the *Middlesex Journal* noted in 1771, 'For some time past it has been a common practice for the press-gangs to seize abundance of honest tradesmen indiscriminately, and carry them to the rendezvous houses, where they extort money from them to let them go again.'[31]

Opposition to impressment was deep-rooted and by no means as sporadic as some historians have assumed.[32] In the opening months of mobilization that prefaced the Seven Years War, at least seven major anti-impressment riots were reported in the press and in letters to the Admiralty; from Bo'ness in Scotland to Deal in Kent, where twenty-seven men, 'armed and Disguised, some having their Faces blacked', attacked the local gang and wrecked the rendezvous.[33] In the western ports of Bristol and Liverpool, where privateering was a passion in wartime, recruiting officers frequently found the going rough, and it was not unknown for armed privateers to rescue members of their crews from the rendezvous and intimidate the gangs into inaction. When Captain Gordon's gang beat up for volunteers in Bristol in January 1759, he reported that 'three hundred Seamen gathered in a riotous manner, almost killed a person whom they thought belonged to us, wounded the drummer ... threatening Death and Destruction of the officers'.[34] By the summer, after further confrontations with the seamen and affrays with the Kingswood colliers and soldiers quartered in the town, Gordon reported that every member of his gang had been wounded (one had been murdered) and urgently requested more men. Otherwise, he confessed, 'the Duty cannot be carried on in this large and Populous City where we have everything to contend with'.[35]

Violent confrontations of this scale and duration were rare in most British ports, although it sometimes required only a few dramatically successful confrontations with the press gangs to transform ports into virtual no-go areas. At Greenock it was reported in 1795 that the gangs had been persistently 'driven off by the People' when they 'attempted landing on different parts of the Shore', and 'rescues have taken place more than once even upon the Quays'.[36] Yet quite apart from these instances of armed resistance, seamen had other methods of evading impressment.[37] Seafaring communities were perennially on the alert for press-gangs, and the slightest whiff of a warrant or sight of a tender would send men scurrying from the quays and into the back country. Seamen also used legal strategies to elude impressment. They enlisted in the militia; they plied a trade in protections, that is, certificates of exemption from the press; they even had themselves arrested for debt in order to secure their release from the navy. Such suits were so frequent at the Nore that the Admiralty Solicitor wondered whether their lordships should not declare the area to be 'upon the High Sea' and therefore outside civil jurisdiction.[38]

The Admiralty adopted various strategies to counter these evasions. It periodically issued warrants for a 'hot press', namely a recruiting drive that allowed the gangs to ignore the exemptions that the Board had itself granted to various seafaring trades and industries. In the summer of 1779, when the search for recruits intensified with the entry of France and Spain into the American war, it technically broke the law, ordering all protections, whether guaranteed by statute or not, to be peremptorily ignored. And it backed up this drive with military force. But essentially the Admiralty knew that it was in the interest of the propertied classes to ensure that the fleet was sufficiently manned. In the last analysis it knew that the merchants and shipowners needed Admiralty convoys for their cargoes and that the local authorities would respond to arguments that stressed the importance of protecting commerce and empire.

The success of impressment rested ultimately on a tacit agreement between the government and the employing classes on the need to sustain Britain's naval power. From the employers' point of view the system of recruitment, however chaotic and arbitrary it sometimes appeared, was not without certain advantages. Impressment reduced property crime; it mopped up a migrant male population that might otherwise steal and pilfer, especially in times of wartime scarcities and high prices.[39] It also allowed portside employers the opportunity to reinforce the fabric of authority and labour discipline. Although merchants, mariners and riverside employers sometimes experienced a serious depletion of men in time of war, impressment did afford them some opportunity of retaining their most valuable men (and, indeed, strengthening their hold over them) through the distribution of protections or the extension of credit to those in hiding. It also enabled them to wean the most refractory from their workforce. In 1808, for instance, the regulating captain at Bristol impressed a ship's carpenter from a homecoming West Indian at the request of the captain 'for his ill usage to the Mate, and threats to the Captain of cutting him down with an *Axe* if he interfered on behalf of the Mate'.[40] Predictably impressment was used to resist demands for better pay. In 1771, for example, the seamen at Shields opposed a reduction of wages by striking the sails of all the ships in the harbour, only to have their protest compromised by the threat of impressment. Six years later, when the sailors rioted for a raise in wages, the ship masters set the press gang upon them.[41] Such a tactic had also been used in the southern ports as early as 1739, for the *London Evening Post* reported that when 'some sturdy Fellows belonging to a Ship near Southampton . . . refus'd to go the Voyage without a Rise of Wages', the master of the vessel 'gave Scent of them to a Press Gang' and had them sent on board a man of war.[42]

Portside employers also used the gang to rid themselves of unruly apprentices, and very occasionally to recover those that ran away.[43] Because they were such important intermediaries in cases of contested impressments, they were able to use their advantage to exact deference and respect from the vulnerable. This was potentially true of all employers, not simply those in the ports, for there were cases where tramping artisans or travelling apprentices were taken up by the civil authorities on the grounds that they were not gainfully employed, and it frequently required a character reference from their masters to have them released.[44] Impressment, in other words, operated like other aspects of the law in the eighteenth century; it allowed for the discretionary favours of the rich and powerful.[45] For these reasons it was the preferred option of many employers to the problem of manning the fleet.

Impressment has traditionally been seen by naval historians as an administrative problem, but it ought also to be viewed within the broader framework of labour relations. Seaman were a conscript labour force in the eighteenth century, at least potentially so, and their coercion was justified not simply in terms of national imperatives but, as Charles Butler's discourse revealed, according to older notions of half-free forms of labour that in other contexts were in decline. The vagrant represented the reverse side of this notion, the masterless men and women who had to be compelled to labour, whose social irregularity was a moral affront to discipline and subordination. The persistence of such notions in the eighteenth century is important, for the advance of free mobile labour was a protracted and, from the propertied point of view, a troubling affair that frequently required extra-economic compulsions to sustain and control it. The vagrancy laws were used in a variety of ways in the eighteenth century to render labour more tractable and proletarian, to strike a suitable balance between mobility and social order, and to redistribute welfare costs between town and country. Impressment was used by port employers to inhibit spiralling labour costs in wartime and to harness a workforce that was largely young, refractory and mobile. To be sure, impressment was often inconvenient and vexatious to merchants and manufacturers, but it did give them more bargaining power, both with the state and their workers, than other bureaucratic systems of recruitment. Like the vagrancy laws, impressment facilitated the highly regulatory, personal and discretionary character of labour control that continued to play an important role in Britain's maturing capitalist economy.

NOTES

1. Cited by James Stephen Taylor, *Poverty, Migration, and Settlement in the Industrial Revolution* (Palo Alto, California, 1989), p. 28.
2. E.E. Lipson, *The Economic History of England* (London, 1920), Vol. iii, p. 265.
3. On the administration of the settlement acts and a reinterpretation of their effectiveness, see James Stephen Taylor, 'The Impact of Pauper Settlement 1691–1834', *Past*

and Present, 73 (Nov. 1976), pp. 42–74; for the contemporary comment on the restrictive nature of the acts, William Hay, *Remarks on the Laws Relating to the Poor with Proposals for their Better Relief and Employment* (London, 1751), p. 9.

4. See David Levine, 'Production, Reproduction, and the Proletarian Family in England, 1500–1851', in Levine (ed.), *Proletarianization and Family History* (Orlando, Florida, 1984), pp. 87–128. Levine shows that while the total population grew sevenfold from 1520 to 1850, the proletariat grew 23-fold.

5. Bernard Mandeville, *A Letter to Dion* (London, 1732: Augustan Reprint Society, no. 41, Los Angeles, 1953), pp. 50–1. See also Philip Harth (ed.), *The Fable of the Bees*, (Harmondsworth: Pelican, 1970), pp. 209–10.

6. Robert Brenner, 'The Origins of Capitalist Development: a Critique of Neo-Smithian Marxism', *New Left Review*, 104 (July/Aug. 1977), p. 27.

7. J.H. Clapham, 'The Spitalfields Acts, 1773–1824', *Economic Journal*, 26 (1916), p. 461.

8. See Mary B. Rose, 'Social Policy and Business: Parish Apprenticeship and the Early Factory System 1750–1834', *Business History*, 31, 4 (Oct. 1989), pp. 5–29. It is noteworthy that pauper apprentices were not indentured for standardized terms of service; rather, until they reached the age of majority. See GLRO, Registers of Apprenticeship, St. Luke, Chelsea, 1791–1802.

9. See A.L. Beier, *Masterless Men* (London, 1985), pp. 171–5.

10. Joanna Innes, 'English Houses of Correction and "Labour Discipline" c. 1660–1780: A Critical Examination' (unpublished paper, July 1983).

11. See Peter D'Sena, 'Perquisites and Casual Labour on the London Wharfside in the Eighteenth Century', *London Journal*, 14, 2 (1989), pp. 130–47; Peter Linebaugh, *The London Hanged* (London, 1991), pp. 417–36.

12. On the Night Poaching bill, see P.B. Munsche, *Gentlemen and Poachers* (Cambridge, 1981), pp. 25–6, 99–101, and Roger Wells, *Wretched Faces. Famine in Wartime England 1793–1801* (Glouceser and New York, 1988), pp. 167–8.

13. See Douglas Hay, 'War, Dearth and Theft in the Eighteenth Century: The Record of the English Courts', *Past and Present*, 155 (May, 1982), pp. 117–60; Nicholas Rogers, 'Confronting the Crime Wave: The Debate over Social Reform and Regulation, 1749–53', in L. Davison, T. Hitchcock, T. Keirn and R.B. Shoemaker (eds.), *Stilling the Grumbling Hive: the Response to Social and Economic Problems in England, 1689–1750* (Stroud, England and New York, 1992), pp. 77–98.

14. The expenses on passing vagrants in Somerset and Yorkshire rose significantly at the end of the American war, for example; information received from Joanna Innes of Somerville College, Oxford. For the end of the Napoleonic war, see the figures presented to parliament by the vagrancy contractor for Middlesex, Thomas David, B.P.P., 1821, iv, p. 151.

15. These figures are based on the vagrancy examinations for Middlesex, 1757–58, 1764–65, 1776–77, housed in the Greater London Record Office. For concerns about pilfering among this mobile population, see *The Times*, 27 July 1786, where Kent was said to be 'sadly infested with a number of idle people, men and women, who come under pretense of picking of hops, or harvest work; and till they can get employment, they support themselves by theft, in robbing the farmers of poultry &c'.

16. The importance of unemployment and industrial accident as causes of vagrancy is evident in the annual reports of the London Mendicity Society, the first being published in 1819. It is less evident, although probably significant, in the formulaic vagrancy examinations of the eighteenth century.

17. On the gender bias of vagrants passed out of London, see Nicholas Rogers, 'Policing the Poor in Eighteenth-Century London: The Vagrancy Laws and their Administration', *Histoire sociale-Social History*, 34, 47 (May 1991), pp. 127–47. On family breakdown as a factor in female poverty, see also David A. Kent, '"Gone for a Soldier": Family Breakdown and the Demography of Desertion in a London Parish, 1750–91', *Local Population Studies*, 45 (1990), pp. 27–42.

18. Saunders Welch, *A Proposal to Render Effectual a Plan to Remove the Nuisance of Common Prostitutes from the Streets of this Metropolis* (London, 1758), pp. 47–50, 56.

19. R.P. Hastings, *Essays in North Riding History 1780–1850* (Northallerton, 1981), p. 154.
20. For an example of the latter, see the case of William Dunn, apprehended in St. Martin-in-the-fields, March 1784, for 'diserting [*sic*] and leaving Mary his wife and their child chargeable to the said Parish'. Westminster Lib., Parish examinations, St. Martin-in-the-fields, F 5069/244–5. For an example of an abandoned apprentice who was apprehended for vagrancy, see the case of Mary Bentley, a fifteen-year-old, who after ten months was 'turned out of Door and never served her said master since'. F 5069/312.
21. Cited in C.J. Ribton-Turner, *A History of Vagrants and Vagrancy and Beggars and Begging* (London, 1887), pp. 214–15.
22. Henry Richard Fox Bourne, *The Life of John Locke* (London, 1876: reprint, 1969), Vol. 2, p. 379.
23. Under 2 & 3 Anne c.6 clause 16. For earlier impressments, see Beier, *Masterless Men*, pp. 161–2.
24. *Public Advertiser*, 6 Jan. 1776. On taking up vagrants, see *Times*, 2 Oct. 1787.
25. *Times*, 2 Oct. 1787. For examples of recruits raised under the vagrancy acts, see PRO Adm 1/1912, H 297, Adm 1/1913, H 144.
26. On this phenomenon, see N.A.M. Rodger, 'Stragglers and Deserters from the Royal Navy During the Seven Years' War', *Bulletin, Institute of Historical Research*, 57 (1984), pp. 56–79.
27. The Newcastle and Liverpool figures are calculated from the returns of the recruiting officers in Adm 1. for the year 1778. For the Seven Years War, see Stephen F. Gradish, *The Manning of the British Navy During the Seven Years War* (London, 1980), 69–70 and Rodger, 'Stragglers', pp. 56–79.
28. Charles Butler, *An Essay on the Legality of Impressing Seamen* (London, 2nd. ed., 1778), pp. 6, 33.
29. Philonauta, *The Sailor's Happiness* (London, 1751), pp. 19–20.
30. R.M.S. Pasley (ed.), *Private Sea Journals, 1778–1782* (London, 1931), p. 61, cited by Daniel A. Baugh, *British Naval Administration in the Age of Walpole* (Princeton, 1965), p. 147.
31. *Middlesex Journal*, 3–5 Jan. 1771.
32. See N.A.M. Rodger, *The Wooden World. An Anatomy of the Georgian Navy* (London, 1986), pp. 164–82.
33. PRO Adm 1/3677/28.
34. PRO Adm 1/1834 (Gordon) 1 Feb. 1759.
35. PRO Adm 1/1834 (Gordon) 17 June 1759.
36. PRO Adm 1/579, Admiral Pringle's report, 1795.
37. For a more detailed discussion, see Nicholas Rogers, 'Liberty Road: Opposition to Impressment in Britain during the American War of Independence', in Colin Howell and Richard J. Twomey (eds.), *Jack Tar in History: Essays in the History of Maritime Life and Labour* (Fredericton, New Brunswick, 1991), pp. 63–5.
38. PRO Adm 1/3680/256.
39. See Hay, 'War, Dearth and Theft', pp. 117–60.
40. PRO Adm 1/1542 (Geo Barker), 21 June 1808.
41. *York Courant*, 19, 26 March 1771; *London Evening Post*, 27 Feb. to 1 March 1777.
42. *London Evening Post*, 3–6 Nov. 1739.
43. PRO Adm 1/1498 (Bover) 6 Jan. 1778; Adm 1/1904 (Hamilton) 18 April 1778.
44. See, for example, PRO Adm 1/3681/112.
45. For an example of a young London servant appealing to his master to have him discharged from the navy, see PRO Adm 1/1612/2124 (Cunninghame).

Freedom at Issue: Vagrancy Legislation and the Meaning of Freedom in Britain and the Cape Colony, 1799 to 1842

ELIZABETH ELBOURNE

'NO MIDWAY BETWEEN SLAVERY AND FREEDOM'

'What is a nation without freedom?' asked Hendrik Heyn, a young Khoi man, in the so-called 'Hottentot' settlement of Kat River in the Cape Colony in 1834.[1] He was participating in a meeting of the peasant inhabitants of the Kat River settlement to protest against the Legislative Assembly's projected reinstatement of vagrancy legislation, which, having been abolished in 1828, would have once again empowered local officials to classify people as vagrants and to compel them either to labour on public works or to be contracted out. 'Better slaves at once than that a man should compel me to work, then can he me also sell, for there is no midway between slavery and freedom.'[2] Andries Hatha, a leading older member of the community made a similar point by example:

> Suppose I have cultivated my ground and sold 10 muids of my barley at Rixdollars 6 per muid, with which I have paid for 3 oxen that I bought, yet I journey to see my friends at Algoa Bay, but have on a ragged jacket and the Veld-Cornet meets me on the way, and inquires from where and whereto I am going. I inform him of all, but he looks upon my ragged jacket, and asks if I have any proof upon me. Upon which having no proof upon me, he seizes me and brings me before the Magistrate, who also gives me into the hands of a Baas. . . . Thus although I am really a free person, yet I am dealt with as a slave.[3]

In the charged atmosphere of 1834, as the Cape Colony neared the official day of emancipation for its extensive slave population, the Khoi and 'free coloured' population of the colony clearly conflated their own former status with slavery itself. In 1828 legislation had been passed both in London and at the Cape explicitly stating the right of Khoi to own land, and forbidding legislation which differentiated between people on the basis of race. Many 'free coloured' people, in the parlance of the time, feared for the repeal of Ordinance 50 in the wake of abolition, and worried that this would open the door to their own enslavement. Rural mission stations were flooded with applications for membership as people came seeking a legal place of settlement to remove them from the ambit of vagrancy legislation. As one slave man said, as he brought his distraught free Khoi wife and the couple's free children to be registered at the Eastern Cape station of Bethelsdorp:

> I know they are free but I could not satisfy my wife without coming here for the purpose mentioned – they say when the slaves are made free the Hottentots will be taken in their place. I myself do not believe the tale – for certainly God who is about to make the slaves free would not permit the Hottentots to be slaves in their stead.[4]

Or as Valentyn Jacobs put it in a meeting held at the mission station of Theopolis to oppose the vagrancy act, 'we are assembled to oppose the introduction of a law, the object of which is to bring us back to slavery'.[5]

The intellectual move in the charged atmosphere of the 1830s of conflating the status of the Khoi before Ordinance 50 with that of slavery is interesting and important. The indigenous Khoikhoi and San, their mixed-race descendants and the 'free black' population centred in Cape Town, largely made up of freed slaves, in fact present a classic example of a so-called 'free' population caught up in the ambiguities of a slave colony. Since the earliest days of Dutch occupation in the mid-seventeenth century the colony had possessed several 'midways between slavery and freedom'. The Dutch East India Company (VOC) had originally decided that it would not be economically viable to enslave the Khoikhoi, despite the recommendations of some of its officers. The Company's small refreshment station for Cape shipping was dependent on a steady supply of meat from the Khoikhoi, and thus on their co-operation; in addition, it was initially too difficult to keep Khoikhoi in a very small settlement against their wishes, and they were considered by some ineffective for hard labour.[6] In consequence, from the very beginning the VOC imported slave labour from its East Indian trading system into South Africa; the wine farms of the Western Cape, in particular, were developed by slave labour, while slave-ownership was also the rule in the urban centre of Cape Town itself. Initially, then, the colony comprised three quite different groups: slaves, white officials and burghers, and the indigenous Khoikhoi who were subject to their own rulers and customs. Over time, a number of processes eroded the ethnic boundaries between groups, hardening some legal boundaries while loosening others – processes which included acculturation, sexual relations, the incorporation of the Khoikhoi as conquered subjects into the legal structures of the Cape colony, the manumission of slaves and the consequent emergence of the legal category of 'free blacks', experimentations with indentured white servants, and the influx into the colony of a small number of other Africans, under a variety of circumstances. By the 1790s there were different legal categories and cultural expectations for 'Hottentots and Bushmen', free blacks, white burghers and illegal labour from outside the colony. Each category contained its own ambiguities and insecurities, and there were considerable regional variations.[7]

The current discussion will focus more narrowly on the colonial Khoisan of the Eastern Cape, primarily Gonaqua, in the early nineteenth century, in the bitter aftermath of late eighteenth-century dispossession. It was in the frontier districts of the Eastern Cape, to which many had in fact fled from the colony before running up against Xhosa occupation, that the Khoi were most numerous in this period. Unlike the better capitalized Western Cape, where imported slaves provided the bulk of the workforce on wine and fruit farms, most cash-poor farmers in the Eastern Cape relied on Khoikhoi labour to tend the cattle which were at the base of the relatively precarious *trekboer* economy. A sense of a separate Khoikhoi ethnic identity persisted longer in the Eastern Cape than it did in the regions closer to earlier white settlement; this, combined with high literacy rates and the economic ideology introduced by the London Missionary Society (LMS) missionaries who worked in the area from 1801 onwards, helped create a tentatively organizing peasant community by the 1830s which was aware of, and eager to benefit from, the abolitionist ferment, and conscious of the evangelical rhetoric of freedom. In light of these paradoxes, this discussion has a double agenda. First, we shall examine the changing legal status of free 'Hottentot' labour in the period of British colonization under consideration, and to look at the implications of that status. Second, we shall argue that there was a debate over the meaning of freedom being carried on, both tacitly and explicitly, at the Cape and in Britain itself as political struggle took place over the legal obligations of Khoi labour. Participants included colonial administrators, European missionaries of different political stripes, white settlers and the Khoisan and other free people of colour themselves. The history of the status of Khoisan labour in South Africa thus sheds useful light on the larger topic of the distinction between freedom and unfreedom in the Atlantic world in the early nineteenth century, in addition to illuminating the particular workings of dispossession of a people who tend to be assumed in South African history books to have had no history after a discreet vanishing act at some point in the eighteenth century.

'PROPER REGULARITY': SOCIAL THEORY AND EARLY BRITISH
LABOUR REGULATION

When the British took over the Cape from the Prince of Orange in 1798,
in order to prevent it from falling into the hands of the Batavian regime
and thus of revolutionary France, they found the frontier regions of the
Eastern Cape in upheaval. Among other local conflicts erupting in the
absence of a central authority, the Gonaqua Khoi were making a last
stand against the Dutch farmers who had invaded their territory. The
Gonaqua were still a relatively intact group, despite the recent devastating impact of dispossession by white settlers with superior technology and
the legacy of a milder period of Xhosa hegemony. They thus stood in
contrast to the longer subdued and more fragmented Khoisan of the
Western Cape and Cape Town region. When the frontier Dutch extended
their original rebellion against the Dutch East India Company into one
against the incoming British, complete with the cockades and slogans of
revolutionary France, the Khoi servants of the Dutch rose against them
and either went further into the interior to join with the Xhosa against the
white settlers, or travelled to join the British, on the assumption that the
British soldiers would drive away the Dutch. Without entering into the
complicated details of turn-of-the-century Cape history and the failure of
the Khoi rebellion, my point is simply that Khoi of the Eastern Cape were
in the process of being conquered.[8] The personal violence and the rough
and ready system of pass laws with which local officials controlled the
Khoi was a means to enshrine their dispossession from land as well as an
attempt to coerce their labour, in two separate but inextricably linked
processes. The *inboek* system on the frontier blurred the boundary
further: farmers raided Khoisan kraals for children to be indentured until
the age of eighteen or twenty-five, following the colonial custom of
indenturing free children born on white farms and simultaneously
entrenching conquest.[9]

When the British finally retook the Cape for good from the Batavian
Republic at the end of 1805, they inherited a turbulent and violent
interior, and a great deal of rhetoric about the wildness of the primitive
Khoikhoi and San. In 1808 the young Tory governor Lord Caledon
dispatched his lieutenant Colonel Collins into the frontier districts of
Graaff Reinet and the Sneeuberg in order to investigate the colonial
frontiers, in response to complaints of labour unrest, cattle raiding and
'banditry' in the remote districts of the colony. Collins' reports and letters
described the Khoikhoi and San as nomadic people, characterized by a
'roving disposition' and a natural love of idleness. He conflated
nomadism with lack of law. It had, for example, been naive of the first

British governor, Macartney, to hope hastily to civilize the bushmen of the northern frontier: 'such multitudes of savages, of the fiercest disposition, dispersed through such a vast extent of country, in no part of which they have a settled residence, and from which they plunder their neighbours in every direction; – without the idea of any Law, divine or human; without any connexion among themselves, except such as arises from the ties of parental, or conjugal affection; and even, without the least knowledge of the manner of cultivating corn, or rearing cattle'.[10]

The way in which Collins perceived and thought about the nomadic peoples of South Africa was of course shaped by his own cultural preconceptions. In particular, one can tease out a couple of relationships between popular conceptions of 'primitive' peoples, and some ways in which the British thought about themselves and the nature of freedom. Before the 1820s, socially conservative colonial adminstrators seeking to justify labour restrictions on the indigenous people tended to make in rough and ready form a distinction between two kinds of freedom. Unbridled liberty characterized individuals in a state of nature, who lived without law and necessarily did damage to one another. True freedom involved voluntary servitude to the public good: rational sacrifices of individual liberty thus permitted the freedom of the whole. This distinction between liberties was of course expressed in more sophisticated form by numerous British theorists of the social contract. Man in a state of nature had a life which was necessarily nasty, brutish and short, in Hobbes' classic formulation; in a state of civilization, men came together either to draw up laws themselves or to vest authority in a leader who could impose order on chaos. In Hannah More's interpretation for the masses, her 1793 tract, *Village Politics*, published by the Association for Preserving Liberty and Property against Republicans and Levellers, false French freedom contrasted with true British liberty. As one of the characters in More's dialogue remarked, in France,

> they are all so free that there's nobody safe. They make free to rob whom they will and kill whom they will. If they don't like a man's looks they make free to hang him with-out judge or jury, and the next lamp-post does for the gallows; so then they call themselves free, because you see they have no king to take them up and hang them for it.[11]

Social contract theory in general, and debates about liberty in particular, were central to late eighteenth- and early nineteenth-century self-understanding, if only because of the political currency of the idea of the British constitution as the product of a social compact, broken by the Stuarts but restored through the revolutionary settlement. Large generalizations are risky, but it seems none the less true that the issue of what nomadism was, and how settled societies ought to interact with nomads, went to the heart of profound debates in British public life and popular self-understanding, even if the average Britisher knew nothing of the Khoisan themselves.

A linked body of ideas with much popular currency in the early nineteenth century related to the development of human society through time. Scottish Enlightenment philosophers, famously, had outlined four sequential phases through which human society passed: 'hunting, pasturage, farming, and commerce', in Adam Smith's formulation.[12] As Smith, in his lectures on justice, and John Millar, in his *Origin of the Distinction of Ranks*, contended, the complication of society in general proceeded from economic complication, and the introduction of private property was both the hinge of economic and intellectual development and the necessary prerequisite of government, 'the very end of which is to secure wealth and to defend the rich from the poor'.[13] The sophisticated economic arguments of the political economists were rarely tackled by colonial administrators; indeed, one speculates that most would have been on the Tory side of opposition to the remaking of society called for by Whig politicians on economistic grounds.[14] Like many others, however, colonial administrators and evangelical missionaries alike shared the basic idea that nomadic pastoralism and hunting and gathering were prior stages of human civilization, to be followed by agriculture and commerce. Nomadism was a state of emptiness, characterized by the lack of social or political organization and the lack of knowledge of more advanced economic techniques.

In more sentimental fashion, British evangelicals also tended to espouse this complex of beliefs about nomadism, the state of nature, and the value of restricted liberty. The most striking example of early evangelical assumptions about the coincidence between nomadism and lawlessness is perhaps the LMS role in the formation of the Griqua polity. When several nomadic groups in Transorangia, of Khoisan and mixed-race background, some of them refugees from the colony, decided to form a settled community and to invite a missionary to provide instruction and diplomatic links, Scottish LMS director and visiting inspector John Campbell drew directly on the basic assumptions of Scottish political theory and general ideas about the relationship between freedom and law as he advised them to draw up a written constitution and thus enter into a formal social contract:

> I endeavoured to explain to them the necessity and design of laws
> for the government of every society ... that by appointing rulers or

judges to execute the laws they might adopt, they were not giving away their power, but only lending it to the judges, for their reciprocal advantage – and that in the history of the world there was no account of any people existing and prospering without laws. I commended them highly for having relinquished a wandering life, and become a stationary people, and said I was happy that they were, from experience, convinced of its utility; and assured them that in proportion to the length of time they remainded here, they and their children would become attached to the spot, and be desirous to promote its prosperity; that they would feel it become a home, of which, while wanderers, they were destitute.[15]

In the wake of the visit of three converted 'Hottentots' to London, where they preached and answered questions before enraptured evangelical crowds, the *Evangelical Magazine* proclaimed in verse the value of Christianity to a people who in a state of nature were devoid of both artifice and law:

> Naked, but as filth arays;
> Artless, but as want constrains;
> Lawless, but as passion sways,
> Or as hapless slav'ry chains.

By bringing people out of the state of nature and instilling a proper sense of law, Christianity created happiness: 'Mark them, – savage once and wild/ Now adorn'd with smiles serene .... Hark! religion joy doth bring' – and so forth.[16] The fact that at least two of these 'converted Hottentots' were half-slave (probably from South-East Asia), half-San farmworkers and already thoroughly embedded in colonial power relationships was irrelevant to the rhetoric of separateness and wildness.

Sharing many of these intellectual tools and preconceptions, and drawing on pre-existing patterns of labour regulation throughout the British empire, it is not surprising that when the British colonial administration turned its attention to regularizing labour relations in the interior, its officials used English vagrancy and settlement legislation as models. The first instinct of Governor Dundas during the third frontier war had been to try to persuade Khoi rebels to 'settle' and to farm. Having put down the settler rebellion in Graaff Reinet, he urged Khoisan 'bandits' who had formed raiding parties in the Zuurveld to return to the Algoa Bay area and to become 'agriculturalists'. One result was the establishment of the first London Missionary Society station in the Cape: Dundas gave grain and tools to the eccentric Dutch missionary, Johannes van der Kemp, and promised government protection in exchange for instruction to the Khoi. In the end this would be all the land the Khoi won from the war; a small land grant to a Khoi captain would be confiscated some years later by Dutch farmers, while negotiations with other rebels were broken off prematurely. Similarly, the negotiating strategy of the Batavian regime, which briefly succeeded the British, was to treat only with rebel leaders who agreed to settle on mission stations or with farmers. Khoisan were expected to 'settle', and yet had never been accorded loan-farms by the VOC, nor possessed the cash to buy land under the British system of private land tenure: the result was a legal limbo which left them peculiarly vulnerable.

In 1809, Governor Caledon issued what became known as the 'Caledon Proclamation', or 'Caledon Code'. The code was designed to ameliorate the condition of the Khoi, particularly in light of Collins' reports and of missionary complaints about the abuse of labour contracts by local farmers. The Proclamation formally instituted settlement and vagrancy laws in the colony on the British model; in the process of so doing it created a legal category of 'Hottentot' labour. From now until emancipation, the term 'Hottentot' was applied in a double sense throughout the colony: in the sense of ethnic origin, and in the sense of a labour category. In the latter sense, 'Hottentot' was clearly an expansive category which came to include all nonwhites working within the colony on a permanent basis. Such classification reflected and entrenched the white colonial conviction that whites and non-whites were in different labour categories. When the term 'Hottentot' is used below, it is to reflect colonial usage and to convey its intrinsic ambiguity.

Explicitly, the Caledon Proclamation ruled that every 'Hottentot' was henceforward to have a fixed 'place of abode'. Since in practice, if not in theory, 'Hottentots' did not have legal title to specific tracts of land, settlements could in effect only be acquired at a mission station, on a farm, or through employment with the Cape Corps, the Khoi regiment founded at Cape Town by the VOC and continued by the British. Hottentots travelling between districts required a certificate signed by the district governor, or *landdrost*, and those travelling within the district needed a pass from an employer or from a local official. Between contracts, Khoi labourers were to be given three days in which to find a new employer, and were to be allowed to travel for that purpose. Those found without documentation were to be charged as vagrants, and could be either compelled to acquire a legal settlement through hiring themselves out to new masters, or thrown into gaol and forced to participate in public works.[17]

Pass law legislation, on the model of Dutch settlement law, had existed in Graaff Reinet since the 1790s, and further towards Cape Town in the

Swellendam District as early as the 1780s; the VOC had turned down earlier requests from colonists for mobility control. The Caledon Proclamation made pass laws more systematic and expanded the power of local officials to control and punish those taken up for 'vagrancy'. In 1822 members of a royal commission of inquiry into Cape affairs (to which we shall return shortly) were shocked to discover 'since the date of this Proclamation, the Hottentots have been considered as being incapacitated by law from holding lands'.[18] No law openly disbarred the Khoi from buying into colonial land tenure systems but prejudicial custom, the weight of pass law legislation, and (under the quitrent system) lack of access to cash excluded most from 'legal' land ownership. The *landdrost* of Uitenhage, Jacob Cuyler, bluntly told the Commission that there had 'never been an instance in this district, where a Hottentot has possessed lands', and that permitting Hottentot land tenure would 'require considerable alteration of the present system, especially while the distinction between the Burgher class and the Hottentot people is so wide'. Others attributed the legal incapacity of the Khoi to hold property to the fact of their not being Christians, despite some counter-examples of Muslim land tenure in the Cape Town region. These were ironic statements in a region once dotted with Khoi kraals. They unintentionally underscore one of the chief implications of stringent vagrancy legislation: that the Khoi were aliens in their own territory. Many Khoi none the less continued to eke out existence in the margins of extensive white land grants, pursuing traditional subsistence strategies, keeping their stock out of the hands of colonists, and sometimes raiding white farms for food and further stock, in the context of an ongoing violent struggle over the ownership of land and cattle. Using a British rhetoric about the need to compel the idle poor to work for the good of society, the Caledon Code lent moral legitimacy to the seizure of such people:

> it is necessary that not only the inhabitants of the Hottentot nation, in the same manner as the other inhabitants, should be subject to proper regularity in regard to their place of abode and occupations, but also that they should find an encouragement for preferring entering the service of inhabitants to leading an indolent life, by which they are rendered useless both for themselves and the community at large.[19]

Despite great pressure, the evident persistence of such small-scale 'indolent' groups through the 1830s might be taken as itself a form of resistance to labour coercion and land theft.

The code also sought to limit the contractual powers of individual employers for the mutual benefit of all. Although the proclamation has been described as an immobilizing statute,[20] at the time Caledon's reforms attempted to open up the labour market by limiting the duration of contracts and thus permitting competition among farmers for labour. Hottentot labour contracts could not exceed a year, and if longer than a month had to be written down. In 1812 a codicil concerning apprenticeship was introduced: children who had been brought up on white farms were to be 'apprenticed' to the farmer until the age of twenty-five, in compensation for their early keep. Again, this law codified existing restraints on Khoi mobility using the language of European labour practices.

As Susan Newton-King has convincingly demonstrated, in rural areas the coercive elements of the Caledon Code were put into practice, while its reformative aspects tended to be ignored.[21] The British system of parochially-based poor relief administered by local magistrates and parish vestries was translated in the Cape Colony into control being given to *landdrosts* and veld cornets over pass law decisions. Cape Town possessed a minimal programme of poor relief but the rural districts had vagrancy legislation without a poor law; consequently, the Hottentot gained no right to poor relief from the fact of a settlement, and the benefit of settlement legislation accrued entirely to employers. The patronage opportunities available to local officials increased dramatically in consequence.[22]

Since the system was administered by those who most benefited from it, there were few judicial checks on abuses before the institution of circuit courts in 1812. These abuses were considerable.[23] Violence pervaded frontier society, as small groups struggled against one another for survival. On the side of whites, the precedent existed of disciplinary violence against slaves. At the same time, colonists were afraid of the Khoi whom they were dispossessing. Some practised against them a sadistic and economically dysfunctional level of violence which went well beyond what could be termed 'disciplinary', for it often incapacitated labourers. Here, for example, is an extract from the testimony of a missionary, James Read, who had married a Khoi woman, Elizabeth Valentyn, and collected information about atrocities:

> We have likewise been informed of the murder of a Hottentot girl by a farmer's wife who might be considered a Monster, but is in this Country, considered a worthy Inhabitant. ... A farmer in her neighbourhood told me, he saw her stab a Hottentot woman with an iron craw that the Child with which she was pregnant fell from her body and expired with the mother. ... An other poor old slave woman came here naked about a fortnight ago who had been so

horridly beaten that she could scarce walk. She had come about six miles upon her hands and knees; her child likewise had been murdered. ... Her Master and Mistress are well known here as famous for cruelty and murder – the latter has been known to throw Hottentot women in the oven and burn them alive, and tear out slaves' eyes while alive with the thumb and finger as if she had a dead sheep's head.[24]

This willingness to resort to violence could be used to ensure that labour relations between Khoi and whites resembled the relationship between slaves and their masters. It enabled farmers to dishonour Khoisan in elaborate ways: might continuous dishonour not be seen as a substitute for the natal displacement and the social death which, Orlando Patterson has claimed, characterize the slave across a variety of cultures?[25] Be that as it may, the sense of being deliberately dishonoured was strongly felt by many labourers. In 1843 Frans Mager tragically attested to his self-hatred as a boy, as his master kept him apart from the white-determined symbols of respectability:

When I was a boy, my Baas spoke to me in the Hottentot language, he would not teach me to speak the Dutch. I got only a few 'semels' to eat and my Nation then was in a miserable state, so much so that I even rubbed myself over with white clay to try to gain acceptance with my master. In those days there was no wages worth while, only a blue Handkerchief and a Knife. ... We were only allowed to make a straw hut before the sun was under on the Sabbath day, when we had to bring the sheep or calves to the Kraal; and if we attempted to make the hut that the cold or wind would not come in, then the Baas would break it open, saying thereby we would sleep too sound in the night, or too late in the morning, it was enough that it kept off the sun. ... Here the chairman asked, if his Baas never instructed him? No Mr. Chairman; we were allowed to live as the beasts. Did you never see a Bible? No, we were hurried away from hearing that, and were never told about God.[26]

Consistent dishonour, such as the stringent guard kept at the portal of the white church and the emasculation of Khoi farmworkers through the sexual exploitation of their women and the compulsory 'apprenticeship' of all children born on the farm, kept at bay the potentially threatening implications of the freedom of so-called 'Hottentots'. Above all, it enshrined the Khoi loss of land.

In 1812 circuit courts were introduced into the interior, partly as a result of Read's testimony and concern in London over reports from other sources of the abuse of farmworkers by 'Dutch' settlers. The court was staffed by local judges and, when forced to investigate substantial charges of assault and murder, its report fell back on the same ideas we have discussed above of the social contract and the need for external restraint upon man in a state of nature. Although the judges found Dutch defendants guilty on several counts of misdemeanour, defendants were absolved of all charges of murder or serious assault, largely because the convention was used that the unsupported testimony of Khoikhoi witnesses was not legally valid.[27] Having disqualified Khoikhoi from testifying on the customary basis that they were constitutively incapable of becoming Christians and thus of testifying on oath, the three circuit commissioners then penned a devastating report destined for imperial eyes. Here they threw into doubt the right of the contemporary Khoi and San to be considered as peoples, and therefore implicitly to exist independently of the white labour market. The Hottentots were 'this people that one can scarcely more consider as such, because that excepting the kraals at the Slange River in the district of George, they have not anywhere an independent subsistence', while the 'Bosjesmen' were 'this people, which one can scarcely consider as such, because that they have not the smallest idea of social order, of Government, or of a head'.[28] The Khoisan were thus signalled as available for absorption into 'organized' society as labourers. Hottentots ought to work for the farmers, the report stated. The farmers would necessarily treat them well, out of 'self interest, this great spring of all human action', in the context of the increasing cost of slaves and recent government legislation. Smithian beliefs about the overall social harmony generated by the pursuit of individual self-interest were thus adopted and turned against the Khoisan, whose own pursuit of perceived self-interest was, ironically, portrayed as invalid. In other words, nomads and primitive pastoralists were not included in the community of economic actors to whom the laws of liberal political economy might be held to apply. This assumption was made even clearer by the distinction drawn by the report between Genadendal, where missionaries instilled 'industry, order and subordination', and Bethelsdorp, where Van der Kemp had 'established such an overstrained principle of liberty as the ground work, that the natural state of barbarism appears there to supercede civilization and social order'.[29] In the latter station, in consequence, 'laziness and idleness, and consequently dirt and filth' flourished without restraint: here again, man in his natural state of barbarism was clearly assumed to be devoid of the virtues of economic man.

What was needed across all social categories was the rule of law, which alone could bring a community out of the state of nature. The Dutch commissioners lauded the British Governor for having already impressed 'on the minds of the landdrosts that the maintenance of *equal right* and *equal protection* to all classes of society forms the basis of His Majesty's Government', and that their function was 'to cause *justice* to be done to all, without respect to persons'.[30] One sees both here and in Caledon's thinking a mixture of ways of considering freedom and equality. The rule of law must apply equally to all individuals in a society. On the other hand, the *legal* concept of vagrancy took the Khoisan, as it took many of the European poor, out of the community of those who were to be considered as equals, thus resolving the dilemma of creating, and indeed adapting, a meaningful language of political and economic equality to a situation of actual racial and class inequality. In both cases, the presumed refusal to work of the vagrant – in other words, his failure to fulfil an obligation to society as a whole – negated the contingent obligations of society to him.

Despite this initial whitewash, the circuit courts were none the less effective over time in reducing somewhat the levels of violence in the frontier districts. All the same, violence remained a subtext to labour relations, in a ballet with the putative rule of law which has characterized South Africa in other centuries as well. In the 1830s Khoi attested that up until 1828 violence was used against them to make them sign contracts, to compel them to leave without wages or to accept extremely low payment, often in drink or in kind, and to deprive them of stock which they already possessed.

Clearly many were involved in contractual relationships which differed from slavery: unlike slaves, they might find masters who would treat them well and permit them to leave at the expiry of a contract. In cases of conflict, however, it was almost always the farmer who won. Jan Abel, for example, had more power than a slave when he negotiated with his boss for a salary increase, but he had no control over the outcome. After ten years of service, by which he accumulated sheep, he asked to receive ten sheep a year rather than five. He recounted in 1834 that he

> was asked whether I deserve so much; and if my baas was to give me so much then he would become bankrupt; and as I insisted he chased me away; and came back to me in the morning, inquiring whether I would agree with him again but still insisting upon my *vee* (sheep), for which I had served for many years, he told me to turn them out early next morning. I came there with some friends and my wife, who had a small switch in her hand: but the baas told her to throw away the switch his staff was baas enough; and to the others he said they [Abel's sheep] must come out from among his sheep;

and whilst I was busy catching my sheep out from his in the kraal, he drove them all out with such a force that those I had picked out for me were carried away, so that I never got them to this day.[31]

In entering into long-term service in return for stock Abel was living out the Khoi tradition of clientage. As Richard Elphick has detailed, Khoi undergoing hard times would enter the service of others in exchange for the right to live with them, be fed and eventually to receive stock in return in order to rebuild economically. The white reluctance to replenish the stock of Khoi labourers cut this cycle of replenishment off, meaning that the Khoi gradually lost their stock.[32] It was not until the 1820s, however, that one finds evidence of Khoi classifying this practice as slavery – although the absence of testimony in the earlier period is, of course, not conclusive given the scantiness of evidence in general. It is clear, however, that from the 1790s through the 1810s, most Khoi served for no wages and, according to missionary testimony, were most concerned with having food and land to live on in exchange for labour. From the 1820s on, however, in an increasingly monetized economy, the withholding of wages or refusal to offer adequate remuneration was increasingly perceived as a means of keeping the Khoi in servitude. Lack of wages had become a further badge of dishonour, associated with slave status.

ORDINANCE 50 AND THE ABOLITION OF VAGRANCY LEGISLATION

As the foregoing discussion suggests, the actual economic status of the Khoisan changed considerably throughout the 1810s and 1820s, in part because of increasing urbanization and monetization of the economy, and in part because of Khoi contact with missionaries dedicated to the reconstruction of Khoi society in the image of a utopian industrializing Britain. To continue a version of their former nomadic pastoralist lifestyle in the margins of white property was fraught with risk, but many were reluctant to work on white farms. The existence of mission stations provided an economic alternative, although local officials did their best to restrict entry to mission stations. Many Khoi were able to use mission stations as bases to learn trades, such as transport-riding; to hire themselves out on a seasonal rather than a permanent basis to farmers; and to leave family, stock and cash wages in a place where they could not be touched by employers.[33]

The 1820s saw the advent of British settlers and the gradual development of small-scale urban centres as a counterbalance to Cape Town.

Greater monetization of the economy and a wider range of economic opportunity in the new towns of Grahamstown and Algoa Bay (later Port Elizabeth) meant that Khoisan were increasingly developing lifestyles which were visibly at odds with their traditional categorization as primitive vagrants from disorganized societies. They were engaged in the white economy on more equal terms with whites than in the past, and were increasingly perceived, by the British settlers in particular, as an economic threat.

Even as the economic options open to the Khoikhoi were expanding, the interstitial status of 'Hottentot' labour was coming under effective political threat from two directions at once: from the powerful evangelical lobby temporarily united around the question of abolition, and from the metropolitan imperial administration itself. During the early 1820s, influential British officials, spearheaded by the liberal reformist William Huskisson at the Board of Trade, sought to establish free trade more fully throughout the empire. The dilemma posed in South Africa by contradictions within a developing British language of liberalism thus became more acute in the 1820s as the imperial administration sought to liberalize the Cape colonial economy, well before Britain fundamentally revamped labour relations across the colonial world with the 1834 abolition of slavery.[34] The metropolitan government deliberately and fundamentally attacked the oligarchic system initiated by the VOC and maintained by the early British administration. In the late 1820s, following reports from a commission of inquiry established by the British Under-Secretary of State for the Colonies, R.W. Horton, London handed control of local government to centrally-appointed officials, liberalized trade, gave teeth to legislation to transform land tenure to a British quitrent system, monetized the economy further, sought to introduce free labour, and, in 1828, abolished disability on the basis of colour. J.B. Peires makes a convincing case that it was to this gamut of fundamental reforms that Afrikaner farmers were reacting when they began the Great Trek, as much as to the immediate events of 1834.[35]

In 1828 the Whig governor Bourke, in response to his mandate to implement a variety of reform measures, promulgated Ordinance 50, which abolished legislation relating to the 'Hottentots' as a legal category, and ordained that all legislation must henceforward pertain equally to all classes of person in the Cape Colony. With specific reference to free labour, the second clause proclaimed that

> whereas by usage and custom of this colony Hottentots and other free persons of colour have been subjected to certain restraints as to their residence, mode of life and employment ... no Hottentot or

other free person of colour, lawfully residing in this colony, shall be
subject to any compulsory service to which other of His Majesty's
subjects therein are not liable, nor to any hindrance, molestation,
fine, imprisonment or punishment of any kind whatsoever, under
the pretense that such person has been guilty of vagrancy or any
other offence, unless after trial in due course of law.[36]

Another crucial provision, under the guise of an affirmation of the
status quo, was the statement that free persons of colour were permitted
to hold title to land. In the meantime, the activist superintendent of the
LMS, Dr John Philip, had travelled to London and had persuaded Sir
George Murray to affirm the civil equality of white and 'coloured' in the
Cape Colony through an Order in Council, and later to entrench the
provisions of Ordinance 50, such that they could not be modified without
the consent of London.[37]

This legislation must, however, be placed side by side with Ordinance
49, which permitted African labour to enter the colony on short-term
contracts only. Such immigrants were to be obliged to carry passes, and
those found without passes could be pressed into public works for up to a
year. The same potential for local abuse and for the manipulation of
'outsiders' was clearly present in this legislation as in earlier vagrancy
legislation. Ordinance 49 throws into relief, however, increased colonial
readiness to see the colonial Khoisan now as citizens of a sort, to be
incorporated into the economic community on different terms than
outsiders, in however inequitable a fashion.

It is of interest for our discussion of free and unfree labour that a
number of British interlocutors in debates over the future of the colony
talked about Dutch settlers, especially the Dutch peasants of the interior,
in terms similar to those previously applied to the Khoisan: the economic
'backwardness' of the peasant farmers caused moral insufficiency. As
early as 1802, Governor Macartney's assistant, John Barrow, had published a description of his sojourn in South Africa which levelled that
charge, linking the idleness, unproductivity, and lack of material wants of
the farmers to their brutal treatment of the Khoikhoi.[38] Despite alliances
between Dutch and British on the ground, the commissioners of inquiry
shared the opinion of Barrow and other commentators that the Dutch
were lazy and unproductive, and that labour and land tenure systems at
the Cape encouraged these qualities. Among other things, the commissioners' final report recommended a head tax on servants hired on an
annual basis, to discourage Khoi clientage and to force 'indolent' Dutch
farmers to put themselves and their 'numerous' families to work.[39] The
commissioners sought thereby to stimulate the economy by replacing

bonded labour with seasonal labour to be paid in cash, and by remaking the supposedly uneconomic and immoral character of the indolent Dutch. The classic evangelical equivalence between immorality and slave-owning found its echo in the economist's assumption that for the good of the economy the controllers of cheap labour also needed to be forced to work: if the slave owner and the slave could generate little moral capital between them, then the same held true of economic capital.

The other substantial source of the attack on the interstitial status of the Khoi labourer was the evangelical missionary lobby. In South Africa the chief missionary proponents of the liberalization of laws affecting Khoi labour were nonconformists from the London Missionary Society who had been through the attacks directed at nonconformity in general, and even at missionary activity in particular, in the suspicious, turbulent 1790s and 1800s. Arguably, some of these first LMS missionaries were more sympathetic to African political concerns than the envoys of the better-established and more 'respectable' Victorian missionary movement, who had been exposed for more of their lives to an increasingly well-entrenched racialist discourse. Certainly, the early LMS movement yielded two figures, Johannes van der Kemp and James Read, who married into the slave and Khoi communities and became deeply involved in local politics. Van der Kemp died in 1811, bequeathing a legacy of radical millenarianism to Khoi religious thought. Read is more important for the current discussion: he was called by the Philipton church to be the minister at Kat River and he and his half-Khoi son, James Read junior, proved an important conduit of knowledge of contemporary British economic debates to the Kat River community. Read's work sparked a substantial Khoisan missionary drive to the hinterland beyond the colony, and helped coalesce a Khoi sense of allegiance to British evangelical anti-slavery activists. At the same time, the white LMS missionary community fractured around issues of race and politics; by the 1830s, Read was an increasingly isolated figure on the ground, even as the LMS higher administration was riding the abolitionist bandwagon and the powerful LMS South African superintendant, John Philip, was mobilizing successfully on the issue of civil rights for the Khoisan. Those Khoisan who aligned themselves publicly with Read were thus maneouvring in a complicated situation of uncertain alliances.

Be that as it may, the more radical wing of the LMS held the public stage in the early 1830s in the heady aftermath of abolition. The society's linked economic and spiritual platform, under the leadership of the Scotsman John Philip from 1819 onwards, depended on the idea of freedom in complicated ways. The economic arena could only function (as it must) as a venue for salvation if individuals were all free economic actors: the free choice to perform economic acts lent moral dignity, whereas forced labour degraded the person doing the forcing and did not permit the enslaved person to gain any moral capital from the workplace. In a parallel fashion, the moral arena both demanded and created freedom. Sin was slavery; true freedom was only to be gained through the knowledge of God and the self won through the process of conversion. Philip's famous statement that all he wanted for the Hottentots was the right to bring their labour to a free market and the rest would follow had many more implications than is immediately apparent.[40]

Through the 1820s and 1830s, leading reformist missionaries and their allies, liberal propagandists such as John Fairbairn and Thomas Pringle, developed much further the theme that the labour practices and indolence of the Dutch caused immorality. Adherence to the sound laws of economics and individual morality were inextricably linked, and idleness was a cardinal sin. 'The master has but one idea in his head,' wrote John Philip of slave-owners in the interior, '& that is how to oppress the people of colour, think of virtue, truth, humanity, apprehension, and one turns from the brutal countenance of the master to repose on the lines of thought and humanity in the face of his slave.'[41] By the 1830s the Khoisan themselves were adopting elements of this language; as several speakers pointed out in public meetings at the time of the Great Trek, 'the Boers over the boundary are the Vagrants'.[42]

There was a longstanding, widespread and very influential body of liberal evangelical social theory behind such pronouncements.[43] Free labour was a means by which the individual expiated guilt and constructed his own salvation; slavery and bonded labour were morally damaging to the slave-owner as well as preventing the slave or labourer from having an equal opportunity to rise in civilization through economic advancement. In their own way, the liberal evangelical social theorists of the early nineteenth century were as convinced of the relationship between morality and market forces, and as optimistically messianic, as the marxist economic historians who, until recently at least, so fervently opposed them in South Africa.

In the early 1830s an evangelically tinged version of liberal economics had considerable political clout. The Whig government both itself contained a number of influential evangelicals and was particularly beholden to the new dissenting electorate which constituted an important plank of its electoral support and tended to favour free labour and 'modern' economics in an evangelical guise.[44] In this context it is worth noting that leading British abolitionists Zachary Macaulay and James Stephen were among the candidates considered as commissioners under the New Poor Law of 1834,[45] which aimed to increase the mobility of labour and to dismantle the paternalist structure of outdoor relief, and that support for the new poor law was a common evangelical characteristic.[46] For both paupers and free coloureds, it was, in David Brion Davis's phrase, the 'very essence of emancipation ... to remove the arbitrary constraints that stifled responsibility and concealed individual worth'.[47]

A third broad trend urging the abolition of racially-biased labour laws was the belated acknowledgement by the Colonial Office through the 1820s of the ambiguous status of 'free' coloured labour in colonial slave societies. In the context of debate about the abolition of slavery, and what might replace it, the legal disabilities of coloureds in a variety of countries were linked and made a potentially highly embarrassing issue by the more radical anti-slavery pressure groups.[48] Activists made particular play of the idea that British subjects ought to be treated equally under the law. London adopted a policy of quietly redressing grievances in response to petitions from individual groups of free coloureds, but refused to make public and programmatic reforms.[49] This context sheds new light on the fact that Murray was willing to give Philip an Order-in-Council affirming that South African law was and always had been colour-blind, on condition that the issue not be made a subject of debate in parliament. More powerful free coloured communities were able to obtain more concrete concessions, as did, for example, the free coloured community of St.Kitts, whose permanent agent in London, Ralph Cleghorn, worked closely with the anti-slavery society during the late 1820s, or the Grenada community which maintained the free coloured proprietor Edward Gibbs as its London agent.[50]

It is against this broad background that Ordinance 50 must be placed, rather than simply in the context of personality politics. The specific processes must not be lost, however, in the maw of debate over general international economic shifts, crucial as these broad changes were. In the context of the interest politics of the early nineteenth century, including the small size of the Colonial Office and its consequent susceptibility to personal influences, it is also extremely important that Philip was able to establish a relationship with Sir Thomas Fowell Buxton, leader of the parliamentay abolitionists and a close colleague of the powerful colonial under-secretary James Stephen. After considerable personal effort, Philip was able to persuade Buxton that the Hottentot cause was a version of the fight against slavery, and to have it taken up directly by powerful abolitionists. Their interest was, however, partly contingent on a rosy view of the capacity of the Khoisan to flourish as novice members of the free market, and to furnish a useful model of free black labour for propaganda purposes. This background is important because it helps explain why the Khoisan experienced such powerful pressures in the direction of Christianization, and why their imperial alliance initially bore such valuable fruit.

The impact of Ordinance 50 has been called into question by some historians, but the passionate support given to it by Khoisan petitioners in 1834 leaves no doubt as to the importance it was accorded by those whom it most directly affected. Land grants to Khoisan at the Kat River settlement offered hope of long-term economic independence as well as some small restitution for the thefts of the past – although the land grants came nowhere near what the Khoi felt they needed and were owed. In addition to heartfelt speeches exalting the principle of free labour and the return of Hottentot land, petitioners also made prosaic comments that revealed the range of economic opportunities opened by the removal of vagrancy legislation, and the passage of 'the 50th Ordinance, which enables you to ride out barley and oats, and to make contracts for supplying the Troops', as Mager Pretorius put it.[51] It is also clear that many Khoisan who had emigrated from the colony returned in order to take up the offer of land, or simply because they now found it tolerable to live in the colony with a greater degree of independence.

As colonists found themselves confronted by the daily sight of free Khoisan on the roads and in small communities scratching a living from the land, and as news reached the Cape of the imminent abolition of slavery, pressure mounted for a renewal of vagrancy law. This time, however, the chief agitators were precisely those British settlers whom the commissioners of inquiry had fondly hoped would embrace the principle of free labour and stimulate the idle Dutch to work.

THE DEFEAT OF RENEWED VAGRANCY LEGISLATION, 1834

The year 1834 was momentous for labour relations in the Cape Colony, and a turning point in relations between Afrikaners and the British. The abolition of slavery took effect in 1834, although former slaves would remain 'apprentices' until 1838. At the same time, the newly formed Legislative Council attempted to pass comprehensive vagrancy legislation, but was snubbed by London in 1835 on the basis that the law contravened the second clause of Ordinance 50, cited above. The failure of this legislation put one of the final, if certainly not the first, nails into the coffin of the relationship between Dutch settlers and the British empire.

The effort of the newly-formed Legislative Council to reinstate vagrancy legislation must again be placed in colonial context. West Indian proprietors, scrambling for ways to retain slave labour in the wake of abolition, fought hard both for the compulsory 'apprenticeship' of freed slaves and for the establishment of vagrancy legislation. Indeed, the

Anti-Slavery Society, headed by Buxton, felt in 1835 that the threat posed by permanent vagrancy laws was so severe that the parliamentary abolitionists could not oppose temporary apprenticeship legislation as strenuously as they would have liked. The directors therefore decided at a meeting of December 1835 that it was injudicious to present a motion in parliament against apprenticeship when the danger lay more in 'some Vagrancy Law' which would 'perpetualise slavery under another name'. Colonial Office staff agreed: at a meeting with Buxton, the minister Grey and the colonial under-secretary, James Stephen, claimed that they hated the apprenticeship system and would accept its abolition if Buxton could secure it, but none the less saw it as 'part of the bargain'; vagrancy legislation, on the other hand, was unacceptable.[52]

Had Colonel Wade, Acting Governor of the Cape Colony, realized the extent of opposition at the heart of the Colonial Office, he might have been less confident in proposing a vagrancy law as his parting shot to London in 1833. Wade and the many other white supporters of vagrancy legislation do not appear, however, to have appreciated the extent to which the wind was changing with regard to the legal status of free persons of colour. A draft ordinance was quickly drawn up by the Legislative Council between the departure of Wade and the arrival of the new Governor, Sir Benjamin D'Urban. Its terms permitted the arrest as a vagrant of any person on the road who was unable to provide an account of how he or she had subsisted over the past three days. The act re-entrenched the provision that all people must have a legal place of abode, and, on pain of a vagrancy charge, forbade such traditional Khoi means of finding food as robbing bees' nests, digging for roots, hunting on government land, or picking berries. A person found guilty of being a vagrant by a local official could either be set to work upon the roads, or compelled to find a master and a legal place of settlement. As in the Caledon Code, there was no distinction between the genuinely destitute and a Khoi person with, for example, cattle but no master.

The draft legislation immediately aroused a storm of controversy. The English-language *Grahamstown Journal* came out strongly in favour of the act, while the bilingual but anglophile *South African Commercial Advertiser*, edited by the redoubtable John Fairbairn, was as equally fervently opposed. The Dutch community tended to be strongly in favour, especially in the rural districts, where vagrancy legislation would have represented a welcome return to 'the old system', as its opponents dubbed it. The British settler community, centred at Grahamstown in the Eastern Cape, vociferously expressed its support in numerous public meetings, and bombarded the Legislative Council with petitions urging that the measure be adopted. Among whites, in sum, there were only a handful of opponents. They included, however, the highly visible and vocal Philip and Fairbairn; other white opponents, including LMS missionaries George Barker, William Anderson and James Read, and a couple of scattered settlers, had less clout but were able to channel information to the press via Fairbairn and to London via John Philip's anti-slavery connections.[53]

With a few notable exceptions, the Khoi community was passionately opposed. Hundreds rushed to register at mission stations in order to maintain legal independence.[54] Mission stations were further used as a base from which to petition the colonial and imperial governments. The most substantial petition, with 400-odd signatures, came from Philipton, in the independent Kat River community. Kat River also saw, however, the only Khoi counter-petition, signed by eighty settlers, mostly members of a group of mixed white and Khoisan descent, who followed colonial parlance in terming themselves 'Bastards', worshipped at the church of the government agent, W. Thompson, and apparently did not feel themselves to be personally at risk.[55] This division reflected tension in the early 1830s between those who identifed themselves as 'Hottentots' (despite mixed ancestry in some cases) and those who claimed higher status for themselves on the basis of mixed-race parentage, as well as class tension based on the fact that the 'Bastard' community tended to have accumulated more stock in contrast to the 'Hottentot' community, and that the former were more favourable to the Dutch than the English-influenced LMS community.

The most obvious point of disagreement among these various positions was economic. White settlers claimed that since the abolition of vagrancy legislation under Ordinance 50, Hottentots had taken to wandering around the countryside, refusing to hire themselves out to local farmers, and living from cattle theft. The Khoi were therefore an economic threat, as well as living in an immoral fashion. Opponents pointed out in response that laws against trespass and theft were adequate defences against such depredations. British settlers rather sought to adopt Dutch labour relations and to have a constant supply of ill-paid labour. Further, Khoi petitioners claimed, white settlers wished to dispossess the last vestiges of the Hottentots still living respectably on their ancient soil, to regain Khoi property such as cattle and sheep, to remove Khoisan from the wage economy and to eliminate economic competition. A more appropriate response would be to return to the Khoi some of the lands which were once theirs, in the form of land grants mimicking those made out to British settlers.

In this extensive public debate, both the largely British settler lobby and their Khoi and British opponents claimed to be the standard-bearers of 'liberty'. Both deployed what might be seen as standard 'liberal' arguments of the day to bolster their positions. Most of the white interlocutors claimed that the values which they were defending were peculiarly English – although for many Khoisan, unnoticed at the time, this debate would mark a key moment in their loss of faith in the English as political allies.[56] The Dutch peasantry tended to be used as whipping boys; the British settlers tended to look down on them as economically unprogressive, many Khoi (despite some who felt more allegiance and had done better out of the relationship) bitterly remembered their loss of possessions to Dutch farmers and the brutality with which many had been treated while in service, and the Philip-Fairbairn circle wrote them off as slave-holders.

On the face of things, the British settler lobby walked something of an intellectual tightrope. The importance of 'liberty' warred with the desire for racially-based labour legislation. This was, however, a dilemma which confronted other British colonists elsewhere in the world. As James Tully has contended, American colonists argued throughout the eighteenth century that Indian groups did not have sovereignty over their lands because they lacked organized political societies and hence could not enter into social contracts. Thomas Jefferson, for example, used a combination of Lockean natural law theories of conquest and the theory that monarchical ownership of land was a Norman innovation imposed on the Saxon developers of England, to contend that land belonged to the settlers who chose to cultivate it, rather than being available as a legal object of treaties between Indians and the British Crown.[57] In this sense, the American declaration of independence was contingent on the use of natural law theory to deny to the original inhabitants of the land the property rights which were the basis of equality and full membership in the political community. This was certainly the Achilles' heel of the use of British constitutional theory by liberal activists.

Many settler agitators for vagrancy legislation indignantly denied the imputation that the legislation was racially biased. A series of resolutions passed at a meeting of settlers at Graaff Reinet, for example, explicitly disavowed, in carefully racially neutral terms, any desire among participants to avail themselves of the 'compelled services of the poor classes', to depress wages, or to oppose land grants 'for the independent settlement of the industrious poor'.[58] Other commentators, however, argued that vagrancy legislation was necessary to help the most 'degraded' sections of society, unavoidably the Hottentots in South Africa. The types of conservative interpretations of social contract theory and of the limits of liberty which we discussed at the beginning of this essay resurfaced among the self-proclaimed proponents of British liberty.

Leading settler Robert Godlonton decried the suffering caused in the Cape Colony by 'the want of some regulation tending to curb that propensity to Vagrancy which prevailed amongst so many of the coloured classes'.[59] The *Grahamstown Journal*, mouthpiece of the 'Grahamstown English' (many of whom were in fact Scottish), cited Hume to support the nobility of legislating with regard to beggary and vagrancy, but quickly slipped into a discussion of coloured insufficiency. More than anyone else, the 'coloured classes' were in need of discipline and instruction: 'bred in the lap of indolence, and with little or no incentive to steady perseverence in industry, they eke out a wretched existence in listless inactivity, or where opportunity presents itself, relieve the tedium of life by an indulgence in the most debasing and ruinous profligacy'. How could this be otherwise with a primitive people?

> Who need be informed that a wandering and nomadic life is the bane of civilization? or who need be told that to reclaim a barbarous people, the first step is to fix them to the soil, and to induce them to create around them those comforts which constitute a Home.

Although it was just that Ordinance 50 relieved the coloured classes from 'an iniquitous infringement on their personal liberty', they deserved more: 'they should have been stimulated to habits of order and industry; education should have been easy of access to them; and they should have been taught to understand the value of the social compact ... '.[60]

The contested concept of liberty formed the centrepiece of the resolutions which were sent by the Legislative Council to London to accompany the final version of the draft. Drawing heavily on ideas of the reconstructibility of man and the insufficiency of a state of nature, the council argued that the Hottentots were 'of an unsettled roaming disposition, fondly attached to the pleasures of nomadic life, averse from fixed or orderly habits and employments, and by far the great proportion of them utterly unacquainted with, and regardless of, even the most ordinary artificial wants and comforts of civilized life'. Consequently, the 'unhappy gift' of 'unrestrained liberty' was impeding their progress in civilization and industry. A further implicit argument from the social contract was marshalled to bring political liberalism to bear against lack of restraints on the Khoi: the current position of the Khoisan subverted the rights and security of property of others, and infringed the civil liberty of all subjects. Such liberty consisted not in a mere absence of restraint but 'in the undisturbed enjoyment of legal rights, alone to be derived from the efficient protection of civil government'.[61]

The white anti-vagrancy lobby came to terms with the social contract argument not by denying the validity of its terms, but by claiming for the

Khoisan equal membership in a unitary political community by virtue of their advance in civilization. As John Philip had once written, as he urged Khoi mission communities to build straight streets, square houses and other presumed signs of rationality in anticipation of a visit from the commissioners of inquiry, the Khoi had to prove themselves 'fit to be free'.[62] Both Philip and his most important London contact, Thomas Fowell Buxton, in fact did not believe in right of conquest arguments: Buxton opposed European settlement in foreign countries altogether, while Philip argued in his *Researches in South Africa* that the Khoi were far better off, and more virtuous, before the advent of Europeans.[63] The public thrust of their arguments none the less drew on natural law theory in a double sense. On the one hand, Khoisan and other free black communities were virtuous and thus could be trusted with freedom. They were on the upward path to civilization, through economic self-improvement. On the other hand, the axis of their ascent was via free labour: morality in the market place could not operate in the presence of constraint. Consequently, they needed to maintain the freedom which they already had and to be given more in order to complete the journey. Khoi communities found themselves called upon to act out ritualistic expressions of themselves as communities saved by free labour, paralleling evangelical ideas about the reconstitution of the self through conversion and the consequent assumption of self-knowledge and responsibility.

Anti-vagrancy agitation, however, permitted Khoisan communitites to speak directly on the public stage for the first time in many years, rather than being represented by missionaries. 'It forms a new era in the politics of the colony, the Hottentots as a nation petitioning for their Civil rights', commented George Barker.[64] At the first session of the Philipton meeting, Andries Stoeffels said that, 'this was the first day and the first time and the first place' that he was allowed to speak on behalf of his nation.[65] After a long period of neglect of Khoi history post-1828, revisionist accounts by Stanley Trapido and Clifton Crais have recently appeared, both of which take account of the evidence of these meetings. Trapido has emphasized the Khoisan use of liberalism to propound a new 'Hottentot nationalism', whereas Crais has stressed the way the memory of past oppression informed, as it continues to inform, the political actions of Eastern Cape peasants.[66] I would want to add some additional points.

A complicated concept of freedom emerges from the speeches made in opposition to vagrancy law. In the case of recently emancipated slaves in the British Caribbean, Nigel Bolland has argued that while 'for many of the former slaves the labor process was to be, unavoidably, the focal point of their struggle for freedom, there is abundant evidence that freedom meant more for them than the freedom to sell or to withhold their own labor power in the marketplace'.[67] A similar claim can be made for the Khoisan, never technically enslaved but in a similarly precarious position and already possessing many family ties to slaves. At the same time, as argued above, many Khoisan had come under the influence of abolitionst thought, and sought to position themselves rhetorically within the terms of European debate. This was probably particularly true of that second generation of converts to Christianity who had been educated from childhood in London Missionary Society schools. There were, then, no pure types of 'African' response to British visions of a free labour world, but rather a series of negotiating positions within a rhetoric that was, to some extent, shared.

A profoundly important difference between Khoi and British positions was that for the Khoi, freedom was linked strongly to the restoration of land. This demand was uppermost in the minds of a people who kept alive a sense that as a community they had been robbed of land – and this despite the ethnic admixture which somewhat diluted the Hottentot claim to land restoration. Immediately after the passage of Ordinance 50, for example, inhabitants of Bethelsdorp had on the strength of it petitioned the colonial government for the return of land which had not yet been 'given to others of His Majesty's subjects', claiming it was just that what remained of the land that 'belonged to their fathers' be reserved for them and their children.[68] Ironically, both the Khoi and Dutch farmers possessed a sense of connection to the land based on long-standing occupation and use of its resources, whether through hunting, gathering, pastoralism or peasant agriculture, standing in contrast to the liberal administrator's conception of land as alienable private property which could be bought and sold without prior possession.[69]

Mobility was also an important part of freedom. The vagrancy law evidently influenced the terms of the debate; other evidence suggests, however, both that mobility remained an important concern for a recently nomadic people, and that the economic consequences of restricted mobility were serious in a colony in which many Hottentots made their living as transport riders and supplemented their incomes by hunting and gathering food, following older subsistence patterns.

Mobility control also enabled forced employment at low wages. For Valentyn Jacobs,

> The law as it now stands is sufficient for every purpose, and there are magistrates and Field-Cornets, but these cannot ask us where are you going, and this is the reason why they want a new law; they cannot ask us where are you going according to law and will have a

> vagrant law to do so .... We must open our eyes, we must oppose
> this act, for if it passes every man will set his own price on our
> labour.[70]

The desire to be honoured also emerged strongly from the testimony of
many, suggesting, as I have argued above, that dishonour was linked to
labour coercion. Badges of honour for some included Western-style
clothing and the right to choose one's own residence. Magerman, at Kat
River, claimed 'I was always naked before but now that I have come here
I appear to be something like a human (showing his red jacket) – my
friends I desire to remain here and not run away any more.'[71] Platje
Jonker of Theopolis attested 'I fear a vagrant is something like a dog, you
may knock him on the head and no notice will be taken of it. A vagabond,
children, is a man who does not know where to find his night cap.'[72]

A final noteworthy trend running through Khoi speeches was strong
awareness of the racial quality of the legislation. As Slinger Booy of
Theopolis put it most bluntly, 'the vagrant law is for black men'. Even in
this, however, many drew, as Stanley Trapido points out, on the rhetoric
of nationhood and of the rights of nations to liberty. Philip Campher
proclaimed, 'I stand here my nation to advocate your cause, and if it
should be that I must die for my nation, I could almost do it, provided that
would secure your liberty.'[73]

As much of the above testimony attests, Khoi speakers were very
aware of 'property rights', as Europeans defined them – of the monetization of the economy, of the fact that they were being significantly
underpaid for their work, and had been refused just wages in the past, of
the symbolic value vested in possessions, of prior Khoi ownership of the
land, and the moral obligation of the government at the very least to
return sections of this land to them. Several said clearly that when they
could not eat they stole to survive, but they would prefer to farm. To this
extent, they had significantly internalized Western notions of property –
if indeed one can ascribe such notions solely to the 'West', which I myself
doubt. Their testimony gave the lie to the myth of the nomad with no
notion of property value or economic theory, propagated by the settler
lobby. It also calls into question the somewhat romantic disparagement
by some recent historians of the absorption of supposedly conservative
capitalist ideology by inhabitants of mission stations. Before reifying
capitalism to the point of meaninglessness, one needs to remember the
conditions against which people were struggling: to recognize the nature
of the market economy and to want to survive within it was not a shameful
goal – especially given the extraordinarily high rates of alcoholism and
other manifestations of social breakdown which ran through the im-

poverished Khoi community. At the same time, these beliefs about property cannot be assumed to have the same ideological freight as they did, for example, for British missionaries or British economists. They seem part of the desire of people of colour to be respected and to be included in an organic economic community of free people. Talking to the colonial state about land and wages thus did not preclude the Khoi and their descendants from sharing, to a point of impoverishment, land, food and possessions with others in need, especially relatives, in accordance with older Khoi custom: one of the reasons given by both Khoi and their LMS advocates for the urgency of increased land grants was that grants to individuals were overrun by clients in times of need and the value 'eaten up'.[74]

However strong the Khoisan commitment to clientage and to communal sharing, and despite the different meanings which many clearly attached to 'freedom', one also notes the use of a rhetoric of 'rights' and liberalism. Such rhetoric is not as surprising as it might seem. Many Khoisan were, far from being untamed children of nature, attending to the colonial debate very closely: many of them did, after all, follow newspapers and subscribe to the European missionary press.[75] The young men who made up the bulk of public interlocutors at Kat River had for the most part been educated in schools under the supervision of James Read junior, or had been trained by him to form an emerging Khoisan school teacher elite. Read junior, educated under Scottish influence at Cape Town and an enthusiastic proponent of European liberalism, proclaimed himself both a 'radical' and a 'liberal', and doubtless influenced a number of young men. John Philip was an additional influence, as the leading LMS proponent of 'Hottentot rights', who frequently visited Eastern Cape stations, had acted as political patron of the mixed Khoi-white Griqua of Transorangia, promoted the evangelization of the African interior by Khoisan converts, and gave political advice to the Khoi.

Given these information sources, it is not surprising that Hottentot speakers competed with colonial critics on their own terms. Here, for example, is an extract from the petition submitted by Theopolis.

> That as far as the Hottentots are concerned, whatever may be the sentiments of his Excellency the Governor and the honourable council, it is impossible for memorialists to look at the spirit of the letters published in favour of the new law, the arguments used at public meetings convened to petition in favour of it, and to recollect how often some of us have already been taunted by being told we have been long enough our own masters, that in a little time we shall find ourselves in other hands, and not to feel that it is for cheap

servants, the 'compulsory service', the compulsory service of memorialists, that the whole of this clamour about a Vagrant Act has been raised. 'It is a law in place of the old law' that is wanted; a law that will tame the 'restlessness' of the Hottentots; a law to punish the Hottentots as felons before a felony has been committed; a law for the 'prevention of crime'; a law that will encourage proprietors and capitalists to engage in extensive 'improvements and speculations'. Hottentots are to be obliged to enter into contract for more than one month and their 'restlessness' is to be subdued for the sole benefit of their masters.[76]

As if a dam had been broken, the meetings also provided a means for the public recounting of stories, as the older members of the community attempted to convince the young of the dangers of vagrancy legislation and recalled the abuses to which they had been subject as bonded labour. This public statement of a collective consciousness of suffering, and awareness of the need for vigilance, was not the least of the legacies of the 1834 vagrancy debate.[77] The Khoisan were no longer prepared to accept being excluded from the political community.

Thus, in these debates, a number of Khoi speakers stressed the danger of different types of liberty in any community where the citizens were biased against one another by racial hatred. The same Hendrik Heyn quoted at the beginning of this discussion acknowledged the argument of the *Grahamstown Journal* that England, the supposed home of liberty, possessed a vagrancy law. In England, however, Heyn argued, 'the people are born under the law and brought up, they all know the Laws and how to defend themselves, and have friends there to plead their cause, and because they are of one colour they have so far an attachment for each other; but here it is not so, here there is no sympathy and we have no friend to come up for us'. Heyn concluded, however, 'that while we are all subjects of one King, so we ought to have one sympathy'.[78] Out of the experience of discrimination came a drive on the part of many to establish themselves as citizens of a common ruler, and to claim equality on that basis with white settlers. Essentially, the limits placed on citizenship by theorists of the social contract were rejected by people of colour claiming equal rights as the reward for their cultural integration and their full incorporation into the polity.

THE AFTERMATH OF VICTORY

In 1835 victory seemed complete for the evangelical missionary and Khoisan proponents of free labour. Away from the limelight generated by the anti-slavery struggle, some dismal years lay ahead, however. In 1841 the legislative assembly passed masters and servants legislation which discretely curtailed some of the rights laid out in Ordinance 50. Reflecting a renewed imperial tightening of labour restrictions in former slave colonies in the 1840s, the Masters and Servants Act was essentially racially biased legislation disguised as legislation to control class relations. None the less, the principle of racial equality under the law, battered and cynically distorted as it was in most instances, prevented a return to explicitly racial coercive labour legislation. Under some circumstances, oral contracts would be valid for up to twelve months; written agreements were compulsory only for contracts of twelve months or more, and the upper limits of a contract were extended to three years. The duties of servants were more rigidly defined, with greater penalties for neglect, refusal to work, desertion, damage to property, violence, insolence and insubordination. The second clause of Ordinance 50, which forbade legislation targeted at the Hottentots in particular was dropped by Governor Napier, who claimed that it branded the free coloured people as an inferior class.[79] These modifications all tended to work against free coloured servants and were clearly, if covertly, targeted at non-whites. This was not, however, a sufficiently large issue on which to call out the evangelical troops, even had they continued to exist in sufficiently large numbers. Instead, the increasingly isolated and out-of-fashion radical wing of the LMS was discouraged as the economic fortunes of the mingled Khoisan and ex-slave communities, now coming to be called 'coloured', took a downturn and the racial hegemony of the Cape economy thwarted the development of a prosperous class of coloured people. These were, however, the trials of liberty, as the abolitionists conceived of it.

Vagrancy legislation remained a central political concern for the Khoisan and ex-slave community, for whom it symbolized the never-forgotten 'old system'. In 1851 self-government was in the wind for the Cape Colony. One among many strains behind the eponymously-named Kat River rebellion of that year, in which Khoisan from all over the colony joined the existing attack of the Xhosa on the colony, was the 'Hottentot' fear of renewed vagrancy legislation. As Crais has argued, many of Khoisan descent, holding to a utopian vision of the protective power of the British empire, fought for the return of imperial control and protection against labour legislation. The rebel Windvogel, cited by Crais, recalled that he had heard

that there was to be *Vagrant Law*, and I heard the Hottentots say that they were to be inbooked as in former times [*sic*], the same as

> Slaves . . . . The Kafirs and Hottentots came together like Bucks and Sheep, and all I heard was that the war was to be against the Settlers and not against the Government.[80]

There were others with different ideas, but the defensive drive against vagrancy legislation was a crucial component in the imperial allegiances of a threatened community. The rebellion was unsuccessful, and reprisals included the break-up of the Kat River settlement through the alienation of its land to white speculators. People of colour none the less received the franchise in the Cape Colony, although property limitations kept their eligibility rates low. In 1856 a severe Masters and Servants Act justified the fears of the 1851 rebels, essentially establishing a form of vagrancy legislation through its severe contract restrictions and punishments for laziness and desertion.[81] The changing debates of the 1850s would be, however, another substantial subject.

The great writer on anti-slavery and Western culture, David Brion Davis, has commented with particular insight on linkages between the ideology of free labour and the British drive to abolish slavery. The South African case has proved him right on several points. The crucial piece of legislation affecting the status of the nominally free was passed in 1828 by a Tory government, in deliberately low-key fashion. The critical groundwork had been accomplished by a commission given the mandate to free up trade and labour flows, which had concluded that the bonded labour status of the Khoi, in personal thrall as they were to white farmers in the rural districts, vitiated the economic wellbeing of the colony. In the prevailing climate of enthusiasm about free labour and the revamping of old vagrancy and poor laws in Britain itself, those many British settlers in South Africa who wanted a return to the semi-free status of Hottentot labour could no longer draw directly on the 'state of nature' arguments which earlier administrators had used to design special laws for the Khoisan. Rather, they were compelled to turn to broader arguments about the control of criminality in order to preserve the liberty of a community as a whole. The abolition of slavery was a tremendous upheaval, which tore apart the Cape Colony: abolition had none the less been heralded some years beforehand in the debates over a group of people who were in theory already free.

The South African case also underscores Davis' argument that anxiety about ways of instilling self-discipline into the working poor accompanied the desire to free labour. The leading white South African proponents of the 'liberty' of the 'coloureds', John Philip, the Reads, Thomas Pringle and the journalist John Fairbairn, all envisaged ideal communities of working Khoi, settled as small-scale peasants and artisans and made prosperous through internalization of work discipline. They seized on Kat River as a utopian community precisely because it seemed to illustrate the internal transformation wrought by free labour and the unfettered right to own property. Indeed, John Fairbairn enthusiastically upheld the New Poor Law. His opposition to the vagrancy act in 1834 was partially based on his comparison of it with the Old Poor Law of Great Britain: it required vagrants and the poor to be taken care of at the public expense, even if in gaol and on public works projects, rather than forcing labourers 'freely' to follow work without a social safety net to make idleness an option. John Philip was less enthusiastic about the New Poor Law, and unlike Fairbairn seems to have become more 'radical' with age, rather than the converse; he too thought, however, that the Khoi ought to be left to depend on the free market.

The one area where the author would want to modify the now-standard account of the transition from slavery to a free labour economy would be to insert some account of the ambiguous enthusiasm of the once-enslaved for the free labour market. In the South African case in particular, recognition of the negative consequences of an unregulated market in free labour in a capitalist environment has muted for many historians the participation of Khoisan and ex-slaves in debates couched in liberal terms. At the time, as South African historiography tends not to recognize, liberalism itself was ambiguous and multi-faceted, and its economic ideology was fought over bitterly by many, including Khoisan and former slaves. This is not in any sense to imply that the Khoisan of Kat River and elsewhere did not suffer tremendously from a capitalist economy, particularly given its profound racial biases. These comments must also be placed side by side with awareness that freedom had a different set of meanings for the Khoisan than for white interlocutors in colonial debates, and was linked with particular intimacy to the restoration of land. None the less, in 1834, Khoisan fought passionately for the principle of 'free labour'. As Andries Stoeffels stated in 1834, 'We rejoiced at the very words freedom and free labour even before it was mingled with water and ground; and now that it is mingled with water and ground it is twenty times sweeter than forced labour.'[82] The day-to-day skirmishes of political argument were thus deeply ambiguous – but so too of course were the allegiances, beliefs and rhetorical participation in public debate of individuals across the faultlines of ethnicity.

ACKNOWLEDGEMENTS

I would like to thank the Social Sciences and Humanities Research Council of Canada for financial support. I would also like to thank Mohammed Mbodj, Catherine Desbarats, James Tully and Daniel Weinstock for reading and commenting helpfully on this article, and also Terence Ranger, Robert Ross and Stanley Trapio, the participants in the 1993 York University conference on 'Unfree Labour and the Development of the Atlantic World', and Leonard Thompson and other members in a panel at the 1992 American Historical Association meeting where I presented part of the current work in a rather different incarnation.

NOTES

1. The terms 'Khoi' and 'San' are used here as substitutes for the colonial terms 'Hottentots' and 'Bushmen', which were originally coined by the European invaders, and are now considered insulting by many. There is debate about the distinction between Khoikhoi and San; here I sidestep the problem by using the widely accepted amalgam 'Khoisan', which at least has the virtue of underscoring ethnic ambiguity. Throughout the nineteenth century the Khoisan were increasingly mingling with other ethnic groups, especially after the ending of slave apprenticeship in 1838. It is none the less the case that well past the mid-century point, a wide range of people, many of ethnically mixed backgrounds, described themselves as 'Hottentots', and mobilized politically around 'Hottentot' land rights and the defence of the 'Hottentot nation' until at least the Kat River rebellion of 1851. I therefore reproduce the term when it was used by the Khoisan themselves or by outside observers: not to do so hides issues of identity and nationalism which deserve to be investigated in their own right. 'Khoi' may be taken as a transliteration of 'Hottentot' in the historical record.

2. *South African Commercial Advertiser* (SACA) 6 Sept. 1834: 'Adjourned Public Meeting at Philipton, Kat River, resumed August 12th'. It is an unavoidable problem that all quotes from public meetings were transcribed from speech and then translated: the original comments were almost certainly made in Dutch or Khoi, although some Khoi were also conversant with English. Scribes of Khoi descent took minutes at the several public meetings held to protest at the reimposition of vagrancy legislation. There is a good chance that these minutes were fairly accurately transcribed: first, because speeches at public meetings were routinely written up for publication during this period; and, second, because the Khoi still had a strong oral culture and cultivated the skill of memorization – contrast reports of Xhosa messengers being able to repeat speeches verbatim. Some speakers (including Andries Hatha, cited below) read their speeches: these may have been transcribed directly into meeting minutes, but there is no way of knowing.

3. Cape Archives (CA) A50: 'Minutes of meeting held at Philipton', reprinted in SACA, 3 Sept. 1834: 'Report of a Meeting held at Philipton, Aug 5th, 1834, to consider the propriety of memorialising his Excellency the Governor and the Honorable the Legislative Council on the proposed Vagrancy Act'.

4. Council for World Missions Archives, School of Oriental and African Studies, London: London Missionary Society, South Africa Correspondence, 14/1/D, William Anderson to LMS, 17 July 1834 (henceforth annotated as LMS-SA 14/1/D).

5. LMS-SA 14/2/B: George Barker to LMS, 6 Oct. 1834.

6. Nigel Worden, *Slavery in Dutch South Africa* (Cambridge, 1985), pp. 7–8 and 34–6.

7. For an overview of processes in the VOC period, Richard Elphick and Robert Shell, 'Intergroup Relations: Khoikhoi, Settlers, Slaves and Free Blacks, 1652–1795', in R. Elphick and Hermann Giliomee (eds.), *The Shaping of South African Society, 1652–1840* (Middletown, Connecticut, 1988), pp. 184–239; R. Elphick and Hermann Giliomee, 'The Origins and Entrenchment of European Dominance at the Cape, 1652–1840', in ibid., esp. pp. 529–30.

8. Susan Newton-King and V.C. Malherbe, *The Khoikhoi Rebellion in the Eastern Cape*

(1799–1803) (Cape Town, 1981).

9. In theory, these children were saved by farmers from commando raids or other life-threatening situations.

10. MSS. Afr.s.1, Rhodes House, Oxford: Col. R. Collins to Alexandre du Pré, Lord Caledon, Governor of the Cape Colony, Cape Town, 30 May 1808.

11. Hannah More, *Village Politics* (London, 1793), p. 4.

12. Adam Smith, *Lectures on Jurisprudence*, edited by R.L. Meek, D.D. Raphael and G. Stein (Clarendon Press, 1978), p. 459; cited in Anand C. Chitnis, *The Scottish Enlightenment and Early Victorian English Society* (London, 1986), p. 2.

13. Smith, *Lectures*, p. 404; Chitnis, *Scottish Enlightenment*, pp. 2–7; John Millar, 'The Origin of the Distinction of Ranks', in William C. Lehmann (ed.), *John Millar of Glasgow 1735–1801: His Life and Thought and his Contributions to Sociological Analysis* (Cambridge, 1960); J. Marshall and Glyndwr Williams, *The Great Map of Mankind: Perceptions of the World in the Age of Enlightenment* (Cambridge, Mass., 1982). Cf also the general historicist thrust of Smith's account of the linkages between the development of economic institutions and the complication of society in *The Wealth of Nations*, Book 1 (Penguin edition, edited by Andrew Skinner, Harmondsworth, 1974), pp. 109–57.

14. Boyd Hilton, *The Age of Atonement* (Cambridge, 1988).

15. John Campbell, *Travels in South Africa Undertaken at the Request of the London Missionary Society; Being a Narrative of a Second Journey in the Interior of that Country* (London, 1822), p. 256. Cf also Martin Legassick, 'The Griqua, the Sotho Tswana and the Missionaries, 1780–1880: The Politics of a Frontier Zone' (unpublished Ph.D. thesis, University of California, 1969); Legassick, 'The Northern Frontier to c.1840: The Rise and Decline of the Griqua People', in Elphick and Giliomee, *Shaping*; Robert Ross, *Adam Kok's Griquas: A Study in the Development of Stratification in South Africa* (London, 1976).

16. *Evangelical Magazine*, Dec. 1803, p. 549.

17. Proclamation issued by the Earl of Caledon, Nov. 1809, given in full in 'Papers Relevant to the Condition and Treatment of the Native Inhabitants of Southern Africa, within the Colony of the Cape of Good Hope, or Beyond the Frontier of that Colony', Part I (London, House of Commons, 1835), reprinted by Irish University Press, *British Parliamentary Papers: Colonies, Africa*, Vol. 19, (Shannon, Ireland, 1970), pp. 459–60; also reproduced in John Philip, *Researches in South Africa* (London, 1828), Appendix II; Susan Newton-King, 'The Labour Market of the Cape Colony, 1807–28', in Shula Marks and Anthony Atmore (eds.), *Economy and Society in Pre-Industrial South Africa*, pp. 176–8. Irish University Press series of British Parliamentary Papers (henceforth BPP).

18. BPP, Accounts, no.584 (1830): 'Report upon the Hottentot Population of the Cape of Good Hope, and of the Missionary Institutions', p. 5. The poet and liberal activist Thomas Pringle testified in 1823 before the Commissioners of Inquiry as to the 'general exclusion of the Colour'd race from the rights of proprietors', with the only exception he knew being a 'free Malay named Fort who was building at Algoa Bay'. Public Record Office, London, CO 414, Vol.1, pp. 21–2.

19. BPP, *Colonies, Africa*, Vol. 19, p. 164.

20. Stanley Trapido, 'The Emergence of Liberalism and the Making of "Hottentot Nationalism", 1815–1834', Collected Seminar Papers of the Societies of Southern Africa seminar, Institute of Commonwealth Studies, London 1992.

21. Newton-King, 'Labour Market', p. 177.

22. Ibid., p. 177.

23. For example, CA A559, 'Statement of Missionary Grievances' (circa 1821).

24. LMS-SA 3/5/B: James Read to LMS, 30 Aug. 1808.

25. Orlando Patterson, *Slavery and Social Death* (Cambridge, 1982). For a more detailed discussion of frontier violence, see Elizabeth Elbourne, 'Concerning Missionaries: The Case of Dr. Van der Kemp', *Journal of Southern African Studies* (March 1991).

26. SACA, 6 Sept. 1834.

27. According to LMS official John Campbell, who was visiting the colony on a tour of inspection, 'most of the cases which came before the court could not be substantiated by *legal* evidence; for, according to the Dutch law, the oath of a Hottentot is inadmissable'. Future circuits would not have much business to attend to, 'till some law be made to admit instructed Hottentots to give evidence on oath; because, in the present state of the colony, it would be one of the most difficult things imaginable, to get one white man to witness against another, if it referred to any injury sustained by a Hottentot'; see John Campbell, *Travels in South Africa among the Hottentots and Other Tribes; In the Years 1812, 1813 and 1814* (London, 1815), pp. 344–5. Wayne Dooling's MA thesis at the University of Cape Town will show that Khoi witnesses were in fact accepted in courts under certain circumstances (Wayne Dooling, personal communication), but this would not be incompatible in my opinion with a particularly severe application of customary law in a situation in which exoneration was as crucial as this one, given that the commissioners of circuit had many local connections.
28. G.M. Theal (ed.), *Records of the Cape Colony (RCC)* vol.IX: 'Report of the Commission of Circuit for the Districts of Graaff-Reinet, Uitenhage and George', pp. 72 and 81.
29. RCC, IX: 'Report of the Commission', pp. 74–5.
30. RCC, Vol.IX, p. 56. Emphasis in original.
31. SACA, 6 Sept. 1834.
32. Richard Elphick, *Kraal and Castle: Khoikoi and the Founding of White South Africa* (New Haven and London, 1977; new edition, Johannesburg, 1985).
33. Elizabeth Elbourne, 'Early Khoisan Uses of Mission Christianity', *Kronos* (Feb. 1993).
34. Stanley Trapido, 'From Paternalism to Liberalism: The Cape Colony, 1800–1834', *The International History Review*, XII, 1 (Feb. 1990), pp. 76–104; Trapido, 'The Emergence of Liberalism'; J.B. Peires, 'The British and the Cape, 1814–1834', in Elphick and Giliomee, *Shaping*, pp. 472–518, esp. 490–99.
35. Peires, 'The British and the Cape', pp. 499–511.
36. 'Ordinance of His Honour the Lieutenant-governor in Council, for improving the condition of the Hottentots and other Free Persons of Colour at the Cape of Good Hope, and for consolidating and amending the laws affecting these persons', in BPP, Colonies, Africa, Vol.19, p. 169.
37. W.M. Macmillan, *The Cape Colour Question: A Historical Survey* (London and New York, 1968; first published 1927), pp. 211–32; Andrew Ross, *John Philip (1775–1851): Missions, Race and Politics in South Africa* (Aberdeen, 1985); Elizabeth Elbourne, '"To Colonize the Mind": Evangelical Missionaries in Britain and the Eastern Cape, 1790–1837' (D.Phil. thesis, Oxford, 1992), pp. 262–81.
38. John Barrow, *Travels into the Interior of Southern Africa. In which are described the character and condition of the Dutch colonists of the Cape of good Hope, and of the several tribes of natives beyond its limits* (London, 1806, 2nd ed.). Cf also the discussions in J.M.Coetzee, *White Writing in South Africa* (New Haven, 1988) and Jean and John Comaroff, *Of Revelation and Revolution* (Chicago, 1991) – although these commentators tend to downplay the violence being described by Barrow and in general fall prey to the temptation of treating an eyewitness account of atrocities as a description of the internal mental state of the commentator.
39. J.T. Bigge, William Colebrooke and W. Blair, 'Reports of the Commission of Inquiry: II. Upon the Finances at the Cape of Good Hope', in BPP, *Colonies: Africa*, Vol. 19, p. 385.
40. John Philip, *Researches in South Africa* (London, 1828).
41. LMS-SA 14/1/C: Philip to LMS directors, 12 June 1834.
42. SACA, 6 Sept. 1834. Commentary of Daniel Hans, 'Adjourned Public Meeting at Philipton, Kat River, resumed August 12th'.
43. Boyd Hilton, *The Age of Atonement: The Influence of Evangelicalism on Social and Economic Thought, 1785–1865* (Oxford, 1988), provides a provocative overview.
44. Richard Brent, *Liberal Anglican Politics: Whiggery, Religion and Reform 1830–1841* (Oxford, 1987).
45. Anthony Brundage, *The Making of the New Poor Law: The Politics of Inquiry,*

Enactment and Implementation, 1832–39, (London, 1978). pp. 76–7.

46. A point made forcefully by David Brion Davis, *Slavery and Human Progress* (Oxford and New York, 1984), pp. 122–3.

47. Davis, *Slavery and Human Progress*, p. 122.

48. For example, *The Anti-Slavery Reporter*, Vol. V, July 1832, pp. 222–3.

49. In 1829, for example, anti-slavery activist Lushington presented a petition on behalf of the free black and coloured inhabitants of the colonies, praying for the extension of the common rights and privileges of British subjects to this group. Murray responded that he was pleased to see petitions from particular groups and individuals in the colonies, and found it desirable that all freemen should have common advantages, but colonial opinion compelled him to proceed with caution. *Anti-Slavery Reporter*, Vol. III, June 1829, p. 16.

50. Edward Cox, *Free Coloreds in the Slave Societies of St. Kitts and Grenada, 1763–1833* (Knoxville, 1984), pp. 92–110, esp. 107.

51. SACA, 6 Sept. 1834. For a more critical view of the overall impact of Ordinance 50, Leslie Clement Duly, 'A Revisit with the Cape's Hottentot Ordinance of 1828', in M. Kooy (ed.), *Studies in Economics and Economic History* (London, 1972).

52. T.F. Buxton to Z. Macaulay, 4 Dec. 1835: Thomas Fowell Buxton papers, Vol. 14, pp. 176–85, Rhodes House, Oxford. Cf. also A. Tyrrell, 'The "Moral Radical Party" and the Anglo-Jamaican Campaign for the Abolition of the Negro Apprenticeship System', *The English Historical Review*, CCCXCII (July 1984), pp. 481–504, although Tyrrell misses the importance of concern over vagrancy legislation in his discussion of the relationship between Buxton and the 'moral radicals' who fought for unconditional abolition and the immediate cessation of apprenticeship.

53. A few Cape Town gentry, such as the astronomer Lord John Herschel and his wife, Margaret, who were in Philip and Fairbairn's circle, also opposed the act, while the attorney general and eventually Governor Dundas himself would come out against the proposition after some hesitation – possibly fortified by the advance knowledge that the act had been judged legally inadmissable by the Attorney General because it transgressed the second section of Ordinance 50.

54. LMS-SA 14/1/D: Anderson to LMS, Pacaltsdorp, 17 July 1834; Lady Margaret Herschel to Mrs. Stewart, 11 July 1835, in Brian Warner (ed.), *Lady Herschel: Letters from the Cape, 1834–1838* (Cape Town, 1991).

55. Although one of the organizers of the anti-vagrancy petition claimed that many of the signatories of the other petition did not realize what they had signed: 'I know not whether it is because they belong to the Government Church, or that it is, as many of them say, that they are not Hottentots, or that it is, as some of them have said, that they belong to the Government, and therefore cannot contradict the Government, even though it should do wrong; – but further I cannot find one that knows what he has signed. They say that no paper was brought forward and explained, and it seems they had no Dutch copy as we had. Thus some say that they have signed for more money for the nation, others say that they were told it was the Governor's letter, which was to be signed; and others of the people seem to be greatly at a loss'; see letter from 'Niet een van de tagtig', original version, *South African Commercial Advertiser*, 24 Sept. 1834; translation, SACA, 4 Oct. 1834.

56. As James Read, jr. would argue much later in *The Kat River Settlement in 1851: Described in a Series of Letters Published in the South African Commercial Advertiser* (Cape Town, 1852).

57. James Tully, 'Placing the Two Treatises', in N. Philipson and Q. Skinner (eds.), *Political Discourse in Early Modern Britain: Essays in Honour of John Pocock* (Cambridge, 1994).

58. 'Public meeting at Graaf Reinet, held June 21, with Joshua Joubert, JP, in chair', *Grahamstown Journal*, III, 134, 17 July 1834.

59. At a Grahamstown meeting to support the legislation. *Grahamstown Journal*, III, 133, 10 July 1834.

60. *Grahamstown Journal*, III, 142, 11 Sept. 1834.

61. 'Resolutions of the Council ... ', in 'Papers referred to in the evidence of the Rev. J. Philip, D.D. 11 July 1836', *Report from the Select Committee on Aborigines (British settlements) with the Minutes of Evidence, Appendix and Index*: Imperial Blue Books, 1836, nr. VII, 538 and 1837, nr VII, 425, 755–57.
62. John Philip, *Researches in South Africa* (London, 1828).
63. T.F. Buxton papers, Vol. 14, p.361, Rhodes House, Oxford: T.F. Buxton to Colonel Torrens, 27 Jan. 1836. Despite this explicit opposition to colonization in the early 1830s, Buxton later became involved in a problematic attempt at establishing a virtuous evangelical colony of recaptives and former slaves in West Africa.
64. LMS-SA 14/2/A, George Barker to John Campbell, 2 Oct. 1834.
65. Cape Archives, A50: 'Minutes of Meeting at Philipton'; reprinted, SACA, 3 Sept. 1834.
66. Trapido, 'Emergence of Liberalism'; Clifton Crais, *White Supremacy and Black Resistance: The Making of the Colonial Order in the Eastern Cape, 1770–1865* (Cambridge, 1992), p.84.
67. O. Nigel Bolland, 'The Politics of Freedom in the British Caribbean', in Frank McGlynn and Seymour Drescher (eds.), *The Meaning of Freedom: Economics, Politics, and Culture after Slavery* (Pittsburgh, 1992), p.139.
68. Cape Archives, CO 362, Incoming Correspondence from Agents and Missionaries in the Interior, 1828: Memorial to Sir Lowry Cole, n.d. Given the fact that many of the signatories were older men whose younger family members signed for them, there is a strong chance that the formal petition was drawn up by an English-speaking missionary (although not James Read, as the handwriting is not his), but there is no reason to suppose that the writer was not conveying the sentiments of the petitioners.
69. On Afrikaner views of land, tenure, Peires, 'The British and the Cape', pp.502–3.
70. LMS-SA 14/2/B: George Barker to LMS, 6 Oct. 1834.
71. CA A50, 'Minutes of a meeting' (also cited by Crais, *White Supremacy*, p.84).
72. LMS-SA 14/2/A, George Barker to John Campbell, 2 Oct. 1834.
73. Trapido, 'Emergence of Liberalism'; LMS-SA 14/2/B: Barker to LMS, 6 Oct. 1834. *White Supremacy*, p.84); LMS-SA 14/2/B: G. Barker to W. Ellis, Theopolis, 6 Oct. 1834.
74. The Memorial from Kat River stated *inter alia* 'that Memorialists cannot contemplate the immediate effects that this Act will have on the prosperity of this Settlement, in driving multitudes to this place for refuge, as it has done to the Missionary Institutions, by which they may be' eaten up and oppressed, and whom in their unfortunate circumstances, humanity will not allow them to turn away, without alarm'; SACA, 10 Sept. 1834. For a discussion of the long-term impact of the persistence of clientage in Kat River, and the problems of over-crowding which it created, see Tony Kirk, 'Progress and Decline in the Kat River Settlement, 1829–1854', *Journal of African History*, 14 (1973).
75. At the Kat River settlement, 'locations' subscribed *en masse* to the *South African Commercial Advertiser* and the *Grahamstown Journal*: in each village, individual copies were read aloud to groups gathered for the purpose.
76. LMS-SA 14/2/B: G. Barker to W. Ellis, Theopolis, 6 Oct. 1834.
77. As Clifton Crais has argued in *White Supremacy*, p.148.
78. SACA, 6 Sept. 1834.
79. W.M. Macmillan, *The Cape Coloured Question: A Historical Survey* (London, 1927).
80. Crais, *White Supremacy*, p.185; testimony of Windvogel from Cape Archives 1/FBF 1/ 1/2, stat. of Windvogel, 28 July 1851.
81. Crais, *White Supremacy*, p.194.
82. CA A50, 'Minutes of a Meeting at Philipton'.

Background to Rebellion: The Origins of Muslim Slaves in Bahia

PAUL E. LOVEJOY

The Muslim uprising in Bahia in 1835, known as the Malé revolt, provides an unusual opportunity to examine the background of enslaved Africans who were brought to the Americas during the era of the transatlantic slave trade. Virtually all of the slaves and former slaves who were responsible for the Malé revolt and another fourteen conspiracies, disturbances and uprisings that rocked Bahia between 1807 and 1835, came from the interior of the Bight of Benin. They included Hausa, Nupe, Kanuri and Yoruba, many of whom were Muslims.[1] An examination of the origins of these slaves and former slaves raises the issue of what specialists in African history can contribute to the study of slavery in the Americas. The present study is an attempt to counteract the continuing marginalization of Africa by historians of other parts of the world and contribute to a fuller appreciation of the background of people of African descent in the Americas.

We are a long way from the interpretation of Stanley Elkins that slavery was a form of cultural death through the trauma of the middle passage, but we are still largely left with 'people without history', whose background is not considered especially relevant to events in the Americas.[2] Enslavement may have involved the 'social death' of slaves at the time of enslavement, as Orlando Patterson has argued,[3] but even in the Americas, slaves were sometimes able to create a new social order that built on their backgrounds. Social and cultural institutions not only survived the middle passage but could be enhanced and reinterpreted in the context of slavery. This active transference of culture appears to have been the case in Bahia in the first half of the nineteenth century when two groups of Africans – Muslims from the Central Sudan and Yoruba, some of whom were Muslims – endangered one of the oldest and most important slave societies in the Americas.

In most studies of slavery in the Americas, a false polarity continues to characterize the study of Africa and the Americas. This polarity does not exist in the study of the relationship of the Americas to Europe. Slave masters are fully examined in the context of European history. The evolution of the economies, societies and cultures of the Americas is perceived in terms of European origins and an ongoing dialectic between developments in Europe and those in the Americas. The process of 'creolization' is understood to have involved such mutual interaction across the Atlantic, with slaves born in the Americas more or less pulled into a hybrid culture that was essentially Christian and European. Scholars argue over the extent to which the development of slave societies was associated with the rise of capitalism and the degree to which political discourse in the mother countries of the different colonies hinged on issues relating to slavery. Yet no one denies an active and continuing dialogue. By contrast, enslaved Africans are still largely considered to have been 'tribal' people, uprooted from their natal homes and thereby divorced from their historical origins, except for occasional 'survivals' that were more or less important in the evolution of slave communities under slavery but otherwise were unconnected with Africa.

This approach has impoverished slave studies, especially with respect to our understanding of the extent and forms of interaction between Africa and the Americas. This impoverishment is understandable in the sense that it is difficult to be a specialist on more than one area, especially crossing the Atlantic. Such is the difficulty of comparative history. The potential pitfalls in examining the African backgrounds of slaves and former slaves in Bahia will be readily apparent to both Africanists and specialists of Brazil, not to mention anyone who knows anything about historiography and historical methodology. This paper must rely on Brazilian experts for its understanding of what happened in Bahia between 1807 and 1835. This author is not an expert. There are even pitfalls on the African side, because this paper also suggests an interpretation of historical events in the Central Sudan and in the Yoruba interior of the Bight of Benin in the early nineteenth century which is in itself problematic. There is no consensus among specialists on the relative importance of the jihad as a factor in Central Sudanic history in the nineteenth century, for example, which is relevant to the discussion of Muslim resistance in Bahia. Nor do historians agree on the genesis of the Yoruba wars of the same period, which, this paper suggests, were more closely linked to the jihad than many Yoruba specialists would probably accept.

This study is problematic in another sense; it uses statistical data on the scale and direction of the transatlantic slave trade that is equally the subject of an ongoing debate. Scholars disagree on how best to apply the quantitative materials that have been assembled in deciphering ethnic and regional origins of slaves who were exported to the Americas. Our attempt to disaggregate the export data for the Bight of Benin in an effort to understand where, when and how slaves reached the African coast for sale to European slavers must thus be considered preliminary. Elsewhere, this author has argued that somewhere between fifteen and twenty-five per cent of slaves leaving the ports of the Bight of Benin in the first half of the nineteenth century came from the far interior – the Central Sudan.[4] A small sample of 108 slaves from the Central Sudan who were sold into the Atlantic slave trade will be analysed below (see Appendix), but this sample itself raises questions of reliability and representation. Chronologically, it includes individuals who were sold into the transatlantic trade in the decade after the 1835 Male revolt as well as slaves who were enslaved before that date. But this paper assumes, tentatively, that the patterns described below are not affected to any significant degree. Tying the tenuous pieces together to link events in the Bight of Benin interior with the uprisings and conspiracies of Bahia requires a degree of faith that will probably test the endurance of specialists and non-specialists alike. The string of events and forces may well break under the tension of closer examination.

Despite the risks and problems, this study addresses several key historical questions: how conceptions of ethnicity and identity evolved in the Americas under slavery; how religion, in this case Islam, contributed to the evolution of community among slaves and former slaves in the Americas; and how and to what extent historical developments in Africa were carried over into the Americas, specifically from the Bight of Benin to Bahia. These questions address the issues of agency and African 'survivals'; the active and passive behaviour of enslaved Africans in the Americas, not only in the narrow sense of resistance to slavery but in the broader sense of ethnicity, identity and community. In the case of Bahia, the culture and society of slaves and former slaves from the interior of the Bight of Benin were intimately connected with resistance. But our concern here is to go beyond a study of slave culture as largely manifestations of resistance to slavery. For Muslims in Bahia in the first half of the nineteenth century, Islamic affiliation was not merely a question of resistance; it often brought with it a commitment to religious and cultural behaviour that emerged from the political history of the Central Sudan. Muslims in Bahia drew no polarity between Africa and the Americas, as have many scholars; they belonged to *dar-es salaam*, the world of Islam. Their cultural heritage was not a set of 'survival' traits brought from Africa; rather Islam involved a way of life and a dedication to community that did not just surface in acts of resistance to slavery, but required the active transferral of culture from Africa and its continued evolution in the dramatically different context of slavery.

HISTORICAL BACKGROUND: BAHIA AND THE BIGHT OF BENIN

To examine the role of Muslims and non-Muslim Yoruba in the conspiracies and uprisings in Bahia between 1807 and 1835, it is first necessary to provide a brief overview of historical events in Bahia and in the interior of the Bight of Benin during this period. It is also important to examine the major characteristics of the trans-Atlantic slave trade between the Bight of Benin and Brazil, especially from the 1780s through the first several decades of the nineteenth century, when virtually all of the slaves and former slaves who were involved in the revolts and conspiracies arrived in Bahia. Once this overview is completed, we will examine the sample of 108 slaves from the Central Sudan who were sold into the transatlantic slave trade during this period in an effort to understand the broad patterns that governed the slaves and former slaves who have been identified with Bahian resistance.

Sugar production in Bahia expanded rapidly in the 1790s after revolution had destroyed the St. Domingue sugar industry. Although sugar had been the staple of the Bahian economy since the middle of the sixteenth century, the Caribbean islands had replaced Brazil as the leading area of sugar cultivation, leaving Bahia an economic backwater. To respond to the opportunity presented by the collapse of St. Domingue, Bahian planters imported tens of thousands of slaves from Africa, particularly from the Bight of Benin, to increase production.[5] In this way, Muslim slaves from the Central Sudan and Yoruba slaves from the interior of the Bight of Benin arrived in Bahia in substantial numbers. Among the newly imported slave population after 1791–92, prime adult males figured prominently; the proportion of adult males who had been born in Africa rapidly became a significant element in Bahia.

The demography of early nineteenth-century Bahia was peculiar in another respect. There was a substantial population of freed slaves in addition to a large number of slaves who had been born in Africa. According to João José Reis, the population of Bahia and the small, neighbouring province of Sergipe del Rey in 1824 was 858,000. Of these, 22.4 per cent were whites, 15 per cent were free blacks and mulattoes, and over 60 per cent were slaves, of whom a majority were African born.[6] Even African-born slaves were able to achieve emancipation through self-help cooperatives, lay brotherhoods, and other means.[7] As the conspiracies and revolts make clear, resistance in Bahia frequently crossed class lines; slaves and former slaves, especially within the Muslim community, collaborated in fighting the slavocracy. African birth and religion were sometimes more important than slave and free status.

Changes in the organization of the transatlantic slave trade after 1793 also affected developments in Bahia. As a consequence of war in Europe, French and Dutch slavers were driven from the high seas. After 1807, British and US ships also withdrew from the trade, leaving only the Portuguese to operate in the Bight of Benin. By the late 1810s, Spanish ships also purchased slaves in the Bight of Benin, but most of these went to Cuba. British pressure to end the transatlantic slave trade after 1807 made it difficult for other countries to operate between Africa and Bahia. Consequently, most of the transatlantic slave trade to Brazil during the period of the sugar boom was in the hands of Brazilian shippers, who virtually monopolized the trade of the Bight of Benin before 1820 and dominated the trade thereafter. Slaves were also imported from west-central Africa, but they were not a significant factor in the uprisings in Bahia. This pattern of trade was unusual in the history of the trans-Atlantic slave trade. The newly imported slaves of Bahia arrived on the ships of the same national carrier, with a heavy concentration from one section of the African coast, the Bight of Benin.

Despite the boom, Bahia was in turmoil between 1807 and 1835. Prosperity from sugar production collapsed under the political uncertainties of British pressures to end the transatlantic slave trade and the struggle for independence from Portugal, which was obtained in 1822. The large, African-born, predominantly male, population took advantage of this political and economic instability to organize the conspiracies and uprisings that earned Bahia the reputation of being the slave society with one of the most prolonged and intensive periods of aggressive slave resistance in the Americas. The economic boom in Bahia, subsequent to revolution in St. Domingue, gave birth to revolutionary conditions which culminated in the 'Male' revolt of 1835.

In the early nineteenth century, resistance in Bahia was concentrated within two overlapping groups of slaves and former slaves; those who identified as Yoruba and those who identified as Muslim. The two groups overlapped because some Yoruba were Muslim and some were not. Muslims from the Central Sudan included Hausa, Nupe, Kanuri and others associated with Borno and the Sokoto Caliphate. In the case of both groups – Muslims and Yoruba – the personal histories of the slaves and freed slaves who resisted the Bahian slavocracy reveal some similarities that were important factors in the conspiracies and revolts. Because virtually all the participants had been born in Africa and had arrived in Bahia on the same Portuguese-Brazilian ships, shipmates formed strong allegiances, and the ethnic backgrounds of slaves further consolidated these ties. There emerged a community of African-born slaves and former slaves in Bahia with the potential for revolt.[8]

The historical and cultural background of the slaves and freed slaves who were involved in the political disturbances between 1807 and 1835 facilitated not only the emergence of common bonds of community; it may also explain their propensity to revolt in the name of Islam. In the late eighteenth and early nineteenth centuries, the powerful state of Oyo dominated the export trade from the Bight of Benin.[9] Oyo funnelled slaves to ports on the Bight of Benin from the far interior, particularly in the 1780s and 1790s. Previously slaves from the interior had not been a significant factor in the export trade from this part of Africa.[10] Oyo continued to dominate the export trade from the Bight of Benin in the first two decades of the nineteenth century. Thereafter the cataclysmic events that resulted in the formation and expansion of the Sokoto Caliphate became a major factor in the trade. The previous state system of the Central Sudan – Borno, Nupe, and the Hausa states of Gobir, Kebbi, Katsina, Kano and Zaria – collapsed before militant Islam. Even Oyo fell to the jihad.[11]

Oyo's collapse in turn prompted the Yoruba wars, the incorporation of the old heartland of Oyo into the Sokoto Caliphate as the Emirate of Ilorin, and the creation of the new Yoruba states of Ibadan, Abeokuta and New Oyo, among others. The result was the export of tens of thousands of Yoruba slaves. As it happened, many slaves of the jihad and its subsequent and related wars found themselves concentrated in Bahia.

Islam was an important factor in the turmoil in Bahia, just as it had been in the interior of the Bight of Benin. Slaves from different ethnic backgrounds combined under the banner of Islam, forming a community whose members were known in Bahia as 'Male'.[12] In the first two decades of the nineteenth century, Hausa Muslims constituted the core of the Male community, although Nupe and Borno Muslims were also in evidence.[13] The revolts and conspiracies of 1807, 1809, 1812, 1816, 1826, as well as the 1835 Male revolt, were associated with Islam. Others sometimes were and sometimes were not. The evidence indicates that Hausa, Nupe, and Borno slaves and former slaves were able to subordinate ethnic loyalties in the interests of a larger identity.

The evolution of the Muslim community began well before the first conspiracy in 1807. Slaves from the Central Sudan, many of whom were probably Muslims, arrived in Bahia in considerable numbers only in the 1780s. Imports continued at a high level into the 1790s and first two decades of the nineteenth century, even though the volume of the slave trade from the Bight of Benin dropped off substantially after 1793, when Portuguese traders were the only European merchants operating there. Between 1800 and 1850, perhaps 75,000–124,000 slaves left the Central Sudan for the Americas, with a majority going to Brazil and especially Bahia.[14]

The predominance of Central Sudanic Muslims, especially Hausa, in the early Muslim population of Bahia had a strong influence on the development of Islam. Hausa, Borno and Nupe clerics assumed a much more influential position within the Muslim community than their numbers might suggest; even after Yoruba Muslims arrived in the late 1810s and the 1820s. Only in the 1820s did Yoruba Muslims become more numerous than Muslims from the Central Sudan. While some Yoruba were already Muslim before leaving Africa, many others appear to have converted to Islam only in Bahia itself, particularly after 1830. According to Reis, 'many of the fighters of 1835 were ardent recent converts'.[15]

The Yoruba community was divided along religious and cultural lines that were more or less permeable. While some were Muslims, others recognized common bonds based on language and traditional Yoruba religious institutions, especially worship of *orisha*. Because of the Yoruba wars, moreover, individuals from the various Yoruba sub-groups (Oyo, Egba, Ilesha, Ijebu, Yagba, among others) were not necessarily friendly with each other. The political divisions arising from conditions among the Yoruba in West Africa remained strong among this population, although the significance of this observation has yet to be explored in detail. Perhaps twice as many Yoruba were forced to move to Bahia as slaves than was the case for slaves from the Central Sudan. Because of their numbers, Yoruba culture, history and religious observance continued in Bahia, as it did in Cuba.

Muslims (including Yoruba and non-Yoruba) and Yoruba (both Muslims and non-Muslims) were overlapping and conflicting categories that competed for the loyalties of slaves and former slaves. Bahian society was complex in its entirety, with the population divided along racial, class and ethnic lines but often finding common interest across those same lines. The slave and former slave populations were no exception. As the interactions among Yoruba and Muslims demonstrates, ethnicity and religion were mixed, partially and incompletely, in the unique historical setting of Bahian society. Static perceptions of ethnicity have failed to capture the centrality of Africa in understanding why and how slaves identified as they did.

ORIGINS OF BAHIAN MUSLIMS

Virtually all of the Muslim slaves who were in Bahia came from the Central Sudan or the adjacent Yoruba country in the interior of the Bight of Benin, as noted above. This situation presents a rare opportunity. Biographical data have been compiled on 108 slaves from the Central Sudan who were destined for the transatlantic traffic in the first half of the nineteenth century (see Appendix, p. 176), which allows an analysis of the background of the Muslim population of Bahia. The sample is significant because it thrusts Africa into the foreground, thereby providing an example of how the false polarity between Africa and the Americas can be overcome. It is assumed that the sample is representative of the Muslim community in Brazil, and specifically that of Bahia, in the period leading up to the Male revolt of 1835.

This analytical technique is suggestive. Scholars have not used sociological methods to examine the African backgrounds of slaves in the Americas. It has generally been assumed that such data do not exist but, as this sample demonstrates, it is possible to generate such information. The biographical material in the sample allows us both to consider African participants of the Male revolt in a new light, specifically relating to their religious, ethnic and cultural identities, and how these changed under slavery and freedom in the Americas, and to address the question of agency in the development of African communities in the Americas.

Several assumptions have to be made in using this sample to explore the backgrounds of Muslim slaves in Bahia. First, it is assumed that the sample is representative of the age, sex and ethnicity of the exported population from the far interior of the Bight of Benin and that the slave population imported into Bahia from the Bight of Benin and the Central Sudan was characterized by the same age, sex and ethnic profile of this exported population. These are reasonable suppositions in the light of the recent research of David Eltis and Stanley Engerman, who have demonstrated that the demographic profile of the exported slave population from each coastal region of Africa tended to be transferred to all receiving areas in the Americas; that is, Bahia, other parts of Brazil, and Cuba, which were virtually the only receiving areas in the Americas after 1807, received cargoes of slaves from the Bight of Benin that shared the same demographic characteristics.[16] Destination in the Americas does not appear to have been a significant factor affecting the make-up of ship consignments of slaves. Consequently, it is reasonable to assume that my sample of 108 slaves is representative of the trans-Atlantic slave trade and the trade to Bahia for the period 1805–50.

It is known that approximately 94–95 per cent of the slaves exported from the Central Sudan to the Americas were males, and the great majority of these were adults, that is in their mid-teens or older. Furthermore, the great proportion of these prime adult males had been enslaved in the jihad, often because they were involved in the fighting, and hence a commitment to Islam and a tendency to promote conversion to Islam were fundamental attitudes of many of the slaves from the Central Sudan when they arrived in the Americas. The data allow a preliminary discussion of the relative proportions of Muslims and non-Muslims among exported slaves from the Central Sudan. It is clear that the tradition of conversion to Islam that was firmly entrenched in the Central Sudan was transferred to Bahia. This tradition involved the conversion of people from the Central Sudan who were not Hausa to Islam, thereby acquiring a 'Male' identity that was an outgrowth of the initial Hausa ascendancy. The ethnic origins of 'Male' identity shifted in the 1820s and early 1830s as Yoruba became predominant within the Muslim community.

The coalescence of a Muslim community of mixed ethnic background that included a Yoruba majority by 1835 demonstrates that many political issues current in West Africa were transferred to Bahia. Slaves and former slaves appear to have united along lines that had as much to do with their African backgrounds as with their plight in Bahia. Our sample provides a body of data that is useful in understanding the background of the Male community and the extent to which events in West Africa and in Brazil were interconnected even after imported slaves had been incorporated into the slave regime of Bahia.

Description of the Sample

The miscellaneous sample of 108 slaves from the Central Sudan between 1805 and 1850 is derived from interviews conducted by d'Andrada in Brazil in 1819, as reported by Menèzes de Drumond (eight observations), the crew of the 1841 Niger Expedition (six observations), slave narratives collected by de Castelnau in the late 1840s (23 observations), the linguistic inventory conducted by S.W. Koelle in Sierra Leone in 1850 (66 observations), and miscellaneous other sources (5 observations). Data on name, age, sex, method of enslavement, route taken from the Central Sudan to the sea and religion are included in the sample, which is summarized in the Appendix and is examined below.

The largest number of slaves were those interviewed by Koelle in Sierra Leone.[17] Koelle identified many liberated slaves from the interior of the Bight of Benin, including Igala (13), Nupe (303), Borno or Kanuri (36), Buduma (1), Fika (5), Karekare (2), Bede and Ngizim (16), Hausa (8), and Fulani (unknown number).[18] Hausa slaves were under-represented in his inventory because Koelle was trying to identify as many languages as possible and therefore contacted and enumerated smaller proportions of the larger linguistic communities. Hence, his data cannot be used to establish the relative importance of different ethnic categories in the exported slave population from the Central Sudan. In 1848 there were 657 Hausa and 163 Nupe in Sierra Leone; the total population being 13,273.[19] When combined with slaves from Borno and elsewhere in the Central Sudan, which we estimate at approximately 420, it is likely that there were at least 1,240 people from the Central Sudan in Freetown, or less than ten per cent of the liberated slave population.

In Brazil, Menèzes de Drumond, of Rio de Janeiro, published the digests of interviews with Hausa slaves in Brazil in 1826. The interviews were conducted in 1819 by M. d'Andrada, a former government minister and author of an essay on the geography of Portugal.[20] Since the slaves are referred to as 'his', it can be assumed that d'Andrada was their master. Unfortunately, de Drumond's data do not include information on non-Hausa slaves. Francis de Castelnau, the French consul in Bahia, interviewed his informants in the late 1840s. De Castelnau's sample includes Hausa and one Fulani cleric who came from Kano.[21]

Miscellaneous data include material from a British officer serving in Sierra Leone in 1821,[22] Clapperton's second expedition to the Sokoto Caliphate in 1826,[23] and the 1841 Niger River expedition.[24] The Niger expedition recruited former slaves in Sierra Leone to serve as interpreters. The Rev. Schön, the chaplain on the *Wilberforce*, who had lived in Sierra Leone for several years, lined up 'a large number of volunteers', from whom thirteen were selected to accompany the expedition as interpreters and agents. These included

> Ibu [Igbo], Kakanda, Yarriba [Yoriba], Bornu, Eggarah [Igala], Haussa, Nufi [Nupe], Benin [Edo], and Filatah [Fulani, Fulbe]; the latter was ... named Mahomed Lamina, the only one who had visited Timbaktuh [Timbuktu]. He was far superior to all the others in intelligence, having had a tolerable Mussulman education. He told us, that he had kept a journal in Arabic, of his former travels; but unfortunately, it was in the possession of his brother, who was away from Sierra Leone.[25]

These various biographies will almost certainly be supplemented by additional material gleaned from future archival research, but a preliminary analysis is useful in suggesting lines of enquiry that might profitably be followed.

Ethnicity

Because of the manner in which slaves or freed slaves were selected, the various samples cannot be used to determine the relative importance of different ethnic groups in the exported slave population. Koelle specifically sought out people who spoke different languages in the compilation of his linguistic inventory, and the samples from Brazil were directed specifically at Hausa slaves. Presumably, other ethnic backgrounds were often ignored in the Americas, and individual slaves tended to identify with one of the major ethnic labels, such as Hausa, Borno and Nupe. The relative proportions of ethnic groups as sources of slaves, therefore, have to be determined in other ways.

Evidence from Bahia indicates that Hausa, Nupe and Borno slaves and former slaves constituted a significant portion of the Bahian population in the first third of the nineteenth century. According to Reis, at least 15.8 per cent of all slaves and former slaves in Bahia in the mid-1830s had come from the Central Sudan. Reis examined the registers of manumitted slaves between 1819 and 1836 and a sample of urban slaves from 1820–35. Among those whose ethnic origins are known (2,441 individuals) were 385 individuals from the Central Sudan, of whom 252 were Hausa (10.3 per cent), 88 were Nupe (3.6 per cent), and 45 were from Borno (1.8 per cent). If Yoruba cast into the trade by the wars stemming from the Sokoto Caliphate are included in this total, the proportion of slaves from the Central Sudan and the expanding jihad from that region would have been higher still. Yoruba slaves and freed slaves constituted 28.6 per cent of the Reis samples (699 persons),[26] and it seems likely that many, if not most, of these slaves were products of the jihad or its aftermath. Because proportions of this magnitude could have been achieved only as a result of a steady import of slaves over the two or three decades before 1835, Central Sudanic slaves must have constituted a substantial proportion of slave exports from the Bight of Benin at that time.[27]

Gender and Age

As already noted, almost all the slaves exported from the Central Sudan who were sold into the transatlantic trade in the nineteenth century were males. This unusual pattern traced its origins to the eighteenth century, when slaves from the Central Sudan first became a recognized component of the trans-Atlantic slave trade. The inventories of eighteenth-century French plantations in the Caribbean, as studied by David Geggus, reveal that the proportion of males to females was 'exceptional' among Hausa slaves, 'very few of whose women entered the Atlantic trade'.[28] Almost 95 per cent of the 227 'Aoussa' and the 60 'Gambari' (the Yoruba term for Hausa) were males.[29] It is likely that the proportion of males among Hausa slaves imported into Bahia at the same time was similar.

The overwhelming preponderance of males among Central Sudanic slaves who were exported to the Americas continued into the nineteenth century. The Hausa slaves whom de Castelnau interviewed were employed in heavy labour at the time of or shortly after the Male revolt;

'la plupart sont employés à Bahia comme nègres de palanquin (cadeira)'.
Indeed 'il est au contraire très rare d'y rencontrer des femmes de leur
nation. Ils viennent à peu pres tous par la voie d'Onim [Lagos]'.[30]
According to Hugh Clapperton, who travelled through the Sokoto
Caliphate in the mid 1820s, 'the greater part of the young Male Slaves are
carried down and disposed of in the Bight of Benin'.[31] Young adult males
comprised 'the vast majority of southbound exports' from the Sokoto
Caliphate in the nineteenth century, according to David Tambo.[32] The
proportion of males in my sample of 108 slaves is 95.4 per cent male. Of
the 108 slaves, only five (4.6 per cent) were females, three adults and two
girls. The preponderance of males among the exported slave population
also characterized the northern Yoruba area.[33]

TABLE 1

AGES OF SLAVES EXPORTED TO THE AMERICAS FROM THE CENTRAL SUDAN

Category	Number	Percentage
'Adults'	30	31.9
Over 30	9	9.6
20–29	38	40.4
15–19	11	11.7
children	6	6.4
Total	94	100.0

Source: Appendix.

Male slaves from the Central Sudan were often seen on the West
African coast, and returned slaves from Brazil and elsewhere in the
Americas were also in evidence in the 1840s and later. Two Hausa men
who had been emancipated in Trinidad were in Freetown in 1837; they
moved to Badagry in 1839 along with a man from Nupe.[34] Male slaves
recruited by the Dutch on the Gold Coast for shipment to Indonesia as
soldiers for its colonial army also included Hausa, and there are other
examples of slaves and former slaves from the Central Sudan, all of whom
were males, on the West African coast.[35] Similar instances of female
slaves from the Central Sudan are rare.

The approximate ages of captives at the time of enslavement, as
estimated from my sample, confirms other observations that the exported
male slaves from the Central Sudan were almost entirely adults (Table 1).
For the 94 slaves whose ages can be estimated approximately, 30 (29 men
and one woman) were identified as 'adults' at the time of enslavement.
Since 23 of these were males who had been captured in battle, it is likely
that they were all in their late teens or twenties. The ages of an additional

38 slaves were 20–29 at the time of enslavement, while 11 were in their mid to late teens. Nine males over age thirty can also be identified, while only six children, two girls and four boys, appear in the sample.

The age and sex profile of the exported Yoruba population was much more balanced than that of the slave population from the Central Sudan (Table 2). Exported slaves from areas near the coast had a high proportion of females, ranging from 38 to 42 per cent. This exported population can be separated into three sections: Ewe/Fon, southern Yoruba and northern Yoruba. It is likely that the first two groups of exported slaves included a relatively balanced proportion of women, men and children but that the northern Yoruba had a higher proportion of prime adult males and lower proportions of women and children. Moreover, the age and sex profile of the slaves exported from the northern Yoruba country probably fell somewhere between the relatively balanced profile of the coastal zone and the extreme imbalance of the exported population from the Central Sudan. All nine slaves in a small sample of Yoruba who were resettled in Sierra Leone were males in their twenties or thirties, and eight were captured in the jihad, seized in one of the Yoruba wars or were kidnapped; the other man was sold for debt.[36]

These data confirm the impression gleaned from Bahian sources. The imported slave population from the Bight of Benin in the late eighteenth and early nineteenth centuries was heavily male, mostly adults. The further from the interior of West Africa that slaves had come, the more likely that this pattern prevailed.[37] Since distance from the coast was also correlated with the likelihood that slaves were Muslim, there appears to have been a high correlation between adult males and Islam as well.

TABLE 2

SEX RATIOS OF THE BIGHT OF BENIN SLAVE TRADE, 1800–66

Sex	Total	Coastal	Interior
Males	330,000	215–262,000	71–118,000
Females	164,000	158–160,000	4–6,000
Total	497,000	373–422,000	75–124,000
Percentage Male	67	58–62	95

Source: For sex ratios for the Bight and Benin as a whole, see David Eltis, 'Fluctuations in the Age and Sex Ratios of Slaves in the Nineteenth-Century Transatlantic Slave Traffic', Slavery and Abolition, 7 (1986), pp. 259, 264. The range of exports from the Central Sudan is calculated at 75,000–124,000; see Paul E. Lovejoy, 'The Central Sudan and the Atlantic Slave Trade', in Robert W. Harms, Joseph C. Miller, David S. Newbury and Michelle D. Wagner (eds.), Paths to the Past: African Historical Essays in Honor of Jan Vansina (Atlanta, 1994). Figures are rounded to nearest thousand.

Patterns of Enslavement

The overwhelming majority of slaves from the Central Sudan were not only prime adult males, but most were also seized in war or raids associated with the jihad. It has previously been observed that slave raiding and enslavement through military engagements associated with the jihad were extensive, but the conscious enslavement of males for export to the Americas has not been appreciated fully.[38] According to one British officer in Sierra Leone in 1821, 'many natives from Houssa, who have been made prisoners by the Foulahs [Fula, that is, Fulani or Fulbe] and [have] been brought overland to the Gold Coast', were subsequently sold to European slave traders.[39] Data from my sample indicate that these slaves were prime males often taken in battle.

TABLE 3

METHOD OF ENSLAVEMENT IN THE CENTRAL SUDAN:
PROFILE OF MALE SLAVES EXPORTED TO THE ATLANTIC COAST

Category	Number	Percentage
Kidnapped	12	15
War/jihad/raiding	62	76
Judicial	3	
Pawning	3	
Sale of domestic slave	1	10
Tribute payment	1	
Total	82	100

Source: Appendix.

In the case of 82 slaves whose method of enslavement is known (Table 3), 62 (75.6 per cent) identified their enslavement with war, Fulani raids, or the jihad specifically. Another 12 slaves (14.6 per cent) had been kidnapped, which may or may not have been related to the jihad. In a few cases, war appears to have been related to secondary or related engagements on the frontiers of the Sokoto Caliphate. Taken together, 90.2 per cent of slaves reported that they had been violently seized.

The correlation between the high percentage of enslavement through violence and the prevalence of adult males in the enslaved population that was exported is suggestive. As noted above, prime males also were common among northern Yoruba exports, although not among Yoruba as a whole. The wars and raids of Nupe and Ilorin appear to have accounted for a significant proportion of these slaves. In some cases, captives had been soldiers, and a few were Muslim clerics, who were often involved in the jihad, which also indicates an adult population. The consolidation and expansion of the Sokoto Caliphate had the effect of producing a pool of adult male slaves for the Americas, many of whom either acquired or were able to transfer a commitment to Islam from the Central Sudan to Bahia.

Judicial enslavement, pawning, the sale of a domestic slave, and the transfer of a slave as part of the payment of tribute account for the other 10 per cent of slaves whose histories are known. While it is likely that many slaves were not directly connected with the jihad, some of the judicial and other forms of transfer may have been a byproduct of the Muslim campaign. It should be noted that the data do not usually distinguish among situations in which Muslim forces were enslaving non-Muslims and Muslim enemies of the Sokoto Caliphate and when soldiers and other Muslims associated with the Caliphate itself were captured. Certainly many Muslims who supported the jihad were among the exported slaves.

While there is only one case in the sample of a slave being sold for judicial reasons, it appears that the sale of domestic slaves accused of violent crimes was a common form of punishment. The few women who were sent to the Americas included slaves suspected of murder, as Clapperton learned in Kano in 1826. When a merchant from Ghadames was found strangled in his bed, several of his concubines who were suspected of the crime were sent to the coast for sale to the Americas. According to Clapperton, 'It had been customary, in cases of this kind, to send the perpetrators of similar crimes to the sea-coast, to be sold to the slave-dealers.'[40] Prime female slaves were not usually exported south. Most female exports went north across the Sahara, but 'criminals' were clearly a separate category.

Brief accounts of other slaves who entered the trans-Atlantic slave trade indicate that many Muslims were deported, sometimes because they were kidnapped, seized by bandits or otherwise enslaved. Clapperton's slave, Pasko, whose real name was Abubakar, was originally from Gobir; he was taken in war during the jihad 'and sold to a Gonja trader', who then sold him to 'a native of Ashantee' who sold him in turn to a trader going to Whydah, where he eventually found himself on a Portuguese ship.[41] Dan Kano, whose name indicates that his family was from Kano, was 'born at Brinee Yawoori [Birnin Yauri] and was there about sixteen or seventeen years ago [before April 8, 1821]'. He was seized by Fulani while on a trading expedition 'and carried to the Gold Coast', where he was sold to a Portuguese ship, probably in the Bight of Benin.[42] Koelle's informants included Ofen or Sam Pratt, whose birth name was Yasgua, born in Nduro. At age 22 he was sold by the chief of the town and in about 1843 was taken to the sea via Asante. Nduro was located seven days from Rabba, east of Goali [Birnin Gwari ?], south-west of 'Hausa', between Kambali [Kambari] country and Nupe.[43] Another of Koelle's informants was Habu, or Sam Jackson, who was born in Kano, seized sometime in the 1840s in a Gobir raid when he was 20 and sold south to Lagos. There was also Mohammadu from Katsina. He was seized by Fulani raiders while working on his farm, then sold in Gobir, taken to Damagaram, and then sent south to Rabba and Ilorin before reaching the coast, probably at Lagos, in the 1840s.[44]

Sarjeant Frazer, serving in the 2nd West India regiment in Sierra Leone in 1821, was born in Hausaland 'and resided there a long time, [before being] taken prisoner in Goingia [Gonja], and brought to the Gold Coast, where he was sold'. Frazer had been a merchant who dealt in natron from Borno.[45] Ali Eisami was seized during the jihad in Borno, taken through the Sokoto Caliphate, and eventually sold in Katunga, the Hausa name for the capital of Oyo. His master sold him to the coast in 1817 because he feared that his slave might become involved in the slave uprising against Oyo in that year.[46] One of de Castelnau's informants was Boué [Bawa ?], who had come from Zaria, apparently in the 1830s or 1840s, taken to Asante, where he was eventually sold to European, probably Portuguese, slavers. De Castelnau reports that most Hausa slaves reached the coast at Lagos, not the Gold Coast, which suggests that Boué found his way back to Whydah or some other port on the Bight of Benin.[47]

The six slaves whom d'Andrada interviewed in 1819 had come from either Nupe or the Hausa region, and all six had been taken prisoner during the jihad and had passed to the coast at Lagos ('Ico'). François was from Kano; Abubakar, alias Guillaume Pasco, was from Katsina; Mathieu was from Daura; Joseph was from Tabarau in Nupe; Bernard was from Gobir; Benoit was from Gaya [Ghuiah]; and Boniface from Kebbi.[48] As prisoners of the jihad, they may not all have been Muslims, but it is likely that they were, at least nominally.

As Clapperton reported from Wawa in Borgu in 1826, 'the slaves sold to the sea coast are generally those taken in war or refractory and intractable domestic slaves. Nyffé at present is the place that produces the most slaves, owing to the civil war raging in that country.'[49] That war was the jihad and eventually resulted in the overthrow of the old aristocracy and the establishment of an Islamic government under the Sokoto Caliphate. Abali, who was born in Kanem, was seized during a Borno raid on Kano, and from there was sold south to Lagos in 1844.[50] Another slave, born in Kano, was captured in a raid on Gobir, 'where he was bought by slave-dealers, and at once carried to the sea by way of Kadzina [Katsina], Zalia [Zaria], Nupe, Ilori [Ilorin], Dsebu [Ijebu], and Eko [Lagos]', also in 1844.[51] Similarly, Mohammadu, alias Jacob Brown, was kidnapped while farming, sold to Damagaram but ultimately reached the coast via Rabba and Ilorin, arriving in Sierra Leone in 1844.[52]

Religious Affiliation of the Exported Enslaved Population

The names of the slaves in the sample provide a preliminary indication of the religious affiliation of the exported, male population of the Central Sudan. Of the 108 slaves, 41 (38 per cent) had Muslim, or what appear to be Muslim, names (Table 4). Some of these slaves also had Christian names given to them by their Brazilian owners. Three others were clearly Muslims, and another 13 were probably Muslim, based on their stated origins. Thirty-nine slaves were referred to by African names that do not seem to have been Muslim. Many of these also had a Christian name, and 12 slaves were listed under Christian names only or no names but were probably not Muslims, based on their stated origins. Although there is no way of knowing how many of the slaves with non-Muslim African names were in fact Muslims or how many slaves with Christian and African names were Muslims, it seems reasonable to conclude that at least 52.8 per cent of the slaves exported from the Central Sudan to the Americas were Muslims. The percentage was probably much higher.

While this analysis of religious affiliation of slaves and former slaves from the Central Sudan is preliminary, it appears that the process of conversion which was underway in the Central Sudan as a result of the jihad continued in Bahia. Names such as 'Keuta' [Kyauta] 'So-Allah' [Sai Allah ?] were common names given to non-Muslim slaves by Muslim masters in the Central Sudan. Such names also indicate that slaves were

TABLE 4

SLAVES EXPORTED FROM THE CENTRAL SUDAN TO THE GUINEA COAST
RELIGIOUS IDENTIFICATION, 1805–50

Names of Slaves	Number	Percentage
Muslim names	41	38.0
Muslim, no name	3	2.8
Probably Muslim	13	12.0
Non-Muslim African names	39	36.1
No indication; no names given, Christial name only	11	11.1
Total	108	100

Source: Appendix.

instructed in the rudiments of Islam. African names that are clearly not Muslim in genesis include Ogbaleye, clearly Yoruba, Odiemi, Adsoro, and others.

Among the slaves and former slaves who were tried for their involvement in the 1835 Male revolt were a number of Muslim clerics. The slave Antonio, for example, was of Hausa origin and had been to Qur'anic school before being captured.[53] Reis has provided the fullest study of these clerics, while Nina Rodriguez collected information on the *imam*, Malam Abubakar, who appears to have led the revolt.[54] Samuel Crowther, himself a freed slave of Yoruba origin, met two liberated Hausa slaves from Brazil at Badagry in 1845. One, Mohama, was a *malam*, with whom Crowther became engaged in a lengthy theological discussion.[55] The French consul in Bahia, de Castelnau, also found out the extent of learning among the Muslim clerics from the Sokoto Caliphate. In 1848, Muhammad Abdullahi described himself as Fulani from Kano. He had been in Bahia for 30 years, having been taken in battle during a campaign against Maradi, the independent Hausa enclave north of Katsina. According to de Castelnau,

> This old man, Mohammed-Abdullad, Filani, who has been in Bahia some thirty years, freed himself from slavery by his work, and today is a carpenter. He is educated and not only knows how to read and write in his language, but also in Portuguese. Moreover, he is very intolerant, very fanatical, and he wants to convert me by all means; and even though I treated him very well, gave him money etc. he refused to come back to my house, telling another Negro that he did not want to go to the house of a Christian dog. He might be seventy years old. He was a *marabout* and had made the voyage to Mecca. ... He makes a lot of fun of the Hausas saying that they grow goatee beards in order to look like men. ... The Hausa Negroes at my house seem to have a great deal of respect for this man and, following his example start to mutter in chanting the verses of the Koran.[56]

The Arabic texts, amulets and other documents seized after the 1835 revolt included the crude writings of students as well as more sophisticated passages from the Qur'an.[57] The presence of mosques and Qur'anic schools was noted by authorities at the time. As the activities of Muslim clerics make clear, resistance was cast in a religious mould that was transferred directly from Africa to Bahia in the first half of the nineteenth century. Nina Rodriguez, himself of African descent, concluded in 1900 that the ideology of jihad was the basis of resistance in Bahia, and this author tends to concur.[58]

CONCLUSION

Bahian slave-owners faced a complex series of problems in controlling their slave population between 1807 and 1835. Resistance was inherent in the institution of slavery, as Eugene Genovese has recognized,[59] but a simple model based on pre-revolutionary and post-revolutionary Europe and North America is misleading. As Jack Goody has observed, the Bahian case does not fit into Genovese's model of slave resistance in the Americas.[60] The internal contradictions within slavery allowed slaves to establish their own communities, maintain a sense of identity as cultural beings, and otherwise resist the incursions of the master culture into their lives. African factors were essential in this quest for autonomy. As John Thornton has argued, Christian practices in syncretic form that arose in Africa might have helped shape the slave communities of the Americas.[61] Similarly, this paper argues that African Islam was a formative influence in Bahia.

The historical context in which specific groups of slaves moved to the Americas has to be taken into consideration in any attempt to understand the evolution of slave culture and society. Because it is often difficult to identify the ethnic, religious and cultural origins of slaves, historians of slavery in the Americas have had trouble examining their importance in the evolution of slave culture. In some cases, however, obvious links between Africa and the Americas emerge clearly. Such is the case of Bahia in the early nineteenth century. Seldom have the data revealed a correlation between slave resistance and the African backgrounds of those in rebellion with such clarity.

The evolution of a Male identity reflected the influence of the ideological and political struggle in Hausa society at the turn of the nineteenth century. When Hausa slaves began to arrive in sufficient numbers to establish a community and redefine their identity under slavery, they brought with them the experience of the political turmoil that preceded the jihad in the Central Sudan. The recognition of Muslims as a community was a controversial factor underlying this turmoil, and when Gobir and other Hausa states tried to regulate the activities of Muslims, even enslaving man of them, the violent reaction manifested itself in the form of jihad. Enslavement of Muslims was another. Ironically, the jihad did not end the export of Muslim slaves to the Americas. New arrivals after the outbreak of the jihad reinforced this link between Africa and the Americas. Muslim identity emerged as the dominant loyalty among Hausa, and by extension to slaves from neighbouring Borno and Nupe. People of other ethnic backgrounds, especially those from the Central Sudan, appear to have been absorbed into the Muslim community, whether or not they had been Muslims before leaving Africa.

The influx of Muslim Yoruba resulted in the 'Yoruba-ization' of the Muslim community, although the correlation between Yoruba ethnicity and Islam was never total because many Yoruba were not Muslims. It seems that Yoruba slaves and former slaves sometimes behaved on the basis of ethnic background and at other times responded as Muslims. In certain contexts, there was solidarity on the basis of Yoruba identity that resulted in a coalition between Muslims and non-Muslim Yoruba, but on other occasions Yoruba resistance was associated with *orisha* worship and especially the *ogboni* cult. Hence, there were two traditions of revolt in Bahia – one Muslim and one based on *orisha*, the first being trans-ethnic and the second being ethnic.[62]

Bahian slave masters had to contend with an imported slave population, whether Muslim or non-Muslim, that was prone to revolt and military action. Many slaves from the Bight of Benin were imbued with a military tradition based on religious solidarity and a commitment to holy war. Other slaves from the same region had suffered as a result of militant Islam and the failure of non-Muslims and less-militant Muslims to combine in effective opposition to jihad. Despite these conflicting backgrounds, slaves from the Bight of Benin coalesced into a community capable of sustaining a tradition of resistance. The slaves and former slaves who were engaged in the conspiracies and uprisings between 1807 and 1835 searched for a strategy of resistance that might result in a safe return to Africa, the formation of autonomous communities in Brazil, or the overthrow of the slave regime. They came closest to achieving the destruction of the established regime on the basis of Islam in 1835.

The ethnic, age and gender profile of the exported population of the Bight of Benin makes it possible to throw new light on the debate over the role of religion and ethnicity in the various conspiracies and uprisings in Bahia between 1807 and 1835. These revolts followed a pattern that suggests strong similarities with the jihad that was underway in the Central Sudan during the same years. In 1835, there was a flag, the use of amulets, the wearing of white Muslim robes, identification by Muslim names, group prayers led by an imam, and the staging of the revolt at the end of the month of Ramadan.[63] Similarly, the Muslim uprising against Afonja in 1817 may well have inspired many slaves in Brazil. As Pierre Verger has observed, the conspirators in both Ilorin and Bahia used silver rings as a means of identifying sympathizers.[64]

The attitude of Muhammad Abdullahi, the Fulani cleric from Kano whom de Castelnau interviewed in 1848, reveals this conscious and clear link with the jihad. As discussed above, Muhammad Abdullahi had made the pilgrimage to Mecca, had fought in the jihad, was seized by enemies of the Sokoto Caliphate, and was deported to Bahia in about 1817 as a result. Other Muslims held him in great respect.[65] There is no question, therefore, that the Muslim leadership was knowledgable of and probably supportive of the jihad. It is inconceivable that this background not only informed the discourse of revolt in 1835 but helped shape the actions of the Muslim community.

The congruence of demand and supply factors created an explosive situation. The demand for prime males to be used in heavy physical labour was met through the importation of Muslims, but the concentration of adult males who were war prisoners, often with military training and experience, was dangerous, especially when they were united by a militant ideology. Government officials and slave-owners in Bahia debated policies on how best to prevent another St. Domingue revolution without recognizing that the jihad in the Central Sudan, the military uprising by slave soldiers in Ilorin in 1817 and the continued involvement of these slaves in Oyo politics in the 1820s were more likely models for action than St. Domingue. The concentration of too many prime males kept Bahian slave society on the edge of revolt. The slavocracy was deceived by ethnic rivalries in a situation in which Islam proved to be a powerful force in overcoming ethnic divisions.[66]

Rarely in the history of slavery has it been possible to correlate the trajectories of the home societies of slaves and the slave regime in the Americas to which the exported slaves were subjected. In the case of the Bight of Benin and Bahia in the nineteenth century it is possible to trace large numbers of slaves from capture in Africa to rebellion in the Americas, a path that follows the slaves from the Central Sudan and the Yoruba country to the Bight of Benin and across the Atlantic to Bahia, where their occupations, culture, and religious observances are reasonably well known. When the background of the Bahian slave population is examined in this fashion, the reasons for revolt and the ability to organize resistance to the slavocracy of Bahia become clearer than might otherwise be possible.

ACKNOWLEDGEMENTS

I wish to thank Louise Lennihan, Nicholas Rogers and Joseph C. Miller for their comments. This paper was presented at the African Studies Center, Boston University, 1 April 1994.

NOTES

1. The literature on the Bahian uprisings of the early nineteenth century is extensive; see Stuart B. Schwartz, *Sugar Plantations in the Formation of Brazilian Society, Bahia,*

1550–1835 (Cambridge, 1985); João José Reis, *Slave Rebellion in Brazil: The Muslim Uprising of 1835 in Bahia* (Baltimore, 1993); Reis, 'Slave Resistance in Brazil: Bahia, 1807–1835', *Luso-Brazilian Review*, 25, 1 (1988), pp. 111–44; and Reis and Paulo F. de Moraes Farias, 'Islam and Slave Resistance in Bahia, Brazil', *Islam and sociétés au sud du Sahara*, 3 (1989), pp. 41–66; Clovis Moura, *Reblioes da Senzala* (São Paulo, 1959); Luis Luna, *O Negro na Luta Contra Escravidao* (Rio de Janeiro, 1967); Raymond Kent, 'African Revolt in Bahia', *Journal of Social History*, 3 (1970), pp. 334–56; Howard Prince, 'Slave Rebellion in Brazil, 1807–1835' (Ph.D. thesis, unpublished, Columbia University, 1972); Katia M. de Queirós Mattoso, 'Os escravos na Bahia no alvorecer do século XIX: Estude de um grupo social', *Revista de Historia*, 47, 97 (1974), pp. 109–35; and Pierre Verger, *Flux et reflux de la traite des Nègres entre le golfe du Bénin et Bahia de Todos os Santos du 17ᵉ et 18ᵉ siècles* (The Hague, 1968), which has been translated as *Trade Relations between the Bight of Benin and Bahia, 17th–19th Century* (Ibadan, 1976), which is the edition used here.

2. Stanley Elkins, *Slavery: A Problem in American Institutional and Intellectual Life* (Chicago, 1964).

3. Orlando Patterson, *Slavery and Social Death: A Comparative Study* (Cambridge, Mass., 1982).

4. Paul E. Lovejoy, 'The Central Sudan and the Atlantic Slave Trade', in Robert W. Harms, Joseph C. Miller, David S. Newbury, and Michele D. Wagner (eds.), *Paths to the Past: African Historical Essays in Honor of Jan Vansina* (Atlanta, 1994).

5. For an overview, see Schwartz, *Sugar Plantations*. Between 1800 and 1850, the total number of slaves imported into Bahia was 301,500; see Reis, 'Slave Resistance in Bahia', p. 115; and David Eltis, 'Welfare Trends among the Yoruba in the Early Nineteenth Century: The Anthropometric Evidence', *Journal of Economic History*, 50, 3 (1990), 538. According to Eltis, *Economic Growth and the Ending of the Transatlantic Slave Trade* (New York, 1987), pp. 243–4, slave imports into Bahia were as follows:

1786–90	20,300	1821–25	23,700
1791–95	34,300	1826–30	47,900
1796–1800	36,200	1831–35	16,700
1801–5	36,300	1836–40	15,800
1806–10	39,100	1841–45	21,200
1811–15	36,400	1846–50	45,000
1816–20	34,300	1851–55	1,900

6. Reis, 'Slave Resistance in Bahia', p. 114. These figures do not add up to 100 per cent, which Reis does not explain.

7. On the lay brotherhoods, see Patrica Mulvey, 'The Black Lay Brotherhoods of Colonial Brazil' (Ph.D. thesis, unpublished, City University of New York, 1976).

8. For example, ethnic origins of 177 slaves on four separate slave ships dating to 1821–22 included 41 Nupe, 34 Hausa, 1 Fulani, or 42.9 per cent, of those whose ethnic origins were stated; see Sierra Leone slave registers, FO 84/9 and 15, as cited in Eltis, *Economic Growth*, 358 fn.

9. Robin Law, *The Oyo Empire, c. 1600–c.1836: A West African Imperialism in the Era of the Atlantic Slave Trade* (Oxford, 1977), pp. 220, 227.

10. Patrick Manning, *Slavery and African Life: Occidental, Oriental, and African Slave Trades* (Cambridge, 1990); Manning, *Slavery, Colonialism and Economic Growth in Dahomey, 1640–1960* (Cambridge, 1982); Manning, 'The Slave Trade of the Bight of Benin, 1640–1890', in Henry A. Gemery and Jan S. Hogendorn (eds.), *The Uncommon Market: Essays in the Economic History of the Atlantic Slave Trade* (New York, 1975); and Lovejoy, 'Central Sudan and the Atlantic Slave Trade'.

11. Law dates the uprising of Hausa slaves in Ilorin to 1817; there was subsequent unrest as a result of runaway slaves, the destruction of Osugun by Fulani and Oyo Muslims in 1821; and Afonja, the Oyo ruler of Ilorin was overthrown in 1823–24. In addition, the

important centre of Owu fell in 1822, which was followed by the destruction of the Egba towns. Further unrest followed in the 1830s with a series of wars staged from the new Oyo base at Ibadan, including the invasion of the Egbado district, which had been an important province of Oyo. See Law, *Oyo Empire*, pp. 246–7, 250–60, 275–6. Also see Schwartz, *Sugar Plantations*, p. 475 for an appreciation of these events by a Brazilian expert. For the routes to the coast, see Lovejoy, 'Central Sudan and Atlantic Slave Trade'; Mahdi Adamu, 'The Delivery of Slaves from the Central Sudan to the Bight of Benin in the Eighteenth and Nineteenth Centuries', in Henry A. Gemery and Jan S. Hogendorn (eds.), *The Uncommon Market* (New York, 1979), pp. 163–80; Paul E. Lovejoy and Jan S. Hogendorn, 'Slave Marketing in West Africa', in Gemery and Hogendorn, *Uncommon Market*, pp. 221–31; and Joseph E. Inikori, 'The Sources of Supply for the Atlantic Slave Exports from the Bight of Benin and the Bight of Bonny (Biafra)', in S. Daget (ed.) *De la traite à l'esclavage du Ve au XIXeme siècle; Actes du Colloque International sur la traite des Noirs, Nantes 1985* (Nantes and Paris, 1988), II, pp. 25–43.

12. The etymology of the term 'Male' has confused scholars; see Reis, *Slave Rebellion in Brazil*, pp. 96–7. Apparently the first use of the term was in 1704 to refer to Muslim merchants from the interior who were on the coast in the Bight of Benin; see Robin Law, *The Slave Coast of West Africa, 1550–1750. The Impact of the Atlantic Slave Trade on an African Society* (Oxford, 1991), p. 188, citing the unpublished report of Labat. Also see Paul E. Lovejoy, *Caravans of Kola. The Hausa Kola Trade 1700–1900* (Zaria and Ibadan, 1980), p. 34, where the 'Malais' on the Dahomey coast in the early eighteenth century are identified with the Muslim Wangara merchants of Borgu, not Hausa; Mahdi Adamu, *The Hausa Factor in West African History* (Zaria and Ibadan, 1978), pp. 113–15, who discusses the Malayes or Malais as Hausa. In 1726, W. Snelgrave, *A New Account of Some Parts of Guinea and the Slave Trade* (London, 1734), p. 80, described the Malayes as merchants who came from 'a nation far inland bordering on the Moors'; they were literate and there were about 40 of them. It should be noted that *imale* was the Yoruba term for Muslims, and variations of the term, with different suffixes and a phonetic shift from 'l' to 'r', were used by the Asante (Marabu) and the Fon (Maremu or Malemu). According to oral traditions collected by Adamu, they were associated with the eighteenth-century Hausa state of Zamfara; see *Hausa Factor*, p. 115. According to William Smith, 'it is not uncommon to find a *Malayan* and sometimes two among a parcel of slaves' brought to the coast early in the eighteenth century; see *A New Voyage to Guinea* (London, 1744), p. 136.

13. The leadership of the abortive 1807 conspiracy was Hausa, while the count of Ponte, the governor, referred to 'slaves principally of the Hausa nation who with total disregard and resistance to the laws of slavery have become revolutionaries and disloyal'. In 1813 there was a plot among Hausa dockworkers. See Schwartz, *Sugar Plantations*, pp. 480, 482, 483.

14. Lovejoy, 'Central Sudan and Atlantic Slave Trade'.

15. Reis, 'Slave Resistance in Bahia', p. 127.

16. David Eltis and Stanley L. Engerman, 'Was the Slave Trade Dominated by Men?' *Journal of Interdisciplinary History*, 23 (1992); also see 'Fluctuations in Sex and Age Ratios in the Transatlantic Slave Trade, 1663–1864', *Economic History Review*, 46, 2 (1993), pp. 308–23.

17. Sigismund Wilhelm Koelle, *Polyglotta Africana* (Graz, 1963), pp. 8–18.

18. Koelle, *Polyglotta Africana*, pp. 1–21; P.E.H. Hair, 'Koelle at Freetown: An Historical Introduction', in *Polyglotta Africana*, pp. 7*–17*; Hair, 'The Enslavement of Koelle's Informants', *Journal of African History*, 6 (1965), pp. 193–203. Numbers in brackets include reported population of each language group.

19. Philip D. Curtin, *The Atlantic Slave Trade: A Census* (Madison, 1969), p. 244. Curtin, who compiled the census from Parliamentary Papers, 1849 [C.1126], includes Nupe recaptives under the Bight of Benin and Hausa recaptives under the Bight of Biafra, although it is likely that most Hausa slaves travelled through ports in the Bight of Benin, not the Bight of Biafra.

20. Menèzes de Drumond, 'Lettres sur l'Afrique ancienne et moderne', *Journal des Voyages*, 32 (1826), pp. 203–5.
21. François de Castelnau, *Renseignements sur l'Afrique centrale et sur une nation d'hommes à queue qui s'y trouverait, d'après le rapport des nègres du Soudan, esclaves à Bahia* (Paris, 1851).
22. Muhammad Misrah, 'Narrative of a Journey from Egypt to the Western Coast of Africa, by Mahomed Misrah. Communicated by an Officer serving in Sierra Leone', *The Quarterly Journal* (Oct. 1822), 6, pp. 15–16.
23. Richard Lander, *Records of Captain Clapperton's Last Expedition to Africa* (London, 1830), I, pp. 204, 206.
24. William Allen and T.R.H. Thomson, *A Narrative of the Expedition sent by Her Majesty's Government to the River Niger in 1841, under the Command of Captain H.D. Trotter, R.N.* (London, 1848), II, p. 184.
25. Allen and Thomson, *Narrative of the Niger Expedition*, I, pp. 178–9.
26. Reis, *Slave Rebellion in Brazil*, p. 140.
27. Curtin, *Atlantic Slave Trade*, pp. 244–9, 289–98. Also see Philip D. Curtin and Jan Vansina, 'Sources of the Nineteenth-Century Atlantic Slave Trade', *Journal of African History*, 5 (1964), pp. 185–208. For Hausa and Nupe former slaves in Sierra Leone, see Christopher Fyfe, *A History of Sierra Leone* (London, 1962), pp. 66, 138, 170, 231, 234, 424 (Hausa), and 170, 231, 289, 293, 320 (Nupe).
28. David Geggus, 'Sex Ratio, Age and Ethnicity in the Atlantic Slave Trade: Data from French Shipping and Plantation Records', *Journal of African History*, 30 (1989), p. 36.
29. Geggus, 'French Records on the Atlantic Slave Trade', 36.
30. De Castelnau, *Renseignements sur l'Afrique centrale*, p. 9.
31. Clapperton to R. Wilmot Horton, 6 June 1825, in E.W. Bovill (ed.), *Missions to the Niger, IV. The Bornu Mission, 1822–25, Part 3* (London, 1966), IV, p. 774.
32. David C. Tambo, 'The Sokoto Caliphate Slave Trade in the Nineteenth Century', *International Journal of African Historical Studies*, 9, 2 (1976), pp. 204–5.
33. According to Elits, 'the adult male ratios of the Yoruba and Nupe slaves in the 1821–2 Sierra Leone sample [of freed slaves] are exceptionally high'; *Economic Growth*, 358 fn.
34. Fyfe, *History of Sierra Leone*, p. 212.
35. Among other sources, see Joseph Raymond LaTorre, 'Wealth Surpasses Everything: An Economic History of Asante, 1750–1874', Ph.D. thesis, Berkeley, 1978, p. 420; Lovejoy, 'Central Sudan and the Atlantic Slave Trade'; Allen and Thomson, *Narrative of the Niger Expedition*, p. 226, refer to 'a native of Bornu, [who] had been sold when a boy by the Nufi traders ... [and subsequently] taken by the Filatahs in one of their predatory excursions'.
36. Koelle, *Polyglotta Africana*.
37. This confirms the findings of Eltis and Engerman, 'Fluctuations in Sex and Age Ratios', p. 313, 'male ratios were likely to rise and child ratios to fall with the length of the interior trade route', although they do not include the Central Sudan in their analysis.
38. See, for example, Michael Mason, 'Population and "Slave Raiding" – The Case of the Middle Belt of Nigeria', *Journal of African History*, 10, 4 (1969), pp. 551–64 and Jan Hogendorn, 'Slave Acquisition and Delivery in Precolonial Hausaland', in R. Dumett and Ben K. Schwartz (eds.), *West African Culture Dynamics: Archaeological and Historical Perspectives* (The Hague, 1980), pp. 477–93.
39. Misrah, 'Narrative of a Journey', p. 14.
40. Clapperton, p. 171
41. Lander, *Captain Clapperton's Last Expedition*, I, pp. 204, 206.
42. As cited in Misrah, 'Narrative of a Journey', p. 6.
43. Koelle, *Polyglotta Africana*, p. 19.
44. Ibid., p. 17.
45. As reported in Misrah, 'Narrative of a Journey', pp. 15–16.
46. See the biography of Ali Eisami, who was seized during the jihad in Borno, in H.F.C.

Smith, Murray Last, and Gambo Gubio (eds.), 'Ali Eisami Gazirmabe of Bornu', in Philip D. Curtin (ed.), *Africa Remembered: Narratives of West Africans from the Era of the Slave Trade* (Madison, 1967), pp. 202, 211–12.

47. De Castelnau, *Renseignements sur l'Afrique centrale*, p. 40.
48. Menèzes de Drumond, 'Lettres sur l'Afrique', pp. 206–16.
49. Clapperton, 1826, 2nd journey, p. 94.
50. Koelle, *Polyglotta Africana*, p. 10.
51. Ibid., p. 17.
52. Ibid.
53. João José Reis, 'Slave Rebellion in Brazil: The African Muslim Uprising in Bahia, 1835' (Ph.D. thesis, unpublished, University of Minnesota, 1983), pp. 146–7; also see Reis, *Slave Rebellion in Brazil*, pp. 102–3.
54. According to the imam of Salvador in the 1890s, the imam at the time of the revolt was Abubakar, which is a Hausa name; see Raymundo Nina Rodrigues, *Os Africanos no Brasil* (São Paulo, 1932), pp. 109–10. Nina Rodrigues based his study on notes collected between 1890 and his death in 1906. Also see Verger, *Trade Relations*, pp. 300, 307. Reis discusses other clerics whom he considers were likely to have been the leader but does not include Abubakar as a candidate; see *Slave Rebellion in Brazil*, p. 130.
55. Adamu, *Hausa Factor*, p. 132, citing 19/5/45; CMS: CA2/031/(b). Crowther, in his journal entry for 12 June 1846, stated that he and Townsend went to Badagry, 'to see the extension of Indian corn, beans, groundnuts, and cassava belonging to the Hausa people. Since last month, I have visited many similar plantations. All this cultivation began this year because when we arrived here [in the middle of 1845] there was no sign of cultivation anywhere in or around Badagry'; CMS, Yoruba Mission, CA2/031(b), as cited in Adamu, *Hausa Factor*, p. 128.
56. De Castelnau, *Renseignements sur l'Afrique centrale*, 46. Also see Verger, *Trade Relations*, p. 287.
57. See Jack Goody, 'Writing, Religion and Revolt in Bahia', *Visible Language*, 20 (1986), pp. 318–43; Vincent Monteil, 'Analyse de 25 documents arabes des Malés de Bahia (1835)', *Bulletin de l'Institute Fondamentale d'Afrique Noire*, sér. B, 29, 1–2 (1967), pp. 88–98; and Rolf Reichert, 'L'insurrection d'esclaves de 1835 à la lumière des documents arabes des archives publiques de l'état de Bahia (Bresil)', *Bulletin de l'Institute Fondamaentale d'Afrique Noire*, sér. B, 29, 1–2 (1967), pp. 99–104.
58. Nina Rodrigues published his preliminary analysis of the importance of Islam among slaves in *O Jornal do Commercio* of Rio de Janeiro on 2 Nov. 1900; see Verger, *Trade Relations*, pp. 285–86. For a fuller analysis, see Nina Rodrigues, *Os Africanos no Brasil*, pp. 93–120. For similar conclusions, see Verger, *Trade Relations*, pp. 294–308. For a critique of the conclusions of Nina Rodrigues and Verger, see Reis, *Slave Rebellion in Brazil*, pp. 120–28.
59. Eugene Genovese, *From Rebellion to Revolution: Afro-American Slave Revolts in the Making of the New World* (New York, 1979). Also see Michael Craton, *Testing the Chains: Resistance to Slavery in the British West Indies* (Ithaca, 1982).
60. Goody, 'Writing, Religion and Revolt in Bahia', p. 331.
61. John Thornton, *Africa and Africans in the Making of the Atlantic World, 1400–1680* (Cambridge, 1992).
62. The 1820s witnessed ten uprisings in Bahia and five in neighbouring Sergipe de El-Rey in which Yoruba slaves and former slaves were involved; see Schwartz, *Sugar Plantations*, pp. 486–7.
63. Nina Rodriguez, *Os Africanos no Brasil*, pp. 93–120; also see Verger, *Trade Relations*, pp. 294–309; Reis, *Slave Rebellion in Brazil*, pp. 115, 117. Withdrawal to the fugitive slave settlements (*quilambo*) that surrounded Salvador should also be noted. Such a withdrawal is consistent with the *hijra*, although there is no evidence that rebels perceived the *quilambos* in this manner.
64. Verger, *Trade Relations*, p. 304; Reis, *Slave Rebellion in Brazil*, p. 104.
65. De Castelnau, *Renseignements sur l'Afrique centrale*, p. 46.
66. According to Duncan, who was at Whydah in the mid-1840s, 'the country ten or twelve

miles round Whydah is very interesting, the soil good, land level, and in many places well cultivated by people returned from the Brazils. . . . I learnt that many of them were driven away from Brazil on account of their being concerned in an attempted revolution amongst slaves there, who turned against their masters. These people are generally from the Foola [Sokoto Caliphate] and Eyo [Oyo] countries. Many, it appears, were taken away at the age of twenty or twenty four years – consequently they can give a full account of their route to Badagry, where they were shipped'; see John Duncan, *Travels in Western Africa, in 1845 and 1846* (London, 1847), I, 64, pp. 185–6.

APPENDIX

PROFILE OF SLAVES EXPORTED FROM THE CENTRAL SUDAN, 1805–1850

Name	Origin	Method of Enslavement	Date of Export	Route to sea	Age of Enslavement
Boniface[1]	Kebbi	jihad	1804–8	Lagos	adult
Benoit[1]	Gaya	jihad	1804–8	Lagos	adult
François[1]	Kano	jihad	1804–8	Lagos	adult
Abubakar,[1] Guillaume Pasco	Katsina	jihad	1805	Lagos	adult
Mathieu[1]	Daura	jihad	1804–8	Lagos	adult
Bernard[1]	Gobir	jihad	1804–8	Lagos	adult
Mama,[3] John Tanner	Nupe	war prisoner of Fulani	1816	Lagos	35
Joseph[1]	Nupe	jihad	before 1818	Lagos	adult
Mohammad Abdullah[2]	Kano	jihad	c.1818	Lagos	adult
Musa Massause[3]	Gwari	civil war	1818	via Egba	24
'Ali Eisami[3] William Harding	Kanuri	Fulani raid	1818	'Aku' Yorubaland	25
Elifo, Peter Mamma[3]	Nupe	sold, probably pawn	1820	Lagos	25
Mahammad, Manuel[2]	Katsina	war prisoner	c.1820	Lagos	20s
Kolo, John Gerber[3]	Igala	Fulani raid	1821	Lagos	27
Ogbaleye, Thomas Johnson[3]	New Oyo	kidnapped by Fulani	1822	Lagos	25
William Dala[3]	Bedde	Fulani raid	1830	'Yoruba'	28
Karo, Manuel[2]	Borno	war prisoner	1830s?	Lagos	adult
Robo,[3] George Macauley	Yagba	war prisoner of Nupe	1835	Lagos	20s
Aeta,[3] Joseph Wilhelm	Yagba	war prisoner of Yoruba	1835	Lagos	adult
Aba-Hama[2]	Borno	war prisoner	before 1840s	Lagos	adult

Soleman[2]	Borno	war prisoner	before 1840s	Lagos	adult
Ali[2]	Borno	war prisoner	before 1840s	Lagos	adult
Aboubakar[2]	Bagirmi	kidnapped	before 1840s	Lagos	adult
Mammarou[2]	Muniyo Borno	war prisoner	before 1840s	Lagos	adult
Kiwa[2]	Zamfara	war prisoner	before 1840s	Lagos	adult
Meidassara[2]	Kano	war prisoner	1840s, earlier	Lagos	adult
Wuene,[3] William Cole	Borgu	war with Ilorin	1842	Yoruba	25
Mahammah Manuel[2]	Kano	war prisoner	c.1842	Lagos	adult
Odiemi,[3] James Wilhelm	Gori, NE Yoruba	Nupe and Fulani raid	1840s, earlier	Lagos	28
Adam, Braz[2]	Zaria	war prisoner	1840s?	Lagos	adult
Habu,[3] Samuel Jackson	Kano	war prisoner	1846	Lagos	20
Muhammadou, Jacob Brown[3]	Katsina	kidnapped	1846	Ilorin	20s
Abali[3]	Kanem	war prisoner	1846	Lagos	22
Gol, Thomas Klein[3]	Bute	war captive of Fulani	1847	Lagos	19
unknown	Bute	war captive of Fulani	1847	Lagos	young boy
unknown	Bute	war captive of Fulani	1847	Lagos	young girl
So-Allah, David[2]	Tangali	child slave (pawn ?)	1850	Lagos	10
Osman, Francisco[2]	Shira	kidnapped	1850	Lagos	20s
Grusa, Augusto[2]	Zaria	domestic slave	1850	Lagos	adult
Dan Kano[4]	Birnin Yauri	Fulani raid	1804	Asante	adult
Abubakar, Pasko[4]	Gobir	war prisoner	c.1807	Asante	unknown
Sarjeant Frazer[4]	Hausa	kidnapped	before 1820	Asante	adult
'Runaway Slave'[4]	Borno	unknown, kidnapped	before 1841	Asante	unknown
Yasqua Ofen, Sam Pratt[3]	Gwari	sold by chief	1843	Asante	22
Hardou,	Katsina	captured	before	Nupe	adult

Elias[2]			1840s	[Asante ?]	
Boue,[2] Antonio	Zaria	war prisoner	1840s, earlier	Nupe, Asante	adult
Keauta[3]	Kambari	kidnapped by Fulani	1816	Rabba	26
Arogu, James Jones[3]	Yagba	war prisoner of Fulani	1836	Rabba	20s
Rescou[2]	Nupe	Hausa raid	1840s, earlier	Rabba	adult
Segbara, Thomas Cocker[3]	Basa	war prisoner	1843	Rabba	24
Lamadsi, John Smith[3]	Gwari	kidnapped, Fulani raid	1847	Rabba	47
Adsi, John Man[3]	Mbarike	war captive	1824	Niger R.	40s
Adsofe, William Davis[3]	Bunu	kidnapped	1824	Niger R.	20s
Sobori, John Pratt	Esitako	Fulani raid	1826	Niger R.	22
Abutso, John Second[3]	Afudu	seized in slave raid	1828	Niger R.	24
Johnson[5]	Idah	unknown	before 1830s	Niger R.	unknown
Adsoro[3]	Igbira	kidnapped	1830	Niger R.	22
Soraga, Thomas Cocker[3]	Boritsu	kidnapped	1830	Niger R.	23
Disile, John Cocker[3]	Tiv	war captive	1830	Niger R.	adult 4 wives
Ali Here[5]	Hausa	unknown	before 1831	Niger R.	unknown
Atumei, Thomas Davis[3]	Igbira	taken in war	1831	Niger R.	30
Wosandse,[3] John MacCormack	Kupa	dispute, sold	1835	Niger R.	married 15 yrs
Ako, George Hall[3]	Igbira	adultery	1835	Niger R.	30–35
Ate, Andrew Parker[3]	Basa	kidnapped	1837	Niger R.	adult 3 wives
Macaulay[5]	Nupe	kidnapped by Fulani	before 1840	Niger R.	unknown
Yono, William Macauly[3]	Bfut	war captive of Fulani	1825	Calabar	18
Ndanga, John Harding[3]	Bakum	war captive of Fulani	1827	Calabar	20s
Mbepe, James John[3]	Ngoala	war captive Fulani raid	1827	Calabar	18
Awazi, Henry Johnson[3]	Burukim	war captive of Fulani	1828	Calabar	20

Kamsi, John Thomas[3]	Balu	war captive of Fulani	1832	Calabar	20
Sise, John Cole[3]	Bagba	war captive of Fulani	1835	Calabar	30
Mehemmet[2]	Kano	jihad	c.1810	unknown	20
Gambo, Thomas King[3]	Ngodsin	unknown	1810	unknown	20s
Muhammadu[3]	Gobir	kidnapped	1810	unknown	17
Andya, William Price[3]	Jukun	unknown	1810	unknown	16
Damoutourou[2]	Borno	jihad	1810s	unknown	adult
Francisco[1] (malam)	Hausa	unknown	1810s	unknown	adult
Sikari, Thomas Sawyer[3]	Musu	unknown	1820	unknown	20
Bilan, Andrew Rikett[3]	Karekare	unknown	1820	unknown	17
Ndsu, John Macauly[3]	Jukun	war prisoner	1821	unknown	17
Batia, John William[3]	Borgu	civil war	1822	unknown	20s
Antonio[4]	Hausa	unknown	before 1835	unknown	unknown
male[5]	Kakanda	unknown	before 1840	unknown	unknown
male[5]	Borno	unknown	before 1840	unknown	unknown
Mahomed Lawina[5]	Fulani	unknown	before 1840	unknown	unknown
male[3]	Bedde	unknown	before 1840s	unknown	young boy
female[3]	Bedde	unknown	before 1840s	unknown	young girl
female[3]	Bedde	unknown	before 1840s	unknown	adult
male[3]	Fika	unknown	1840s, earlier	unknown	unknown
male[3]	Fika	unknown	1840s, earlier	unknown	unknown
female[3]	Fika	unknown	1840s, earlier	unknown	unknown
female[3]	Fika	unknown	1840s, earlier	unknown	unknown
Griss, Quacho[2]	Lafia	war prisoner	1840s, earlier	unknown	adult
Bague[2]	Nupe	unknown	1840s, earlier	unknown	adult

Ibrahim[2]	Hausa	unknown	1840s	unknown	young man
Abarsi, Andrew Aitkin[3]	Tuareg	kidnapped	1843	unknown	28
Ali, Moses Twin[3]	Bedde	unknown	1844	unknown	17
Madsinda, Thomas Cocker[3]	Kamuku	pawn	1844	unknown	25
male[3]	Fika	unknown	1845	unknown	23
male[3]	Fika	unknown	1846	unknown	29
Made[3]	Muniyo	kidnapped	1846	unknown	20s
Dsetham, George Harding[3]	Jaba	war prisoner	1846	unknown	23
Gbala, Sam John[3]	Koro	war prisoner	1846	unknown	19
Abare, Andrew Sewell[3]	Karekare	unknown	1846	unknown	18
Albarka[3]	Jarawa	tribute payment	1847	unknown	12
Adamu, Edward Klein[3]	Kano	war prisoner	1847	unknown	20s
Momadu, Robert Dixon[3]	Nguru	unknown	1847	unknown	26
Ali[3]	Muniyo	unknown	1840s, earlier	unknown	unknown

Sources: 1. Interviews conducted by d'Andrada, as reported in Menèzes de Drumond, 'Lettres sur l'Afrique ancienne et moderne', *Journal des Voyages*, 32 (1826), pp. 205–16.
   2. François de Castelnau, *Renseignements sur l'Afrique centrale et sur une nation d'hommes à queue qui s'y trouverait, d'après le rapport des nègres du Soudan, esclaves à Bahia* (Paris, 1851). François de Castelnau, the French consul, interviewed his informants in the late 1840s.
   3. Sigismund Wilhelm Koelle, *Polyglotta Africana* (Graz, 1963), pp. 8–18.
   4. Miscellaneous data includes data from *Clapperton's Last Expedition to Africa*, I, pp. 204, 206; Information on two slaves is included in Muhammad Misrah, 'Narrative of a Journey from Egypt to the Western Coast of Africa, by Mahomed Misrah. Communicated by an Officer serving in Sierra Leone', *The Quarterly Journal* (Oct. 1822), pp. 6, 15–16. William Allen and T.R.H. Thomson, *A Narrative of the Expedition sent by Her Majesty's Government to the River Niger in 1841, under the Command of Captain H.D. Trotter, R.N.* (London, 1848), II, p. 184, also refer to a runaway slave from Kumasi at Cape Coast, who effectively made the trip to the coast, although he was not exported.
   5. Freed slaves on the Niger Expedition of 1841, as reported in Allen and Thomson, *Narrative*, I, pp. 79, 252, 330; II, pp. 117–18.

Part III

Aftermath of Abolition

The Transition from Slavery to Migrant Labour in Rural Brazil

NANCY PRISCILLA NARO

During his journey to colonial Brazil, the British traveller John Luccock observed a rural order where the planter class ruled rural society, semi-nomadic landless freemen effectively occupied the margins or boundaries of alienated land, and slave labour sustained the rural order.[1] At the time of his travels, in the decade following the arrival of the Portuguese monarch and the court at Rio de Janeiro in 1808, the hinterland of Rio de Janeiro was undergoing rapid settlement in response to increasing international demand for coffee. The 'first phase' of the coffee economy expanded into the sparsely settled forested Western Paraíba Valley, including eastern São Paulo and rural Rio de Janeiro, where it reached its heyday in the 1840s and 1850s. By the 1870s the 'first phase' was showing signs of economic reversal but the 'second phase' was at its height in the Eastern Paraíba Valley. A decade later, coffee production extended to the north-eastern tip of Rio de Janeiro province where the cycle lasted until the 1940s.

Coffee in the nineteenth century was Brazil's leading export product and accounted for the expansion of the plantation complex in South Central Brazil. The plantation complex is defined by Philip D. Curtin as 'the economic and political order centering on slave plantations in the New World tropics'.[2] This paper argues that the conventional idea of the plantation complex holds up in general but takes no account of important processes in the coffee economy that developed in the Fluminense region from about 1820 to 1940. Slave labour was the preferred form of labour on prominent coffee estates during the initial and dynamic phases of coffee expansion. However, in the aftermath of the suspension of the trans-atlantic slave trade to Brazil in 1851, important changes in slave family units and the increasing incorporation of the free non-white population into the coffee economy during slavery established the bases for the social relations of production that characterized the post-emancipation plantation complex.

Throughout the Paraíba Valley, the suitability of high altitudes, cool temperatures and hillside cultivation for coffee production contributed to the emergence of a dominant plantation arrangement associated with the *fazenda*.[3] The migration and settlement of the first generations of planter families and their slave and free labour forces are an unwritten chapter in the history of migration and, given the nature of overland and river travel in the early nineteenth century, was probably fraught with unexpected challenges brought on by climate changes, disease, death and isolation, similar to those recorded in the letters of migrants who moved west and south-west in the United States.[4]

Access to land and labour were vital factors in the expansion of the coffee economies. Throughout the colonial period, official crown land grants, called *sesmarias*, had been issued to court favourites from Lisbon. In the decade after 1808, speculation over the nascent international coffee market generated demand for official land grants in the mountainous regions west of Rio de Janeiro. Detailed analysis of the social status and nationality of the land grant recipients has not been done, although it is known that migration into the Paraíba Valley originated from the exhausted mining areas of Minas Gerais and from the expanding court city of Rio de Janeiro. Official land grantees, their families and free and unfree labour forces settled choice areas near the Paraíba River and its tributaries. Foreign travellers, who did not account for how land was acquired by their landowning hosts, did observe that those landowners consented to the presence of semi-nomadic landless freemen on the margins or boundaries of alienated land as buffers to potential land claimants.[5] Opportunities for settlement on fertile land and assurances of cheap labour from the transatlantic slave trade from Africa also attracted unofficial claimants and fortune-seekers who squatted on and effectively cultivated unoccupied stretches of public and private land and made their livelihood by the provision of foodstuffs and services not readily available in areas of recent settlement.

Under the dictates of the 1850 Land Law and the regulatory statutes of 1854, squatters could claim and register those public lands that they had effectively cultivated. Although the 1850 Land Law restricted purchase of public lands to moneyed interests, post-mortem inventories and legal cases from a number of Fluminense *municípios* reveal that land was easily transferred through sale, inheritance or exchange.[6]

Official and unofficial claimants to land co-existed as long as land was abundant. By the 1850s the uncontrolled production and expansion of coffee had moved into areas dedicated to small scale production of basic staples for the regional market.[7] The comparatively higher price of coffee also led foodstuff producers to convert from subsistence production to the more lucrative production of coffee.[8] By mid-century, planters were complaining of the prohibitive local costs of foodstuffs and one Vassouras planter was commissioning corn and beans from his factor in Rio de Janeiro.[9] The French traveller, Charles de Ribeyrolles, entreated Brazilians to preserve the sources of nutrition and not be bound by the immediate gains offered by coffee:

> Brazilians, do not look down upon the pig, or vegetable dye plants or the silkworm, or the bee or the banana. Plants, fruits and animals may be lesser priorities but they are nourishing; one only drinks coffee at dessert. ... Ah, but, coffee sells so handsomely![10]

THE SLAVE POPULATION

The frequent uprooting and the constant replacement of the African and Brazilian slave populations to satisfy the demand for abundant cheap labour were integral parts of the plantation complex. When the trans-atlantic slave trade all but ended in the 1850s, the slave population was unable to maintain its numbers through natural reproduction. The low ratio of females to males, infrequency of marriage and family life, poor and unsanitary food and housing and a customary disregard for slave progeny were among the reasons why deaths exceeded births among slaves in Brazil.[11] By 1874 slaves were 10 per cent of the total population of the North-East, 16 per cent of the extreme North, 15 per cent of the West and South, and 22 per cent of the centre South. Of Brazil's entire population of 9,761,449, approximately 16 per cent were enslaved.[12] In the leading coffee *municípios* (towns and their surrounding rural areas) of Rio de Janeiro, steady supplies of slave labour coming from the North-East of Brazil in the 1850s and from the city of Rio de Janeiro in the 1860s and 1870s fed the demands of the Fluminense regional slave markets. Abrupt declines in the slave population at the Court and in the capital city of Rio de Janeiro from 100,000 in 1864 to half that number, 47,084, a decade later, may be explained by inaccurate population counts, but could also be attributed to manumission of urban slaves and to the effects over time of the cholera epidemic of the 1850s and related diseases. In light of the higher prices offered for slaves in the highland coffee-producing areas in this period, it seems plausible that slave-owners in the Court were selling excess labour to the highlands plantations of the interior.[13]

Two ongoing trends in population movement accompanied the expansion of the coffee economy in the Paraíba Valley. The first was the shift of the slave population from the lowlands foodstuffs-producing *municípios* to the highlands coffee export areas in response to increasing demand and rising prices for male slaves. The continuous supply of male slaves to the highlands coffee *municípios* during the decade prior to emancipation is revealed by the sex ratio of 123:100 for the *município* of Vassouras, one of the foremost producers of coffee for the foreign market. This represents a marked contrast to the sex ratio of 74.6:100 in the lowlands foodstuffs producing *município* of Rio Bonito, where small scale foodstuffs and commodities production for regional markets was prevalent. The gradual substitution of the slave population by free farmers was accompanied by the declining proportions of male to female slaves (Table 1). For both Vassouras and Rio Bonito, post-mortem inventory listings of slaves have been taken at five-year intervals from 1860 to 1885 and the slave adults in the productive age category of 15–44 have been divided into those younger and older. The resulting dependency ratio of 64 confirms the preponderant nature of the active slave population between the ages of 15 and 45 well into the decade when slavery met its demise. It also suggests high infant and child mortality and a shortened life expectancy for adults.[14] In Rio Bonito, the dependency ratio was 99, suggesting an older population and one where life expectancy was greater for children and adults.

The second trend involved changes in the slave family units. The slave population of the province of Rio de Janeiro declined nine per cent between 1874 and 1884, yet a perusal of post-mortem inventories between 1860 and 1885 reveals that the proportion of partial slave families to the total was increasing. Partial slave families, as listed in post-mortem inventories, were heavily weighted to include women: a slave woman and some of her children, grandchildren, and nephews and nieces; siblings; mother and child; father and child; father, mother and some of their children.[15] In Vassouras, half of the slaves in slaveholdings with fewer than 20 slaves were listed in the inventories as kin under one or more of the above arrangements. In holdings of 21 to 40 slaves, at least one quarter of the slaves had family ties. In large slaveholdings of over 100 slaves, over 40 per cent of the slaves were living with children, siblings or parents. This trend has also been identified in the coffee-producing *município* of Paraíba do Sul, suggesting that although natural replacement of the slave population was not sufficient to offset the overall decline, multi-generational slave families were a growing reality in the coffee-export areas.[16] In lowlands areas where there was a general decline in the slave population between mid-century and 1872, slave families with kinship ties were a significant part of the rural slave population.[17] The infrastructure of post-emancipation labour arrangements was already in place and operating during slavery through fixed family-based production units that were indicative of changing social relations on coffee *fazendas* in both *municípios* where coffee was exported to the world market and in *municípios* where coffee and foodstuffs were produced for local consumption.

PLANTER STRATEGIES

Control over labour and access to land sustained the social relations of production in the hands of prominent coffee and sugar planters. Although census data show that the slave population was not reproducing

TABLE 1

SLAVE SEX RATIOS IN POST-MORTEM INVENTORIES OF RIO BONITO AND VASSOURAS, 1845–55, 1860–70 and 1875–85

Vassouras

Years	Number of Inventories	Total Slaves	Sex Ratio[2]
1845–55[3]			
1860–70	19	3,528	186:100
1875–85	18	2,206	123:100
1872 Census		18,480	132.8:100

Rio Bonito

Years	Number of Inventories	Total Slaves	Sex Ratio[2]
1845–55	18	3,351	186:100
1860–70	19	1,722	90.6:100
1875–85	18	1,344	74.6:100
1872 Census		7,201	98.4:100

1. Inventories were selected for years ending in 0 and in 5.
2. The sex ratio is the number of males per 100 females.
3. Data not available.

Sources: Vassouras: Ordem dos Advogados do Brasil/Cartório Público do Primeiro Oficio de Notas; Post-mortem Inventories for the years 1860, 1865, 1870, 1875, 1880, 1885. Rio Bonito: Cartório Público do Primeiro Oficio de Notas; Post-mortem Inventories for the years 1845, 1850, 1855, 1860, 1865, 1870, 1880, 1885; *Brasil. Recenseamento da população, 1872*. In 1872 the sex ratios for the lowlands municipality of Capivary and the highlands coffee municipality of Paraíba do Sul were 113:100 and 136:100, respectively.

itself, planter delegates from the Central South who met at the Agricultural Congress in 1878 were mindful of the need to relieve potential and real labour shortages on their units of production. Methods were proposed for the labour use of the children of slaves and ex-slaves, a potential 'class in formation', many of whom would enter productive age in the 1880s.[18] The Rio Branco Law of 27 September 1871, stipulated that these children were legally free (*ingênuos*) but must remain with their mothers until eight years of age, when the state would reimburse their owners for their freedom. Another provision permitted children to remain with their mothers until twenty-one years of age when they would be freed without compensation.[19] The prominent Vassouras planter, the Baron of Rio Bonito, warned that the freed children could be an element of disorder unless measures were forthcoming to oblige them to work. Concerning the *ingênuos*, who according to Conrad's estimates were almost half a million children in Brazil, the Baron stated: 'It is a new class of individuals that constitute an exception and for which there must be special regulations; moreover, as their numbers increase, they may, instead of becoming useful, become an element of disorder unless there is a means of obliging them to work.' The Baron lent his approval to proposals that the state assume the costs of educating slave children for agricultural labour up to twenty-one years of age, at which time they would be prepared to contribute to the rural labour market.[20]

Despite the 1871 law, and despite diminishing yields, shortages of slave labour and other signs of reversal in the initial coffee areas by the 1870s, many planters clung to the belief that slave labour would serve their needs until the end of the century.[21] Pressed for solutions to foreseeable shortages of field labour and their implications for the structure and organization of the rural wage labour market, delegates to the Agricultural Congress reviewed labour alternatives. Population transfers and trans-oceanic migrations were among the most seriously considered possibilities as some lauded the tireless energy of Chinese labourers. São Paulo planters, in particular, extolled the benefits to Brazil of European rural labour, and a general accounting was made of labour solutions encountered in other post-slave societies of the Americas. Planters expressed concern whether to regulate the free semi-nomadic rural Brazilian population but only grudgingly admitted that there were advantages to be gained from employing the locally available 'national' free and freed farm labourer. In comparison with possible or imagined labour alternatives, the 'national' worker stood little better in the eyes of the planter class of the 1870s than in the earlier accounts of travellers such as J.J. Tschudi in the 1850s, or Auguste St. Hilaire, Tollenare and Henry Koster at the beginning of the century.[22]

TANGIBLE SOLUTIONS

The composition of the rural labour force was affected by the ageing of African slave labour, the freeing of slave children who were born after passage of the Rio Branco Law in 1871, and the increase of the 'national' population which in 1874 was almost six times greater than the slave population.[23] The non-white population of slave, freed and free rural labourers that numbered 61 per cent of the total population in the province of Rio de Janeiro in 1872 represented an abundant locally available resource. In the three parishes of Vassouras, where coffee production was intensifying in 1850, the free non-white population varied from 12 to 14 per cent. Twenty-two years later, the marked increases in the free non-white population in the same three parishes suggest that although elite planters were opposed to replacing slave labour with other alternatives, the municipality as a whole was incorporating free non-white labour in agricultural production. In the parish of Nossa Senhora da Conceição, that included the town centre of Vassouras, the total population did not increase but the free non-white segment was almost three times larger in 1872 than in 1850. As the town centre expanded, this population became absorbed into the growing urban infrastructure of formal and informal markets, artisan trades, domestic service, railroad construction, commerce and civil service. In Paty de Alferes the total population increased slightly, but the free non-white segment more than doubled. In the third parish, Sacra Familia de Tinguá, the total population declined between the two dates but the free non-white population almost doubled (Table 3). Holdings of land were smaller in this parish than in Conceição and Paty de Alferes, and the terrain was steep and mountainous. Free non-white farmers and ex-slaves made up the majority of the population, suggesting that within the *município* of Vassouras, foodstuffs farming for the local market developed with coffee production and, in this parish, was holding its own in what has been presented as a major coffee-export economy.[24]

As Stanley Stein has argued, foodstuffs producers were displaced during the dynamic stages of the coffee economy.[25] In both Vassouras and Valença, however, the increase of the free non-white rural population in all parishes occurred between 1850 and 1872, when the initial coffee phase began to show signs of reversal. Despite the preference of prominent coffee planters for slave labour, the plantation complex, including the foodstuffs, artisan, and civil service sectors, was making adjustments to accommodate the free non-white population by the early 1870s. In the newer coffee areas of Paraíba do Sul and Cantagalo, the declining proportion of free non-whites in the population between the two dates

TABLE 2

POPULATION OF VASSOURAS, 1850 and 1872

Parish	1850					1872				
	Total	Free	%	Slave	%	Total	Free	%	Slave	%
N.S. de Conceição	10,086	3,291	33	6,795	67	10,644	4,461	42	6,203	58
Ferreiros						4,666	2,123	45	2,543	55
Paty de Alf.	11,489	3,040	25	8,449	75	14,440	6,353	44	8,087	56
Mendes							3,340	1,647	49	1,693	51
Sac. Fam. de Tinguá	7,063	3,097	44	3,966	56	6,143	4,501	73	1,642	27
Totals	28,638	11,428		19,210		39,253	19,085		20,168	

Source: Rio de Janeiro, Relatório do Presidente da Provincia (1850); data from 1872 are based on the revised calculations of the 1872 census of Clothilde Paiva, CEDEPLAR, Universidade Féderal de Minas Cerais.

TABLE 3

POPULATION OF VASSOURAS, 1850 and 1872

Parish	1850			1872		
	Total	Free Non-White	%	Total	Free Non-White	%
Conceição	10,086	1,238	12	10,664	4,421	32
Ferreiros				4,666	874	19
Paty de Alf.	11,489	1,648	14	14,440	3,053	21
Mendes				3,340	943	28
Sac. Fam. de Tinguá	7,063	1,178	17	6,143	2,139	35

Source: Table 2.

TABLE 4

POPULATION OF FOUR FLUMINENSE MUNICÍPIOS, 1850 and 1872

Município	1850			1872		
	Total	Free Non-White	%	Total	Freee Non-White	%
Vassouras	28,638	4,064	14	39,253	10,430	27
Valença	17,621	1,806	10	47,131	7,043	15
Cantagalo	16,478	2,492	15	29,453	3,312	11
Paraíba do Sul	16,753	4,228	25	37,461	7,314	20
N.S. Natividade	n.d.	n.d.	n.d.	5,635	1,669	30

Sources: Rio de Janeiro, *Relatório do Presidente da Provincia, (1850)*; *Recenseamento, 1872*.

suggests that, as had initially been the case in Vassouras, the free non-white population was not incorporated into the local economy because of heavy reliance of planters on slave labour. As supplies of slave labour, capital and available land became scarce, the proportion of free and non-white family-based labour increased. In lowlands foodstuffs and commodity-producing areas where land was available for purchase and for settlement, family-based units of free non-white labour combined semi-subsistence with coffee production, a pattern that also became the norm for expansion of the coffee frontier to the emerging Northern Fluminense towns. In Nossa Senhora da Natividade de Carangola, for example, the free non-white population was already 30 per cent of the total population in 1872, suggesting that the infrastructure of the post-emancipation coffee economy was in place before coffee began to flourish there in the 1880s and 1890s.

CABINS AND SMALL FARMS

What is known about the free and freed non-white population? John Luccock has described *sitiantes* (temporary workers) as lazy, ignorant and 'prone to acts of violence which knew no limits, killing any being which crossed their way'. Most of the families had no local roots and stayed only long enough to harvest their crops and settle with the landowner before moving on, abandoning their homes with no regrets (*sem pesar*) and settling again with no other concern than to avoid rivalries and annoyances with their neighbours.[26]

Some court cases later in the century deal with transient populations but most reveal more fixed populations that include overseers, semi-subsistence producers (including ex-slaves who continued to farm garden plots), go-betweens of various kinds, artisans, mule-train drivers, poor cousins of planters who provided manpower for the private protection of the landowner and his family, thieves and providers of various and sundry part-time pleasures and services. Many were born in or near the *município* or claimed local residence for a number of years.[27] Free resident farmers worked as auxiliary labour and kept small livestock on plots of land within the confines of a *fazenda* or *engenho* unit. In addition to providing extra labour on the premises these arrangements enabled landless farmers to take advantage of an infrastructure not otherwise available: transportation, credit mechanisms and markets for surplus production.

The precarious structure of the dwellings suggests that people lived modestly. Their transient lifestyle was in accord with the needs of the plantation economy, which accommodated a sizeable resident free labour force while supplies of slave labour were plentiful.[28] The cabins, which varied in size according to the amount of capital invested in improvements, were wattle-and-daub structures of one or two rooms with earthen floors, thatched roofs, shutterless windows and wooden doors. Because of the unpredictability of tenure, the meagre possessions of landless farmers were all moveable: slaves, animals, manioc presses, earthenware pottery, copper cooking pans, carts and wagons. Improved cabins had limestone outer coatings, tile roofs and wooden floors, an indication of assured tenure for the landowner's kin, long-term free or freed artisans and overseers.

Before the 1870s, garden plots, cabins and livestock changed hands without prior consultation of the landlord, a workable arrangement that operated along horizontal lines among landless farmers and attests to the frequent turnover of occupancy on estates.[29] De jure claims of landless farmers to the land they farmed on the basis of effective occupation were almost exclusively ruled out since all property on an estate was subject to appraisal at the time of the landowner's death. The accommodation of free farmers, including a growing number of ex-slaves, and the compensation for improvements made to the property depended on individual arrangements that were made with the heirs to the estate.[30]

The plantation complex accommodated shifting numbers of short-term labourers. As a result, tenuous horizontal networks developed that were essential to the continued operation of the economy. As the second half of the nineteenth century progressed, more settled and permanent labour arrangements emerged, but because unequal hierarchical relations and planter dominance continued, labour relations changed in form but did not radically alter the unfree or migratory nature of labour in the plantation complex.

As a court case reveals, the group solidarity of ex-slaves could reinforce, not threaten, the hierarchical social relations between the planter class and their social inferiors during the process of transition from slave to free labour. The case involved the slave, Caetana, whose master freed her and other slaves upon his death and granted them use of farm land on his estate. When she was beaten by the lover whom she had invited to share her cabin, the other freed people amongst whom she lived and earned her livelihood came to Caetana's rescue. Her initial reaction, common among small landless farmers, was to move away; but her request to a neighbouring landowner for a place to live was denied. She then sought her deceased master's brother, who was a priest and who resided on an adjoining fazenda. He sent his Portuguese overseer to 'administer justice' which resulted in the beating and physical removal of the boyfriend from Caetana's cabin. Caetana's recourse to the planter class to solve her problem reinforced traditional vertical ties that bound landless occupants to the *senhor* or master; in this case, to the master's extended family. Caetana's case demonstrated how horizontal solidarity was also operative in rural social relations. The overseer's aggressive treatment of the boyfriend reinstated forms of oppression that had been permissable with impunity under slavery and generated a new protest from Caetana's freed neighbours. Freedom had not altered the social hierarchy or the place of the hated oppressor in that hierarchy, but the complaints of the lover, an ex-slave, backed by Caetana's peers, resulted in the arrest and prosecution of the overseer by the local authorities.

Traditional ties of dependency on the master class protected Caetana in the first instance. It also led to the ex-slaves' settlement of past scores with the overseer, and, most importantly, did not implicate or involve the priest, her former master's brother. The pervasiveness of vertical ties, strengthened by mutual obligations between masters and dependants, gave some leeway to freedmen and free farmers to manipulate the rigid social hierarchy dominated by the planter class. However, the wide range of favours that secured those dependencies in the post-emancipation period made these same men unfree in terms of the way in which they perceived their freedom and with regard to how society perceived their autonomy.

FROM SLAVE TO MIGRANT LABOR

The 1880s were a period of intense readjustment as the plantation system responded to the abolition movement, to legislation in 1886 that prohibited the whipping of slaves and freed slaves over sixty years of age, to foreclosures on property, and to shortages of credit and of capital. Impoverished planters and small farmers forfeited improvements; they sold or took their slaves and moved on. The crisis in commercial plantation agriculture was irreversible as the abolition movement spread from its urban bases into the interior and reached its culminating point when slaves walked away from the São Paulo *fazendas* in 1887.[31]

Brazil's principal export continued to be coffee in the post-emancipation period. Brazil exported 216,000 tons in 1871 and until the 1930s was the supplier of more than one half of the coffee sold in the international trade.[32] By the close of the nineteenth century, however, the planter-merchant nobility, whose claims to social, political and economic prominence rested on the cultivation by slave labour of the coffee bean for the foreign market, had been disfranchised by the downfall of Brazil's monarchy and the onset of a republic. They were outdistanced by technically progressive planters. Planter groups tied to the emerging coffee economy of western São Paulo, who were supported by government projects to introduce European immigrant labour, engaged in modernizing efforts at increased productivity and profits under capitalist conditions, including the use of labour-saving devices for drying and transporting coffee beans.[33]

The legal emancipation of slaves in 1888 did not diminish the need for a disciplined dependent labour force in the plantation complex. The demand for administrative services, artisan skills, and for both semiskilled and cheap and abundant unskilled labour was satisfied by workers from decaying coffee regions who moved into and out of the coffee economy as the production needs and commercialization networks required. The rigidly hierarchical social relations characteristic of slavery persisted in the post-emancipation coffee areas; although the availability of land for settlement in the early stages of the coffee boom in the northeastern tip of Rio de Janeiro served as an incentive for sharecroppers, tenant farmers, wage workers, small landowners and immigrant *colonos* to create a more open social milieu than was the case under slavery. Yet it may be argued that semi-nomadic rural labourers only preserved their mobile lifestyles in the post-emancipation coffee economy because they lacked viable alternatives. The working and sanitary conditions of the post-emancipation production units were not designed to maintain large numbers of labourers on more than a seasonal basis. There was little chance that a transient labour force, even if judicially free, could permanently alter or even challenge the rigid social hierarchy that had characterized the plantation complex since its inception in the sixteenth century.

NOTES

1. John Luccock, *Notas sobre o Rio de Janeiro e partes meridionais do Brasil* (São Paulo, 1975), p. 194.
2. Philip D. Curtin, *The Rise and Fall of the Plantation Complex. Essays in Atlantic History* (Cambridge, 1990), p. ix. By the decade of the 1830s, coffee had replaced sugar as Brazil's leading export and the Centre South of the country, including Rio de Janeiro, Espírito Santo, Minas Gerais and western São Paulo, were the dynamic centres of the coffee economy.
3. A *fazenda* was an agricultural establishment which included a main dwelling for the owner, slave quarters and cultivated fields and forests. Charles Ribeyrolles, *Brasil Pitoresco* (São Paulo, 2nd ed., 1976), Vol. II, p. 31.
4. Elizabeth Fox-Genovese, *Within the Plantation Household: Black and White Women of*

the Old South (Chapel Hill, 1988). Vilma Paraiso Ferreira de Almada documented the migration of Vassouras families to the newly developing coffee areas of Espirito Santo; see *Escravismo e Transição. O Espirito Santo (1850/1888)* (Rio de Janeiro, 1984). Studies of family history have not dealt with childhood experiences of moving, and to date no biographical accounts of migrant Brazilian families have supplemented land records, census data, post-mortem inventories and criminal records as sources for migration studies.

5. Henry Koster, *Viagens ao Nordeste do Brasil* (Recife, [1817], 1978); L.F. Tollenare, *Notas Dominicais tomadas durante uma residência em Portugal e no Brazil nos anos de 1816, 1817 e 1818: parte relativa a Pernambuco* (Recife, 1905); Sérgio Milliet, *Roteiro do Café e Outros Ensaios*, 3rd ed. (São Paulo, 1941); Auguste de Saint-Hilaire, *Viagem pelas Províncias do Rio de Janeiro e Minas Gerais* (São Paulo, 1975); and John Luccock, *Notas*.

6. Nancy Priscilla Naro, 'O Trabalhador Nacional: O Legado da Emancipação' (unpublished report), Centro de Estudos Afro-Asiáticos, Aug. 1992. For a detailed examination of misrule through claims to land, see James Holston, 'The Misrule of Law: Land and Usurpation in Brazil', *Comparative Studies in Society and History*, 33 (1991), pp. 695–725.

7. Stanley J. Stein, *Vassouras: A Brazilian Coffee County, 1850–1900* (Cambridge, Mass., 1957).

8. J.J. von Tschudi, *Viagem às províncias do Rio de Janeiro e São Paulo* (São Paulo, 1976), 48.

9. The planter was Francisco Peixoto de Lacerda Werneck (Barão de Pati do Alferes). See Eduardo Silva, *Barões e Escravidão: Três gerações de fazendeiros e a crise de estrutura escravista* (Rio de Janeiro, 1984), pp. 229–30.

10. Charles de Ribeyrolles, *Brasil Pitoresco* (São Paulo, 1980), Vol I. pp. 229–30.

11. Robert E. Conrad, *The Destruction of Brazilian Slavery* (Los Angeles, 1972), p. 24. See also Philip D. Curtin, *The Atlantic Slave Trade: A Census* (Madison, 1969), p. 29.

12. Conrad, *Destruction of Brazilian Slavery*, Appendices, Table 2, p. 284.

13. See Robert W. Slenes, 'Grandeza ou decadencia? O mercado de escravos e a economia cafeeira da provincia do Rio de Janeiro, 1850–1888', in Iraci de Nero da Costa (ed.), *Brasil: Historia Econômica e Demográfica* (São Paulo, 1986), pp. 126–9, for an analysis of comparative slave prices.

14. According to Stuart Schwartz, the dependency ratios for Bahian parishes in 1788 were 143 for whites and 69 for all slaves; see *Sugar Plantations in the Formation of Brazilian Society: Bahia, 1550–1835* (Cambridge, 1985), p. 359. The dependency ratio is calculated as A + B/C times 100, where A = 0–14 years, B = 45 years and over, and C = 15–44 years.

15. For Stuart Schwartz, a partial slave family and kin relationships had to be recognized as such by the slave-owner; see *Sugar Plantations*. For the literature on slave families, see Naro, 'Revision and Persistence: Recent Historiography on the Transition from Slave to Free Labour in Rural Brazil', *Slavery and Abolition*, 13, 2 (1992), note 30, p. 84.

16. João L.R. Fragoso and Manolo G. Florentino, 'Filho de Inocência Crioula. Neto de Joana Cabinda', *Estudos Econômicos*, 17, 2 (1987), pp. 151–73.

17. See Hebe Maria Gomes de Castro, *Ao Sul da História* (São Paulo, 1987). My study of the transition from slave to free labour in the *município* of Rio Bonito from 1845 to 1888 has produced similar findings.

18. *Congresso Agrícola*, facsimile edition, Introdução de José Murilo de Carvalho (Rio de Janeiro, 1988); and Conrad, *Destruction of Brazilian Slavery*, p. 117.

19. *Coleção de Leis do Imperio do Brasil em 1871*, Lei 2.040, Tomo XXXI, Parte I, pp. 147–51.

20. 'E uma classe nova de individuos, que constitue uma excepção, e para a qual e forçoso haver regulamento especial; até porque augmentada ella em numero crescido, bem longe de tornar-se útil, pode constituir um elemento de desordem, desde que não haja recurso para obrigar-a a trabalhar'; see *Congresso Agrícola*, 1878, 238. See also Peter Eisenberg, 'A Mentalidade dos Fazendeiros no Congresso Agricola de 1878', *Homens*

Esquecidos. Escravos e Trabalhadores Livres no Brasil. Séculos XVIII e XIX (São Paulo, 1989), pp. 147–8; and Conrad, *Destruction of Brazilian Slavery*, Ch. 6–7.

21. Slenes, 'Grandeza ou decadência?', pp. 141–2.
22. *Congresso Agrícola*, 1878. Expressions of planter sentiment can be found in official speeches of politicians analysed by Celia Marinho de Azevedo, *Medo Branco. Onda Negra* (São Paulo, 1987). One might suggest, on the basis of a front page article in the *Jornal do Comercio*, 28 de junho de 1894, that the reference to 'too many parties' as the reason for the lack of assiduousness on the part of the 'national' labourer reflected little change in planter attitudes.
23. Conrad, *Destruction of Brazilian Slavery*, Table 2, p. 284.
24. Analysis of parish land records has made it possible to question whether Vassouras was exclusively a producer of coffee. In other *municípios*, where public land was available for purchase and where mixed production for domestic markets predominated, the free non-white population was made up of small-scale family producers of crops for local markets. See Naro, 'Customary Rightholders and Legal Claimants to Land in Rio de Janeiro, Brazil, 1870–1890', *The Americas*, 48, 4 (1992), pp. 485–517.
25. Stein, *Vassouras*, Ch. 3.
26. Luccock, *Notas*, p. 194.
27. Maria Sylvia Carvalho Franco, *Homens Livres na Sociedade Escravocrata* (São Paulo, 1972); Jacob Gorender, *O Escravismo Colonial* (São Paulo, 2nd ed., 1985), p. 289 *passim*. Coffee and sugar estate appraisals in postmortem inventories from all of the Vassouras parishes and from at least ten Fluminense *municípios* currently under study contain listings of families of farmers who lived on and farmed small-scale *sítios* or *situações* with fruit trees, coffee, manioc and cornfields. For a listing of these studies, see Naro, 'Revision and Persistence, pp. 68–85; and Stuart B. Schwartz, *Slaves, Peasants and Rebels* (Champagne/Urbana, 1992). Ciro F.S. Cardoso has argued that the garden plots or provision grounds allotted to slaves contributed to the formation of a proto-peasantry; see *Escravo ou camponês? O Protocampesinato negro nas Américas* (São Paulo, 1987).
28. Hebe de Castro, *Ao Sul*.
29. Ibid.; and Naro, 'Customary Rightholders'.
30. Naro, 'Customary Rightholders'.
31. Joseph E. Sweigart has dealt with the credit crisis in the Rio de Janeiro coffee sector; see 'Financing and Marketing Brazilian Export Agriculture: The Coffee Factors of Rio de Janeiro, 1850–1888' (Ph.D. dissertation, University of Texas at Austin, 1980). In *Da Casa Grande à Senzala* and more recently in *Luso Brazilian Review*, 29, 2 (1992), pp. 145–50, Emilia Viotti da Costa has dealt with the departure of São Paulo slaves from the coffee *fazendas* in 1887. The departure of slaves is recently evaluated by Celia Maria de Azevedo, 'On Hell and Paradise: Abolitionism in the US and Brazil, A Comparative Perspective' (Ph.D. dissertation, Columbia University, 1993).
32. Warren Dean, 'The Brazilian Economy, 1870–1930', in Leslie Bethell (ed.), *Cambridge History of Latin America* (Cambridge, 1985), Vol. 4, ch. 19, pp. 694–5.
33. Octavio Ianni, *Raças e Classes Sociais no Brasil* (Rio de Janeiro, 1966), pp. 75–114.

Slavery, the International Labour Market and the Emancipation of Slaves in the Nineteenth Century

MARTIN A. KLEIN

The creation of a world economy by European capitalism and the reconstruction of economic relations in almost all parts of the world created in their wake tremendous demands for labour, which could only be met by various forms of labour coercion. European expansion brought in its train an increase in the use of unfree labour in Asia and Africa as well as in the Americas. If the Atlantic world experienced the greatest demands it was because large fertile areas were underpopulated and because some densely populated areas were decimated by disease.[1] There were large movements of free labour, but they were inadequate to the demands of an expanding European economy. Both in the Atlantic basin and elsewhere in the world, slavery was the most common form of unfreedom, in large part because slavery gave the slave's owner greater control over the slave's productive labour. In the Atlantic basin, slaves were also attractive because they could be moved long distances and because Africans had a lower mortality rate than Europeans in such movement.[2] Other forms of unfree labour coexisted with slavery, for example, indentured labour and peonage in the Americas, bondage in India, debt servitude in South-East Asia, pawnship in Africa, and these forms were used to control labour when slavery was abolished.[3]

None of these types was unique, all were widespread and few were ever actively questioned anywhere before the eighteenth century. It is not slavery that was unique, but emancipation. Ironically, slavery was systematically questioned only after a capitalist Europe created in the Americas a particularly systematic form of slavery.[4] The major arenas of the battle over emancipation were in the Atlantic basin, but it shaped all parts of the world. This paper tries to set the question of emancipation in an international and comparative context. It will argue that the struggle for emancipation involved not simply the imposition of a policy that was in the interests of the very powers that created a modern form of slavery, but that acceptance also required the acceptance of different ideological systems.[5]

In all parts of the world, the slave was seen both as an outsider and as property. Thus, Patterson writes: 'Not only was the slave denied all claims on, and obligations to, his parents and living blood relations but, by extension, all such claims and obligations on his more remote ancestors and on his descendants.'[6] For Watson, the property relationship differentiates slavery from other forms of involuntary labour.[7] Reid uses saleability to differentiate slavery from other forms of bondage.[8] For most contemporary writers, the idea of property is derivative from the slave's deracination, but the two notions were linked. The marginality of the slave made him or her dependent and thus more exploitable.[9] The property relationship maintained that marginality and was probably responsible for slavery replacing or absorbing other forms of unfree labour. Most important, the reification of the person in slavery gave the master control. Slaves were valuable not because they were better workers, but because more could be extracted from them.

Slave systems can be divided into two groups. First, there was elite slavery. In African and Asian societies, many slaves were found within the courts, in elite households and within the political system.[10] Slaves were concubines, officials, soldiers, servants, entertainers, and artisans. In some cases, there was no other kind of slavery. The wealth that supported the elite was produced through taxation, tribute, corvée or by other means. Within these systems, slaves were important not as producers but as part of the structure that extracted wealth or spent it. Many slaves exercised great power, particularly eunuchs and slave soldiers. Most played humble roles, but within the households of the rich and powerful. Thus, Martin Wilbur originally conceived of his study of slavery in Han China 'as one way to learn more about the condition of the lower classes in Han times, but it now appears to reveal much more about the ruling group, and to contribute only indirectly to a knowledge of the common people'.[11] This does not mean that slavery was unimportant. The existence of a mass of dependent persons was essential to the power of the state and the privileges of the elite. The Middle East and the Arab world rarely used slaves for productive activities, but the hunger of this area for slaves has been a factor in its history for over two thousand years, and has influenced its relations with Slavic areas around the Black Sea and with Africa.[12]

The second type was productive slavery, in which slave labour was used primarily for productive purposes.[13] In some, slave labour was the only important source of income for the state and the elite. In others, slavery functioned alongside other kinds of obligation, as in India and South-East Asia, or alongside free labour, as in the US South. In some, like ancient Rome, reliance on slave labour resulted from military success.[14] Often, for example, as on American slave plantations, slave labour replaced other forms of labour because it offered those with land or capital higher profits. In these, slaves were replenished by purchase, slave-producing societies developed to supply the market, and economic calculation imposed increasingly intensive labour on the slave. The result was that larger numbers of slaves were gathered in large units of production.[15] On the Atlantic islands and in the Americas, slaves were sought almost exclusively for productive purposes.

In general, slave-using societies were those where control of persons was more valuable than land or other kinds of wealth. Reid's remarks about South-East Asia could be extended to other societies:

> The key to Southeast Asian social systems was the control of men. Land was assumed to be abundant, and not therefore an index to power. ... The wealth of the rich, and the power of the strong, lay in the dependant man- (and woman-) power they could gather around them. For the poor and the weak ... security and opportunity depended upon being bonded to somebody strong enough to look after them ... the important question was to whom you were bonded rather than the abstract legal quality of your bondage.[16]

In the Americas, land was freely available but labour was in short supply. American planters did not need clients, but they did need workers, particularly where work was harsh, as on sugar plantations.[17] Where population densities were high, control of land brought with it control of persons and made slavery redundant. Thus, in China slavery was widespread, but totally unimportant as a source of production.

INDIGENOUS SLAVERY AND EUROPEAN EXPANSION

Slaves were often the subject of struggles for the control of their productivity and their services, usually a struggle between kings and aristocrats or between military, commercial and agrarian elites. Soon after the first Portuguese ships made contact with African and Asian peoples, Europeans became part of this struggle.[18] During the centuries of expansion, European traders became involved with slavery in two ways. First, they became involved in moving slaves. In the fifteenth century, the Portuguese on the coast of West Africa bought slaves not only for use in Portugal and the Atlantic Islands but for sale to labour-short Akan gold-miners in what is now Ghana.[19] As sugar cultivation moved from the Atlantic islands to Brazil, the slave trade expanded to meet the needs of the new market. In the East, a slave trade economy evolved that linked the Indian Ocean and the South China seas. Africans were sold in India, the Persian Gulf and Indonesia.[20] Malays were sold in south China and at the Cape of Good Hope.[21] Slaves were moved from the outer islands of Indonesia to Java and various trading cities in South-East Asia.[22]

Second, and linked to this, Europeans in both Africa and Asia used slave labour themselves. As outsiders, they had little call on labour in societies where labour was provided largely within social relationships. They used slaves as sailors and as labourers, but most important, they used slaves within their own households. The more successful had large and often lavish houses, staffed by slave gardeners, cooks and servants. Even the more modest had slave concubines and servants.[23] In South-East Asia, a Chinese diaspora was linked to its European counterpart and, like it, consisted largely of males, who often purchased sexual and domestic services.[24] Thus, throughout the growing colonial empires, in Asia and Africa as in the Americas, slavery was part of the domestic life of both the Europeans and new middleman groups.

Economic growth and a European taste for tropical products created an opportunity for Europeans to move from commerce to production. They tended to do so in areas where population was low or had been decimated by diseases the Europeans introduced, first, on such Atlantic islands as Madeira and São Tomé. In Brazil and the West Indies, Europeans started by pressing native labour to work for them, but when harsh rule and European diseases decimated native populations, this proved inadequate. The import of Africans became the cheapest and often the only way to find labour, particularly after the growth of sugar production in the West Indies in the seventeenth century.[25] Similarly, in the Banda Islands of Indonesia, Jan Pietrzoon Coen's brutal conquest left population so low that spice production could only be maintained by importing labour to produce the spices the Dutch wanted.[26]

From commercial empire in the sixteenth century and settlement in the seventeenth century, Europeans moved to control massive populations in India and Indonesia by the late eighteenth century. Their intervention in the local economy took two forms. First, they tended to rely heavily on traditional systems of general obligation. Forced labour was widely used in India and South-East Asia, just as it was earlier used by Spanish to procure labour for their mines.[27] In Asia, the corvée was first used for public purposes, and then increasingly for commmodity production.[28] The new colonial rulers could use these systems to their own advantage. At the same time, colonial taxation and a new legal framework encouraged cash crop production and the extension of market relationships. Many prospered, but debt, landlessness, population growth and the restrictions of caste left most of the poor with few options. Though no statistics are available, it seems certain for India and probable for much of the rest of East and South Asia that the extension of market relationships stimulated the growth of debt bondage – and perhaps also the sale of children.[29]

Even though the Atlantic slave trade was withdrawing huge numbers from eighteenth- and nineteenth-century Africa, or perhaps because of it, slave use was increasing within Africa.[30] The same networks that fed the Atlantic market supplied African users, and the loss of population made control of persons even more necessary. The end of the Atlantic slave trade was paralleled by the development of commodity exports, which created a demand for slaves and pawns within Africa.[31] A disguised export trade also persisted as the slave trade was used to produce supposedly free labour in Senegal[32] and on the Atlantic islands.[33] The fiction of an indenture contract often covered what was really a continuation of the slave trade.[34] By contrast, in India and South-East Asia, use of servile labour was declining. Feeny argues that in Thailand other kinds of labour became cheap, largely because of population growth and large-scale migration from China.[35] In India, the decline of slavery involved both a shift into debt bondage and the development of more efficient wage labour systems.[36]

THE ABOLITION OF SLAVERY

There were times in many parts of the world when slavery declined, often replaced or absorbed by other forms of exploitation. During the late medieval period, slavery disappeared in northern Europe,[37] and in seventeenth-century Russia it was absorbed within a rather harsh form of serfdom.[38] The use of slaves was declining in South-East Asia during the nineteenth century, most strikingly in Thailand.[39] There is no evidence, however, that slavery was seriously attacked in any part of the world before the eighteeenth century. The abolition movement had its origins in a change in European consciousness. In the eighteenth century, Enlightenment thinkers in England and on the Continent increasingly called slavery into question. Montesquieu dissected classical justifications of slavery and attacked it as contrary to natural law.[40] Adam Smith and his followers argued that free labour was more productive because it was better motivated.[41] More important for its later consequences, in 1758 the Philadelphia Yearly meeting of the Quakers voted to exclude any members who bought or sold slaves.[42] Within a generation, abolition had a solid base in evangelical Protestant churches on both sides of the Atlantic.

Slavery was held to be illegal in England in 1772 and by the end of the century upper Canada and most of the northern United States had abolished it. In 1794 revolutionary France followed. The abolitionists were hostile to slavery, but they focused first on ending the trade. The United States constitution provided for the end of slave imports in 1808. The Danes abolished the colonial slave trade in 1803, the British in 1807, and the Dutch in 1814.[43] There was a difference between the British and French abolition movements. In Britain, a powerful movement based in the dissenting churches developed methods of shaping public opinion and was a major force in British politics for 50 years. On the Continent, it remained more a movement of ideas, which never mobilized the masses. Napoleon re-established slavery in the French colonies in 1802, and the Catholic Church was hostile to abolition for much of the nineteenth century.[44] Nevertheless, for the heirs of the Enlightenment throughout the nineteenth century, slavery was seen as contrary to natural law and reason. The revolutionary regime in 1848 again abolished slavery throughout the French empire. It did so without any hesitation, without any transition period, and without any qualifications.

The success of the British abolitionists in persuading Parliament to abolish colonial slavery in 1833 did not end their struggle. The law passed was less than the abolitionists wanted. They were opposed to its apprenticeship provisions. The slaves in the West Indies, however, quickly undercut any idea of a transitional status, but that still left slavery elsewhere.[45] Rival nations reaped the benefits of British abolition. The slave trade continued in foreign ships, only slightly riskier due to the efforts of the Royal Navy, and slave-based production remained prosperous in Brazil, the United States and Spanish Cuba.[46] The British and Foreign Anti-Slavery Society was formed in 1839.[47] During its early years, it was concerned primarily with the Americas, particularly with Cuba, Brazil and the United States. Increasingly, however, it confronted other issues. European explorers described the horrors of the slave trade in Africa.[48] The 1833 abolition did not affect India, Burma or Ceylon, which were controlled by the East India Company. And wherever British authority was extended on the African mainland, concern about relations with slave-holding neighbours compromised British policy.[49]

By 1839 Great Britain had treaties with all major maritime powers except the United States providing for the right to search each other's merchant vessels.[50] The Royal Navy eliminated the trade in some areas, but the skill of the slavers and international law, which required that slaving ships be taken to a Prize Court, limited these efforts. The only Court in West Africa was at Freetown. Under Palmerston, however, as the Royal Navy began to cut more deeply into the trade, British pressure extended its field of operations. In 1845, Sayyid Said of Zanzibar agreed to prohibit the export of slaves from his African territories.[51] Similar treaties were signed with various West African rulers.[52] Initially, the Ottomans refused to institute any action against slavery, but in 1847, they closed the Constantinople slave market and banned the slave trade in the Persian Gulf. Ten years later, they prohibited the trade in African slaves. These actions had the effect of driving the slave trade into back alleys and private homes.[53]

British attacks on the slave trade produced a particularly vehement response in the Muslim world because slavery was seen as an institution legitimated by the Prophet. During the late nineteenth century the most persistent export trade from Africa was from the Horn across the Red Sea into the Hijaz.[54] The major effect of European intervention was to make the trade less public.[55] Finally, in 1880 a stronger treaty was signed. The trade declined, though a regular trade in African slaves to the Hijaz continued well into the 1920s.[56] The pilgrimage to Mecca remained the occasion for a clandestine slave trade even after that. Egypt closed its slave markets in 1854 and, in 1877, agreed to an anti-slavery convention with Great Britain.[57] The slave trade was abolished in Tunisia in 1846, and after French occupation in 1881, this ban was made more effective. In Morocco, Islam bolstered resistance to foreign intervention. For a long time, British attentions only made the trade more secretive. A formal ban on the trade came only in 1922, but French occupation of the Niger valley during the 1890s effectively reduced its scale.[58]

It was not just British pressure. The British were often resented, but abolition made steady, if sometimes slow progress. Haitian slaves rose in revolt in 1791 and freed themselves in a bitter and violent revolution that ended only with recognition of Haitian independence in 1804.[59] The leaders of the revolutions against Spain were less radical, but all of the newborn American republics abolished the slave trade after independence. Chile abolished slavery in 1823, and Mexico and Central America followed soon afterwards. The others passed gradual emancipation laws, which freed all children born after the law was enacted. These free womb laws involved a long transition period. As a result, in countries with important slave systems slave prices remained high and planters bitterly and successfully resisted emancipation for a generation. In spite of this, the Hispanic republics ended slavery one by one, finishing with Peru in 1854.[60] Denmark abolished slavery in 1848, the Netherlands in 1863, and the United States between 1863 and 1865. When slavery was abolished in Cuba in 1886 and Brazil in 1888, it was partly a result of internal forces, in Brazil's case a mass abolition movement subsidized by the British.[61] In Cuba, David Eltis argues, it was because the price of sugar was no longer adequate to cover the costs of importing slaves.[62]

Also in 1888, a series of Catholic abolition societies were founded in

Europe under the leadership of Cardinal Lavigerie and with the blessing of Pope Leo XIII.[63] The French Catholic abolition movement used quiet pressure more than open propaganda, but it was backed by a strong missionary presence. In France, the Catholic abolitionists refused to collaborate with the more secular movement that had long existed, but they were probably able to put more pressure on the government because they could mobilize Catholic public opinion. More important than any single movement was the equation in late nineteenth-century Europe of bondage with backwardness and the belief held throughout Europe that slavery was profoundly immoral.

MOTIVES FOR ABOLITION

The major debate on abolition has been whether it was a triumph of moral principle[64] or a victory of economic interest. The debate was provoked by Eric Williams' *Capitalism and Slavery*,[65] which argued that accumulation of capital in the slave trade and in slave-based production was crucial to the industrial revolution, but that by the end of the eighteenth century the West Indian slave plantations had declined in profitability and in their importance to Great Britain. Most contemporary writers accept the link between anti-slavery and industrial capitalism, while rejecting the economic determinism of Eric Williams. Thus Seymour Drescher has proven that there was no such decline at the time of the anti-slavery debate; 'The key to the timing of slavery's ultimate demise in the Western economy lies not in its economic functioning but in its social peculiarity'.[66] Eltis argues that the period from 1820 to 1860 was the most profitable period for the Atlantic slave trade.[67] None the less, as David Brion Davis has observed, 'antislavery cannot be divorced from the vast economic changes that were intensifying social conflicts and heightening class consciousness . . . in Britain it was part of a larger ideology that helped to ensure stability while accommodating society to political and economic change.'[68]

For Howard Temperley, the key question is not what the abolitionists thought but why they were so successful at convincing others. It was not, after all, the market that ended slavery, but the state.[69] The two leaders of abolition, Great Britain and the northern United States were free labour zones which had experienced extraordinary growth, and the dominant political leaders in both were convinced that individual freedom was crucial to that growth. Continental Europe was still freeing itself from traditional restraints on labour. The abolition movement lacked the organizational base provided by evangelical Protestantism, but a similar capitalist, free labour ideology predominated in Europe by the end of the nineteenth century.[70] Slavery was seen both as immoral and irrational. Public opinion shaped the strategies of imperial statesmen and pro-consuls. Leopold, the King of the Belgians, made alliances with slave-dealers when he first penetrated the Congo, but when confronted by the problem of how to finance his colony, he found it necessary to wrap himself in an anti-slavery cloak.[71] The French officers, who gave slaves to their soldiers and allies after military victories, often justified their actions in terms of an eventual abolition.[72] Lugard proposed eventual abolition in northern Nigeria and sold himself at home as an anti-slavery crusader, but in the short run he reinforced the control of slave-owners over their slaves.[73] The contrast between metropole and colony was quite sharp. By the end of the nineteenth century, an Enlightenment discourse on slavery was generally accepted within Europe, but not always in the colonies.

This is most vividly illustrated by the Brussels conference of 1889–90, at which the major European powers agreed to measures against the internal African slave trade, the export of slaves from Africa and the trade in arms and liquor.[74] The Brussels Act came a decade before most colonial powers were willing to act against the slave trade within Africa. It provided a cloak of moral legitimacy for the partition of Africa, but there was a gap between the rhetoric and the reality of Europe's moral crusade. The problem was that Europe's proconsuls lacked resources.[75] The quest for African empire was often backed by well-organized public relations efforts, but the real interests involved were often very limited and most European statesmen were well aware of this.[76] Leaders such as Bismarck and Salisbury viewed the claims of the colonial lobby with great scep-ticism. European parliaments were willing to approve colonies as long as they did not cost anything. Colonies were forced to pay their own way, but the revenue that could be extracted from most areas being colonized was limited. Thus, European armies were small and made up primarily of soldiers recruited in the colonies.[77] Booty, particularly human booty, attracted allies. In addition, European generals were often anxious to prevent their enemies from uniting. It was therefore important not to undermine the existing social order, which depended on slaves.[78] The practice was often to free the slaves of enemies but to reinforce the control of allies and those who submitted willingly over their slaves.

EUROPEAN ABOLITION AND NON-WESTERN SLAVERY

Until the middle of the nineteenth century, the abolition movement focused on the exploitation of slaves by Europeans or people of Euro-pean descent. The act of 1833 did not apply to India. There were probably more slaves in India than in all of the Americas, but they were mostly owned by Indian masters.[79] More important, British India was being ruled by a small number of British officials allied to Indian princes, commanding Indian soldiers and dependent on Indian subalterns and intermediaries. They lacked both the desire and the administrative capacity to force abolition on reluctant Indian ruling classes. When the issue of Indian slavery was raised in Britain, the response was vigorous. One official insisted that 'the lower classes are glad to bind themselves and their posterity to such perpetual service, in order to be secure of subsistence in sickness and in old age ... and in periods of scarcity'.[80] Self sale or the sale of children was seen as an effective way of dealing with such disasters as the Bengal Famine of 1833.

But the attack was equally vigorous. The trade in women and children offended Christian sensibilities. So too did the castration of young boys and the operation of roving bands of thugs who made kidnapping a business. From the renewal of the East Indian Company charter in 1833, efforts were made to force the East India Company to act. Finally, in 1843, it did so, albeit reluctantly. The crucial provision of the Abolition Act was that the courts were no longer to recognize claims rising out of slave status.[81] No compensation was paid to slave-owners and no effort was made to provide alternative employment to the slaves. The hope was that slaves would not notice, that they would quietly continue to work under their masters, and that, in the absence of recruits, slavery would eventually die out. Only in 1860 did it become illegal to own slaves. In 1859 the control of the former masters was strengthened by the Workmens' Breach of Contract Act.[82] Such masters and servants legislation was passed in most British colonies within a generation after the end of slavery.[83] For Sudipto Mundle, the Workmens' Breach of Contract Act was one of several factors that contributed to the dramatic expansion of debt bondage.[84]

CONTRACT LABOUR

The attack on slavery took place while slavery was still profitable. Abolition was successful well before the demand for unskilled labour in the tropics could be met by an international free labour market. The most important problem was the production of sugar. The intensity of labour on the sugar plantation and the distasteful nature of the work was such that it was difficult to recruit labour without coercion.[85] When the slave trade was abolished, the continuing decline of local population created a labour shortage. In the West Indies, this was intensified with the ending of slavery; many former slaves, particularly women, withdrew from the onerous labour of the plantation.[86] Indentured labour systems designed primarily to provide labour for expanding sugar production in Guyana, Trinidad, Natal and Cuba were also important in older areas like Jamaica and were used to get labour for other labour short areas. Indenture systems based in Africa looked very much like the slave trade they were supposedly replacing.[87] Within Africa, slave caravans continued to move down to the coast, and the use of pawns increased because it was difficult to recruit other forms of labour for expanding commodity production.[88]

Unfree labour was recruited on a large scale in India, China and, to a lesser degree, Java and Japan, where poverty and landlessness created a pool of willing migrants. While the Chinese 'coolie' trade involved people purchased and sold,[89] the Indian indentured system was essentially a voluntary migration, though there was some coercion and strong economic pressures on the migrants. Emmer argues that the Indian trade tapped into existing migrating patterns within India and to areas like Ceylon and the Straits Settlements.[90] The system provided labour not only for sugar plantations but also for tea in Ceylon, rubber in Malaya, railroads in North America and gold mines in South Africa. Watched by abolitionist interests, the British imposed controls on recruitment, which gradually became effective. The other powers were less conscientious. The French indenture system remained a disguised slave trade until 1862 and slaves were provided to Europeans from East Africa for a generation more.[91] The Portuguese abolished slavery in 1878 but continued what amounted to a slave trade until 1910.[92]

According to Kumar, 28 million Indians left India between 1846 and 1932, mostly as indentured labourers and mostly to other tropical colonies. This is more than twice the number of slaves estimated to have been exported in the Atlantic trade.[93] In addition, there were large-scale movements in Indonesia from Java to the outer islands and in India to the jute industry of Bengal and the tea plantations of Assam. The argument of Eltis, Fogel and Engerman that slavery was abolished in the Americas while still profitable can be extended elsewhere; capitalist enterprises operating in distant corners of the world were still hungry for unskilled labour and would pay what was necessary no matter how it was obtained.[94] The continued importance of labour coercion suggests that capital could not get the labour it wanted in other ways, at least in some areas.

THE PERSISTENCE OF SLAVERY

While European enterprise used new forms of coerced labour, slavery, slave use and slave raiding were expanding in many areas outside

European control. In West Africa, the end of the Atlantic trade and the decline in the Saharan trade hardly affected the price of slaves because demand within Africa was so high.[95] Slaves were used in West Africa to produce palm oil and peanuts for European markets, grain and cloth for Saharan markets, and soldiers for the slaving armies.[96] In East Africa, they produced cloves on Zanzibar and grain, coconuts and sesame on the coast.[97] In the Arab world, markets were being closed, but slave use seems to have increased. Clarence-Smith suggests that the 'rise in real incomes and the expansion in the numbers of the wealthy elite contributed to greater demand'.[98] Ricks describes an increase in slave use in Persia.[99] With the slave trade restricted elsewhere, the Red Sea route expanded and the Hijaz served as a base for trade to other parts of the Middle East.[100] Enslavement was clearly increasing within Africa during the second half of the nineteenth century with slaves being exploited both within Africa or in the Middle East.[101]

James Warren's study of the Sulu Sultanate gives us a similar picture for South-East Asia. Located between Borneo and the Philippines, the Sulu islands were the home of slave-raiding pirates. In the eighteenth century, they sold their slave booty along with spices and other Indonesian goods to Dutch and Chinese merchants.[102] During the nineteenth century slave-raiding expanded, but the export of slaves declined. The slaves were sold instead within the 'Sulu zone' – the coasts of Borneo, Celebes and the islands in between. Many slaves manned the ships that enslaved others or took part in productive labour. Women often became concubines or servants. The Sulu pirates took most of their slaves in the southern Philippines where the Spanish were at first helpless to block them. Only after 1860 did steamships enable European powers gradually to establish their control over slavers in both Atlantic and Pacific waters.

ENDING THE SLAVE TRADE

Colonial regimes were usually reluctant to act against slavery, both because they relied on slave-holding elites and because the administrators themselves did not see slavery as an evil. Sir Stamford Raffles abolished the import of slaves into Java in 1813 during British occupation, and the Dutch prohibited the slave trade elsewhere in Indonesia in 1818. Even though the Dutch moved during the early nineteenth century toward more intensive use of corvées and compulsory cultivation, they did not prohibit slave ownership until 1860, and then immediately began making exceptions for indigeneous slave-owners in the outer islands.[103] Only after 1878 was abolition pursued more vigorously, but in some areas no serious action was taken until the twentieth century. Elsewhere in

South-East Asia, abolition laws were enacted later. In Cambodia, the French signed treaties in 1877 and 1884 which had anti-slavery clauses, but acted decisively only with definitive occupation in 1897. The law prohibited the sale of persons but merely regulated debt slavery. With the imposition of colonial taxes and the elaboration of a money economy, debt slavery increased much as it had earlier in India.[104] In British-ruled Malaya, abolition of slavery and debt bondage came piecemeal, state by state, and was not complete until 1915.[105] In Burma, the British moved with similar caution, acting in parts of eastern Burma only in 1926.[106]

In Africa, serious abolition also came late. Slaves were freed at the Cape in 1833 by the same measure that freed slaves in the West Indies, but this only drove Afrikaner farmers into the interior, where they were less restrained in their efforts to coerce the labour of others.[107] The legal status of slavery was abolished on the Gold Coast in 1874.[108] In 1901 the British 'freed' the slaves in Southern Nigeria, and then immediately forbade them to leave their masters.[109] In spite of Freetown's historic role in the anti-slavery struggle, slavery was not abolished in the interior of Sierra Leone until 1926.[110] In 1848 the French were reluctant to apply an emancipation law which threatened the colony's relations with its neighbours. The major concern of colonial administrations was often to limit the damage which these islands of liberty did to their relations with African states.[111] Africa was largely conquered with armies recruited from slaves. Many of these armies, like the French, rewarded their troops and allies with slave booty.[112]

Conquest was usually followed by a ban on slave-trading and slave-raiding, but some laws were clearly written for outside consumption and local administrators were often reluctant to enforce anti-slavery legislation. As in Asia, colonial administrators distinguished slaving from slavery and argued that slavery was benign. Furthermore, they believed that compulsion was necessary to maintain production, and they tended to identify their own interests with those of slave-owning intermediaries. Invariably, slaves were seen as lazy workers who had to be coerced. Even when forced to abolish slavery, colonial administrators tried to reinforce the control of former masters over their ex-slaves or secure other forms of labour. This was particularly true in areas that were economically important or strategic. Thus, in East Africa, the British allowed slavery to die on the coast and killed it on Zanzibar, but tried other ways to guarantee labour supplies to the Zanzibar slave plantations.[113] In West Africa, the French recognized the property rights of the former masters in the fertile inner delta of the Niger, and former masters were able to use control over land to maintain control over labour.[114] In Northern Nigeria, masters continued to exercise control over supposedly free persons. The legal status of slavery for all people was abolished only in 1936.[115] In the Sudan, a British administration tolerated both slavery and slave trade until about 1930.[116]

For the colonial empires of Asia and Africa, the Indian formula of 1843 was a more attractive model than the American one. In West Africa, the French withdrew recognition of slave status in 1903, but with the state no longer standing behind the masters, more than a half million slaves returned to earlier homes.[117] In Northern Nigeria, Lugard freed only slaves who had been mistreated, but insisted on the slave's right to purchase redemption. Many, however, fled.[118] Once slavery lost its legal status, the official line was that it no longer existed. From that time on, colonial administrators were generally reluctant to involve themselves in conflicts that arose over the issue. In many areas, a small clandestine slave trade in children persisted well into the twentieth century, and slave status has often remained important up to the present.[119] An important difference between Africa and the Americas is that in the Americas slavery ended, while in Africa, slaves who knew no other home often remained embedded in traditional relationships.

While slavery persisted in Africa, though often in fossilized forms, in the Americas new forms of labour coercion developed. Former slaves often dreamed of '40 acres and a mule', but usually found themselves landless and dependent.[120] In Jamaica, Guyana and Brazil slaves were able to withdraw from plantation economies onto less commercial land.[121] In Barbados, in the American South, and in Cuba, control of land gave the former slave-owners the whip hand in the struggle to control the labour of their former slaves, who were tied by debt and landlessness to peonage and share-cropping arrangements.[122] Increasingly plantations turned to hired labour or gave way to share-cropping arrangements.

Colonial regimes in Africa and Asia generally lacked the funds to develop infrastructure and expand administration and thus turned, often massively, to forced labour. The Dutch in Indonesia relied more on a system of compulsory labour than on declining slave systems. In India, forced labour was particularly important in the early nineteenth century. In Africa, the Belgians relied very heavily on forced labour.[123] Forced labour was used by the French until 1946 and in Portuguese Africa into the 1970s.[124] Systems of forced cultivation similar to the Indonesian cultivation system were also used by the Portuguese and Belgians.[125]

SLAVERY AND REFORM

Neither the issue of slavery nor the slave trade was confined to colonial domains. During the nineteenth century, much of the world struggled with the problem of how to limit, resist and understand the West. African and Asian rulers were sometimes simply interested in fending off international pressure and creating alliances. This was certainly true of Menelik of Ethiopia. Between 1876 and 1908, when he suffered a stroke, Menelik issued edicts restricting and banning the slave trade. During the same period the taking of slaves helped finance the conquest of southern Ethiopia and rewarded the military commanders.[126] Khedive Ismail of Egypt actually asked for a British demonstration against Egyptian slavery in 1872, which was then arranged.[127] When Sultan Barghash of Zanzibar agreed to ban the slave trade in 1873, he did so only because he depended on British power.

Anti-slavery was also part of a more profound reaction. Just as the Russian reformers of 1861 saw emancipation of the serfs as a way of liberating productive energies from the restraints of an archaic social order, many reformers elsewhere saw abolition as part of a programme of reform. Both the Turks[128] and the Thais[129] were anxious to fend off imperialist threats to their sovereignty, but in both cases they sought to do so by transforming the nature of their own societies. In China, the last years of the Empire saw a series of sweeping reform proposals, one of which was finally approved in 1910.[130] Furthermore, some reformers looked to their own traditions to sanction anti-slavery action. Ottoman reformers sought justification in the humane principles of Islam.[131] Chou Fu, a Chinese reformer, argued that Chinese practice had strayed from early principle.[132] And Ahmed al-Nasiri, a Moroccan historian, wrote:

> The basic condition of the human being is freedom ... The reason in the Holy Law which existed in the Time of the Prophet and the pious forefathers for enslaving people – namely being capture in a jihad which has the object of making the Word of God supreme and bringing men to His religion – does not exist in these days.[133]

CLASS STRUGGLE

Those who abolished slavery were often concerned to maintain the social order and, in many cases, to confirm the authority of masters over those supposedly emancipated. Slaves, however, often refused to do what was expected of them. In the Americas, they rejected apprenticeship and withdrew their labour from the plantations, often retreating into upland areas. In Africa, slaves left their masters, usually to go home, but often to seek other opportunities elsewhere. Many, moreover, were born in slavery or had spent long years in slavery. Throughout Asia and Africa, the vast majority of slaves remained where they were. They gradually asserted control of their productive and family lives while often remaining subservient to former masters. In the Sulu archipelago, Warren describes people enslaved as children who had lost all memory of their original homes.[134] In Malaya, Endicott tells us that most freed slaves had no desire to return to aboriginal homes in the hill region. The desire of freed slaves to remain where they were was particularly strong when they had been effectively assimilated into a new culture, or where land was valuable or work remunerative.[135] These events often involved new forms of class struggle. Former slaves were usually successful in getting control of their family lives, but there were many ways in which masters were able to maintain their control over labour. In India, it was through the extension of debt bondage, in Senegal through control of the housing and job markets.[136] In both cases former masters were successful, but their success reflected their ability to protect and reward.[137] In parts of Africa, there was an increase of pawning in the twentieth century.[138]

In general, there was a complex process of negotiating new relationships. Thus, in many parts of the American South freed slaves forced masters to bid for their labour and in the process, asserted their social autonomy. Eventually, however, the plantation owners were able to use land ownership, control over credit and the coercive power of the state to force former slaves into dependent relationships, most often involving sharecropping.[139] The same thing was true in the more densely populated areas of Asia, Africa and the Americas. Shortage of land restricted the freedom of the bonded. State and master struggled to develop new ways of expropriating the labour of their former dependants, while slave and bondsman sought to circumscribe their ability to do so or to extract in exchange greater security. Even where masters were not successful in maintaining control of labour, they generally maintained their social ascendancy and, as a result, the stigma of slave origins has persisted to the present.[140]

CONCLUSION

Most slave systems were functioning well when slavery came under attack. While there are a few cases where slave labour was ceasing to be competitive or where masters acquiesced in emancipation because they had other ways of obtaining labour, this author knows of no case where slave owners as a class voluntarily rejected the institution. Emancipation came at a time when an expanding capitalism was still hungry for labour, and free labour migration was not capable of meeting that demand.

Within Africa and parts of South-East Asia, this was largely because slavery tied up so much of the population. There was simply no pool of free labour available.[141] Only in the twentieth century has free labour migration been capable of meeting the demand for labour in diverse parts of the world.

The attack on slavery involved a change in European conciousness. In the context of European history, it is impossible to argue that society became more humane, but people certainly began to regard certain kinds of exploitation as immoral. Slavery eventually became redundant, an inefficient way of getting labour, but emancipation took place long before that happened. Abolition was often forced on the periphery by a centre committed to a free labour ideology and convinced that free labour was essential to the dramatic growth and transformation of the capitalist world. This ideology was given its loftiest expression by the abolition movement spawned by and consistently supported by Christian churches. It was also powerful enough that those non-Western elites who sought to understand Europe's ascendancy invariably saw free labour as a crucial part of that ascendancy. It is only these ideological agendas that can explain why Europe turned against slavery when it was still profitable. Ironically, that ideology was resisted vigorously by colonial administrations willing to protect and exploit different kinds of servitude. To be sure, the freeing of labour from traditional restraints was often part of the colonial agenda, but it was usually put off into the distant future. Dependent on democratically elected European parliaments for their budgets, colonial administrations were vulnerable to the pressures of abolitionist groups and increasingly had difficulty controlling the flow of information about their policies. The timing of action against slavery was often motivated more by political pragmatism than by abolitionist principle. This also often shaped the way emancipation policies were carried out.

NOTES

1. Herbert Klein, *African Slavery in Latin America and the Caribbean* (Oxford, 1986); Richard Dunn, *Sugar and Slaves. The Rise of the Planter Class in the English West Indies 1624–1713* (London, 1973); Stuart Schwartz, *Sugar Plantations in the Formation of Brazilian Society. Bahia, 1550–1835* (Cambridge, 1985). For a recent provocative look at the process, see John Thornton, *Africa and Africans in the Making of the Atlantic World, 1400–1680* (Cambridge, 1992).
2. Philip Curtin, 'Epidemiology and the Slave Trade', *Political Science Quarterly*, 83 (1968), pp.191–216. See also Kenneth Kiple, *The Caribbean Slave. A Biological History* (Cambridge, 1984).
3. The literature on comparative slavery is limited. The classic is H.I. Nieboer, *Slavery as*

an Industrial System: Ethnological Researches (The Hague, 1910). The only comparable recent examination of slavery in broad cross cultural perspective is Orlando Patterson, *Slavery and Social Death* (Cambridge, Mass., 1982). The literature is, however, growing rapidly; see especially Léonie Archer, *Slavery and Other Forms of Unfree Labour* (London, 1988); Claude Meillassoux (ed.), *L'esclavage en Afrique précoloniale* (Paris, 1975) and *Anthropologie de l'esclavage* (Paris, 1986); Suzanne Miers and Igor Kopytoff (eds.), *Slavery in Africa* (Madison, 1977); Paul Lovejoy, *Transformations in Slavery: A History of Slavery in Africa* (Cambridge, 1983); Claire Robertson and Martin Klein (eds.), *Women and Slavery in Africa* (Madison, 1983); James L. Watson (ed.), *African and Asian Systems of Slavery* (Oxford, 1980); Anthony Reid (ed.), *Slavery, Bondage and Dependency in South-East Asia* (St. Lucia, 1983). For more bibliography, see Joseph Miller, *Slavery: A World-wide Bibliography* (New York, 1985).

4. David Brion Davis, *The Problem of Slavery in Western Culture* (Ithaca, 1966) and *Slavery and Human Progress* (New York, 1984).

5. The ideas developed here are expounded more fully in Martin Klein (ed.), *Breaking the Chains. Slavery, Bondage, and Emancipation in Modern Africa and Asia* (Madison, 1993). See also on emancipation in Africa, Suzanne Miers and Richard Roberts (eds.), *The End of Slavery in Africa* (Madison, 1988).

6. Patterson, *Slavery and Social Death*, p. 5; Meillassoux, *Anthropologie de l'esclavage*, pp. 23–42. See also Moses Finley, 'Slavery', in *International Encyclopedia of the Social Sciences* (New York, 1968) and 'Between Slavery and Freedom', *Comparative Studies in Society and History*, 6 (1964), pp. 233–49.

7. Watson, 'Introduction: Slavery as an Institution: Open and Closed Systems', in Watson, *African and Asian Systems of Slavery*, pp. 8–9.

8. Anthony Reid, 'The Decline of Slavery in Nineteenth-Century Indonesia', in M. Klein, *Breaking the Chains*, p. 65.

9. James McCann, 'Children of the House: Slavery and its Suppression in Lasta, Northern Ethiopia, 1916–1935', in Miers and Roberts, *End of Slavery*.

10. Ehud Toledano, 'Ottoman Concepts of Slavery in the Period of Reform, 1830–1880s', in M. Klein, *Breaking the Chains*; and *The Ottoman Slave Trade and Its Suppression, 1840–1890* (Princeton, 1982); Alan Fisher, 'Chattel Slavery in the Ottoman Empire', *Slavery and Abolition*, 1 (1980), pp. 25–45; Watson, 'Transactions in People: The Chinese Market in Slaves, Servants and Heirs', in Watson, *Asian and African Systems of Slavery*.

11. C. Martin Wilbur, *Slavery in China during the Former Han Dynasty: 206 B.C.–A.D. 25* (Chicago, 1943).

12. Fisher, 'Chattel Slavery'; Halil Inalcik, 'Servile Labor in the Ottoman Empire', in A. Ascher, T. Halasi-Kun and Bela Kiraly (eds.), *The Mutual Effects of the Islamic and Judeo-Christian Worlds: The East European Pattern* (New York, 1979); W. G. Clarence-Smith (ed.), *The Economics of the Indian Ocean Slave Trade* (London, 1989); Bernard Lewis, *Race and Slavery in the Middle East* (London, 1990); and Murray Gordon, *Slavery in the Arab World* (New York, 1987).

13. The distinction between elite slavery and productive slavery is the same Finley ('Slavery', p. 308) makes between slave societies and slave-owning societies.

14. Keith Hopkins, *Conquerors and Slaves* (Cambridge, 1978).

15. Finley, 'Slavery', suggests that there have been only five 'slave societies'. Clearly, however, many African societies and some Asian ones meet his definition. See also for a discussion of this topic, Hopkins *Conquerers and Slaves*, pp. 99–102. On Africa, see Lovejoy, *Transformations in Slavery*.

16. Reid, *Slavery, Bondage, and Emancipation*, p. 8.

17. Dunn, *Sugar and Slaves*; Schwartz, *Sugar Plantations*; Curtin, *Plantation Complex*.

18. Tanika Sarkar, 'Bondage in the Colonial Context', in Utsa Patnaik and Manjari Dingwaney (eds.), *Chains of Servitude: Bondage and Slavery in India* (Madras, 1985); Reid, '"Closed" and "Open" Slave Systems in Precolonial South-East Asia', in Reid, *Slavery, Bondage, and Emancipation*.

19. Lovejoy, *Transformations in Slavery*, pp. 35–43; K.Y. Daaku, *Trade and Politics on the Gold Coast, 1600–1720* (Oxford, 1970); John Vogt, *Portuguese Rule on the Gold Coast, 1469–1682* (Athens, Georgia, 1979). On São Tomé, see Robert Garfield, *A History of Sao Tomé Island 1470–1655* (San Francisco, 1992).
20. Joseph Harris, *The African Presence in Asia: Consequences of the East African Slave Trade* (Evanston, 1971).
21. On the Cape, see Nigel Worden, *Slavery in Dutch South Africa* (Cambridge, 1985).
22. Reid, *Slavery, Bondage, and Emancipation*.
23. For Asia see Reid, *Slavery, Bondage, and Emancipation*, pp. 14–28 and 25–7. For Africa, see Mohammed Mbodj, 'The Abolition of Slavery in Senegal, 1820–1890: Crisis or the Rise of a New Entrepreneurial Class?', in M. Klein, *Breaking the Chains*; George Brooks, 'The Signares of St. Louis and Gorée: Women Entreprenurs in Eighteenth-Century Senegal', in Nancy Hafkin and Edna Bay (eds.), *Women in Africa* (Stanford, 1976); James Searing, *West African Slavery and Atlantic Commerce: the Senegal River Valley, 1700–1860* (Cambridge, 1993).
24. Reid, *Slavery, Bondage, and Emancipation*.
25. Dunn, *Sugar and Slaves*; Schwartz, *Sugar Plantations*; Philip D. Curtin, *The Rise and Fall of the Plantation Complex: Essays in Atlantic History* (Cambridge, 1990); H. Klein, *African Slavery*.
26. Bruno Lasker, *Human Bondage in South-East Asia* (Chapel Hill, 1950).
27. On the *encomienda*, see Leslie Byrd Simpson, *The Encomienda in New Spain* (Berkeley and Los Angeles, rev. ed., 1966).
28. Dharma Kumar, 'Colonialism, Bondage and Caste in British India', in M. Klein, *Breaking the Chains*; David Feeny, 'The Demise of Corvée and Slavery in Thailand, 1782–1913', in ibid.; Reid, *Slavery, Bondage, and Emancipation*; and Reid, 'Slavery in Indonesia'.
29. Sarkar, 'Bondage in the Colonial Context'; Watson, 'Chinese Market in Slaves'; and Dharma Kumar, H. Fukuzawa, B. Chaudhuri, and E. Stokes, 'Agrarian Relations', in Dharma Kumar (ed.), *The Cambridge Economic History of India* (Cambridge, 1983), Vol. II.
30. Lovejoy, *Transformations in Slavery*; Paul E. Lovejoy, 'Plantations in the Economy of the Sokoto Caliphate', *Journal of African History*, 19 (1978), pp. 341–68; Martin Klein and Lovejoy, 'Slavery in West Africa', in Henry A. Gemery and Jan S. Hogendorn (eds.), *The Uncommon Market: Essays in the Economic History of the Atlantic Slave Trade* (New York, 1979); Martin Klein, 'The Impact of the Atlantic Slave Trade on the Societies of the Western Sudan', in Joseph Inikori and Stanley Engerman (eds.), *The Atlantic Slave Trade. Effects on Economies, Societies, and Peoples in Africa, the Americas, and Europe* (Durham, 1992).
31. Martin A. Klein, 'Slavery, the Slave Trade, and Legitimate Commerce in Late Nineteenth Century Africa', *Etudes d'histoire africaine*, 2 (1971), 5–28. On the widespread use of pawns, see Toyin Falola and Paul E. Lovejoy (eds.), *Pawnship in Africa: Historical Perspectives on Debt Bondage* (Boulder, 1994).
32. Mbodj, 'Abolition of Slavery in Senegal'.
33. W.G. Clarence-Smith, 'Cocoa Plantations and Coerced Labor in the Gulf of Guinea, 1870–1914', in M. Klein, *Breaking the Chains*.
34. François Renault, *Libération d'esclaves et nouvelle servitude* (Dakar, 1976).
35. Feeny, 'Corvée and Slavery in Thailand'.
36. Kumar, 'British India'.
37. Marc Bloch, 'How and Why Ancient Slavery Came to an End', in *Slavery and Serfdom in the Middle Ages* (Berkeley, trans. W.R. Beer, 1975); David Pelteret, 'Slave Raiding and Slave Trading in Early England', *Anglo-Saxon England*, 9 (1981), pp. 99–114; Pierre Bonnassie, *From Slavery to Feudalism in South-Western Europe* (Cambridge, 1991).
38. Richard Hellie, *Slavery in Russia, 1450–1725* (Chicago, 1982).
39. Feeny, 'Corvée and Slavery in Thailand'.
40. Davis, *Problem of Slavery*, pp. 402–8.
41. Adam Smith, *The Wealth of Nations* (New York, 1937 [1776]), 365.

42. Davis, *Slavery and Human Progress*, p. 107.
43. C. Duncan Rice, *The Rise and Fall of Black Slavery* (London, 1975), Ch. 6.
44. Seymour Drescher, 'Two Variants of Anti-Slavery: Religious Organization and Social Mobilization in Britain and France, 1780–1870', in Christine Bolt and Seymour Drescher (eds.), *Anti-slavery, Religion and Reform: Essays in Memory of Roger Anstey* (Folkestone, 1980) and *Capitalism and Antislavery: British Popular Mobilization In Comparative Perspective* (Basingstoke, 1986).
45. Eric Foner, *Nothing But Freedom. Emancipation and Its Legacy* (Baton Rouge, 1983); Philip Curtin, *Two Jamaicas* (Cambrdige, Mass., 1955); William Green, *British Slave Emancipation: The Sugar Colonies and the Great Experiment 1830–1865* (Oxford, 1976).
46. David Eltis, *Economic Growth and the Ending of the Transatlantic Slave Trade* (New York, 1987); and David Eltis and James Walvin (eds.), *The Abolition of the Atlantic Slave Trade* (Madison, 1981).
47. See for example Howard Temperley, *British Antislavery, 1833–1870* (London, 1972); and Suzanne Miers, *Britain and the Ending of the Slave Trade* (New York, 1975).
48. See for example James Richardson, *Travels in the Great Desert of the Sahara in 1845 and 1846* (London, 1848).
49. Raymond Dumett and Marion Johnson, 'Britain and the Suppression of Slavery in the Gold Coast Colony, Ashanti, and the Northern Territories', in Miers and Roberts, *End of Slavery*; Miers, *Britain and Ending of Slave Trade*, pp. 163–6. Of course, other colonies were afraid of offending slave-owning and slave-traiding African states. The seeming clarity of French legislation was ignored by local policy-makers; see Mbodj, 'Abolition of Slavery in Senegal'.
50. Miers, *Britain and the End of the Slave Trade*, Ch. 1.
51. Frederick Cooper, *Plantation Slavery on the East Coast of Africa* (New Haven, 1977), p. 45.
52. K.O. Dike, *Trade and Politics in the Niger Delta* (London, 1956); and Miers, *Britain and the End of the Slave Trade*, Ch. 2.
53. Toledano, *Ottoman Slave Trade*.
54. Ralph Austen, 'The 19th Century Islamic Slave Trade from East Africa (Swahili and Red Sea Coasts): A Tentative Census', in Clarence-Smith, *Indian Ocean Slave Trade*; and Janet Ewald, 'The Nile Valley system and Red Sea Slave Trade, 1820–1880', in ibid.
55. William Ochsenwald, 'Muslim-European Conflict in the Hijaz: The Slave Trade Controversy, 1840–95', *Middle Eastern Studies*, 16 (1980), pp. 115–26.
56. Suzanne Miers, 'Diplomacy versus Humanitarianism: Britain and Consular Manumission in Hijaz', *Slavery and Abolition*, 10, 3 (1989), 102–28; Paul Lovejoy and Jan Hogendorn, *Slow Death for Slavery. The Course of Abolition in Northern Nigeria, 1897–1936* (Cambridge, 1993), p. 275.
57. Gabriel Baer, 'Slavery in Nineteenth Century Egypt', *Journal of African History*, 8 (1967), pp. 417–41.
58. Daniel Schroeter, 'Slave Markets and Slavery in Moroccan Urban Society', in Elizabeth Savage (ed.), *The Human Commodity. Perspectives on the Trans-Saharan Slave Trade* (London, 1992).
59. Carolyn Fick, *The Making of Haiti: the Saint Domingue Revolution from Below* (Knoxville, 1990); David Geggus, *Slavery, War and Revolution: The British Occupation of Saint Domingue 1793–1798* (Oxford, 1982).
60. H. Klein, *African Slavery*; Peter Blanchard, *Slavery and Abolition in Early Republican Peru* (Wilmington, Del., 1992); and John Lombardi, *The Decline and Abolition of Negro Slavery in Venezuela, 1820–1854* (Westport, Conn., 1971).
61. Eltis, *Economic Growth*, pp. 207–17; Leslie Bethell, *The Abolition of the Brazilian Slave Trade* (Cambridge, 1970); Robert Conrad, *The Destruction of Brazilian Slavery, 1850–88* (Berkeley, 1972); Robert Brent Toplin, *The Abolition of Slavery in Brazil* (New York, 1975).
62. Eltis, *Economic Growth*, pp. 218–19; Rebecca Scott, *Slave Emancipation in Cuba:*

The Transition to Free Labour (Princeton, 1985); Manuel Moreno Fraginals, Frank Moya Pons and Stanley Engerman (eds.), *Between Slavery and Free Labor. The Spanish-Speaking Caribbean in the Nineteenth Century* (Baltimore, 1985).

63. François Renault, *Lavigerie, l'esclavage africain et l'Europe, 1868–1892* (Paris, 1971).

64. Reginald Coupland, *The British Anti-Slavery Movement* (London, 1933); Roger Anstey, *The Atlantic Slave Trade and British Abolition, 1769–1810* (Atlantic Highlands, NJ, 1975).

65. Eric Williams, *Capitalism and Slavery* (Chapel Hill, 1944). For the most recent assessments of the Williams thesis, see Barbara Solow and Stanley Engerman (eds.), *British Capitalism and Caribbean Slavery. The Legacy of Eric Williams* (Cambridge, 1987) and Barbara Solow (ed.), *Slavery and the Rise of the Atlantic System* (Cambridge, 1991).

66. Seymour Drescher, *Econocide: British Slavery in the Era of Abolition* (Pittsburgh, 1977), p.5.

67. Eltis, *Economic Growth*.

68. David Brion Davis, 'Capitalism, Abolitionism and Hegemony', in Solow and Engerman, *Legacy of Eric Williams*, p.218, citing argument in Davis, *Problem of Slavery*.

69. Howard Temperley, 'Capitalism, Slavery and Ideology', *Past and Present*, 75 (1977), p.96.

70. Except for the work of François Renault on Lavigerie, anti-slavery movements on the continent have not been studied. Most research on continental movements focuses on the first half of the century.

71. Neil Ascherson, *The King Incorporated* (London, 1963).

72. Martin Klein, 'Slavery and Emancipation in French West Africa', in Klein, *Breaking the Chains*.

73. Louise Lennihan, 'Rights in Men and Rights in Land: Slavery, Labor and Smallholder Agriculture in Northern Nigeria', *Slavery and Abolition*, 3 (1982), pp.111–39; Lovejoy and Hogendorn, *Slow Death for Slavery*; Hogendorn and Lovejoy, 'The Reform of Slavery in Early Colonial Northern Nigeria', in Miers and Roberts, *End of Slavery*; Hogendorn and Lovejoy, 'The Development and Execution of Frederick Lugard's Policies toward Slavery in Northern Nigeria', *Slavery and Abolition*, 10 (1989), pp.1–43.

74. Miers, *Britain and the Ending of the Slave Trade*.

75. Dennis Cordell, *Dar al-Kuti and the Last Years of the Trans-Saharan Slave Trade* (Madison, 1985) and 'The Delicate Balance of Force and Flight: The End of Slavery in Eastern Ubangi-Shari', in Miers and Roberts, *End of Slavery*; M. Klein, 'Slavery and Emancipation in French West Africa'.

76. A.G. Hopkins and Peter Cain, *British Imperialism* (London, 1993).

77. Myron Echenberg, *Colonial Conscripts. The Tirailleurs Sénégalais in French West Africa, 1857–1960* (London, 1991).

78. Michael Twaddle, 'The Ending of Slavery in Buganda'; Don Ohadike, 'The Decline of Slavery among the Igbo People'; and Linda Heywood, 'Slavery and Forced Labor in the Changing Political Economy of Central Angola, 1850–1949', all in Miers and Roberts, *End of Slavery*.

79. Temperley, *British Antislavery*; and D.R. Banaji, *Slavery in British India* (Bombay, 1933).

80. Temperley, *British Antislavery*, p.95.

81. Temperley, *British Antislavery*, p.107; Kumar, 'British India'.

82. Sarkar, 'Bondage in the Colonial Context'; Kumar, 'British India'.

83. See contribution by Paul Craven and Douglas Hay in this volume. See also Hilliard Pouncy, 'Colonial Racial Attitudes and Colonial Labour Laws in British West Africa, 1815–1946' (Ph.D. thesis, unpublished, Massachusetts Institute of Technology, 1981); Gerald McSheffrey, 'Slavery, Indentured Servitude, Legitimate Trade and the Impact of Abolition in the Gold Coast: 1874–1901', *Journal of African History*, 24 (1983), pp.349–68; Stanley Greenberg, *Race and State in Capitalist Development* (New Haven, 1980), pp.73–8.

84. Sudipto Mundle, *Backwardness and Bondage. Agrarian Relations in a South Bihar District* (New Delhi, 1986).
85. Stanley Engerman, 'Servants to Slaves to Servants: Contract Labour and European Expansion', in Pieter Emmer (ed.), *Colonialism and Migration: Indentured Labour before and after Slavery* (Dordrecht, 1986).
86. Temperley, *British Antislavery*, pp. 124–36.
87. Renault, 1976; Miers, 1975, pp. 28–30; Johnson Asiegbu, *Slavery and the Politics of Liberation, 1787–1861: A Study of Liberated African Emigration and British Anti-Slavery Policy* (New York, 1969).
88. Falola and Lovejoy, *Pawnship in Africa*.
89. Watt Stewart, *Chinese Bondage in Peru* (Durham, NC, 1951).
90. Emmer, 1986; Hugh Tinker, *A New System of Slavery: The Export of Indian Labour Overseas, 1830–1920* (London, 1974); Shula Marks and Peter Richardson (eds.), *International Labour Migration: Historical Perspectives* (London, 1985).
91. Renault, *Libération d'esclaves*.
92. W.G. Clarence-Smith, *The Third Portuguese Empire, 1825–1975* (Manchester, 1985), pp. 74–6, 107–9; Leroy Vail and Landeg White, *Capitalism and Colonialism in Mozambique* (London, 1980); Heywood, 'Central Angola'.
93. Kumar, 'British India'. On Africa, see Paul Lovejoy, 'The Impact of the Atlantic Slave Trade on Africa: A Review of the Literature', *Journal of African History*, 30 (1989), pp. 365–94.
94. Eltis, *Economic Growth*; Robert Fogel and Stanley Engerman, *Time on the Cross: The Economics of American Negro Slavery* (Boston, 1974).
95. E.A. McDougall argues that in many areas prices actually increased, see 'In Search of a Desert-edge Perspective: the Sahara-Sahel and the Atlantic Slave Trade, c. 1815–00', in Robin Law, (ed.), *The Ending of the Atlantic Slave Trade and its Impact on Western Africa*, (Cambridge, forthcoming). See also Martin A. Klein, 'Women and Slavery in the Western Sudan', in Klein and Robertson, *Woman and Slavery*; Martin A. Klein, 'The Slave Trade in the Western Sudan during the Nineteenth Century', in Savage, *The Human Commodity*; Richard Roberts, *Warriors, Merchants and Slaves* (Stanford, 1987), p. 117.
96. Lovejoy, *Transformations in Slavery*, Chs. 8 & 9; A.G. Hopkins, *An Economic History of West Africa* (London, 1973); Richard Roberts, 'The End of Slavery in the French Soudan, 1905–1914', in Miers and Roberts, *End of Slavery*; and E. Ann McDougall, 'Salt, Saharans, and the Trans-Saharan Slave Trade: Nineteenth Century Developments', in Savage, *The Human Commodity*.
97. Cooper, *Plantation Slavery*; Abdul Sherriff, *Slaves, Spices and Ivory in Zanzibar* (London, 1987).
98. Clarence-Smith, *Indian Ocean Slave Trade*, p. 5.
99. Thomas Ricks, 'Slaves and Slave Traders in the Persian Gulf, 18th and 19th Centuries: An Assessment', in Clarence-Smith, *Indian Ocean Slave Trade*.
100. Janet Ewald, 'The Nile Valley System and Red Sea Slave Trade, 1820–1880', in Clarence-Smith, *Indian Ocean Slave Trade*.
101. Jan Vansina, *Kingdoms of the Savanna* (Madison, 1966), Ch. 8; and M. Klein, 'French West Africa'; Clarence-Smith, *Indian Ocean Slave Trade*.
102. James Francis Warren, *The Sulu Zone, 1768–1898: The Dynamics of External Trade, Slavery and Ethnicity in the Transformation of a South-East Asian Maritime State* (Singapore, 1981), pp. 13–14.
103. Reid, 'Slavery in Indonesia'; Heather Sutherland, 'Slavery and the Slave Trade in South Sulawesi, 1660s–1800s', in Reid, *Slavery, Bondage, and Emancipation*, p. 277.
104. Alain Forest, *Le Cambodge et la colonisation française* (Paris, 1980), 342–57. A major concern in Cambodia was to put slaves on the tax rolls.
105. Kirk Endicott, 'The Effects of Slave Raiding on the Aborigines of the Malay Peninsula', in Reid, *Slavery, Bondage, and Emancipation*.
106. Anthony Reid, 'Introduction: Slavery and Bondage in Southeast Asian History', in Reid, *Slavery, Bondage, and Emancipation*, p. 34.

107. Elizabeth Eldridge and Fred Morton (eds.), *Slavery and South Africa: Captive Labor on the Dutch Frontier* (Boulder, 1994).
108. Dumett and Johnson, 'Slavery in the Gold Coast'; MacSheffrey, 'Abolition in the Gold Coast'.
109. Don Ohadike, 'The Decline of Slavery among the Igbo People', in Miers and Roberts, *End of Slavery*, p. 446; T.N. Tamuno, *The Evolution of the Nigerian State* (London, 1972), pp. 317–38.
110. John Grace, *Domestic Slavery in West Africa* (New York, 1975).
111. Miers, *Britain and the Ending of the Slave Trade*, pp. 157–66; Klein, 'French West Africa'.
112. Klein, 'French West Africa'; Lovejoy and Hogendorn, *Slow Death for Slavery*, p. 33; Echenberg, *Colonial Conscripts*, Ch. 2.
113. Frederick Cooper, *From Slaves to Squatters: Plantation Labor and Agriculture in Zanzibar and Coastal Kenya, 1890–1925* (New Haven, 1980); and Fred Morton, *The Children of Ham. Freed Slaves and Fugitive Slaves on the Kenya Coast, 1873 to 1907* (Boulder, 1990).
114. Martin A. Klein, 'From Slave to Share-Cropper: An Effort at Controlled Social Change in the French Soudan', *Itinerario*, 8 (1983), pp. 102–15.
115. Lovejoy and Hogendorn, *Slow Death for Slavery*, Ch. 9.
116. Martin Daly, *Empire on the Nile: The Anglo-Egyptian Sudan, 1898–1934* (Cambridge, 1986), pp. 231–7.
117. Martin Klein and Richard Roberts, 'The Banamba Exodus of 1905 and the Decline of Slavery in the Western Sudan', *Journal of African History*, 21 (1980), 375–94.
118. Hogendorn and Lovejoy, 'Lugard's Policies'.
119. Lovejoy and Hogendorn, *Slow Death for Slavery*, pp. 262–4; and C.N. Ubah, 'Suppression of the Slave Trade in the Nigerian Emirates', *Journal of African History*, 32 (1991), pp. 447–70.
120. Foner, *Nothing But Freedom*; Michael Wayne, *The Reshaping of Plantation Society. The Natchez District, 1860–1880* (Baton Rouge, 1983); Jay R. Mandle, *The Roots of Black Poverty: The Southern Plantation Economy after the Civil War* (Durham, 1978); Roger Ransom and Richard Sutch, *One Kind of Freedom: The Economic Consequences of Emancipation* (New York, 1977); and Claude Oubre, *Forty Acres and a Mule: The Freedmen's Bureau and Black Land Ownership* (Baton Rouge, 1978).
121. H. Klein, *African Slavery*; Green, *British Slave Emancipation*; Robert Toplin, *The Abolition of Slavery in Brazil* (New York, 1972); Robert Conrad, *The Destruction of Brazilian Slavery, 1850–1888* (Berkeley, 1972).
122. Foner, *Nothing But Freedom*; Scott, *Slave Emancipation in Cuba*; and Wayne, *Reshaping Plantation Society*.
123. David Northrup, 'The Ending of Slavery in the Eastern Belgian Congo', in Miers and Roberts, *End of Slavery*; Bogumil Jewsiewicki, 'African Peasants in the Totalitarian Colonial Society of the Belgian Congo', in Martin Klein (ed.), *Peasants in Africa* (Beverly Hills, 1980).
124. Clarence-Smith, *Third Portuguese Empire*, p. 215.
125. Ibid., pp. 182–4; and Jewsiewicki, 'Belgian Congo'.
126. Timothy Fernyhough, 'Slavery and the Slave Trade in Southern Ethiopia in the 19th Century', in Clarence-Smith, *Indian Ocean Slave Trade*; and McCann, 'Slavery in Lasta'.
127. Miers, *Britain and the Ending of the Slave Trade*, p. 78.
128. Toledano, 'Ottoman Concepts'.
129. Feeny, 'Corvée and Slavery in Thailand'.
130. Marinus Meijer, 'Slavery at the End of the Ch'ing Dynasty', in Jerome A. Cohen (ed.), *Essays on China's Legal Tradition* (Princeton, 1980).
131. Toledano, 'Ottoman Concepts'.
132. Meijer, 'Slavery of the Ch'ing Dynastry', p. 327.
133. Cited by John Hunwick, 'Black Africans in the Meditteranean World: Introduction to a Neglected Aspect of the African Diaspora', in Savage, *The Human Commodity*, p. 7.

134. Warren, *Sulu Zone*, Ch. 11.
135. Endicott, 'Slave Raiding in the Malay Peninsula'.
136. Mbodj, 'Abolition of Slavery in Senegal'.
137. Gyan Prakash, *Bonded Histories: Geneologies of Labor Servitude in Colonial India* (Cambridge, 1990).
138. Falola and Lovejoy, *Pawnship in Africa*.
139. Foner, *Nothing But Freedom*; and Wayne, *Reshaping Plantation Society*.
140. Watson, 'Chinese Market in Slaves', pp.245–8; Miers and Roberts, *End of Slavery*.
141. This was also true where work was unpleasant, as for example with sugar or the guano islands of Peru, or where population densities were low; see Stewart, *Chinese Bondage in Peru*.

Slavery and Pawnship in the Yoruba Economy of the Nineteenth Century

TOYIN FALOLA

Slaves were kept for non-economic purposes.[1]

The system of pawning that gave rise to *iwofa* labour was not a common practice of the Yoruba and ... it only became an important mode of labour recruitment in the 1890s.[2]

These two opening quotations are misleading, but their author, Adeniyi Oroge, pioneered the study of slavery and pawnship among the Yoruba, and it is important to examine the reasons why he reached his conclusions. His approach is based on the assumption that Yoruba slavery and pawnship differed from labour institutions elsewhere because they were not oppressive. Despite the evidence that he presents on the ubiquity of slavery and pawnship, he believed that kinship was at the core of labour organisation and that a kinship idiom defined the practice and ideology of both slavery and pawnship.[3] Writing in the late 1960s, the golden age of nationalist historiography, Oroge maintained a comfortable distance from scholars such as Walter Rodney, who realized that slavery was a form of social oppression.[4] Oroge used his impressive data to demonstrate a contrary thesis: that slaves and pawns were harmoniously integrated into the households of their masters and shared the fruits of their own labour. For Oroge, African slavery differed from that of the American plantation economy. He moralized that it was no sin to keep slaves and pawns in Africa because they were well treated: the so-called slaves generally discharged their duties with apparent efficiency and with the minimum of either supervision or compulsion, thanks largely to the operation of a system of incentives.[5] He objected to the use of the term 'slave', suggesting instead the use of other labels, including 'villenage', 'subject', 'servant', 'serf', or even 'pawn'.[6] When later he studied pawnship as an independent scholar, he settled for the Yoruba word, *iwofa*, apparently to implement his preference for using local terms to emphasize the non-oppressive character of pawnship.[7]

To a large extent, Oroge was an heir to a long-standing position among the Yoruba elite, cultural nationalists who considered slavery and pawn-ship as benevolent social institutions that were used to recruit labour and to assist the needy. Samuel Johnson, the nineteenth-century scholar and guru of Yoruba history, made the same point in his comments on both institutions.[8] Many of his successors, including academic scholars, con-tinue to argue that Yoruba slavery was benevolent and that the term 'slavery' itself is inappropriate.[9] Other studies on African societies have tended to reach different conclusions and move the subject in a different direction. The mainstream research examines servile institutions in the broader context of the development of the transatlantic system.[10] For these scholars, it is important to understand the historical background which made it possible for large numbers of slaves to be moved from Africa to the Americas. Since the Yoruba region was particularly impor-tant as a source of slaves for Brazil and Cuba in the nineteenth century, it is especially important to understand the operation of servile institutions in the Yoruba region at the time, as well as subsequent to the abolition of the transatlantic slave trade from the region in the 1850s. The present contribution is intended to analyse the role of slaves and pawns in the economy of the Yoruba states in the nineteenth century, specifically in the context of the major changes in the region during the century. In so doing, it will be shown that both institutions were widespread; moreover, new light will be shed on the African dimension in the study of unfree labour in the development of the Atlantic economy.

THE ORGANIZATION OF LABOUR

Four historical phenomena affected the organization of labour and its supply during the century: the abolition of the Atlantic slave trade; the expansion of agriculture; the rise of military states; and colonization by the British. The abolition of the Atlantic slave trade had, as elsewhere, the effect of diverting slaves to internal requirements.[11] The gradual impact of abolition resulted in a lengthy transition to a new economy based on the export of raw materials rather than labour. This shift to the so-called 'legitimate' trade was the second major development. As the successor to the Atlantic slave trade, the export of raw materials en-couraged the extensive use of slaves in local production to meet the demands of the international market, especially in the second half of the century. Western industrialization was felt in the Yoruba economy as a demand for oils and fats; in general the end of the Atlantic slave trade increased Euro-African interaction.[12]

Slaves had been used for production before the nineteenth century, but

'legitimate' trade expanded the market and thus put pressure on productive resources. The single most successful response to this pressure
was to put more labour to work, and the major way to increase labour was
through domestic slavery and pawnship. To those who had no reason for
immediate cash, using slaves for production was more profitable than
selling them, and those with access to capital were able to supplement
their labour requirements through pawning. 'Legitimate' trade provided
an excellent option for those with slaves and pawns. Those who wanted to
sell their slaves abroad still had the opportunity to do so in the first half of
the century, since the external market did not close all at once, and if
necessary pawns could be acquired when slaves were scarce or too
expensive.

While there is as yet no major study of Yoruba agriculture in the
nineteenth century, one conclusion that will be hard to challenge is that
farming expanded in scale and scope during the second half of the
century, partly to meet the demands of external markets.[13] As farming
expanded so did the use of slave labour and pawns. Trade, too, expanded, and the shipment of export products from the hinterland to the
coastal towns required a large amount of slave and pawn labour. Unlike
slave exports, many people, including the poor, participated in the
production of palm oil and kernels because of low capital and labour
requirements per unit of production. However, accumulating wealth in
this industry was a different matter. Without the facilities of modern
technology, many workers were necessary to produce large quantities of
oil and kernels and to transport them in heavy pots over long distances.

The third development was the rise of military states created and
nurtured by the use of force. Following the fall of Oyo, new city-states
emerged[14] at Ibadan, Ijaye, new Oyo, Oke-Odan, Abeokuta and Ilorin.[15]
These new city-states were governed by military or authoritarian regimes
which dispensed with or modified previous monarchical traditions.[16] Each
of the key operators of these states needed hundreds of people to fight,
farm and trade. Their answer was to perfect the use of warfare, kidnapping and raiding as enslavement mechanisms. In the intense competition
between these rival states on the one hand, and between the leaders of
each state on the other, slaves occupied a prominent position. Large
households, large farms and a large band of followers became essential
requirements in the maintenance of power. The acquisition of pawns was
also instrumental in the accumulation of power.

While the character of the military and political elite is clear, there is
very little on the sociology of the households that they built. While a
household had all the attributes of a lineage, a study of Ibadan has
demonstrated that these households controlled its members differently

from those of kinship groups. Furthermore, households experienced a continuous process of fission.[17] Households were economic units with slaves providing the most valuable labour; pawns supplemented these requirements. In effect, there was a range of relationships disguised within households, which might appear to uninformed outsiders as merely based on kinship but in fact included many unrelated servile members, both slave and pawn.

The fourth and final historical development which had an impact on labour mobilization was the gradual establishment of political authority by the British in the second half of the century. British forces occupied Lagos in 1851; a formal colony was announced in 1861; and the imperial move inland began in the 1890s, resulting in the swift transformation of the hinterland into a British Protectorate.

The British presence had a significant impact. The interests of 'legitimate' trade were promoted, even though they interferred with local politics. British officers began to criticise slavery and later pawnship as social institutions, promoting instead peasant production and the use of wage labour. While the export of slaves across the Atlantic ended in the 1850s, there was little the British could do about domestic slavery and virtually nothing about pawnship. Indeed, in the second half of the nineteenth century, virtually all British officials considered slavery and pawnship necessary evils, and it was feared that their prohibition would affect the economy in negative ways.[18] The British imposed conditions on the conquered Yoruba states that none the less led to a number of important changes in labour organization. The colonial regime used forced labour, but such impositions were considered temporary measures until wage labour undermined slavery and pawnship.

THE YORUBA ECONOMY

The Yoruba economy of the nineteenth century has been poorly studied. It is well known that tens of thousands of Yoruba slaves were exported to the Americas, especially between 1815 and the early 1850s, and the shift to palm oil and kernels as the major exports by mid-century had important repercussions in the interior. The few detailed works on different aspects of the economy reveal a society that was highly stratified and urbanized, dynamic in economic function, developed in its market institutions, and well connected to regional and international markets;[19] and the available evidence indicates that there was a very large number of slaves and pawns among the population.

The nineteenth-century economy revolved around agriculture, manufacturing and trade in a period of intense warfare and demographic change. Agriculture was dominated by crop cultivation; livestock production never developed beyond the keeping of small animals for occasional uses, and large-scale fishing was restricted to areas close to the sea and lagoons. Farming was the primary occupation for most of the population. Production was for both domestic consumption and for surplus to sell in local and international trade. Local manufacture supplied agricultural tools and goods for household use, while internal and regional trade was well connected to the international market in slaves, palm products and cotton, with slaves disappearing as an export in the 1850s, but with rubber and cocoa becoming important after the 1880s. The service sector included entertainment and medicine, both of which flourished, especially in the urban areas.

Slaves were used in the domestic economy to a much greater extent in the nineteenth century than ever before, as far as can be discerned from the available documentation. There is ample evidence to conclude that the economies of the big towns, the commercial centres and the military city-states relied on the large-scale use of slaves. Almost everywhere, slaves were essential in building new political bases and the economy to sustain them. To the military and political leaders, slavery was the best way to organize labour. Imperial Oyo had relied on slavery in the eighteenth century and continued to rely on slave labour in the early nineteenth,[20] as Clapperton and the Lander brothers observed in the late 1820s.[21] The successor states of imperial Oyo, notably new Oyo, Abeokuta, Ibadan and Ijaye, subsequently made use of slaves in the thousands. The incidence of pawnship, especially in the first half of the century, is difficult to discern, but there is no reason to assume that it was unimportant.

The careers of Atiba of new Oyo, Kurunmi of Ijaye, Oluyole of Ibadan and Ogedengbe of Ilesa reveal a careful strategy of building households through massive recruitment of slaves. Atiba relied on large numbers of slaves in relocating his supporters to new Oyo. Kurunmi migrated to his new home with hundreds of slaves and then expanded his following considerably. Oluyole combined his connections with the Oyo royalty with a large following that comprised hundreds of slaves to establish a base at Ibadan; while Ogedengbe imitated the Ibadan generals by acquiring comparable numbers of dependants and war boys at Ilesa. Similarly, Afonja of Ilorin recruited slaves in his campaign against the Alaafin, and after Afonja was overthrown by his own slaves, the new Muslim emirate continued the tradition of relying on slave labour.

Because these political actors and their subordinate officials promoted the expansion of households, their needs probably do more to explain the intense slave-raiding expeditions of the first half of the century than the requirements of the transatlantic slave trade. As slave raiding increased in the first twenty years of the century, military men found it more profitable to divert slaves to their own households than to sell them abroad. Since no one could have achieved power without a large number of followers, the personal households of the elite had to be maintained and also supplied with the resources to fight. It was possible to assemble a following through the manipulation of available resources for enslavement; armed slave supporters were used to make other slaves. The labour of slaves was also used to amass fortunes in more productive ways. Besides their importance in agriculture, occupations such as horse-tending, rope-making, barbing and cow-herding were probably dominated by slaves.[22]

The relocation of people to the new city of Oyo after the destruction of the imperial capital in the early 1830s was typical of the new social order of the nineteenth century. The Muslim rebellion of 1817 and continued Muslim unrest thereafter undermined the heartland of imperial Oyo, and, when forced to evacuate the old capital in the early 1830s, Atiba engaged in slave expeditions to recruit personal followers and labour in order to establish a new base to the south.[23] As in old Oyo, slaves played 'traditional' roles in the palace, served in the army and diplomacy, and were used on the farms and as porters in the caravan trade.[24]

At Kurunmi's Ijaye, slavery was also integral to society. Although it was a new city-state, the area was already well known as a market for slaves exchanged between Oyo and the Egba. As one missionary observed, Are Kurunmi was able to accumulate slaves, wealth and power through outright plunder. Kurunmi's household was so full of slaves and wealth that his compound was:

> a fortress and covered about eleven acres of ground. He had 300 wives and 1,000 slaves. His steward or manager of his domestic affairs was a slave only in name, for he himself owned 300 slaves and had a large domestic establishment of his own. Within the vast labyrinth enclosed by the outer walls of his compound, were stored away an untold amount of treasures of many kinds.[25]

Kurunmi could not have emerged as a political leader and a wealthy entrepreneur without slaves. His other chiefs, although subordinate to him, also employed slaves. One of Kurunmi's farm was over a hundred acres worked by an army of slaves.[26]

At Ibadan, the use of slaves was also part of the strategy of political and economic expansion. In its early years in the 1830s, slave raiding was very intense and the careers of its early leaders were dependent upon it.[27] The number of slaves belonging to Oluyole, for instance, was estimated in the 'thousands'.[28] His fellow chiefs also acquired slaves in the hundreds. Hinderer, the first European missionary to live there, compared the place with London in the 1850s in terms of its rate of population increase, which he attributed to the acquisition of new slaves through warfare.[29] According to his report of 1859, the overwhelming number of slaves raised fears of an uprising.[30] In 1877 the Yoruba missionary, the Rev. James Johnson, estimated that there were more slaves than freeborn.[31]

The situation at Abeokuta was similar.[32] In 1846, according to Townsend's estimate, the bulk of the population was enslaved;[33] the number of slaves being 'exceedingly large and contribut[ing] a very considerable proportion of its population'.[34] In 1880, its wealthiest citizens boasted of possessing 200–500 slaves; some slave-owners did not even have an accurate count of their possessions.

Neighbouring Ijebu also had an elite that depended on slaves, as Johnson reported in 1898.[35] There are similar descriptions for Ondo and Ilorin.[36] The war heroes that emerged in the east were particularly greedy in acquiring slaves.[37] For instance, Ogedengbe of Ilesa counted his slaves in the thousands, although the figures attributed to him were probably exaggerated to inflate his importance.[38]

The use of slaves was thus not limited to the economy, the focus of this essay. Slaves were used in such diverse activities as the palace bureaucracies and the 'public' sector in general. Samuel Johnson made it very clear that slaves were essential to the military of Oyo and later states, as well as in the building of households and harems.[39] As numerous scholars, including Oroge and Smith, have confirmed, the evolution of the new dynasties and kingdoms was closely linked to slavery.[40] Ojo has established that slaves were used in the palaces for a multiplicity of functions,[41] and Idowu has pointed to their role in religion as objects of sacrifice. This importance extended to the economy.[42]

THE ECONOMIC ROLE OF SLAVERY

To those who had access to slaves, especially in large numbers, there was no need to rely on co-operative work groups with the reciprocity that it involved. Neither was it economical to make use of the labour of the lineage for the simple fact that lineages did not tolerate exploitation. Indeed reliance on lineage labour slowed the expansion of economic activities because of the lack of reliability and limited nature of lineage support. Hence those who acquired substantial wealth in one way or another were connected with slavery, either through large-scale farming or extensive trade in local and imported goods.

Most big farms and commercial ventures were connected with men and women with large households. While most households had many free-born members, the slave population was usually more numerous. As some contemporaries described them, households had some characteristics of 'military barracks' because of the importance of slave raiding and warfare, but their functions extended to farming and trade. While the wealthiest slave-owners had hundreds, even thousands of slaves, a British officer in the mid-1860s defined anyone with ten slaves or more as rich. One Lagos chief so described had between twenty and thirty slaves.[43]

Holdings of ten to twenty slaves were insignificant compared to what the influential warriors had, however. At Epe in the 1850s, Kosoko, the exiled king of Lagos, and his lieutenant, Tapa Osodi, each had over five thousand slaves working on their various plantations.[44] According to Samuel Johnson, writing at the end of the century, 'The chiefs have large farms and farm houses containing a hundred to over a thousand souls. These extensive plantations not only support their huge establishments but also supply the markets.'[45] A local historian has tabulated the number of influential households at Ibadan at 104,[46] which accounted for much of the estimated population of 100,000 in 1877.[47] Efusetan Aniwura had 2,000 slaves on her plantation, according to Johnson.[48] At Abeokuta, a literate resident and himself a Yoruba wrote that there were wealthy individuals with at least 400 slaves, and the largest farmers had between 100 and 500 slaves on their plantations.[49] In Ijebu, the *Balogun* of Ikorodu was reported to be in possession of over 400 slaves in 1892,[50] while the *Lisa* of Ondo, a high-ranking chief, had over 800 slaves.[51]

Plantations, whether small or big, were devoted to a variety of crops to meet the requirements of subsistence and trade. These plantations had a number of common features. Since slaves and other farmers resided on them for long durations, they consisted of hamlets and farm houses where slaves and their masters or the representatives of their masters resided. If security was a problem, the plantation or at least the farm houses were fortified. If a plantation was not within walking distance of a town, a small village was founded to house the farmers, who included free persons and slaves who did not necessarily work on the same land or belong to the same master. In general, male slaves farmed the land, and female slaves produced palm oil, gathered kernels and processed other agricultural products.

Villages and farms defined the character of rural life and thus of slaves who worked on the plantations. Villages were never centres of power, entertainment or culture in the Yoruba country, which had already become noted for its urbanization before the nineteenth century. The elite who owned the plantations tended to be absentee landlords who relied on occasional visitations and the use of supervisors. A village had a head, a part-time administrator who settled minor problems and reported to his overlord in town. Livestock-keeping was part of village life. In some areas, tending cattle was assigned to slaves of northern origin because they were more knowledgeable in rearing livestock than local people.[52] Craft production developed more fully in the cities, but the larger villages had smiths to repair tools. Hawkers of small items and itinerant men and women who performed a variety of occupations visited these settlements.

Slaves divided their time between working for their masters and for themselves, as noted in 1857: 'In general the labourer [had to work] from early morning till about 11 o'clock for his master; after his breakfast and rest during the heat of the day, he [continued to work but] for himself the remainder of the day.'[53] Not all worked for such short hours, as many farmers returned to the fields in the evenings. In some places slaves had a day or two free in a seven-day week and were also allowed some hours in the day to rest and to undertake activities of their own choice.[54] It was estimated that an active slave was capable of supplying the needs of five people and generating additional surplus for the market.[55]

The existence of free time has been used as evidence of the relative leniency of African slavery, thereby demonstrating that Yoruba slaves lived a blissful life.[56] The working hours on the fields of their masters were not different from those of free-born farmers, but the slaves did not control the output of their labour, unlike the free-born. While farm work generally was avoided in the afternoon heat when productivity was low, slaves still had to fend for themselves and hence had to work extra hours. They were responsible for their own medical and other domestic needs. Slaves were at the mercy of their masters in the allocation of land to farm, although, as Anna Hinderer observed, slave plots usually adjoined the fields of the masters.[57]

Slaves were also put to extensive use in the distribution sector of the economy. Although trade and farming often went hand in hand, there were entrepreneurs who concentrated mainly on trade. To the rich or free-born who engaged in their own trade, slaves were needed as agents and carriers. Political officials relied on trusted slaves to conduct their business, a practice which was common throughout the century and is well documented by the European travellers and missionaries who were impressed by the trust that was placed in such slaves.[58] The entrepreneurs who were successful were dependent on the use of slaves, especially those who had no time to travel. According to Hinderer, 'slaves are employed by their masters in trading and they [are] so implicitly trusted, that they are sent on expeditions which involve an absence of several months at a time, and return when their commission has been fulfilled'.[59] When masters issued instructions that produce be sold on the farms, slaves doubled as farmers and traders of foodstuffs and raw materials, rendering accounts to their supervisors or owners. Many, in fact, shuttled between the farms and local markets on a regular basis in order to sell perishable items. There were also cases of slave entrepreneurs who either traded on behalf of their masters or used political offices associated with slave titles to trade. Such slave entrepreneurs came to the notice of Europeans in Lagos.[60]

Slaves provided essential transport services as porters. As I have pointed out elsewhere, Yoruba trade usually employed caravans in regional and long distance trade, and caravans needed large numbers of porters to carry articles of trade and other necessities for their masters. Slaves also formed part of the armed guards to protect traders from brigands. Some slaves were even sold if business turned disastrous and the trader needed money to settle debts or recoup losses.

Slavery was connected with the economy in other important ways. Slaves served as toll collectors,[62] as Townsend observed in the case of Kurunmi.[63] Slaves were counted among the canoe men and fishermen making use of the sea and the lagoons.[64] They were involved in salt making, textile production and indeed virtually all other occupations. As disposable items and trade goods, they were sources of wealth to those who traded in them on a regular basis. The state and its leaders sold slaves to procure firearms for warfare and state security, while the military disposed of slaves for immediate cash.[65] Slave prices were considered high for most of the period, in spite of occasional fluctuations.[66] As Hinderer noted, the high-ranking officials in the Ibadan military were slave-traders, making use of their houses as markets, a practice that continued at least until the 1880s.[67] The states along the coast which did not base their reputation on military strength had to acquire captives, and hence selling slaves was a lucrative enterprise. As Biobaku and Ayantuga have shown, the Egba and Ijebu profited from their middleman position in trade in which slaves and other key items were involved.[68] Slavery enabled owners to invest money in property that was relatively secure in economic value and negotiable in times of trouble. Acquiring slaves was an investment considered 'absolutely necessary' for work and better than 'investments upon cloths and beads and which may be easily consumed by fire'.[69]

WORKING CONDITIONS

Samuel Johnson and other contemporary observers recognized that slavery was important, but they argued that its practice was relatively benign, just as Oroge was later to do. Oroge concluded that profits from the export trade enriched slave-owners, but greater wealth enabled masters to be more humane to their slaves:

> Contrary to what one would expect, instead of causing the working hours of the farm slave to be increased, the growing incidence of legitimate commerce led to a further reduction of the time a slave was expected to spend in working for his master, especially by the heathen slave-owners. In view of the increasing returns which the cultivation of cotton brought to agriculture in the late 1850s, the heathen chiefs, in order to forestall any ill will on the part of their slaves, spontaneously gave their slaves from one to three free days in which to work exclusively for themselves.[70]

However, Oroge supplies little evidence for this important conclusion, and he did not explore changes in the working conditions of slaves in the nineteenth century or contrast practices over a period of time. As a result, both his theoretical premises and his analysis of empirical data are open to question.

Slaves were integrated into society and some were allowed to redeem themselves; a few were granted bureaucratic and political power which they manipulated to become influential and to acquire property of their own, including slaves. The ideology underlining slavery as an institution allowed the integration of slaves to a certain extent. It provided opportunities for select numbers of slaves as mechanisms of reward which also helped to rationalize the system, weaken the determination of slaves to resist, and ensure control over the labour of the bulk of the slave population.[71]

Although the empowerment and integration of slaves are useful counterpoints to those contrasting slavery in Africa and the Americas, these features of slavery should not be used to obscure the extent of exploitation of the Yoruba slave population. There is evidence to suggest that slaves were sometimes treated generously and benefited from humane treatment, but there is also evidence of considerable exploitation. The slaves who received the best treatment were personal attendants in the large households and soldier-slaves who helped to sustain the military. These favoured slaves had opportunities of redemption and could themselves benefit from wars to acquire slaves.

The majority of slaves had to take care of themselves, however. Those on large farms were allowed to take what they could eat but otherwise did not profit from their masters' crops. Slaves were allowed to use their free time on their own farms or engage in other enterprises. While many received plots, there were complaints that these were located on land that was overworked and hence infertile. Some masters even denied their slaves spare time to work on their own. Ijebu masters did not set aside a free day for slaves and expected them to work from 6 a.m. to 2 p.m.[72] The numerous changes during the turbulent century probably affected many slaves in other ways; chronic warfare, religious observances and 'legitimate' trade each affected relations between slaves and their masters. The impact of these factors on slave exploitation is unclear, and there is a need to investigate in detail the impact of Christianity and Islam on the condition and status of slaves. Accumulation and profit from trade did not necessarily predispose masters to liberal treatment; on the contrary, the ambition was to accumulate more, which explains the expansion of the households and the continuation of slaving expeditions in the second half of the century. In order to yield profits to traders and to provide resources to procure firearms and guns, 'legitimate' trade and the role of slavery in its promotion were crucial. Slavery could be rationalized in cultural and religious terms, but its linkage to large-scale production also meant that it was rationalized in economic terms as well. Oroge failed to build into his analysis this economic dimension.[73]

In general, slaves complained about their lack of freedom, powerlessness and suffering; at least until they gained redemption or some level of mobility which entitled them to a number of privileges. When the opportunity to escape was available and there was the need to flee, slaves readily did so.[74] There were limits both to the extent to which a kinship ideology rationalized the status of slaves and the degree to which slaves accepted their oppression and exploitation.[75]

PAWNSHIP

Those who had the means to own slaves were the same people who had access to pawns, since they had the money to acquire them.[76] Consequently, the history of pawnship in the nineteenth century is closely associated with slavery. Pawns were not derived from warfare but from contracts on loans. Hence it was the free-born members of society who were pawned, because pawnship did not imply a loss of liberty or political freedom. Pawns were usually cheaper to obtain than slaves; a small loan was sufficient to conclude a pawning transaction. Like slavery, pawnship enabled a lineage or household to expand its numbers and have access to more labour for its own ends. Unlike slavery, pawns were not derived from warfare, raiding expeditions, kidnapping, or other violence.

Again, Oroge's analysis pioneered the study of pawnship among the Yoruba, and indeed, his study is one of the earliest scholarly treatments of the subject of pawnship in Africa.[77] Basing his analysis on contemporary sources, Oroge initially argued that 'the system of pawning that gave rise to *iwofa* labour was not a common practice of the Yoruba ... it only became an important mode of labour recruitment in the 1890s.'[78] Later he demonstrated the ways in which 'wars, raids, famine, scarcity of cowries [money] and imperative heavy expenses that could not be met by normal efforts were potent factors in the growth of the institution' of pawnship, which suggests that pawnship was practised before the 1890s.[79] Whether or not Oroge would have resolved this contradiction had he lived longer is unclear.

There is information, some from the nineteenth century, some later, to reconstruct the essential features of the institution of pawnship and to suggest its relative importance in the nineteenth century.[80] By the early twentieth century, pawning was very important, precisely because it provided a means of acquiring labour and dependants through the extension of credit. Most pawns, like slaves, worked in the farms of their creditors, but the creditor had the right to assign other duties and services. Consequently, pawns were found in virtually all sectors of the economy as well as in households. The basic features, as described in early colonial reports, applied fully to the nineteenth century. As one colonial administrator noted, pawnship was, 'a contract entered into for the purpose of obtaining a sum of money on loan. The terms are that until the debt is paid the "Iwofa" or borrower shall provide labour either of himself or of his child for the 'Olowo' or lender in lieu of interest'.[81] There is one important historical problem, however. The sources do not always accurately differentiate between slaves and pawns, and hence it is more difficult to analyse the relative importance of slavery and pawnship in the nineteenth century.

The extent of the financial burden of borrowing money with pawns as surety was heavy. The debtor was not even entitled to the entire amount of the loan. In some communities, the creditor was entitled to receive a 'bonus' of about ten per cent on a loan. This 'bonus' was either deducted from the actual amount of money given to the debtor or added to the loan, although the fee itself did not attract interest. This additional clause on loans, which further increased the burden of debtors, was prevalent largely among the Egba and Egbado, where 'it was looked upon as a bonus due to the lender for the service rendered to the borrower in lending him the money to meet his requirements'.[82] In addition, an intermediary, *onigbowo*, collected a nominal fee from the debtor for providing surety. The *onigbowo* collected the money and handed it over to the debtor in the presence of the creditor and witnesses. As a party to the contract, the *onigbowo* was the contact and middleman between the creditor and the debtor. He ensured that the loan was repaid and that the creditor did not maltreat the pawn.

A loan could be repaid at any time, a few days or many years after the money had been received. All contracts were terminated when the loan was repaid, but in many cases it took a long time, fifteen to twenty years, to settle the debt, thus ensuring that pawns worked for that many years. A debtor had the option of either paying the loan in full or in instalments, except that the latter arrangement still required the continued labour of the pawn until the full loan was paid.

Terms of contracts were always specified in advance. There were two types, one for children and the other for adults. The differences involved the maintenance of the pawn and the number of days in a month and the hours in a day that the pawn worked for the creditor. Adults were expected to cater for themselves and pursue their own tasks while at the same time working for their creditors. An adult began his or her life as a pawn the day after the loan was consummated. A married woman was allowed to live with her husband and went to the creditor's (usually a woman's) house, in the morning. Alternatively, the woman made a weekly payment to the creditor instead of providing her labour.[83] Widows sometimes lived with their creditors, who were expected to provide food and other minor necessities. Should the female pawn be accompanied by her children, whatever assistance they gave their mother was to the creditor's advantage.

The most important aspects of the contract were the required number of days of service and the daily working hours. With respect to time, the creditor took the best part of the day, from the early morning to noon, the time most suited for farm work, before midday fatigue set in, and also the time most suitable for trading in morning markets. The pawn could spend the rest of the day as he or she wished. During the period of service, the pawns were either supervised to ensure that time was well spent or were assigned specific tasks to be completed. If a pawn was working for a farmer, for example, the usual expectation was the completion of 160 yam heaps between 6 a.m. and 11 a.m. In terms of the number of days of service, the most common contract required a pawn to work for the creditor for half a month, with the remainder of the month belonging to the pawn. According to the Yoruba calendar, the pawn was committed to the creditor for either nine or seventeen days, with the following nine or seventeen days free.

The half-month contract was the maximum that could be required of a pawn, if the loan was large.[84] For instance, in Egbado at the end of the nineteenth century, any amount above the equivalent of £8 meant that the pawn worked two days in four. For smaller loans, a pawn might only be in service one day in four.[85] In Ibadan, Oyo, and the surrounding areas, a loan above £10 was considered high, and a pawn, working under a contract known as *kosinko*, was expected to fulfil the maximum in terms of the days and hours of work. A loan of between £7 and £12 attracted the minimum conditions. This was known as the *ijagbo*, and the pawn worked one in five days, being expected to make 200 heaps or its equivalent in enterprises other than farming.[86] There were other variations to the arrangement, especially if the loan was small. At Ife, a colonial report, which probably reflects the conditions in the late nineteenth century as well as the early twentieth, indicates that a pawn was required to make a certain number of heaps in a year or work every morning for one week in each month.[87]

In the case of children, contracts were negotiated and 'signed' on their behalf by their parents, guardians, or other relations. A minor could be used by the parents or those related to the parents to acquire a loan. When children were pawned by relations, it was either because they had lost their parents or the lineage (as distinct from the nuclear family) or had an urgent need for money. In 1915 the *Alake* of Abeokuta described two common situations in which young people were forced into pawnship by their relations:

> A is the head of a family. He has a younger brother B and a son C. A incurs a debt in the building or repair of the family compound and borrows money on this account from D to whom he consequently becomes IWOFA. The brother B who is 17 or his son C who is 14 seeing this, says 'no, it is a disgrace to us and the rest of the family that its head be an IWOFA on account of debt incurred on the common interest of the family when we the younger relations are there; one of us – either the younger brother or son – as is duty bound, must voluntarily offer to substitute his services for those of the Head of the family to his OLOWO'.[88]

> A is the head of a family and has a son B who has C and D, grandchildren to A. A dies and in order to meet the funeral expenses, his son B has to borrow money from E to whom he consequently becomes IWOFA. D the younger son of B and the youngest of the family, a lad of 15, says 'it is a disgrace to us that our father should be an IWOFA on account of our grandfather's funeral expenses when we are there. I voluntarily offer to substitute my services in place of my father's to his OLOWO'.

Again, the account comes from the early twentieth century but the conditions prevailed earlier.

The *Alake*'s evidence was not peculiar to the Egba; saving the 'honour of the house' was a common reason for 'requesting' any young member of a lineage to enter into pawnship for either the collective interest of the lineage (as in repair of houses or the burial of a prominent elder) or the specific purpose of paying the medical expenses of a relation.

The child was not a debtor but a pawn, and it was not required of him/her to repay the loan but to work for the creditor as interest on the loan. The borrowed funds did not have to be spent on the child or anything of direct benefit to him/her. In making use of children in this manner, the underlying assumption was that children were obliged to reciprocate the support and protection offered by their parents, and pawnship was one way of so doing. In any event, it was believed that parents had the right to control and use the services of their children as they deemed fit. The consent of the children was usually taken for granted.[89] It was generally assumed that the decision to pawn rested with the father or other male relation, but it was expected that this should be discussed with the child's mother. Cases in which women pawned their children required the consent of their husbands.

Child-pawns were handed over to creditors in the presence of the *onigbowo* and other witnesses, and the child lived with the creditor until the debt was paid. Creditors preferred children above the age of eight, that is, those who were old enough to do minor chores, carry small loads, and help with weeding. There were cases of pawns less than eight years of age – those whose 'labour [was] of little value'.[90] Such situations arose if the loan was small and the parents were very poor. Young children in this situation usually lived with the creditors for a long time before the parents could find the money to pay off the loan. Little girls were acceptable pawns because of the possibility that the creditors or their relations might marry them later in life; in the meantime, girls could provide some domestic services (namely, serving food, cleaning, playing with other children, etc).

A creditor was entitled to the entire labour and commanded the full custody of a child-pawn. When creditors changed residence within a town, the children had to move with them. Relocation to another town had to be discussed with the parents so that they would still be able to see their children. If a child refused to co-operate at any time in the contract, the creditor had the right to request a substitute or the immediate repayment of the debt. Parents had the right to visit their children, a common occurrence to ensure the co-operation of the children and to reassure children that loans would be paid. At the same time, such visits protected children from bad treatment. Pawns could also visit their parents, especially during major social and religious events.

It was likely that the majority of pawns were girls, although this should be taken as a tentative statement.[91] As much as possible, creditors rejected boys under the age of eight, but took girls, even in their infancy.

In some cases of small children, creditors might even try to keep them in 'complete ignorance'[92] of their real parents, despite the normal expectations discussed above. A father forced by circumstances to pawn his boy usually struggled hard to redeem him because he, too, needed the boy's labour. In the case of girls, the chances were higher that there would be no need to repay the loan. Indeed, in most cases, a girl stayed with the creditor till marriageable age, making pawnship in some cases a clever disguise for early marriage with all or part of the bride wealth being already paid. Should the creditor or any of the creditor's relations marry the pawn, not only was the loan cancelled but the parents also collected the bride wealth. If marriage was intended, it was in the best interests of the creditor to discuss his plans with both the girl and her parents to avoid being accused of using force and thus violating one of the terms of the contract. There were instances when debtors in fact urged the creditors to marry their daughters as a way of terminating their loans.[93] Should the girl marry someone else, her husband had to pay the loan, in addition to the bride-wealth. If it was clearly established that the creditor sexually abused a girl, the loan was cancelled and the pawn's services terminated. The same results obtained if the creditor tried to force a marriage.[94] If a girl was raped, the creditor lost the pawn and his money, and if the rape led to pregnancy, the creditor had no rights over the baby, which reverted to the parents of the pawn.[95] Should the pawn be already betrothed when sexual abuse occurred, the creditor had to pay a huge fine to the girl's fiancé and to the indigenous authorities.

Girls were more often pawned than boys for three other reasons. First, the rate of desertion and the incidence of resistance was lower for girls than for boys. Secondly, a debtor often anticipated that the creditor or one of the creditor's male relations would be attracted to the pawn and thereby either propose marriage or be tempted to request sex, both of which constituted gross violations of the terms of contracts and therefore resulted in the cancellation of the loan. Thirdly, for farmers and others engaged in labour-intensive occupations, it was more profitable for them to retain their own male children than to pawn them to others. The value of a boy's labour was also perceived by potential creditors as well, and creditors often put pressure on debtors to pledge their boys. If forced by circumstances to relinquish a boy, the debtor was bound to incur the loss of male labour, which was considered more valuable than that of girls.

If a pawn died, a period of grace was allowed for the debtor to repay the loan. If the pawn had served for more than four years, some deduction was usually allowed on the loan. The debtor was not obliged to replace the deceased with another pawn. What was important was the liquidation of the loan, and the interest no longer became an issue. However, if the debtor could not settle the loan for a long period, it was expected that a new pawn would be provided. Should a debtor die, the pawn continued to serve until the loan was paid by either the pawn or any of his/her relations.

Pawns could redeem themselves. For girls, marriage brought immediate redemption. For a boy, the attainment of adulthood automatically changed the contract to the one described for adults, although the pawn could continue to stay with the creditor and could also hope that the creditor would assist him in achieving an independent existence. If a farmer, the creditor was expected to allocate land to the adult-pawn. The pawns could then use part of their income to repay the loan and liberate themselves.

Adult pawnship seem to have generated less tension than child-pawnship. In the case of adults, it was a voluntary decision, one taken when all other available options to raise money had failed. In the case of children, the decision was taken on their behalf, which explains why the terms of the contract had to be modified when the children matured. The real source of tension was that child-pawns lived with the creditors who shouldered the responsibilities of feeding and accommodation. Other needs, such as clothes and medicine, were optional, and the pawn had to go to parents or relatives for these. The expectation was that the creditor would treat the pawn as an adopted child, with all due love and care; but, unlike biological children, there was no expectation that all of the needs of pawned children would be provided. As a British officer observed during this century, 'the boy or girl is treated exactly as a member of the family of the lender's own children. These pawns generally enter the families of those in better circumstances than themselves. Great care is often taken in teaching them trades, such as that of a leather worker, blacksmith, weaver, etc.'[96] The creditor was not obliged to train the pawn, however. The pawn was lucky if the creditor had a skill that could be learnt by observation.

While in theory a creditor could not maltreat a pawn, oral evidence and the very rich folklore on pawnship and slavery indicate that pawns frequently suffered, and sometimes pawns were illegally sold into slavery. Whilst the children of a creditor could say 'no' to their parents, pawns had no freedom of choice with the creditor. Pawns were not expected to refuse difficult assignments. Yoruba folklore contrasts this difference, as the following example notes: 'The master knows the thorny patch, he doesn't hoe there; . . . it is the iwofa that bends his back over the thorny patch.' Sources are unanimous in the conclusion that pawns were expected to be hard working, to accept assignments without question, and to avoid making unnecessary complaints. A widespread saying sums up this expectation:

If the iwofa starts shivering,
They will say he's up to his tricks again
If it was the child of the creditor
They would rub him lavishly with palm oil.

The message here is that the creditor's child, who did little, could fall ill and expect immediate care, while the pawn, who worked hard all the time, would be accused of malingering or laziness should he or she complain of fatigue or sickness. Fadipe has concluded that a child worked not out of any sense of duty but as an 'act of perseverance'. To him, children were deprived of the opportunity to play with their age-mates, as their masters demanded the full use of their time.[97] Fadipe also adds that a pawn could work for an indefinite number of years, a real constraint on freedom:

> Where the *iwofa* system entailed hardship was in the matter of the repayment of a loan in order to redeem the pawned person. To be forgotten in the 'creditor's farm', as the act of serving in peonage is styled, was not an infrequent occurrence, and was often the cause of boys and girls running away. A boy or a girl who was in pawn as a result of celebration of funeral customs of his father might be forgotten by his brothers and sisters whose job it was to repay the loan. A man who pawned his younger brother in order to pay bride price for his wife might forget his obligation to redeem the child. Lastly, girls often got neglected in peonage. Such a girl often had to wait until a young man came along who paid the amount owed in lieu of bride price and other incidental payments made before being married. Girls who were already betrothed were also often pawned by their impecunious fathers, their fiances being afterwards called upon to redeem them in discharge of all obligations in respect of bride price.[98]

Much also depended on the character of the creditor. Oral evidence refers to 'wicked people', in reference to high-handed individuals who abused their own children and hence who had no compunction about abusing pawns. There are also reports of creditors with limited means who wanted to increase their own income and social standing by exploiting the labour of their pawns. Whilst the creditor was expected to maintain the pawn, oral evidence again refers to creditors who asked the parents of the pawns to pay medical bills or to collect their children for treatment and return them when they were healthy again.

Oral evidence strongly suggests that there were important differences between the treatment of pawns and the treatment of kin, including the degree of exploitation of pawns and the failure on the part of creditors to show love or concern for pawns, especially when they had a prolonged illness or got into major trouble. The very fact that the training of a pawn was optional indicates that pawns were exposed to the risk of neglect.

Child-pawns reacted to ill-treatment by reporting creditors to parents or otherwise resisting their oppression. On the latter, the evidence of Fadipe is most revealing and unique:

> a child who could not put up with the continued ill-treatment of his master could ask to have the debt on his head transferred to some other master. The loan could always be repaid at a moment's notice. If parents or relatives refused to heed his complaint, the child could always refuse to go on serving, in which case someone else would have to be substituted for him. The older the child, the greater his chances of rebelling in this way.[99]

A pawn who left the creditor could not be compelled to return.

However, irrespective of the problems that a pawn could encounter, neither the society nor the contracts confused pawnship with slavery. This distinction interested (and sometimes amused) British officers in the early twentieth century. A common statement was that 'An "Iwofa" or "pawn" is a free man; his social status remains the same; his civil and political rights are intact, and he is only subject to his master in the same general sense that "a borrower is servant to the lender".'[100] Ross, the Resident of Oyo Province, thought that there was no stigma attached to pawnship and that a pawn (presumably an adult) was a 'perfectly free agent, at liberty to regulate his own life and to follow his own pursuits when the daily task set by his master is over'.[101]

In spite of the clear differences between slaves and pawns, it should be repeated that a pawn did not have full control over the use of his/her labour. The slippage into debt, in many cases, was evidence of poverty, and in a stratified society where people were motivated by the desire for wealth and power, pawnship represented to many the marginalization of an individual. A popular saying uses a few words to point to the diminished prestige and self-assertion involved in pawnship: 'A pawn cannot boast in the presence of his creditor'.

CONCLUSION

The widespread use of slaves and pawns in nineteenth-century Yoruba-land calls into question a number of assumptions on the nature of servile institutions in the Yoruba region. First, the suggestion that slaves were not important has to be rejected. It also seems likely that pawnship was important much earlier than the last decade of the nineteenth century. That the members of society with small farms and other businesses were able to function without slaves and pawns cannot be denied, although even small-holders probably resorted to slavery and pawnship at times. More often, however, small-holders were the source of pawns and the targets of slave raids and capture in war. There is no evidence that slaves were put to any extensive use in the small villages and areas that failed to develop the military machines that characterized the larger polities. In these places both pawnship and slavery were probably marginal institutions. Studies of the communities raided for slaves (Akoko, Igbomina, Yagba) are few and far between, and existing studies concentrate on the effects of slave raiding and warfare, not local use of slaves.[102] While slavery and pawnship were known in these areas, instability and imperialism limited the ability of their elites to acquire slaves and pawns.

Evidence of large-scale production and trade or of military elites and 'wealthy personages' inevitably meant that slaves were used to maintain production and distribution and to uphold the lifestyle of the elite. Without a single exception, all the great names of the nineteenth century built large households with considerable numbers of slaves, and almost certainly pawns as well. It is possible to construct a multiple model of political economy that includes two modes of production, with a slave mode as the dominant one in the military states, next to a lineage mode in other areas. It may also be argued that as individuals expanded their enterprises, they also increasingly relied on the use of slaves and pawns. Slavery and pawnship did not displace family labour, and it is likely that the majority of free-born people did not make use of slaves or pawns to any appreciable extent simply because they had no access to them. Neither did slavery and pawnship destroy established co-operative work-groups like the *aro* and *owe*, which enabled family labour to be supplemented through networks of friends, relations and neighbours at critical moments in the production process or for public works. Unless inherited, most members of society had no access to slaves because of their cost and the violent nature of their procurement, and the distribution of pawns depended upon the possession of capital that could be extended on credit. Oral and written evidence makes it clear that the ambition of many people was to own slaves and to acquire pawns in order to expand their economic operations. The *oriki orile* ('praise poems') and traditions attest to their importance.[103] Owning slaves was not just for status but an opportunity to accumulate, and wealth provided the means to obtain pawns. Slaves and pawns were assets, markers of wealth. According to the evidence supplied by the missionaries who commented on wealth among the Yoruba, to own slaves was second in importance only to polygamy.[104] The ambition of redeemed slaves, too, was often to own slaves as a means of personal accumulation.[105] This ambition was both a reflection of the extent to which slaves imbibed the ideology of success and status as defined by the elite. To a poor free-born, buying one or two slaves was a sure way of overcoming poverty; to a rich person, it was to 'continue to increase his stock'.[106] Pawns fulfilled the same function.

This analysis of slavery and pawnship among the Yoruba demonstrates that servile institutions developed extensively in one of the most important areas from which slaves were exported to the Americas. While the interconnection between the demand for slaves in the Americas and the evolution of servile institutions in the Yoruba states of the nineteenth century cannot be fully explored here, it is important to realize that the domestic demand for servile labour in Africa was strong. Any analysis of the relative importance of slavery and its abolition in the Americas has to take into account this internal, African dimension.

NOTES

1. E. Adeniyi Oroge, 'The Institution of Slavery in Yorubaland with Particular Reference to the Nineteenth Century' (Ph.D. thesis, unpublished, University of Birmingham, 1971), p.i.
2. Ibid., p.180.
3. Oroge did not use the concept of 'kinship idiom', but this is what his interpretation is all about.
4. Walter Rodney, 'African Slavery and other Forms of Social Oppression on the Upper Guinea Coast in the Context of the Atlantic Slave-Trade', *Journal of African History*, 7, 3 (1966). For the debate on slavery, see, for instance, R. I. Harms, 'Slave Systems in Africa', *History in Africa*, 5 (1978), pp. 327–35; F. Cooper, 'The Problem of Slavery in African Studies', *Journal of African History*, 20 (1979), pp. 103–25; J.L. Watson (ed.), *Asian and African Systems of Slavery* (Oxford, 1980); M.I. Finley, *Ancient Slavery and Modern Ideology* (London, 1980); and Suzanne Miers and Igor Kopytoff (eds.), *Slavery in Africa: Historical and Anthropological Perspectives* (Madison, 1975). Since the 1970s the study of Yoruba slavery has not been well integrated into the mainstream debate.
5. Oroge, 'Institution', p.v.
6. For a rewarding discussion on the problems of term and definition, see the controversial discussion by Igor Kopytoff and Suzanne Miers in *Slavery in Africa*.
7. E.A. Oroge, 'Iwofa: An Historical Survey of the Yoruba Institution of Indenture', *African Economic History*, 14 (1985), pp. 75–106.
8. Samuel Johnson, *The History of the Yorubas* (Lagos, 1921).
9. See N.A. Fadipe, *The Sociology of the Yoruba* (Ibadan, 1970), pp. 186–7; J.F. Ade Ajayi, 'The Atlantic Slave Trade and Africa: An Overview', Conference on Slavery, Arewa House, Kaduna, Nigeria, 1989; and Funso Afolayan, 'Slavery, Warfare and Society in the Nineteenth Century: The Witness of Samuel Johnson', in Toyin Falola (ed.), *The Pioneer, Patriot and Patriarch: Samuel Johnson and Yoruba History* (Madison, 1993), pp. 183–96.
10. The literature is extensive, and grows every year. See, for instance, J.E. Inikori and S.L. Engerman (eds.), *The Atlantic Slave Trade: Effects on Economies, Societies, and*

Peoples in Africa, the Americas, and Europe (Durham, 1992); and Paul Lovejoy (ed.), *Africans in Bondage: Studies in Slavery and the Slave Trade* (Madison, 1986). For a synthesis, see Paul Lovejoy, *Transformations in Slavery: A History of Slavery in Africa* (Cambridge, 1983).

11. See for instance, Lovejoy, *Transformations in Slavery*, Ch. 7.
12. Philip D. Curtin, *The Rise And Fall of the Plantation Complex: Essays in Atlantic History* (Cambridge, 1990), Ch. 13.
13. The production of the major export products of palm oil, palm kernels, cotton and rubber increased in the second half of the century; see Sara S. Berry, *Cocoa, Custom and Socio-Economic Change in Rural Western Nigeria* (Oxford, 1975), p. 23; A.G. Hopkins, 'An Economic History of Lagos, 1880–1914' (Ph.D. thesis, unpublished, University of London, 1964).
14. On this process and its consequences, see J.F.A. Ajayi and R.S. Smith, *Yoruba Warfare in the Nineteenth Century* (Cambridge, 1964); B. Awe, 'The Rise of Ibadan as a Yoruba Power, 1851–1893' (D. Phil, unpublished, Oxford, 1964); and S.A. Akintoye, *Revolution and Power Politics In Yorubaland 1840–1893* (London, 1971).
15. Ilorin was a class by itself, drawing both from Yoruba practice and ideology described here, but also from the Sokoto Caliphate for its Islamic ideology. B. Agiri has mentioned in brief the impact of Islam on slavery, but his data and interpretations do not indicate the extent to which we can connect Ilorin to studies of the Caliphate by Lovejoy, Hogendorn and others. It is hoped that the ongoing study by Ann O'Hear on slavery in Ilorin will clarify the problem. On Ilorin and the ideology of Islam, see the introduction and the chapter by Agiri in Paul E. Lovejoy (ed.), *The Ideology of Slavery in Africa* (Beverly Hills, 1981). On slavery in the Sokoto Caliphate, see Lovejoy, 'The Characteristics of Plantations in the Nineteenth-Century Sokoto Caliphate (Islamic West Africa)', *The American Historical Review*, 84, 5 (1979), pp. 1267–92.
16. Toyin Falola and G.O. Oguntomisin, *The Military in 19th Century Yoruba Politics* (Ile-Ife, 1984).
17. Toyin Falola, *The Political Economy of a Pre-colonial African State: Ibadan, 1830–1900* (Ile-Ife, 1984), Ch. 3.
18. Cd 4957, Moloney to Rowe, 12 May 1881 (enclosure 2 in Rowe to Kimberley, 2 July 1881).
19. See, for instance, I.A. Akinjogbin and S.O. Osoba (eds.), *Topics on Nigerian Economic and Social History* (Ile-Ife, 1980); Ann O'Hear, 'The Economic History of Ilorin in the 19th and 20th Centuries: The Rise and Decline of a Middleman Society' (Ph.D. thesis, unpublished, University of Birmingham, 1983); and R.J. Gavin, 'The Impact of Colonial Rule on Ilorin Economy', *CentrePoint*, 1, 1 (1977), pp. 16–29.
20. Peter Morton-Williams, 'The Oyo-Yoruba and the Atlantic Slave Trade, 1670–1830', *Journal of the Historical Society of Nigeria*, 3, 1 (1964), pp. 25–45; R.C. Law, *The Oyo Empire c. 1600–1836: a West African Imperialism in the Era of the Atlantic Trade* (Oxford, 1977).
21. Richard Lander and John Lander, *Journal of an Expedition to Explore The Course and Termination of the Niger* (London, 1832), pp. 183–4.
22. Lander and Lander, *Journal*, pp. 189–90.
23. On his career and strategies, see S.O. Babayemi, *The Fall and Rise of Oyo c. 1706–1905: A Study in the Traditional Culture of an African Polity* (Lagos, 1990), Ch. 3.
24. See, for instance, Lander and Lander, *Journal*, p. 129; and Babayemi, *Fall and Rise*.
25. R.H. Stone, *In Afric's Forest and Jungle or Six Years Among the Yorubas* (London, 1900), p. 60.
26. CMS CA2/085b, Journal of H. Townsend for the quarter ending 25 Sept. 1852.
27. I.B. Akinyele, *Iwe Itan Ibadan* (self-published, c. 1911), pp. 35, 47, 247.
28. CMS CA2/049(b) David Hinderer, Journal for the Quarter ending 25 Sept. 1851.
29. CMS CA2/049a, Hinderer to Venn, 25 May 1856.
30. CMS CA2/049b, Hinderer, Half Yearly Report of Ibadan Station ending April 1859.
31. CMS CA2/056, Report from Rev. J. Johnson, Aug. 1877.

32. For details, see S.O. Biobaku, *The Egba and their Neighbours, 1842–72* (London, 1957).
33. CMS CA2/085b, Journal of H. Townsend for the quarter ending Sept. 1846.
34. CMS CA2/056, James Johnson to Wright, Annual Report, Jan. 1880.
35. C.O. 147/133, Evidence of Rev. James Johnson, enclosed in Denton to Chamberlain (confidential), 4 June 1898.
36. CMS CA2/098, Extract from C.N. Young's Journal for the third quarter ending Sept. 1875; J.A. Leigh, *History of Ondo* (Self-published, 1917), p. 49.
37. For the career of the notable ones, see S.A. Akintoye, *Revolution and Power Politics in Yorubaland 1840–1893* (London, 1971).
38. CO 147/48, Haastrup to Lt. Governor, 16 Feb. 1882 (Enclosure in Rowe to Kimberley, 14 March 1882).
39. Johnson, *History of Yoruba*, pp. 324–5 (and in many other passages).
40. Oroge, 'Institution', Ch. 1; R.S. Smith, *Kingdoms of the Yoruba* (London, 1969).
41. G.J.A. Ojo, *Yoruba Palaces: A Study of Afins in Yorubaland* (London, 1966).
42. E.B. Idowu, *Olodumare: God In Yoruba Belief* (London, 1962).
43. Parliamentary Papers 1865, Vol. 1 (412), Report from the Select Committee on Africa(Western Coast), Q. 1891, 81 [evidence of McCoskry].
44. See, for instance, FO 84/1175, Beddingfield to McCoskry, 26 Jan. 1862 (Enclosure in McCoskry to Russell, 8 Feb. 1862).
45. Johnson, *History of Yoruba*, p. 325.
46. I.B. Akinyele, *Iwe Itan Ibadan*, 246ff.
47. CMS CA2/056, Report from Rev. J. Johnson, Aug. 1877.
48. Johnson, *History of Yoruba*, p. 354.
49. CO 147/133, Denton to Chamberlain; evidence of J.P.L. Davies.
50. CO 147/134, Denton to Chamberlain, 3 Aug. 1898.
51. CMS CA2/098, Extract from C.N. Young's Journal for the third quarter ending Sept. 1875.
52. See Hinderer, *Seventeen Years*, p. 198; Johnson, *History of Yoruba*, p. 123.
53. FO 2/20, 'Replies to the Queries submitted by the Cotton Supply Association of Manchester dated Sept. 1857', enclosed in Campbell to Clarendon, 12 Nov. 1857.
54. See, for instance, FO 84/1031, Campbell to Clarendon, 14 March 1857; CO 147/133, Denton to Chamberlain (evidence of J.A.O. Payne; enclosure of 4 June, 1878).
55. Interviews with Chief Ojo Bada of Saki, a distinguished local historian with first-hand experience of the use of slaves.
56. Oroge, 'Institution', pp. 199–204.
57. A. Hinderer, *Seventeen Years in the Yoruba Country: Memorials of Anna Hinderer* (London, 1872), p. 61.
58. See for instance, Lander and Lander, *Journal*, pp. 109–13; Johnson, *History of Yoruba*, p. 194.
59. Hinderer, *Seventeen Years in the Yoruba Country*, pp. 61–2.
60. See FO 84/950, Campbell to Clarendon, 1 June 1854.
61. Toyin Falola, 'The Yoruba Caravan System of the 19th Century', *International Journal of African Historical Studies*, 21, 1 (1991), pp. 111–32.
62. Toyin Falola, 'The Yoruba Toll System: Its Operation and Abolition', *Journal of African History*, 30, 1 (1989), pp. 41–63.
63. CMS CA2/085 b, Journal of H. Townsend for the quarter ending 25 Sept. 1852.
64. Parliamentary Papers, 1865, Vol. 1 (412), Report from the Select Committee Appendix I.E.: Taiwo and others to Col. Ord 27 Dec. 1864, pp. 380–81.
65. See Johnson, *History of Yoruba*, p. 325.
66. See, for instance, CMS CA2/049a, Hinderer to Venn, 26 Oct. 1855; CA2/056, J. Johnson to C. C. Venn, Annual Letter, March 1879.
67. CMS CA2/049b. David Hinderer, Journal for the quarter ending 25 Sept. 1851.
68. Biobaku, *Egba and their Neighbours*; O.O. Ayantuga, 'Ijebu and its Neighbours, 1851–1914' (Ph.D. thesis, unpublished, University of London, 1965).
69. CMS CA2/056, Johnson to Wright, 21 June 1878.

70. Oroge, 'Iwofa', pp. 76.
71. There are many leads to pursue, as suggested by Paul Lovejoy and his collaborators in *Ideology of Slavery*.
72. CO 147/133, evidence of J.A.O. Payne, Denton to Chamberlain.
73. The theme of economic rationalization has to be further pursued as part of the changes in the economy and the contribution of an enterprising aristocracy to production.
74. See for instance, E.A. Oroge, 'The Fugitive Slave Crisis of 1859: A Factor in the Growth of Anti-British Feelings Among the Yoruba', *Odu: a Journal of West African Studies*, 12 (1975), pp. 40–53.
75. Toyin Falola, 'Power Relations and Social Interactions among Ibadan Slaves, 1850–1900', *African Economic History*, 16 (1987), pp. 95–114.
76. For details on this institution among the Yoruba and elsewhere, see Toyin Falola and Paul Lovejoy (eds.), *Pawnship in Africa: Historical Perspectives on Debt Bondage* (Boulder, 1994).
77 . For a review of the literature on pawnship, see Falola and Lovejoy, 'Debt Bondage in Historical Perspective', *Pawnship in Africa*.
78. Oroge, 'Institution', p. 180.
79. Oroge, 'Iwofa', p. 76.
80. See, for instance, 'The Oni of Ife, "Iwofa"', *ODU: Journal of Yoruba and Related Studies*, 3 (1956); NAI, Ije Prof 3/c.8/1923, Pawning of children; Ije Prof 3/c.8/1927, Pawning of children; and CSO 26/06827 Vol. II, Tribal Customs and Superstitions.
81. NAI, Abe Prof 3/4/40/23, Iwofa or Pawning.
82. NAI, Abe Prof 3/4/40/23.
83. This was a special condition borrowed from the regulations from other loan arrangements.
84. See for instance, NAI Abe Prof 3/4/40/23.
85. NAI, CSO 26/06827, Vol. I; Memorandum on the Native Custom of Ofa.
86. NAI CSO 26/06827 Vol. II; evidence supplied by Ross, Oct. 1924.
87. NAI, *Report on Native Organization of the Ife Division* by J.A. Mackenzie Esq., DO.
88. NAI, APP 3/1/47; A. Edun to Commissioner, 5 Nov. 1915.
89. See, for instance, NAI, Ije Prof 4/J.1095, Custody of Children of a Native Marriage.
90. NAI, CSO 26/06827 Vol.II; Ross to Secretary, Lagos, 14 March, 1923.
91. This conclusion is derived from archival sources only. In two-thirds of cases where pawns were mentioned by name and in cases that ended in courts, they were girls. In places where child pawnship was less prevalent, most of the few cases that were mentioned were also girls.
92. NAI Abe Prof 3/4/40/23.
93. NAI Ije Prof 3/9/c.8/1923.
94. NAI, CSO 26/0682; Memorandum on Iwofa.
95. NAI, Ije Prof/J.1095.
96. NAI, CSO 26/2/11604; extract from SSP.
97. N.A. Fadipe, *Sociology of the Yoruba*, p. 191.
98. Fadipe, *Sociology of the Yoruba*, p. 193.
99. Ibid., p. 192.
100. NAI, CSO 26/06827 Vol, I.
101. Ibid.
102. See, for instance, M. Mason, 'The Jihad in the South: An Outline of the Nineteenth-Century Nupe Hegemony in North-Eastern Yorubaland and Afenmai', *Journal of the Historical Society of Nigeria*, 5, 2 (1970), pp. 193–210; and Ade Obayemi, 'The Sokoto Jihad and the Okun Yoruba: A Review', *Journal of the Historical Society of Nigeria*, 9 (1978), pp. 61–87.
103. See for instance CMS CA2/049a, Hinderer to Venn, 26 Oct. 1855; and CMS CA2/098, Extract from C.N. Young's Journal for the first quarter of 1876.
104. See, for instance, CMS CA2/056, Johnson to Wright, Annual Report, Jan. 1880.
105. CMS CA2/056, Johnson to Wright, Annual Report, Jan. 1880.
106. Ibid.

Freedom and Slavery and the Shaping of Victorian Britain

JAMES WALVIN

The granting of freedom to Britain's 750,000 slaves in 1838 was a defining moment, not merely for the ex-slaves but for the British themselves. It was a crucial event in the development of a national cultural identity and was basic to the British sense of themselves in their dealings with the outside world through the rest of the century. The belief that the British were uniquely, even divinely, qualified to promote freedom flowed, however, not solely from the campaign against slavery, but traced its roots back to that titanic clash, which spanned a generation, between Britain and the French. In that confused debate which swirled back and forth in the years of revolutionary ferment after 1789, the rhetoric of freedom was basic. There was, of course, a much older tradition of debate about freedom, reaching back to the revolution of the seventeenth century and to the events of 1776–83, but it was the heightened tensions of 1789 which reignited the debate. Initially it was highly polarized, with minority lower-class radicals on the one side, propertied orders on the other. But both sides couched their political ambitions in terms of traditional freedoms. After the 1790s, a decade of deep divide and uncertainty when the nation itself seemed threatened by the unstoppable power of French arms, the debate about freedom was subsumed within a necessary upsurge of patriotism. To win the war against the French it was essential to offer a united, national front; a front which could claim patriotism and freedom as its emblems.

The British believed that the French wars had been fought, and won, on behalf of freedom. British freedom triumphed over aggressive French despotism and Britons had united in destroying French militarism. This national unity was, to a marked degree, bogus. In reality, the fissures in British life were unmistakable. But they were kept carefully in check and did not become obvious again until the years of social and economic dislocation after 1815. For more than a generation, the British had been organized for war (on an all-consuming scale and with a single-mindedness which was not to be repeated until 1914–18) around the ideology of freedom.[1]

The language and imagery of freedom of those years are there for all to see. Newspapers, prints, cartoons and iconography of all kinds bear public testimony to the ideological foundations of the French wars. Time and again, they addressed the question of freedom; freedom against invasion, freedom to remove foreign conquerors, freedom to defend a political system which was, the British claimed, the envy of the world. The war was more easily fought because the British were a freedom-loving people. Although it is easy to dismiss this as propaganda, the British began to believe it. Above all other peoples, they believed themselves to be blessed by an attachment to the pursuit of freedom.

There was, of course, irony here, one not lost on those bands of radicals and reformers who argued for different kinds of freedom; for working people and for subject peoples. It was, in essence, the prototype of a debate which was to flourish many years later in a different British empire. How could the British argue, and fight, for freedom while denying the same experience to millions of their subject peoples?

The debate about freedom between 1789 and 1838 became basic to the shaping of British cultural identity. Stated crudely, when Victoria ascended the throne in 1837, it had become a matter of great national pride that the British had girded up their collective loins and, within a few short years, had overthrown French tyranny *and* then had destroyed the British slave system. This conjunction of events is important. Although the campaign against the slave trade was initially obstructed by fears generated by the French Revolution, in time the vocabulary of abolition blended neatly with the language of freedom which was itself the vernacular of the French wars. Here were two struggles which pitched the lovers of freedom, the British, against forces of evil. In a political world which liked to present complex issues as simple ethical alternatives, the British had triumphed over the forces of darkness.

The sense of national and cultural identity in existence by the early nineteenth century was that of a British people whose attachment to freedom had been shaped by a total war and tempered by a crusade against slavery. Looking back from 1838, the British found plenty of reasons to feel pleased with their efforts. Having secured the freedom of Europe from French aggrandizement they had recently liberated their slaves. They contrasted the actions of their statesmen with the gory achievements of Napoleon. Wilberforce, said Samuel Romilly, saved 'so many of his fellow creatures' while Napoleon was wading 'through slaughter and oppression'.[2] Thereafter they embarked on ensuring that others were not denied their freedom by being sold into slavery in the Americas; hence the Atlantic anti-slave patrols by the Royal Navy.

The British now felt strengthened to embark on a crusade that would bring freedoms to other deprived peoples. Such a crusade would, of course, have the added advantage of helping to secure Britain's wider economic well-being, in Africa or elsewhere. For here was the crux of the matter. As much as they persuaded themselves (and tried, less successfully, to persuade others) of the altruism of their global crusade for freedom, the British had economic irons in the fire. Their rivals, notably the French and the Americans, could see the formula; that freedom, and especially certain kinds of free trade, were perfectly congruent with British economic interests. The British attachment to freedom, for all its high-flown principles, had obvious material benefits.[3]

The British economy – industrializing, hinged on an increasingly urban population, unable now to feed itself adequately – needed to look to all corners of the world: for raw materials, foodstuffs, markets, in short for whatever commercial opportunities presented themselves. The restrictions of the old empire were gradually cast aside; most notable among them was chattel slavery. At home and abroad, freedom to trade, to import and to sell went hand-in-hand with a greater freedom in the management of labour.[4] It was as if the material benefits of freedom had arrived to confirm the older struggles for political freedom. If the years before 1838 had been couched as a struggle for political freedom, the years thereafter saw attention switch to economic matters. The Victorian economy began to flourish in an ideological atmosphere of freedom.

A growing number of economic historians now accept that, for all the contemporary bravado about matters of freedom as basic ingredients in the making of Victorian Britain, the loosening of restraint was indeed crucial in transforming the economy. Yet the century before had been no less vital.[5] It seems clear enough now that the closely-controlled mercantilist state and empire of the eighteenth century laid the basis for much that followed. What many have taken to be profligate expenditure on military forces in fact secured the British conditions for economic growth and rising domestic well-being. The great wars of the eighteenth century not only maintained British dominance and expanded the British empire, but may even have paid for themselves. In the long run, no major power emerged to challenge British economic hegemony until the late nineteenth century.

It made perfect sense in 1838 to speak of freedom as a key cultural characteristic because it seemed to speak to the British political experience of the past half century and also pointed the way forward to enhanced economic prosperity. On the basis of freedom, the British had maintained their own national security and had bestowed the same on others. In the name of freedom they could now advance, through trade and informal empire, to levels of well-being scarcely imagined.

The British drive to end their own slave empire had taken half a century, though success (in 1807 and 1833) had come relatively swiftly. When the 750,000 West Indian slaves celebrated their full freedom at midnight, 1 August 1838, their British friends were propelled forward by a political and organizational momentum. Theirs was a crusade of an indignant and pious people, organized and prepared to tackle slavery wherever it existed. Other nations saw the matter differently. The French, still conscious of the wounds inflicted by the British in the Revolutionary and Napoleonic Wars, were in no mood to accede to British diplomatic calls for abolition. Indeed, the British abolitionists' efforts to win the French over to black freedom may have been counter-productive, and France only ended their own slave systems in the revolutionary confusions in 1848.[7]

The biggest challenge to British abolitionists was, of course, the United States. A great deal of British political effort, money and moral fervour was invested in the campaign to persuade the United States to abandon slavery. Publications and speakers criss-crossed the Atlantic; sister churches hummed with moral indignation. But there were powerful political, and popular, antipathies to British efforts. The United States had not gone its own way simply to defer to British moral posturing. And, like the French before them, there were Americans who pointed to the curiosity of the poacher turned international gamekeeper; the pre-eminent eighteenth-century slaver now masquerading as guardian of the world's morality. British calls for freedom had a hollow ring to American ears, when they came from the nation which had conceded American freedoms in 1783 only at the point of a gun. For all their efforts at home, and however influential the tactical example of their earlier campaign, British abolitionists remained marginal to the domestic American debate about slavery and freedom.

Other regions seemed more amenable to British argument, if only because they were under direct British control or influence. But here the British faced a different moral dilemma. Indian slavery, for instance, unlike black chattel slavery in the Americas, owed nothing to European lineage. It was indigenous and rooted in structures which the British had scarcely begun to understand, still less appreciate. Yet slavery in India seemed ubiquitous, massive (involving perhaps 16 million people) and proffered a number of offensive forms to British evangelicalism. To attack Indian slavery, as the British did from the 1830s onwards, was to confront Indian cultures head-on. This was quite different from ending slavery in the Caribbean.

The British onslaught on Indian cultures was set back by the events of the 'Mutiny' of 1857. British confidence that they might be able to recast the subcontinent in their own image was abruptly undermined. The more ambitious and aggressive of missionaries were henceforth kept in check and the post-1857 political arrangements went out of their way to avoid alienating local peoples by trespassing on their customs. Victoria's proclamation of 1858 stated the case boldly; that the British renounced 'the right and the desire to impose Our convictions on any of Our subjects'. Henceforth, the greatest efforts went into bringing material improvement, 'the importation of the body of the west without its soul'.[8] Foremost among those material improvements was the creation of the Indian railway system which, among other benefits, enhanced the British ability to govern more effectively. In India at least it had become clear enough that the export of British freedoms was more difficult than many had hoped, and colonial governance might be more readily achieved without undermining existing local social systems.

The Indian troubles only deflected the British urge to impose freedom and dislodge slave systems, for there were other regions which beckoned. The Islamic slave trade, for example, continued to flourish. It is now clear enough that, whatever the statistical uncertainties, there was a dramatic increase in enslavement within Africa in the wake of the ending of the Atlantic slave trade. Slaves were moving, in large numbers, within Africa and it was these phenomena which Europeans encountered as they made the explorations into Africa in the second half of the nineteenth century.[9] While the British congratulated themselves on the effectiveness of their Atlantic anti-slaving policies, African slaves were being distributed elsewhere; perhaps three millions to Islamic regions in the nineteenth century. British ships continued their anti-slave trade patrols off East Africa until the end of the century. In fact British vessels continued to stop dhows to examine them for slaves as late as the 1920s.[10]

The British were, however, as interested in events within Africa as they were in the enforced migrations of enslaved Africans overseas. They developed a remarkable curiosity for news about Africa, and much of what they heard served to confirm their aggressively-evangelical instincts. Stories about the continuing horrors of slaving in and from Africa were given added strength from the mid-century by reports of missionaries. Whatever we may think of their aims, and their consequences, the stories which they relayed to their backers and supporters in churches throughout Britain helped to keep alive the British commitment to anti-slavery. The urge to convert Africans had to confront many of the moral and tactical problems posed by the earlier cultural onslaught on India. How could the British and other Europeans disentangle and destroy those cultural habits they disliked without allowing the whole fabric of local society to unravel? Whatever the problems, and however successful their efforts, the missionaries' stories became the stuff of vivid fantasy and widespread public curiosity in Britain. And none more so than the epics of David Livingstone.

Few today would accept the image of the Victorian missionary so beloved of contemporaries. He had inherited the mantle of an earlier generation of British heroes who had set out to put the world to rights. Like abolitionists up to the 1830s, the missionaries from mid-century tapped into a highly-sensitized public interest which is hard to imagine today. And Livingstone, struggling against unimaginable physical odds, personified the British determination to bring enlightenment and salvation to benighted regions of the world. In an age which elevated civic and public heroism to new heights, Livingstone took on heroic proportions. The British public wanted their heroes to be British; to be manly and tough, Christian and persevering in the Lord's cause. The paradox is that there was a chasm between Livingstone's achievements and his fame. In so many respects Livingstone was a failure – notwithstanding his epic explorations – yet he was revered in his homeland; perhaps one of the most famous people in the English-speaking world in his lifetime, and certainly after his death. Such fame is rarely accorded to failures. Once again, the context is crucial.

Britain itself had changed, both in its physical environment and in its cultural outlook. A majority of Britons now lived in urban areas, where, among other things, the printed word was easily available. The British, with the obvious exceptions across the social divides, were now a literate people, keen on the printed word which flew at them in ever-increasing volume and forms. There were few groups or specialist interests which did not promote themselves through print; from local political radicals through to the local church. Cheap newspapers, magazines, comics and children's literature of all kinds completed the circle. From the earliest days of childhood literacy, through to old age, the pleasures of reading were catered for. Time and again, with a minority, critical voice, this was a literature steeped in the heroics of empire.

So many people are familiar with this tradition from their own childhood reading, for instance, that it seems unremarkable. But we need to remind ourselves of the newness and the potency of popular literature. Cheap, imaginative, ever-changing, the popular literature of mid- and late-Victorian Britain spawned a popular culture which paid inordinate attention to issues of empire and exploration. Best remembered in boys' adventure stories, this interest spilled beyond the realms of story-telling into the business of cult creation. And Livingstone was perhaps only the most famous of a host of British heroes portrayed as the agent of freedom and Christianity.[11]

Like other popular heroics, Livingstone's exploits contained a kernel of reality, but one hidden beneath layers of popular fantasy and cultural mythology. Yet here was a story which the British never tired of hearing, right down to that classic encounter with Stanley, and Livingstone's reply as he raised his cap, politely, in quiet greeting. Understated and restrained, it was the very essence of British modesty, in a moment when others might have shown a more exuberant response. Here was an incident which spoke to British qualities. (And even Stanley, though sent by *The New York Times*, was a Welshman.)

Of course a more modern question might be, what was a Scot and a Welshman doing in Ujiji in 1871? Contemporaries had no doubt; that one was about God's work, the other reporting back to a reading public gripped by the drama of the project. It also helped to prompt further interest in Africa and to persuade shoals of young·men to commit themselves to a life of missionary work. As a direct result of Livingstone's efforts dozens of young men in Cambridge set out to open 'a path for commerce and Christianity'.[12] And here was the rub. What the British wanted was the opportunity to convert and to profit.

Here was further confirmation of a truth which the British took to be self-evident; that in the process of establishing themselves as the pre-eminent imperial power (their European dominance secured after the wars in 1815) the British had secured a reputation (at least to their own satisfaction) of moral integrity. In the words of Linda Colley, British supremacy, thanks largely to abolition, provided 'irrefutable proof that British power was founded on religion, on freedom and on moral calibre, not just on a superior stock of armaments and capital'.[13]

What has become clearer in recent years, thanks to work on the nature of British abolitionism to 1838, is the paradoxical consequences of the abolition efforts. Firstly, the campaign itself had politicized millions of Britons, notably women and working people, to a degree which no one had planned and whose consequences none could predict. It was a process of politicization which fed into subsequent movements for reform and provided a model for others to emulate. But at another level abolitionism gave the governing orders a powerful weapon in their dealings with the outside world. The British, the destroyers of black slavery in the Americas, now claimed to be 'the arbiters of the civilized and uncivilized world'.[14] It was, however, a mission in which, again, moral superiority rested comfortably with commercial self-interest. Take for example the comment of Lord Palmerston in 1842.

Let no man imagine that those treaties for the suppression of the slave trade are valuable only as being calculated to promote the great interests of humanity, and as tending to rid mankind of a foul and detestable crime. Such was indeed their great object and their chief merit. But in this case as in many others, virtue carries its own reward; and if the nations of the world could extirpate this abominable traffic, and if the vast population of Africa could by that means be left free betake themselves to peaceful and innocent trade, the greatest commercial benefit would accrue, not to England only, but to every civilized nation which engages in maritime commerce. The slave trade treaties therefore are indirectly treaties for the encouragement of commerce.[15]

It was as if the circle had been completed. Africans were now viewed as producers and consumers, not as the raw manpower for American plantations.

Time and again, Palmerston, and other British statesmen adopted a simple line. They saw themselves as the inheritors of an abolition sentiment which it was their duty to impose on the world. Informed of atrocities in Zanzibar, Palmerston wrote to the British consul in 1846 to 'take every opportunity of impressing upon the Arabs that the nations of Europe are destined to put an end to the African slave trade and that Great Britain is the main instrument in the hands of Providence for the accomplishment of this purpose'.[16]

It was not quite the case that God was British, but that the British were uniquely blessed to carry out His work. And basic to that work was the imposition of freedom around the world. To ensure freedom, the British had to confront and destroy various forms of slavery.

For the governing orders, this crusade, after 1838, had the political bonus of being remarkably popular. They were able to capitalize on the continuing groundswell of public abolitionist sentiment, which was itself sustained by abolitionist organizations and periodicals. But from mid-century this spilled over into a much broader public attachment to freedom as a cultural export. Statesmen knew that public opinion was behind them. Indeed, the campaign up to 1838 had been propelled by public support to a degree that many found uncomfortable.

Yet, even here, there was a hidden political benefit. The concentration on distant problems distracted attention from more pressing, domestic difficulties. Here, after all, was a source of great irritation to those radical leaders who complained, over a number of years, of the way anti-slavery could achieve this deflection, though the hunger, frustration and simple explosion of plebeian anger, most notably in the Chartist outbursts in the 1830s and 1840s, were too strong and aggressive to be deflected by tales of horrors done to the slaves.

On the whole, however, the British abolition campaign had the effect of securing the attachment of millions to the political culture of their homeland. For the really hungry and desperate, this was scarcely enough. But there were many others, measured in their millions, whose loyalty and cultural sense of identity was shaped and refined by anti-slavery. No other campaign attracted such numbers, accumulated so many names to its side, commanded such space in print, built up such parliamentary support and commanded such public backing as the campaign against slavery. Anti-slavery had become a defining quality of being British; a proof of the distinctive and divinely-inspired qualities of the British people. And all this at a time when other peoples hesitated. The Americans continued to rely on and benefit from slavery, the French dragged their feet on abolition, and large parts of Hispanic America struggled to preserve their own form of slavery. Who else in the West could compare with the British in their forthright and aggressive pursuit of freedom?[17]

ANTI-SLAVERY AND VICTORIAN IMPERIALISM

It is a coincidence that the era between the end of the British slave empire and the apogee of a new form of British imperialism was neatly spanned by the reign of Queen Victoria. That monarch came to personify British overseas expansion, her name scattered and appended to distant parts of the globe. By the end of the century, Victoria was a region of Australia, a lake in Africa, a city in Canada, a river in Uganda, and more. All this in addition to her lifelike statues perched in city-centres from Calcutta to Kingston, from Aden to Colombo. Victoria represented to the British, and especially to the British overseas, a personification of all they prided themselves in. Her statues show a small person, but one shrouded in the panoply of formality and power; stern in appearance, imposing in her presence and, in her sculptured, colonial format, close to the divinity which British imperialists knew lay at the heart of their global calling.[18]

The later years of Victoria's reign marked the high-water line of the tide of British imperial sentiment and settlement. Yet it would be wrong to imagine that here was a phenomenon to be explained purely in material and military terms. Obviously, it was fuelled by an expansionist economy yearning for markets and materials and bolstered by a relatively unchallenged military (especially naval) power. But it was also rooted in an ideology of empire which, in that new age of mass literacy, cheap print, mass education and new popular cultures, quickly penetrated to the very grass roots of British life. Notwithstanding that critique of imperialism which formed a descant to the whole process, the British became a fiercely imperial people from top to bottom. Imperial victories were celebrated, setbacks mourned, in the most collective and public of fashions. Nor was this simply the organs of state whipping up imperial theatre. Wherever we look at British popular culture in the last twenty years of the nineteenth century, there we will find an enthusiastic and often belligerent imperialism. Indeed to be imperialist was to be patriotic; and patriotism was one of the most marked inventions of the nineteenth century, to be placed alongside the greatest of other British inventions of those years (though like other inventions it was based on earlier models).[19]

Two simple examples will illustrate the point. In that most popular of British cultural forms, soccer, new stadiums took the name of a battle, Spion Kop, in the South African War. And in that other great forum for popular culture, the Music Hall, the greatest voice was given to that amazing song, 'Rule Britannia'. Though written in the 1740s, to commemorate the accession of the Hanoverians, it came into its own in Victoria's reign. In the process its words were changed, by popular usage. Initially, the song asserted, 'Britannia, rule the waves'; an injunction, not a description. A century later, when it had become a popular song, the popular grammar had been subtly changed; 'Britannia rules the waves'. The injunction of the eighteenth century had become the simple description of the nineteenth century. In the course of the nineteenth century, dozens of arrangements of the song for instruments, for orchestras and for voice, were published, part of that broader drive to satisfy the voracious British appetite for printed music, much of which was inspiring and patriotic.[20]

Perhaps the most curious aspect of 'Rule Britannia' was the line 'Britons never will be slaves.' Here was a statement which was intended to be merely a rousing finale to a song (whose popularity the composer could never have imagined) but which, in fact, stands as a *leitmotif* to Britain's dealings with the outside world. At the time the song was written, the British had established themselves as the most prominent and aggressive of the slave traders in the Atlantic economy. But when the song reached its peak of widespread popularity, the British had transmuted themselves into the zealous and equally aggressive advocates of abolition and freedom. Here was a verse, almost a national anthem, which seemed ideally suited to Britain's new (self-appointed) global role as scourge of the slave trader and guardian of the world's liberties.

The British trumpeted their intention of safeguarding freedom on a global scale; a sign of their remarkable self-confidence if not their political grasp. Naturally enough it proved a complex, up-hill struggle, especially in their dealings with indigenous peoples in India, Africa and the Gulf. But, in public at least, British statesmen and a host of pressure groups, remained steadfast in their attachment to the concept of freedom as an instrument of British colonial and foreign policy. Inevitably, of course, things were not as simple as many believed.

There were difficulties at every turn. The first task the British set themselves was apparently the easiest; to seal off the routes from Africa and to staunch that flow of people which had provided the muscle for the development of the Americas but which was such a haemorrhage for Africa. Viewed from London, or rather looking at a map in London, the problem seemed manageable. With a Slave Trade department in the Foreign Office, and a distinct anti-slave trade squadron in the Royal Navy, the British clearly meant business, notwithstanding the inevitable friction with other Atlantic maritime powers. As we know, the British were unable completely to staunch the flow. It was sixty years before their efforts were counted successful, and even then at a cost of £40 million (seizing in the process some 1600 ships and 150,000 slaves). It was a massive expenditure of time, money, resources and will power; indication enough of the early Victorian commitment to freedom, of a kind.

There were few voices raised against the idea that the British should henceforth redirect their moral crusade in favour of freedom on a global scale. Critics were generally ignored or dismissed in what was an emergent consensus that the British had a 'calling'; a divine mandate which demanded action and which would brook no interference from more earthly powers. When British imperialists looked back to earlier empires, they liked to point to the Roman empire in the Age of Constantine; a Christian evangelical empire which imposed its orthodoxy across Europe. After all, it was the Roman Empire which had abolished slavery in England. Directly or indirectly, imperial conquest could be used to advance a moral position. But the British did not need to look back for justification for their cultural imperialism. It was a God-given imperative.

It is easy, now, to see how this view, so assiduously promoted by the British in everything from children's books to newspapers, was central to that 'culture of complacency' which underpinned the British view of themselves and shaped their dealings with the outside world.[21] It was a culture which also had fundamental domestic consequences because it played a major role in undermining the resolve to tackle pressing domestic matters. Problems at home could be passed off as mere blemishes when attention was drawn to the grander view of Britain's moral, global crusade. Of course, it was no comfort to the wretched, growing in number, density and despair, to learn that the blessings of British freedom were currently being lavishly sprinkled around the world. The contrast, between imperial grandeur and colonial paternalism on the one hand, and domestic squalor on the other, was not fully articulated until late in the century, and did not gain full political direction until the disasters of the South African war. True, there had been a tradition of complaint, Dickens' telescopic philanthropy, but it made little headway against that self-confident, British identity shaped by the collective attachment to freedom and antipathy to slavery.

CONCLUSION

In most of the literature about the ending of British slavery, pride of place has gone, rightly, to the consequences for the freed slaves. Viewed from the British perspective, most historical interest has focused on the economic implications of the British switch from mercantilism towards a freer trading system. The purpose of this paper has been to suggest another, related, line of development.

Securing black freedom, if only at first in the Americas, was the culmination of a much longer process of British public debate about freedom. Taken together, the French Wars and the abolitionist movement had helped redefine British collective identity. The recent work of Linda Colley has suggested the powerful sense of British cultural identity in place at the accession of Victoria. Believing themselves to be empowered to export freedom, the British embarked on that creeping confrontation with other peoples, eager to secure their products, their markets, and eager to impose on them the blessings of Christian freedoms which were the hallmark of the British themselves.

After 1838 the British were especially keen to assault slavery. Inevitably their imperial ventures brought them into contact with indigenous cultures which offended their new-found love of freedom. Their dilemma was how best to confer freedom while securing the best material and strategic advantage to themselves. But whatever the local outcome, and it varied enormously around the world, and however varied the tactical British response, they never lost sight of their ideological impulse.

It is easy, in retrospect, to see how this enterprise was doomed to failure. Yet it speaks to British self-confidence that they could even contemplate so awesome a task. But this too was part of the formula. British cultural identity by the mid-nineteenth century pivoted on a national self-confidence which was itself a potent political force. It was a self-confidence born of some dramatic political (and military) successes in the years between 1789 and 1838. But it went much deeper than that. And it is at this point that we need to recognize the domestic changes in Britain itself. An urbanizing, literate people, linked by a web of political and religious institutions, and instructed through a plethora of printed materials, absorbed the language and ideals of freedom. This was not simply a case of a political or religious elite cleverly orchestrating a public debate. For good or ill, the British, of all sorts and conditions, had become wedded to the idea that they were, above all others, a freedom-loving people with an obligation to export their freedoms.

There is another, quite different story to be told about the British urge to imperial expansion and dominance in the years after 1838. The history of indentured labour, the ruthless conquest and heavy-handed treatment of millions of subject peoples, all this scarcely needs repeating in a volume of this kind. But few Britons saw the unfolding of imperialism in this light. Most remained wedded to that mythological ideal of themselves as crusading lovers of freedom, tough when necessary but resolute in their determination to bestow freedom whatever the local obstacles. The British belief that they were agents for freedom round the world was mythological, but no less powerful for all that. Moreover, it was a myth which proved even more durable than British imperial control itself. Long after their empire, like so many before it, had collapsed and the emperors had gone home, the British continued to take comfort from the knowledge that they had made the world a better place by enabling local peoples to enjoy the benefits of freedom.

NOTES

1. Clive Emsley, *British Society and the French Wars* (London, 1979).
2. Quoted in Linda Colley, *Britons: Forging the Nation* (London and New Haven, 1992), p.359.
3. See in particular, David Eltis, *Economic Growth and the Ending of the Transatlantic Slave Trade* (Oxford, 1987), Ch. 2.
4. See essays in Patrick O'Brien and Rolan Quinault (eds.), *The Industrial Revolution and British Society* (Cambridge, 1993).
5. On the development of the eighteenth-century state, see John Brewer, *Sinews of Power; War, Money and the English State, 1688–1783* (London, 1989).
6. Patrick K. O'Brien, 'Political Preconditions for the Industrial Revolution', in O'Brien and Quinault (eds.), *Industrial Revolution*, pp.149–51.
7. Details of French abolition can be found in Seymour Drescher, *Capitalism and Antislavery* (London, 1987).
8. Bernard Porter, *The Lion's Share: A Short History of British Imperialism* London, 1975), pp.39–40.
9. See essays in Elizabeth Savage (ed.), *The Human Commodity. Perspectives on the Trans-Saharan Slave Trade* (London, 1992).
10. Raymond C. Howell, *The Royal Navy and the Slave Trade* (London, 1987), p.209.
11. On the broader history of popular imperialism, see essays in John M. MacKenzie (ed.), *Imperialism and Popular Culture* (Manchester, 1986).
12. Porter, *Lion's Share*, p.69.
13. Colley, *Britons*, p.359.

14. Ibid., p.361.
15. Quoted in James Walvin, *Black Ivory. A History of British Slavery* (London, 1992), p.309.
16. Colley, *Britons*, p.360.
17. On the broader debate on post-slave freedom see Frank McGlynn and Seymour Drescher (eds.), *The Meaning of Freedom* (Pittsburgh, 1992).
18. Victoria's statue in Dublin was removed from its plinth in 1947 and, curiously, sold to Australia for their bi-centennial celebrations in 1988.
19. See E.J. Hobsbawm and T. Ranger, *The Invention of Tradition* (Cambridge, 1983).
20. Alexandria Scott (ed.), *Musica Britannica* (London, 1981); J.J. Fuld, *The Book of World Famous Music* (New York, 1966), p.477; J.N. Ander-Bach (ed.), *The Catalogue of Printed Music in the British Library to 1980*, Vol.2, (London, 1981), pp.148–51.
21. Colley, *Britons*, p.260.

Notes on Contributors

Paul E. Lovejoy is Professor of History, York University, Canada, and currently holds a Killam Fellowship from the Canada Council.

Nicholas Rogers is Professor and Chair, Department of History, York University, Canada.

O. Nigel Bolland is Professor of Sociology and Anthropology at Colgate University, USA.

Elinor G. K. Melville, Associate Professor, Department of History, York University, Canada, has recently been awarded a Rockefeller Fellowship.

Hilary McD. Beckles is Head of Department of History at the University of the West Indies, Barbados.

Cynthia Radding is Assistant Professor, Department of History, University of Missouri, St. Louis, USA, and will be joining the Department of History, University of Illinois, Champaign-Urbana, in 1995.

Paul Craven is Associate Professor in the Division of Social Sciences, York University, Canada.

Douglas Hay is an Associate Professor in the Division of Social Sciences, York University, Canada.

Elizabeth Elbourne received her doctorate from Oxford University and is now Assistant Professor in the Department of History, McGill University, Canada.

Nancy Priscilla Naro, Universidade Federal Fluminense, Niterói, Rio de Janeiro, Brazil, is currently Visiting Scholar (1992–94), Latin American Cultures Program, University of Pennsylvania.

Martin A. Klein, formerly President of the African Studies Association (USA), is Professor of History, University of Toronto, Canada.

Toyin Falola, previously of Awolowo University, Ile-Ife, Nigeria, is Professor of History at the University of Texas in Austin.

James Walvin, co-editor of *Slavery and Abolition*, is in the Department of History, University of York, UK.

INDEX

Printed in the United States
by Baker & Taylor Publisher Services